Conflict, Inequality and Ethnicity

CU00749943

Titles include:

Frances Stewart (*editor*)
HORIZONTAL INEQUALITIES AND CONFLICT
Understanding Group Violence in Multiethnic Societies

Forthcoming:

Graham Brown
THE POLITICAL ECONOMY OF SECESSION
Ethnicity, Inequality and the State

Arnim Langer, Frances Stewart and Rajesh Venugopal (*editors*)
POST-CONFLICT RESOLUTION AND HORIZONTAL INEQUALITIES

Conflict, Inequality and Ethnicity
Series Standing Order ISBN 978–0–230–24608–9 (hardback) and
978–0–230–24708–6 (paperback)
(*outside North America only*)

You can receive future titles in this series as they are published by placing a standing order. Please contact your bookseller or, in case of difficulty, write to us at the address below with your name and address, the title of the series and the ISBN quoted above.

Customer Services Department, Macmillan Distribution Ltd, Houndmills, Basingstoke, Hampshire RG21 6XS, England

Also by Frances Stewart

TECHNOLOGY AND UNDERDEVELOPMENT

ADJUSTMENT WITH A HUMAN FACE (*with Andrea Cornia and Richard Jolly*)

DEFINING POVERTY IN THE DEVELOPING WORLD (*with Ruhi Saith and Barbara Harriss-White*)

WAR AND UNDERDEVELOPMENT (*with Valpy Fitzgerald and associates*)

Vol. 1: THE ECONOMIC AND SOCIAL CAUSES OF CONFLICT

Vol. 2: COUNTRY EXPERIENCES

Horizontal Inequalities and Conflict

Understanding Group Violence in Multiethnic Societies

Edited by

Frances Stewart

Centre for Research on Inequality, Human Security and Ethnicity, Department of International Development Oxford University, UK

Foreword by Kofi Annan

First published in hardback 2008
This paperback edition published 2010 by
PALGRAVE MACMILLAN

Palgrave Macmillan in the UK is an imprint of Macmillan Publishers Limited, registered in England, company number 785998, of Houndmills, Basingstoke, Hampshire RG21 6XS.

Palgrave Macmillan in the US is a division of St Martin's Press LLC, 175 Fifth Avenue, New York, NY 10010.

Palgrave Macmillan is the global academic imprint of the above companies and has companies and representatives throughout the world.

Palgrave® and Macmillan® are registered trademarks in the United States, the United Kingdom, Europe and other countries.

ISBN-13: 978-0-230-51680-9 hardback
ISBN-13: 978-0-230-24550-1 paperback

This book is printed on paper suitable for recycling and made from fully managed and sustained forest sources. Logging, pulping and manufacturing processes are expected to conform to the environmental regulations of the country of origin.

A catalogue record for this book is available from the British Library.

Library of Congress Cataloging-in-Publication Data
Horizontal inequalities and conflict : understanding group violence in
   multiethnic societies / edited by Frances Stewart.
      p. cm.
   Includes bibliographical references and index.
   ISBN 978-0-230-51680-9 (alk. paper) 978-0-230-24550-1 (pbk)
   1. Ethnic conflict. 2. Social conflict. 3. Violence. 4. Intergroup
   relations. 5. Group identity. I. Stewart, Frances, 1940–
   HM1121.H67 2007
   305.8001—dc22   2007050066

10 9 8 7 6 5 4 3 2 1
19 18 17 16 15 14 13 12 11 10

Printed and bound in Great Britain by
CPI Antony Rowe, Chippenham and Eastbourne

Contents

List of Figures and Tables

Figures

Tables

Foreword

With increasing globalisation, the aftermath of colonialism and migration, almost every country in the world contains a multiplicity of ethnic and religious groups. A critical issue then is how societies can best be organised so that they flourish, in economic, political and cultural terms. The majority of multiethnic societies *do* succeed in establishing the conditions for peaceful and stable development. Yet many countries do not, lapsing instead into ethnic or religious violence, with unacceptable consequences, in terms of loss of lives, loss of livelihoods, forced migration, shattered families and a breakdown in intercommunal relations and trust.

As United Nations Secretary General, I repeatedly witnessed the terrible damage wrought by such conflicts at first hand and today the examples of Sudan, Afghanistan and Iraq remind us daily of their devastating costs. Unfortunately, the list of countries *at risk* of experiencing armed conflict is even longer, with post-conflict countries of particular concern. Even countries which have been relatively stable and prosperous for many years, such as Côte d'Ivoire, can become embroiled in violence, with disastrous socioeconomic consequences.

Hence it is vital and urgent not only to improve our understanding of the underlying causes of these violent conflicts but also to identify the policies that can help avoid these catastrophes, and secure peaceful conditions across the world.

This book makes an extremely important contribution to both these issues. It shows, through careful and well-supported research, that a major cause of violent conflict between groups lies in inequalities between them in political participation and economic resources and well-being, as well as in respect for their cultural differences. These inequalities are termed here 'horizontal inequalities'.

There are clear policy implications from this research which are laid out in the book: above all is the need to establish inclusive societies, and from this simple imperative a large number of specific policy suggestions follow.

Preventing violence is far better and less costly than trying to control it once started, just as avoiding the economic devastation that such violence brings about is clearly greatly to be preferred to the painful and difficult reconstruction of war-devastated economies. Policies that contribute to conflict prevention should therefore be at the forefront of development policy.

I hope that this book will be read by both international and national decision-makers, and that the sorts of policies recommended will be taken up. The need to create inclusive societies and avoid sharp horizontal inequalities should become an accepted norm of policy-making in multiethnic societies.

Kofi Annan

Preface

This book is the result of a global team effort – bringing together some of the main findings of the research of the Centre for Research on Inequality, Human Security and Ethnicity (CRISE). The centre is a Development Research Centre, funded by the Department for International Development. The work would not have been possible without this support. CRISE is a worldwide partnership; the centre at the Department of International Development, University of Oxford, works with scholars in Bolivia, Côte d'Ivoire, Ghana, Guatemala, Indonesia, Malaysia, Nigeria and Peru. We are very grateful for all their work and insights, and for discussions at workshops held in these countries which have had a pervasive influence on the book. We would like to mention, specifically, the team leaders of the regional research groups: Adolfo Figueroa, George Gray Molina, Rotimi Suberu, Riwanto Tirtosudarmo and Dzodzi Tsikata. Throughout, we have enjoyed and are grateful for unfailing and enthusiastic support from the Department of International Development, especially from Barbara Harriss-White, Julia Knight and Rachel Crawford. We would also like to thank the excellent administrative support within CRISE, including Nicola Shepard and Jo Boyce – Jo, together with William Danny, has been immensely supportive in the editorial work on the book. Needless to say, the errors remain those of the authors, while many of the insights come from the network of international scholars with whom we have had the privilege to work.

Various parts of this book have been presented at seminars. We are particularly grateful for ideas and comments from participants at the first PEGNet Workshop in Kiel, April 28, 2006; the Economics Research Seminar at ISS in The Hague, March 2005; the PIDDCP (Political Institutions, Development and a Domestic Civil Peace) Workshop in Oxford, November 10–12, 2005; the National Conference on Political Science, Bergen, Norway, January 4–6, 2006; and several Department of International Development seminars. We have also received many insightful comments and suggestions on parts of the book from James Foster (Chapter 5), and Scott Gates, Håvard Hegre, Eric Neumayer, Håvard Strand and Martha Reynal-Querol (Chapter 7). We also acknowledge the inputs of the whole CRISE team – in particular, besides helpful interactions among the authors, we thank Rachael Diprose, Adam Higazi, Maritza Paredes, Andrea Portugal and Marianna Volpi. We would like to thank Centro Militare di Studi Strategici (CeMISS), Italian Ministry of Defence, Rome, for their generous funding of the survey research in both Ghana and Nigeria, reported on in Chapter 10.

F.S.

Acknowledgements

Table 4.3 is reprinted from Songsore, J. 2003. *Regional Development in Ghana: The Theory and the Reality*. Accra: Woeli Publishing Services.

Table 4.4 is reprinted with permission of Rowman & Littlefield from Shapiro, T.M., and Kenty-Drane, J.L. 2005. The racial wealth gap. In Conrad, C.A., Whitehead, J., Mason, P., and Stewart, J., eds, *African Americans in the U.S. Economy*. Lanham, MD: Rowman & Littlefield.

Table 4.5 is reprinted with the permission of Simon & Schuster Adult Publishing Group, from Thernstrom, S., and Thernstrom, A. 1997. *America in Black And White: One Nation, Indivisible*. Copyright © 1997 by Stephan Thernstrom and Abigail Thernstrom. All rights reserved.

Table 4.7 is reprinted with permission of Sage Publications Inc. Books from Sakamoto, A., and Xie, Y. 2006. The socioeconomic attainments of Asian Americans. In Pyong, G.M., ed., *Asian Americans – Contemporary Trends and Issues*; permission conveyed through Copyright Clearance Center, Inc.

Table 8.2 is reprinted from *The Political Economy of Ivory Coast*, edited by I. William Zartman and Christopher Delgado. Copyright © 1984 by Praeger Publishers. Reproduced with permission of Greenwood Publishing Group, Inc., Westport CT.

Table 8.3 is reprinted with permission of the World Bank from Den Tuinder, B. 1978. *Ivory Coast: The Challenge of Success – A Report for the World Bank*. Baltimore: Johns Hopkins University Press.

Table 8.4 is reprinted with permission of the World Bank from Glewwe, P. 1988. The Distribution of Welfare in Côte d'Ivoire in 1985. *Living Standards Measurement Study Working Paper No. 29*. Washington: World Bank.

Table 8.7 is reprinted from Szereszewski, R. 1966. The macroeconomic structure. In Birmingham, W.B., Neustadt, I., and Omaboe, E.N., eds, *A Study of Contemporary Ghana*. London: George Allen and Unwin.

Table 8.8 is reprinted with kind permission of Springer Science and Business Media from Ewusi, K. 1976. Disparities in levels of regional development in Ghana. *Social Indicators Research* 3 (1): 75–100. Table 3. Copyright © 1976 by D. Reidel Publishing Company, Dordrecht-Holland.

Table 11.1 is reprinted with permission of Cambridge University Press from Yashar, D. 2005. *Contesting Citizenship in Latin America*. Cambridge: CUP.

An earlier version of Chapter 11 was published in *Bulletin of Latin American Research* 25 (4), October 2006. Reprinted with permission of Blackwell Publishing.

Every effort has been made to trace all copyright holders for material included in this book and the publishers would be happy to correct any errors or omissions.

Notes on the Contributors

Graham K. Brown is Research Officer, Southeast Asia, at the Centre for Research on Inequality, Human Security and Ethnicity at the Department of International Development, University of Oxford.

His research interests include separatist conflict in Southeast Asia; local elections and ethnic conflict in Indonesia; historical analysis of the emergence and development of ethnic identities in Southeast Asia, particularly Indonesia and Malaysia; Islamic politics in Southeast Asia; and the electoral process in Malaysia.

Corinne Caumartin is Research Officer, Latin America, at the Centre for Research on Inequality, Human Security and Ethnicity at the Department of International Development, University of Oxford.

Her research is focused on Latin American politics, ethnic politics and inequalities, as well as public security, civil–military relations, policing and police reform.

Matthew J. Gibney is Reader in Forced Migration and Senior Researcher specializing in political theory at the Centre for Research on Inequality, Human Security and Ethnicity at the Department of International Development, University of Oxford.

His research focuses on the evolution and future of political asylum in liberal democratic countries, the normative/ethical issues associated with forced and voluntary migration, democratic political institutions and the representation of ethnic difference.

George Gray Molina is the coordinator of the Bolivian Human Development Report at UNDP-Bolivia and partner researcher at the Centre for Research on Inequality, Human Security and Ethnicity at the Department of International Development, University of Oxford.

Arnim Langer is Research Officer in Economics and Politics, West Africa, at the Centre for Research on Inequality, Human Security and Ethnicity at the Department of International Development, University of Oxford.

His research focuses on the causes and consequences of conflict, post-conflict economic reconstruction, sustainable peace building, inequality, group behaviour and identity formation, and Africa (particularly Côte d'Ivoire, Ghana and Nigeria).

Luca Mancini is Research Officer in Applied Econometrics at the Centre for Research on Inequality, Human Security and Ethnicity at the Department of International Development, University of Oxford.

His research interests include applied development economics, the economics of civil conflict and inequality.

Gudrun Østby is a PhD candidate in Political Science at the University of Oslo and part-time Researcher at the International Peace Research Institute, Oslo (PRIO).

Her research interests include horizontal inequalities, polarization and conflict; cultural factors and civil conflict; natural resources and conflict; subnational conflict studies; child soldiers; and ethnicity and politics in sub-Saharan Africa.

Frances Stewart is Professor of Development Economics, Director of the Centre for Research on Inequality, Human Security and Ethnicity at the Department of International Development and a fellow of Somerville College at the University of Oxford.

Her research interests centre on horizontal inequalities, poverty and human development, group behaviour and the causes and consequences of conflict. She is vice-chair of the United Nations Committee on Development Policy and an overseer of the Thomas Watson Institute at Brown University. She was named one of 50 outstanding technological leaders for 2003 by *Scientific American*. She has been president of the British and Irish Development Studies Association and has been elected as President of the Human Development and Capability Association for 2008–2010.

Her previous books include *War and Underdevelopment* (2001), with Valpy Fitzgerald and others, and *Adjustment with a Human Face* (1987), with Giovanni Andrea Cornia and Richard Jolly.

Rosemary Thorp is University Reader in the Economics of Latin America and Senior Researcher responsible for the Latin American Programme at the Centre for Research on Inequality, Human Security and Ethnicity at the Department of International Development, University of Oxford. Her research examines institutions behind the market, the functions of the market in Latin America and the making of economic policy in Latin America.

Her previous books include *Progress, Poverty and Exclusion: An Economic History of Latin America in the 20th Century* (1998).

Ukoha Ukiwo is Research Fellow at the Centre for Advanced Social Science (CASS), Port Harcourt, Nigeria, and a visting scholar at the Institute of International Studies, University of California, Berkeley, USA. He was a CRISE scholar at the Department of International Development, University of Oxford, UK, from 2003 to 2006.

Part I
Concepts and Issues

1
Horizontal Inequalities and Conflict: An Introduction and some Hypotheses

Frances Stewart

1.1 Introduction

Violent conflict within multiethnic and multireligious countries is a major problem in the world today – from the former Yugoslavia and USSR to Northern Ireland and the Basque country, from Rwanda to Darfur, Indonesia to Fiji, numerous bitter and deadly conflicts are fought along ethnic or religious lines. In addition to the direct injuries and loss of life both on and off the battlefield that result, violent organized conflict is also a major cause of poverty, often leading to economic regress, with much the highest incidence of such conflict found in the poorest countries of the world. Seeking a way of preventing these conflicts is thus of paramount importance.

Yet not all multiethnic or multireligious societies are violent. Indeed the vast majority are not (Fearon and Laitin, 1996). So it is not the case that those with cultural, ethnic, religious or racial differences cannot live together peacefully, as is suggested by the view that there is an unavoidable 'clash of civilisations' (Huntington, 1993). The question, then, is why ethnic or religious conflict breaks out in some circumstances and not others. If we can answer that, we may be able to identify ways of preventing such conflicts and their enormous costs in terms of deaths, injuries, and economic and social collapse.

This book explores one important cause of such conflicts: the existence of major horizontal inequalities (HIs). Horizontal inequalities are inequalities in economic, social or political dimensions or cultural status between culturally defined groups. The book considers the role of horizontal inequalities in causing conflict, and policies that would contribute to reducing HIs and thereby reduce the likelihood of conflict.

This chapter provides the general framework for our discussion: the next section briefly indicates the significance of the problem of conflict between identity groups, within and across nations; Section 1.3 discusses the complex issue of how groups, which potentially provide the basis for conflict, are formed and mobilized; Section 1.4 defines HIs in more detail and explains why they may lead to violent group mobilization, drawing on the example of South Africa; Section 1.5 develops the main hypotheses on the relationship between HIs and conflict to be considered in the rest of the book; and the final section explains the organization of the book.

1.2   Groups in conflict

The incidence of violent conflict among poor countries is high – seven out of ten of the poorest countries in the world are undergoing or have recently experienced some sort of civil war. These conflicts involve very heavy costs. The immediate human costs in terms of deaths, injuries and refugees are most obvious and well known. Deaths as a result of the fighting itself vary from a few thousand to hundreds of thousands; the civil war in Afghanistan claimed an estimated 560,000 direct battle deaths between 1978 and 2002; while nearly 2 million are estimated to have been killed in Southern Sudan and the Nuban mountains from 1983 to 1998 (Burr, 1998). Refugee movements often amount to millions. 'Indirect' deaths as a result of war-induced famine, following disruptions in production, marketing and purchasing power, are often far greater than the direct deaths. The war in the Democratic Republic of Congo from 2000, for example, is estimated to have accounted for nearly 4 million deaths, including both direct and indirect fatalities (Coghlan *et al.*, 2006). Moreover, there are many other heavy indirect costs as a result of the economic and social disruption war causes. Violent conflict is one of the biggest obstacles to development, reducing incomes and investment and undermining human development, as well as causing immense suffering among the belligerents and the countries' populations more generally. Regression analysis suggests an average loss in gross domestic product (GDP) *per capita* of between 2.00 and 2.40 per cent *per annum* among countries experiencing conflict (Imai and Weinstein, 2000; Hoeffler and Reynal-Querol, 2003), while case studies show huge variability in costs, with the worst conflicts leading to far greater losses. For example, one estimate suggested a cumulative loss of half of GDP in the case of Iraq in the Iraq–Iran war, while the increase in infant deaths during the Uganda conflicts amounted to 2 per cent of the population (Stewart *et al.*, 2001).

Violent conflict, of course, is not confined to poor countries, even though its incidence is greatest among them. The conflict in Bosnia that accompanied the breakup of the former Yugoslavia led to over 100,000 deaths and over 2 million refugees and internally displaced persons (IDPs) (Tabeau and Bijak, 2005). Similarly, many violent conflicts were associated with the disintegration of the USSR. Some, notably that in Chechnya, continue to this day – again with heavy costs.

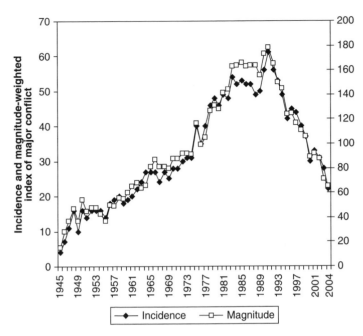

Figure 1.1 Incidence and magnitude of major episodes of political violence, 1946–2004
Source: Calculated from Marshall (2006).

The incidence of violent conflicts rose quite steadily from the 1950s, accelerating following the end of the Cold War, but then declining as the old Cold War–inspired conflicts (such as those in Mozambique and Nicaragua) came to an end, while the often violent transition to new regimes in the former Eastern Bloc gradually subsided (Figure 1.1); a similar pattern can be observed in the magnitude of refugees (Figure 1.2).

During the Cold War many conflicts presented themselves as wars about ideology or class, following the ideological East/West division, with each side supported by the major powers along ideological lines. The conflicts in Vietnam, Cambodia, Mozambique and El Salvador are examples. But even then, some conflicts were overtly conducted along identity lines – for example, the Catholic/Protestant troubles in Northern Ireland and a number of Middle Eastern conflicts (between Christians and Muslims in Lebanon, Sunnis and Shias in Iraq/Iran and Jews and Muslims in Palestine/Israel), as well as the recurrent ethnic conflicts in Burundi and Nigeria. Moreover, in many of the ideological wars, the conflicts had an implicit ethnic or racial base. This was the case, for example, in Mozambique, where the Xitsonga and the Ndau from the south and centre fought northern ethnicities; or in Guatemala and Peru, where the conflicts were presented as ideological and

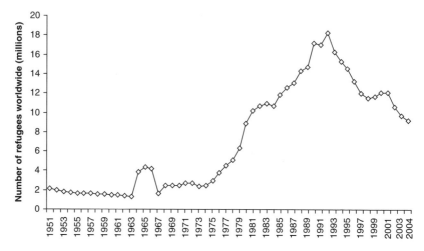

Figure 1.2   Refugee trends, 1951–2004
Sources: UNHCR (2000, 2006).

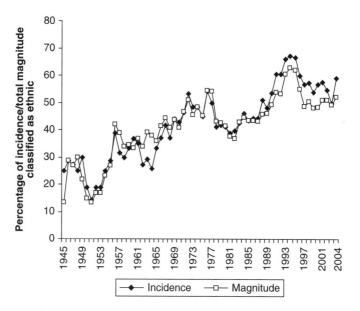

Figure 1.3   Ethnic violence as a proportion of major political violence, 1946–2004
Source: Calculated from Marshall (2006).

led by intellectuals of European origin, but the vast majority of those killed were indigenous (Caumartin, 2005; Figueroa and Barrón, 2005).

The identity basis of conflicts has become much more explicit since the end of the Cold War, as ideological differences have diminished and socialism no longer seems to be a serious alternative nor is using it as a banner a guarantee of external financial support. According to the Center for Systematic Peace (CSP) 'a virtual cornucopia of these seemingly intractable (and previously 'invisible') social identity conflicts exploded onto the world scene and captured the public and policy eyes.'[1] Data on conflict show a major increase in the proportion of all conflicts that are labelled as 'ethnic': from 15 per cent in 1953 to nearly 60 per cent by 2005 (see Figure 1.3)

These identity conflicts have also acquired global dimensions, with Islam versus the West replacing the ideological divisions of the Cold War, with the wars in Afghanistan and Iraq and the Israel/Palestine conflict as clear examples. Today, then, mobilization along group identity lines has become the single most important source of violent conflict. The next section will consider how such identities are formed.

1.3 Group formation and mobilization

People see themselves in many different ways; they have many identities. Some are fluid, short-lived and insignificant (for example, being a member of an evening class), while others are more permanent and more significant personally and socially (for example, gender, ethnicity and religion). The importance people attribute to different aspects of their identity also varies according to context and over time. Clearly, where violent conflicts are mobilized and organized by identity, such identities must be sufficiently important to enough people to make them prepared to fight, kill and even die in the name of that identity. Personal motivation also obviously plays a part in causing people to fight (Collier and Hoeffler, 2004; Keen, 1998), but it is our contention that in many conflicts people are primarily motivated by their group identity – their religion or ethnicity – and consequently group motives are a vital driving force. For this to happen, the group boundaries must be relatively clearly defined and have some continuity over time.

People may be divided into groups in many ways – according to geography, behaviour, language, physical characteristics and so on. Yet only those divisions that have or may acquire strong social significance – that is, such meaning for their members and for others in society that they influence behaviour and well-being in a significant way – are likely to form the basis of identity conflicts. Group identities arise partly from individuals' *own* perceptions of membership of and identity with a particular group – that is, the self-perceptions of those *in* the group – but they are also determined by the perceptions of *those outside the group* about others.[2] The important question, then, is why and when some differences are perceived as being socially significant and others are not, both by group members themselves and by others. Anthropologists have differed sharply on this question. At one extreme are the so-called primordialists, who argue that 'ethnicity is a cultural given, a quasi-natural state of being determined by one's descent and with, in the extreme view, socio-biological determinants' (Douglas, 1988). 'Basic group identity consists of the ready-made set of endowments and identifications which every individual shares with others from the moment of birth by chance of the family into which he is born at that given time and given place' (Isaacs, 1975, quoted in Banks, 1996: 39–40). For primordialists, ethnic identity is etched deep in the subconscious of the individual from birth.

The primordial view, however, doesn't explain why ethnic groups change over time – why they are of pre-eminent significance at some points and then the boundaries and characteristics of groups change. For example, Cohen (1969) has shown how some rural people moving to towns in Nigeria became 'detribalized', while tribal identity became more important for other urbanized Nigerians. Furthermore, it is widely agreed that many tribal distinctions in Africa were invented by the colonial powers:

> Almost all recent studies of nineteenth century pre-colonial Africa have emphasised that far from there being a single 'tribal' identity, most Africans moved in and out of multiple identities, defining themselves at one moment as subject to this chief, at another moment as a member of that cult, at another moment as part of this clan, and at yet another moment as an initiate in that professional guild. (Ranger, 1983: 248)

> Modern Central Africa tribes are not so much survivals from a pre-colonial past but rather colonial creations by colonial officers and African intellectuals. (van Binsbergen 1976, quoted in Ranger, 1983: 248)

One example is the distinction between Hutus and Tutsis, which some historians argue was largely invented by the colonial powers for administrative convenience (Lemarchand, 1994).

Instrumentalists, in contrast, see ethnicity as being developed instrumentally, to be used by groups and their leaders in order to achieve political or economic goals. Cohen, cited above, explained the development of Hausa consciousness and customs in this way.[3] Similarly, Glazer and Moynihan (1975) argued that ethnicity was maintained and enhanced by migrant groups in the US in order to promote their economic interests. The colonial inventions, according to the instrumentalist view, served administrative purposes. Further, the use of ethnic symbols and the enhancement of ethnic identities, often through the reworking of historical memories, is frequently used as a powerful mechanism for the mobilization of support for conflict. Numerous examples, presented in Alexander *et al.* (2000), as well as by Cohen (1969, 1974), Turton (1997) and others, have shown how ethnicity has been used by political and intellectual elites prior to, and in the course of, wars. In international wars, this takes the shape of enhancing national consciousness, with flag waving, historical references, military parades and so on. In civil wars, it is a matter of raising ethnic or religious consciousness. An example here would be the radio broadcasts by the extremist Hutus before the 1994 massacre in Rwanda, in which the Tutsis were repeatedly depicted as subhuman, like rats to be eliminated, echoing Nazi anti-Jewish propaganda of the 1930s. Similarly, Osama bin Laden has appealed to Muslim consciousness, arguing that the conflict he and his followers are waging against the West is 'in essence a religious war' (*The Observer*, 4 November 2001).

A third perspective, with much in common with the instrumental one, is that of 'social constructivists'. Constructivists too believe that ethnicities are frequently used instrumentally for political purposes, but their emphasis is on the 'making' and 'remaking' of ethnic boundaries that must occur to make such instrumentalism possible. Differences are emphasized, even invented, by leaders in order to construct social groups. Such construction is an ongoing process which may reinforce existing group boundaries or develop new ones following the political and social motivation of the leaders responsible for such construction. Group boundaries, it is argued, are made and remade (Anderson, 1983). For example, Akindès (2003) has analyzed how identities are 'marketed' by the media as well as by political leaders in the case of Côte d'Ivoire.

Yet both instrumentalists and constructivists generally recognize that there need to be some felt differences in behaviour, customs, ideology or religion to make it possible to raise ethnic or other consciousness in an instrumental way. For example, Glazer and Moynihan (1975: 379) state that 'For there to be the possibility for an ethnic community at all, there will normally exist some visible cultural differences or "markers" which might help to divide communities into fairly well defined groupings or ethnic categories.' Thus some shared circumstances are needed for group construction – for example, speaking the same language, sharing cultural traditions, living in the same place or facing similar sources of hardship or exploitation. Past group formation, although possibly constructed for political or economic purposes at the time, also contributes to present differences. Whether the origins of a group are instrumental or not, the effect is to change perceptions and make the differences seem real to group members – this is why group identities are so powerful as sources of action. As Turton (1997: 82) puts it, the power of ethnicity or 'its very effectiveness as a means of advancing group interests depends upon its being seen as "primordial" by those who make claims in its name.' Hence, what was a dependent variable at one point in history can act as an independent variable in contributing to current perceptions.[4]

Construction of a cohesive identity can be effected by leaders of a group, or others, including the state, who classify or categorize people into groups

(Barth, 1969; Brubaker and Cooper, 2000). Such categorization can be quite arbitrary, as is argued to have been in the case of the Belgian colonial classification of Hutus and Tutsis, or, despite some arbitrariness, it may follow some visible markers. The Nazi classification of Jews and the classification of 'blacks' in the US historically are examples of such categorization, combining arbitrary decisions on boundaries with some common 'markers' of ancestry. Where categorization by others is the source of group boundaries, what people themselves feel about their own identities may not be important at all: what matters is what others think they are.

Group identities can potentially provide the basis for violent conflict mobilization whether they are primarily own-constructed identities – when they may be used to motivate people to demand rights and to rebel – or identities constructed by the state or other groups – when they may be used to discriminate against (and sometimes fight against) particular groups. Whether group boundaries emerge out of the felt identities of the group itself or through categorization by others, groups which mobilize in a way that threatens social stability generally have some shared characteristics, which usually makes it quite easy to identify members; and they also have some continuity. Yet in almost every case, there is also some fluidity and uncertainty about precise group boundaries, which evolve over time in response to circumstances – for example, during the Biafran war, the Iwerri in Nigeria chose to reject their prior Ibo identity; while in India the Telugu-speaking people, who were an apparently homogeneous group seeking autonomy from the state of Madras, became quite sharply divided once they had gained this autonomy (Horowitz, 1985: 66). Similar developments are occurring in Aceh now that it has achieved the autonomy for which it fought.

This book argues that group mobilization along lines of identity is a central feature of many conflicts, taking a broadly social constructivist view of group formation. The salience of particular identities is increased by political action – by political leaders, media or the education system – sometimes in order to raise consciousness of own identities, sometimes of that of others. Yet, though we take a social constructivist line, we also argue that people themselves can become strongly convinced about the *essential* nature of their identities and that of others – which is why mobilization by identity can work. Moreover, while people can choose which identities are important to them, for the more enduring aspects of their identity they are not free to choose any identity, as it were, 'off a shelf', shifting to whatever seems most convenient at a given moment. Thus, while someone can readily choose to change their social club or to abandon it altogether, Kenyans without mixed parentage cannot choose to stop being Kikuyu and become Luo, though they can choose to downplay their 'Kikuyuness'. In any particular case, history and social context will determine the possibilities. For example, in Europe today a change in religion is relatively easy, but this was much less so in earlier centuries, when religious divisions were a major cause of conflict;

and in some contexts it is almost impossible in some contemporary developing countries.[5] In Peru today, someone who is of indigenous origin can choose to define themselves as *mestizo* but they still cannot choose to avoid all racism. It is where there is limited freedom to switch group that groups' boundaries are particularly important in terms of creating potential group grievances, and hence in terms of political mobilization. Where people can shift groups in an instantaneous and costless way, then group distinctions and boundaries matter much less.

While many conflicts have a cultural dimension, that is the groups involved perceive themselves as belonging to a common culture (ethnicity or religion) and are partly fighting for cultural autonomy, it is evident that cultural differences are not a sufficient explanation for conflict, since the peoples of many multicultural societies live together relatively peacefully. Indeed, Fearon and Laitin (1996) have estimated that from 1960 to 1979, of all the potential ethnic conflicts in Africa (defined as occurring where different ethnic groups live side by side) only 0.01 per cent turned into actual violent conflict. In some cases, groups may live together peacefully for decades and then conflict erupts.

We need, therefore, to go beyond cultural explanations of conflict to economic and political explanations. As Abner Cohen argued,

> Men may and do certainly joke about or ridicule the strange and bizarre customs of men from other ethnic groups, because these customs are different from their own. But they do not fight over such differences alone. *When men do . . . fight across ethnic lines it is nearly always the case that they fight over some fundamental issues concerning the distribution and exercise of power, whether economic, political, or both.*
>
> (1974: 94, italics added)

In other words, cultural differences do not lead to violent conflict unless there are also major economic and/or political causes.

The motivation of the participants is clearly at the root of any violent situation. Many contemporary economists emphasize the pursuit of individual economic advantages as the prime force-driving conflicts (see, for example, Collier and Hoeffler, 2004; Keen, 1998). But the majority of internal conflicts are *organized group* conflicts – they are neither exclusively nor primarily a matter of individuals committing acts of violence against others. What is most often involved is group mobilization of people with particular shared identities or goals to attack others in the name of the group. While young men may fight because they are unemployed, uneducated and have few other opportunities, they also generally fight out of loyalty to a group (or sometimes to an ideology or a cause). Examples include the militia in Najaf in Iraq, the Hutus in Rwanda, the Tamils in Sri Lanka and the Catholics in Northern Ireland, amongst others. Sometimes, indeed, the power of their beliefs or loyalties is so strong that they are prepared to sacrifice their own interests – in the extreme case their own lives – for the wider objectives of the group. Often governments, dominated by a particular identity group, are involved: sometimes instigating attacks against other groups, and sometimes under attack. In fact, Holsti (2000) argues that state violence has more often than not been the initiating cause of recent conflicts.

In contemporary conflicts, group affiliations occur along a variety of different lines. In some cases it is religious affiliation that provides the relevant binding and categorizing identity for the groups involved (for example, the conflicts in Northern Ireland; Muslim/Hindu conflicts in India; and the Muslim/Christian conflicts in the Philippines). In other cases the salient cleavage seems to be racial (for example, in Fiji). Ethnicity is a binding factor in some conflicts (as in Rwanda and Sri Lanka), while in other cases clans are the main source of affiliation (for example, in Somalia). There are also many overlapping distinctions: in some situations, for example, both ethnic and religious affiliations are pertinent (such as in Jos in Nigeria, and in Poso in Indonesia and in the Balkans), while class and ethnicity overlap in Central America, and caste and ethnicity are intertwined in Nepal.

Large-scale *group* mobilization – particularly for violent actions – is unlikely to occur in the absence of serious grievances at both leadership and mass level. The role of leaders is important in political mobilization, in choosing the grounds for mobilization (whether, for example, religion, class or ethnicity) and in 'selling' the importance of the chosen identity to the people being mobilized. At the leadership level, the main motivation may be political ambition and hence such mobilization is particularly likely to occur where there is political exclusion of the group's leaders; while the followers may also be concerned with the political representation of the group as a whole, their primary motivation is more likely to be grievance concerning the economic and social position of their group relative to others. Both leaders and followers may become strongly motivated where there are severe and consistent economic, social, and political differences between culturally defined groups, termed here *multidimensional horizontal inequalities*.

It should be noted that it is not necessarily the relatively deprived who instigate violence. The privileged may also do so, fearing a loss of power and position. The prospect of the possible loss of political power can act as a powerful motive for state-sponsored violence which occurs with the aim of suppressing opposition and maintaining power.

1.4   Horizontal inequalities and mobilization

As noted above, horizontal inequalities are inequalities between culturally defined groups or groups with shared identities. They are called *horizontal* to distinguish them from inequalities among individuals, which we refer to as *vertical inequalities* (VIs). These identities may be formed by religion, ethnic ties or racial affiliations, or other salient factors which bind groups of people together, following the discussion in the previous section.

For simplification, we can categorize HIs into four areas: political participation; economic aspects; social aspects; and cultural status. Each of these contains a number of elements. For example, HIs in political participation can occur at the level of the cabinet, the parliament, the bureaucracy, local government or the army, amongst others. HIs in economic aspects encompass access to and ownership of assets (financial, land, livestock and human and social capital), employment opportunities and incomes. HIs in social aspects encompass access to various services (education, health, water, sanitation and housing), and human outcome indicators (such as measures of health and educational achievements). HIs in cultural status include the extent to which a society recognizes (or fails to recognize) a group's cultural practices (for example, in matters of dress, holidays and so on).

While the four broad categories are relevant to *every* society, the elements that are relevant in a particular case depend on the nature of the society, its political system, its economy and its social structure. For example, land may be irrelevant in modern urban societies but is clearly of paramount importance in many developing rural economies such as in Zimbabwe, while employment seems to be important in most countries. In natural-resource–rich economies, the control over such resources, either directly or via the state, is an important source of group competition. Access to housing is of critical importance in more developed economies, such as Northern Ireland, but is less important where people mostly construct their own housing (as in many African countries), where access to public sector employment is particularly important as a way out of poverty.

There are causal connections between different HIs. For example, inequalities in political power often lead to similar social and economic inequalities. A biased distribution of government jobs and provisions of infrastructure is common, with the group in power discriminating in its favour. For example, in Burundi in the 1990s, half of government investment went to the Bujumbura region and its vicinity, which is the home of the elite Tutsi group (Gaffney, 2000). In some countries, the president and his coterie have taken a massive share of state resources for their private use, such as the Duvaliers in Haiti and the Somoza family in Nicaragua (Lundahl, 2000; Pastor and Boyce, 2000). Moreover, there are connections between economic and social elements. Lack of access to education leads to poor economic opportunities, while low incomes tend to result in poor educational access and achievements in a vicious cycle of deprivation. There are also reinforcing cycles of privilege and deprivation because of the way that one type of capital requires others to be productive. (These cycles, which help explain the persistence of HIs, are explored in Chapter 4.)

The presence of sharp HIs provides a general motive for political mobilization. If governments fail to respond to demands – or indeed repress them violently – this political mobilization may become violent, with the power of identities binding people together. Where there are sharp political HIs, then group leaders may find that violence is the only way to secure political power. Similarly, where groups are denied high-level jobs (for example, in the bureaucracy) educated people have a strong source of resentment. For the masses, in contrast, resentments can be caused by lack of access to land and employment, as well as social services. Lack of cultural recognition can be a running source of resentment, while particular attacks on cultural symbols can be a trigger for conflict (for example, through the desecration of a holy place, as in the destruction of the Babri Mosque in Ayodhya in India).

HIs may be spatially distributed: that is, particular regions of a country may be deprived (or privileged) compared to other regions. In such cases, HIs can lead to separatist claims where resource-rich provinces seek autonomy, resenting the redistribution of local resources to other parts of the country (for example, Biafra in Nigeria or Aceh in Indonesia). Yet, sometimes it is poorer regions which feel exploited by the richer areas (for example, in Bangladesh and Eritrea). Different types of conflict emerge, however, where people from competing groups live in the *same* geographic area, as in Rwanda or Burundi. In such cases, the deprived may seek political and economic rights, or control over government institutions. There may also be attacks on particular groups and pressure for ethnic cleansing without direct government involvement.

The four categories of HIs, and some major elements within each, are presented in Table 1.1, together with examples of where particular HIs appear to have been instrumental in provoking conflict.

1.4.1   Horizontal inequalities in South Africa

The case of South Africa is illustrative of the role of HIs, their pervasive and multidimensional nature and how they can be politicized, leading to political mobilization, protest and eventually violence.

Historically, during the apartheid era, the South African case was an extreme example of very sharp HIs of every type. HIs between blacks (77 per cent of the population in 1996) and whites (10.9 per cent) were entrenched by a white political elite (initially colonial) over the centuries preceding the democratic transition in 1993.

As one scholar observed,

> The history of South Africa's polity is dominated by the use of political power to attain and maintain socio-economic ends. A white minority inherited political power in 1910 and during the next eight decades used this power to entrench itself politically and to enhance its economic, cultural and social interests.
>
> (Schrire, 1996: 59–60)

Table 1.1 Some examples of horizontal inequality in conflict situations

Political dimension	Economic dimension		Social access and situation	Cultural status recognition
	Assets	Employment and incomes		
Participation in government Fiji, Burundi, Bosnia and Herzegovina, Uganda, Sri Lanka	*Land* Fiji, Cambodia, El Salvador, Haiti	*Incomes* Malaysia, South Africa, Fiji, Chiapas	*Education* Rwanda, Burundi, Haiti, South Africa, Northern Uganda, Kosovo	*National holidays*
	Privately owned capital Malaysia, South Africa, Burundi	*Government employment* Sri Lanka, Fiji	*Health services* Burundi, Northern Uganda, Chiapas	*Respect for cultural sites* India, Northern Ireland
	Government Infrastructure Chiapas, Mexico, Burundi	*Private employment* Fiji, Uganda, Malaysia	*Safe water* Northern Uganda, Chiapas	*Respect for cultural behaviour* Latin America, historically
Army/police Fiji, Northern Ireland, Burundi, Kosova	*Aid* Afghanistan, Sudan, Rwanda	*'Elite' employment* South Africa, Fiji, Northern Ireland	*Housing* Northern Ireland	
	Natural resources Liberia, Sierra Leone, Indonesia	*Unemployment* South Africa, Northern Ireland	*Poverty* Chiapas, Uganda, South Africa	

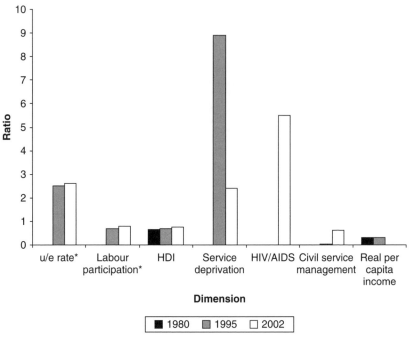

* ratio of black to other.

Figure 1.4   Ratio of performance of black South Africans to white South Africans
Source: UNDP (2003).

The large and consistent HIs that existed under the white-dominated government are well known (see Figure 1.4).

- *Economic HIs*: Real *per capita* GDP of blacks in 1980 was 8 per cent of that of whites; this had risen to 10 per cent by 1990 and just over 12 per cent by 2000 (van der Berg and Louw, 2004). Whites still owned 90 per cent of the land in 2007.[6]
- *Social HIs*: State education expenditure on each white student was 14 times that on each black student in 1980 and adult literacy among blacks was two-thirds that of whites. In 1993, there was only one formal-sector brick house for every 43 Africans compared to one for every 3.5 whites (Knight, 2001). Infant mortality rates among blacks were six times those of whites in 1980 and life expectancy was 56 among blacks and 70 among whites (UNDP, 2003). The ratio of the Human Development Index (HDI) of blacks to whites was 0.64 in 1980 and only 0.60 in 1990 (ibid.).

- *Political HIs*: Throughout the period, the whites had all the cabinet posts, and in 1994 accounted for 94 per cent of the higher echelons of the civil service, and all the senior positions in the police and army (UNDP, 2000).

Following unsuccessful peaceful protests, the sharp HIs in every dimension led to armed rebellion from 1976, until the transfer of power in 1993. Over this period there was some diminution in HIs, partly for economic reasons and in a very partial and unsuccessful effort to secure peace without transferring power.

An overriding objective of the black-majority post-1993 government has been to reduce black/white differentials, but these efforts have been constrained by limits on government expenditure and by the economic liberalization agenda. There was a complete reversal in political inequalities at the top, and a major reduction in HIs in managerial posts in the civil service, where the black share had risen to 63 per cent by 1996. There was a substantial improvement in service access for the black population, and the ratio of blacks/whites on an index of service deprivation fell from nine in 1995 to 2.4 in 2002 (UNDP, 2003). The poverty rate among blacks, which had been over 40 times that of whites in 1995, fell to eight times in 2002. Differentials in infant mortality rates, life expectancy and adult literacy initially narrowed but are rising again with the unequal incidence of HIV/AIDS. The ratio of the HDI of blacks to whites rose from 0.60 in 1990 to 0.73 in 2000 (ibid.).

Efforts to reduce economic inequalities were less successful. While the blacks' share of national income rose from under half in 1985 to three-quarters in 1995, their share of population also increased and there was only a small decrease in the differential of real adjusted GNP *per capita*. Efforts to 'empower' black business by increasing their role in private capital ownership, with a target of 30 per cent ownership, appear to have faltered with the share of quoted companies with significant black influence at just 5 per cent in 2007 (*Financial Times*, 29 June 2007), while Sherer (2000) finds evidence of persistent labour-market discrimination in the post-apartheid era. In general, differentials are diminishing, but remain extremely high. According to a 2005 report, 'Vast racial and gender inequalities in the distribution of and access to wealth, income, skills and employment persist' (Republic of South Africa, 2005: para. 1.5). Nonetheless, with political power and increasing socioeconomic opportunities, the black population give broad political support to the government, while the white population remain the gainers economically. There seems little danger of renewed conflict, but the extremely high level of criminality testifies to the unsatisfactory nature of the economic inequalities.

1.5 Horizontal inequalities and conflict: The main hypotheses

This section considers the main hypotheses concerning the relationship between HIs and violent conflict, to be explored in the rest of the book. In this book when we talk of violent conflict, we are referring to serious political violence, that is violence that primarily has political objectives. Thus we are *not* referring to criminality, domestic violence or relatively minor episodes of political violence, of which there are many. Such serious violent political conflicts can be of different kinds. One important distinction is between conflicts that involve the state, as one significant actor, and those that do not. Within the former category, there are conflicts in which state repression, sometimes spontaneous and sometimes in response to rebellion, is an important source of violence. A second type of violence in which the state is integrally involved is separatist conflict. There are also communal conflicts in which the state is *not* one of the parties to the conflict, though it might intervene on one side or the other. The violent conflicts discussed in this book include examples of each of these kinds.

The hypotheses concern the political outcomes likely to be associated with HIs, where HIs are observed inequalities between groups. We are aware that people take actions on the basis of their *perceptions* of others and of their relative position rather than *actual* inequality. However, in much of this book we will investigate the relationship between *externally measured* inequalities, rather than *self-perceived* HIs, and conflict. The validity of this approach rests on the assumption that perceptions broadly reflect the observed reality. This assumption is being investigated by surveys of perceptions in seven countries.[7] Chapter 10 reports on the findings of two of these surveys – in Ghana and Nigeria – permitting some insights into the relationship between observed and perceived HIs.

1. *Our first hypothesis is that conflict is more likely where there are significant political or economic HIs, or both.*

    Both political and socioeconomic inequalities are of major relevance to political outcomes: strong political HIs mean that leaders of groups feel politically excluded and are thus more likely to lead opposition and possibly rebellion; while socioeconomic inequalities mean that the people as a whole have strong grievances on ethnic lines and are thus likely to be more readily mobilized.

2. *Our second hypothesis is that political mobilization is especially likely where there are consistent HIs, that is both political and economic HIs run in the same direction.*

    Where HIs are inconsistent (that is, there are political HIs but not economic, or there are economic HIs but not political), it seems probable that they are less conflict-promoting than where they are consistent. This is because where there are political HIs but not economic, that is, the economically privileged are politically excluded, the group may mind less about their political exclusion. This seems to have been the case, for example, among the Kikuyu under Moi in Kenya. Similarly, where the economically underprivileged are politically included, the stimulus to opposition will be less, because the potential leaders gain from their political inclusion, and the mass of people may get some satisfaction from that and from the prospect that political inclusion will confer economic benefits. This describes the situation in South Africa post-apartheid.

3. *Our third hypothesis is that lack of cultural recognition and equity, or cultural status HIs, will be provocative, while cultural inclusion will help sustain peace. A change in either direction may be particularly relevant to group mobilization.*

   As we proceeded with our research into HIs, it became apparent that as well as political and socioeconomic HIs, cultural events and *mores* were highly relevant to group grievances. These include issues such as language and education policy, recognition given to particular groups in terms of national holidays, formal and informal attitudes to dress and other types of group behaviour. While it is difficult to measure 'cultural HIs', they do form a component of the overall picture, and one which Langer and Brown explore further in Chapter 3.

4. *Our fourth hypothesis is that political mobilization and possibly conflict will become more likely where HIs are widening.*

   The direction of change in HIs is also likely to be relevant to political outcomes, since if the situation is worsening it seems probable that this is provocative, and if it is improving it will be ameliorative.

Apart from these formal hypotheses, the context in which HIs occur also matters. In particular, political conditions (including the nature of the state), cultural demographic conditions and economic conditions all affect the likelihood of conflict for any given state of HIs.

1.5.1 Political conditions

The nature of the state is of fundamental importance in determining both the cause and the duration of conflict. Several aspects are of relevance:

- *The structure of the state and of power.* Some political systems are highly concentrated, lacking division of powers or geographic decentralization of power. In general, one might expect conflict to be more likely with highly centralized systems than in less decentralized systems (such as federations, or where power is diffused across institutions, or there is substantial decentralization), because in centralized systems more is at stake when determining who controls the state (Bakke and Wibbels, 2006; Suberu, 2001).

- *How accommodating the state is.* People may feel grievances and mobilize politically, but such mobilization need not take a violent form. Those with grievances may acquire power, or be accommodated, peacefully. Violent mobilization is more likely where there is little accommodation. In general, one would expect democratic systems to be more accommodating, especially where the economically deprived group is in a majority. However, fragile democracies can be conflict provoking so there is no simple equation between democracy and conflict (Snyder, 2000; Stewart and O'Sullivan, 1999). Relevant to this is the nature of the democratic system. A first-past-the-post, winner-takes-all system (the Westminster model) is likely to be much more conflict-prone than one involving more power-sharing of a formal or informal nature. Thus proportional representation (PR) systems have been found to be less conflict-prone. This may be because the presence of PR and other power-sharing mechanisms tends to reduce political HIs, as well, probably, as reducing the likelihood of conflict for any given political inequalities.

Whether democratic or not, governments can be accommodating and inclusive making violent opposition less likely. In contrast, governments (especially nondemocratic ones) may make no attempt to meet people's demands, and can react to opposition with harsh repression, which may provoke a further violent reaction.

1.5.2   Cultural demography

The potential strength of any violent movement depends also on the geographic location and relative size of the population in different groups. Where groups are concentrated geographically (or largely so), separatism or irredentism often becomes a political aim. But this is not a possibility where members of each group are dispersed across the country. In the latter case, groups may mobilize in order to gain control over the state, or improve their political and economic rights, without separatist ambitions.

As far as relative size is concerned, at one extreme many small groups may find it difficult to mobilize collectively. At the other, if there is a homogeneous population violence may be less likely, though it can still occur as new and different identities emerge from what appears to be a homogeneous whole – for example, Somalia and Haiti, both relatively homogeneous in some ways, have been subject to endemic conflict (Bangura, 2006; Collier and Hoeffler, 2004; Fearon and Laitin, 2003). In between there are many possibilities. If the privileged group forms the vast majority and the underprivileged group a small minority then any violent protest is likely to be readily suppressed (as in the northern part of Kenya), although foreign support can prolong the conflict (as in northern Uganda). Where there is a small privileged group and a large underprivileged one, the deprived can be mobilized against the privileged – the Jews, the Chinese and the

Lebanese, for example, have been subject to such attacks periodically over many centuries.[8] The presence of a few large groups may be conducive to conflict, as each fights for political supremacy (an example is Fiji; but such conflict is not always violent, as shown in the case of Guyana).[9]

A further relevant feature is the cohesion of the group; strong cohesion and hence mobilization potential may be the outcome of cultural unity, or of political leadership emphasizing group unity. As we have argued, leadership, the media and treatment by others are important in determining which identities are felt so strongly that people mobilize for political violence behind them. However, cohesion is inherently easier in some contexts. Thus, where there is cultural fragmentation (for example, many languages being spoken), mobilization behind some overarching identity may be less likely, and geographic dispersion may also make cohesion less likely. For example, in Peru, one possible overarching identity is an 'indigenous' identity, which would bring together about half the population – a powerful political entity. Yet differences within the indigenous population as to language, history and location mean that such an overarching identity is not strongly felt and hence political action on the basis of indigeneity may be unlikely. Yet it seems that powerful leadership, plus discriminatory treatment, can get people to overcome such differences, as we observe among the Orang Asli in Malaysia, where a pan-Asli identity has emerged. This group contains at least 17 distinct subgroups, yet they came together to protest colonial and later postcolonial discrimination against them (Nicholas, 2000).

Two features seem to determine a group's potential for mobilization. One is whether others categorize people as belonging to a single group, thereby stimulating unity through external pressure; the other is the presence of leadership (normally, but not always, from within the group) which is effective in mobilizing people as a group. In some situations it seems deprived groups can be mobilized because of their felt grievances, yet not in the name of the group but under some other (often ideological) banner. This seems to have been common in the Cold War era.

1.5.3 Economic conditions

The nature of the economy is another type of conditioning factor which helps determine the outbreak (or not) of violent conflict. Countries with low incomes per head are more prone to violence according to econometric investigations (Auvinen and Nafziger, 1999). This may reflect lack of viable occupations among poor populations, who therefore find war an attractive proposition; or lack of state resources, so that the state offers too little to its citizens to persuade them to respect their civic obligations; or it could be that low incomes are associated with weak states which are unable to repress violence effectively.

Low-growth economies seem to be more violence-prone than high-growth. This is probably because with higher growth often all groups benefit to some extent, and so inequalities seem to matter less. If the economy is growing then peaceful economic opportunities expand, so people may be less likely to want to disturb the economy and become involved in conflict.

Many econometric investigations also show that the presence of natural resources raises the risk of conflict (Ross, 2004). There are a number of possible mechanisms which explain this (Humphreys, 2005). In many contexts, the presence of high value natural resources is an important source of HIs, both regionally, as the resource-rich areas are richer than the rest of the country, and locally, as particular groups within a locality gain control over the resources. Sometimes, moreover, it's a matter of 'aspiration to inequality' (Tadjoeddin, 2007) when the populations of regions rich in natural resources find themselves relatively poor in terms of levels of living, and resent the redistribution of 'their resources' to the rest of the country. There are also mechanisms which may explain the connection between natural resources and conflict which have nothing to do with HIs. For example, natural resources offer finance for the prosecution of conflict; it may enrich those fighting (or offer them the prospects of enrichment); and natural resource availability can weaken state capacity and the state's relationship with its citizens because of the high levels of corruption that often result. It is plausible that more than one mechanism is in play in any particular case. What this suggests for our work is that the presence of natural resources may generate an additional propensity to conflict, at times operating by causing sharp HIs, and at times independently of them.

The presence of particular political, demographic and economic conditions of the sort just discussed will mediate the relationship between HIs and conflict. For example, conflict may be less likely to break out, given sharp HIs, where there is a growing economy, or where a very strong state represses any conflict, or where political accommodation occurs. Moreover, HIs are not, of course, the sole source of conflict. Other economic explanations of conflict include the following: private incentives where war provides opportunities of enrichment and where alternative opportunities are very poor (with low incomes, high unemployment), fighting may offer an attractive alternative; environmental pressures have also been argued to lead to conflicts over resources, especially land; and conflict may arise from a failure of the social contract, where the state fails to deliver public services, security and incomes. Each of these explanations has some statistical and case study support. Moreover, different conflicts may have different explanations, with more than one often appearing to be relevant. For example, the north/south conflict in Sudan was both an example of horizontal inequality (with the south being heavily deprived) and one of powerful private gains that perpetuated the struggle (Keen, 1994); and while it has been argued plausibly that environmental poverty was a significant element in the conflict in Rwanda (André and Platteau, 1996), HIs were clearly also important.

It thus follows that we should not expect an automatic relationship between HIs and conflict, not only because particular factors intervene to make conflict more or less likely, but also because there are other factors which may cause conflict even where HIs are limited. Nonetheless, if we conclude that HIs can be an important source of violent conflict, this is of major significance since it points to a range of policies that could help prevent conflict by reducing HIs. The rest of this book is devoted to exploring whether HIs indeed do cause conflict, and under what conditions, following our four hypotheses above.

1.6   Plan of this book

The book is divided into four parts. The first part deals with general and conceptual issues pertaining to HIs. First, Gibney analyzes an important aspect of political inequalities – notably how the concept of citizenship can be used as a mechanism of exclusion; second, Brown and Langer take up the issue of cultural status inequality, analyzing the concept and showing its relationship to group mobilization. One of the reasons HIs are so significant for individual well-being is that they are often very persistent, lasting generations and sometimes even centuries, so that they trap individuals in situations of inequality. The question of why such inequalities are so persistent in some contexts but not in others is dealt with by Stewart and Langer in Chapter 4.

Part II of the book deals with issues of measurement and statistical analysis. It starts with a general discussion of how to measure HIs (Chapter 5). This is followed by two chapters that use econometric analysis to investigate the relationship between HIs and violent conflict: Mancini (Chapter 6) does this across districts within Indonesia in the 1990s and Østby (Chapter 7) uses cross-country data and investigates how political as well as socioeconomic inequalities affect conflict.

Part III presents material from in-depth studies, including Côte d'Ivoire, Ghana and Nigeria in West Africa; Bolivia, Guatemala and Peru in Latin America and secessionist movements in Southeast Asia. This includes a comparative analysis of HIs in Ghana and Côte d'Ivoire by Langer (Chapter 8), followed by a comparison of two cities in Nigeria by Ukiwo. To complete the analysis of the West African case, Chapter 10 reports on surveys of perceptions of identity and inequality in Ghana and Nigeria. Chapter 11 presents a comparative analysis of Bolivia, Guatemala and Peru by Caumartin, Gray Molina and Thorp; and Brown provides an analysis of secessionist movements in Southeast Asia in Chapter 12.

The concluding section (Part IV) first presents findings from the book as a whole (Chapter 13). The final chapter then analyzes a wide range of policies that would contribute to reducing HIs, and considers some political problems and constraints in introducing them.

Notes

1. CSP, Global; Conflict Trends, http://members.aol.com/CSPmgm/conflict.htm
2. Summed up in an advice given in 1858 by a Jew in Prussia to his son: 'Always remember that you are a proud citizen of Prussia, entitled to equal rights. And never forget that you are a Jew. If you do, there will always be others to remind you of your origins' (Frister, 2002: 58).
3. He argued that 'Hausa identity and Hausa ethnic exclusiveness in Ibadan are the expressions not so much of a particularly strong "tribalistic" sentiment as of vested economic interests' (Cohen, 1969: 14).
4. Smith has argued that 'the [past] acts as a constraint on invention. Though the past can be "read" in different ways, it is not any past' (1991, quoted in Turton, 1997: 85).
5. Reynal-Querol (2001: 2) argues for developing countries that 'religious identity is fixed and non-negotiable'.
6. *The Black Star News*, 'South Africa: Whites Own 90% Land', 16 March 2007.
7. The Centre for Research on Inequality, Human Security and Ethnicity has carried out surveys of perceptions in Ghana, Nigeria, Peru, Bolivia, Guatemala, Malaysia and Indonesia.
8. The type of violence analyzed by Chua (2003).
9. See the case studies in Bangura (2006).

2
Who Should be Included? Noncitizens, Conflict and the Constitution of the Citizenry

Matthew J. Gibney

2.1 Introduction

A central hypothesis of this book is that severe inequalities between ethnic groups are likely to give rise to violent conflict. If one makes the plausible assumption that violence involves great costs and huge risks for those participating in it (loss of life, bodily injury, the destruction of property, and so on), it is reasonable to ask why groups would seek to address their grievances in this way. A number of answers suggest themselves, including the desire for revenge, the goal of total victory or revolutionary change, or an inadequate estimation of the consequences of violence.

But most often, it seems safe to assume, violence is employed because political routes for addressing the inequalities in question are blocked. Inequalities in the distribution of economic and social goods (income, housing, education, and so on) exist hand in hand with unequal political influence. Some ethnic groups are thus driven to achieve on the streets what they cannot attain through parliament or resort to gunfire because reliance on the ballot box is futile.

One form of blockage that can exist in ethnically divided societies is the domination of political institutions by an ethnic group or groups to the exclusion of participants in other ethnic groups (Lewis, 1965). The recognition that democratic systems may result in ethnic group domination has resulted in a voluminous literature in political science in recent years. In ethnically divided societies, elections, as Donald Horowitz (1991: 97–8) has put it, may be more like a census than a competition for votes. The result is an unstable and (arguably) undemocratic 'tyranny of the ethnic majority'. In response to this problem, academics have fiercely debated the character of appropriate political institutions for divided societies (Ejobowah, 2001; Shapiro, 1999). They have proposed a range of different models that aim to reduce the salience of ethnic identities (Dorf, 2004), reorganize political

25

institutions around them (Lijphart, 1977), or provide incentives for elec-
tioneering across ethnic divisions in the hope of moderating political rule
(Horowitz, 1991).

These have been important political debates. They have helped to identify
the key and (often) conflicting values involved in the design of political
institutions in societies with deep ethnic divisions. But a significant limitation of these debates is that they have focused solely on the question of how
best to represent an established (if divided) citizenry (whether, for example,
to represent ethnic groups or regions or individual citizens). Consequently,
the question of how the citizenry is itself *constituted* has been largely ignored.
This latter question demands reflection upon the possibility that, in divided
societies, the issue of who is a member of the *demos* (the citizenry) may be
a matter of interest and dispute.

In this chapter, I will focus in a preliminary way on this vexed and
important question. I will do so by considering the issue of access to citizenship (and the rights it typically entails) for noncitizens in divided societies.
In Section 2.1, I define the scope of this analysis. In Sections 2.3 and 2.4,
I look at how individuals, both on their own and as members of ethnic
groups, become noncitizens and the factors that often force them to remain
so over time in the country in which they reside. In Section 2.5, I explain
why it is important for those interested in horizontal inequalities to consider
how the issue of citizenship is distributed across a society and particularly
across ethnic groups. In the final section of this chapter, I will reflect upon
the question of what it means to distribute citizenship fairly. I conclude with
a discussion of the challenges associated with citizenship reform. I will have
achieved my task if, by the end of this chapter, I have shown why those
who desire to avoid the 'tyranny of the ethnic majority' also have reason
to concern themselves with the potential for a 'tyranny of the citizens' –
the rule by those with formal membership in a state over residents unfairly
deprived of membership.

2.2   The scope of the analysis

The term *citizenship* conjures up a number of meanings that correspond to
different topics of analysis. Citizenship may refer simply to *nationality*, the
possession of formal legal membership in a specific nation state, recognized
under both international and domestic law. Following Judith Shklar (1991:
2–3), a second, fundamental understanding of citizenship involves what is
called *standing*, the idea that an individual is deserving of equal respect
along with other members of the polity. Equal respect in this context fundamentally involves the recognition that the individual possesses the same
rights (and duties) as other citizens, including the right to vote, to stand
for public office, and so on. A third understanding of citizenship is more
explicitly normative and can be drawn from the *republican* tradition. In this

view, citizenship is not simply a matter of reciprocal rights and duties, but a distinct and key form of activity. Rooted in ancient Greek and Roman republics, this participative understanding of citizenship sees involvement in the activities of 'ruling and being ruled' as fundamental to a full human life. While initially formulated in small polities where political participation in collective societal decisions was a practical reality, the understanding of citizenship as a noninstrumental good – as not just a means to being free but a form of freedom itself – still exercises a strong influence on contemporary understandings of citizenship (Ignatieff, 1995: 32). In this chapter, however, my focus will be on citizenship as nationality and standing and, in particular, on the implications of exclusion from these aspects of citizenship for people who are not members of the states in which they live.

Citizenship is inherently exclusive. To define a state's citizenry is simultaneously to define who is not a citizen. However, noncitizens are not a homogeneous group. They may be subdivided in a variety of ways, such as between those passing through (visitors), living in (residents), or living outside (nonresidents) a particular state. Amongst those living in the state, the focus of my concern here, four distinct groups of people are evident.

1. Residents who are stateless; those, that is, who hold nationality neither in the state in which they live nor in any other state. Consequently, they are also excluded from the benefits of citizenship as standing. Palestinian refugees living in Lebanon are one example of this group.
2. Residents who lack citizenship where they are currently living but who hold it elsewhere. This group is composed mostly of immigrants who have moved from their state of origin for a variety of reasons including the search for better economic opportunities for themselves or their children.
3. Individuals who are nationals of the country in which they are living but who *formally* lack full standing in the society. These 'second-class citizens' typically share both the title and some of the rights of citizens but live in societies where there is a legal basis to their inferior status as citizens.[1] For example, women in many Middle Eastern countries (or countries under Sharia law) may not vote or pass on citizenship to their children. In some countries, such as South Africa until recently, certain ethnic or racial groups have not had the right to vote in national elections.
4. Residents who might be referred to as 'stunted citizens'. In contrast to 'second-class citizens', these individuals possess both nationality and formal legal equality in their society of residence, but their ability to exercise the rights and privileges of citizenship is effectively 'stunted' by *informal* features of the society in question, for example, racism, sexism, and economic deprivation. Many immigrant groups (for example, Turks in Germany or North Africans in France) find themselves at the centre of a gap between the stated principles of a society built on equal citizenship and the reality of social, economic, and political forces that generate

inequality. The presence of at least some stunted citizens is a feature of every modern state.

In what follows, I shall primarily be concerned with groups one and two (resident noncitizens that are stateless or living outside their country of origin). In the course of discussing the situation of noncitizens, however, I shall engage in some discussion of group three (second-class citizens), in part because the existence of this group suggests that not all societies may accept the Western idea that all citizens are entitled to equal concern and respect. The situation of stunted citizens (group four) will not be considered here. Important as this phenomenon is to the analysis of horizontal inequalities, my discussion in this chapter is limited to formal (legal) modes of exclusion.

2.3 The creation of noncitizenship

Every contemporary state is populated at any particular time by a combination of citizens and noncitizens (aliens). Those without formal membership may include tourists, illegal migrants, economic migrants, guestworkers, foreign diplomats, or refugees. By far, the most common way for noncitizenship (or alienage) to be generated is through *boundary crossing*: moving out of a state in which one holds formal membership (nationality) into another sovereign state. Individuals may make such a move in a wide variety of ways: temporarily (students, tourists) or permanently (economic migrants, retirees); in order to pursue better economic or material conditions (immigrants) or to escape conflict or persecution (refugees, forced migrants); to a neighbouring state or one on the other side of the world. In an international system where political membership is defined by territorial sovereign states, moving outside the state in which one possesses citizenship almost always (with the exception of people holding dual nationality) means taking on the often ill-defined status of noncitizen.[2]

Boundary crossing can also have important intergenerational effects. Despite having spent their entire lives in the countries in which they live, second- or third-generation children of immigrants may be ineligible for citizenship under some systems for allocating membership (Carens, 1995). This is typically the case in countries (such as Germany, until recent citizenship reforms) that allocate citizenship exclusively (or, more commonly, *almost* exclusively (Green, 2004)) on the basis of parents being citizens. Generations of noncitizens may result.

Second-class citizenship may also result from boundary crossing. In Nigeria, for example, citizens can lose some of their rights by crossing political boundaries *within* their own country. The federal system of governance in Nigeria privileges the 'indigenous' members of an internal state (province). Moving between states can deprive nationals of the right to run for office and to claim various privileges and entitlements where they reside. While in most federal systems the local states or provinces differentiate between the rights of residents and visitors, the Nigerian system is extreme in grounding this distinction upon an immutable characteristic like indigeneity rather than period of residence (Bach, 1997).

A second, less common, generator of noncitizenship is the *revocation* or *withdrawal* of citizenship by a country in which a person previously held nationality. Most states claim the right to revoke citizenship under certain circumstances. However, such laws typically apply only to dual nationals (for example, post–September 11 legislation in the UK enabled the withdrawal of British citizenship from suspected terrorists who also held another nationality). Only the most authoritarian of states takes citizenship from people lacking any other nationality, thus making them stateless. The Nazi regime notoriously stripped Jews of citizenship in the 1930s and 1940s, ensuring that all those sent to concentration camps could not be described as German (Arendt, 1986). Significantly, it did so only after first making Jews second-class citizens by depriving them of previously held rights.

The line between making someone stateless and making them reliant on another nationality is often blurred in practice. A person stripped of citizenship may only have nominal links to another country in which they hold nationality. Moreover, that country may not want them. For example, while Kenyan Asians held British passports when they began to leave Kenya and make their way to the UK in the 1960s, legislation was hurriedly put in place by the British parliament to strip them of entrance rights (Hansen, 2000).

State revocation or withdrawal can also result in second-class citizen status. The situation of Jews in Nazi Germany is mentioned above, but even nonauthoritarian regimes may take away some of the citizenship rights of certain groups of nationals. For example, in many southern states in the US, including Florida, criminals convicted of felonies may lose temporarily or permanently their right to vote in national and state elections (Manza and Uggen, 2006).

A third and final way that noncitizens can be generated is through *fundamental changes* in a citizenship-granting state, such as cessation or division. The state in which a citizen held citizenship may cease to exist, or have its identity so transformed that it is profoundly changed. Examples of state disappearance are rare (though the disappearance of Palestine with the formation of the state of Israel in 1948 approximates the phenomenon); state division is more common. After the Czech Republic separated itself from Slovakia in the early 1990s, the Roma population of the former Czechoslovakia became effectively stateless, fully attached to neither of the two new entities. A fundamental transformation that often results in profound changes in citizenship laws is liberation from an existing power. Many Russians forced to migrate to Estonia and Latvia when they were under Soviet occupation found themselves without citizenship when the collapse of communism enabled these countries to construct their own citizenship laws in the early 1990s.[3]

2.4   The reproduction of noncitizenship

As the previous discussion shows, the factors that generate noncitizenship and second-class citizenship are many and varied. The social and political implications of noncitizenship for individuals and groups also vary widely. For tourists and visitors, noncitizenship is typically a temporary and short-term affair that is not usually experienced as a situation of insecurity or vulnerability. For immigrants, on the other hand, who must interact more deeply with the society in which they lack citizenship because they live and work there, the rights withheld from noncitizens are likely to be much more important. For example, the absence of a right to join a union, to work, to have one's family migrate with one, to receive welfare or government assistance, to be protected from deportation, or to run for public office may have a profound impact upon one's quality of life or life chances. For those that are stateless, the nonrecognition of certain rights is of even greater consequence because it is likely that there is no alternative state in which they can reside.

The nature of a noncitizen's experience is therefore determined by a number of factors. The most important of these are as follows: the length of time they hold the status (the longer one is deprived of certain rights, the more onerous the deprivation becomes); the rights respected by the country they find themselves in (whether noncitizens can work, are protected from deportation, and so on); and the category of noncitizenship into which they fall (whether they are illegal migrants, legal permanent residents, refugees, or diplomats, for example).

These factors make it difficult to generalize across societies about the significance of holding or not holding citizenship. Nonetheless, it is evident that in virtually all countries noncitizens occupy a status subordinate to citizens, and in many situations this is a status that may continue for many years, or even a lifetime. This raises the question of why resident noncitizens are not integrated into citizenship in the countries in which they live. One obvious answer may be that they do not wish to take on the status of membership in the countries in which they reside. They may, for example, not feel loyalty or attachment to this country. This is indeed sometimes the case. However, to understand the persistence of noncitizenship status over time, it is necessary also to appreciate a range of barriers external to individual choice. These barriers range from unintentional obstacles to deliberate and orchestrated exclusion.

One such barrier may be *bureaucratic*. This rather banal reason for exclusion is surprisingly common. Noncitizen residents in a state may lack the documentation or proof necessary to apply for citizenship. They may lack proof of their place of birth or evidence of the time period they have been resident in the state of which they wish to become a citizen. Such situations are not rare in countries with poor or incomplete record-keeping. Alternatively, potential applicants might have failed to meet a deadline (perhaps due to lack of knowledge) by which to change their status. Deadlines are often used in regularization campaigns for illegal migrants, though their use is not always so confined. More than 18,000 former citizens of the other former Yugoslavian republics residing in Slovenia at the time of its independence in 1991 lost both the opportunity to apply for naturalization and their status as permanent residents because of a failure to meet a state-imposed cut-off date (Advisory Board on Human Security, 2004: 12). Finally, the process of becoming a citizen may simply be slow or complicated, leaving people without citizenship for a long period after they have applied to transfer their status. Around 300,000 Estate Tamils in Sri Lanka are still waiting for citizenship over 15 years after legislation allowed them to change their status because of a combination of administrative red tape and difficulties with required documentation (ibid.: 11).

Bureaucratic hurdles may be unintentional, a product simply of government inefficiency. But sometimes they reflect the *political interest* of those controlling naturalization in excluding certain groups. Those most commonly excluded from citizenship for political reasons are groups perceived to be 'disloyal' or potential or actual 'competitors' for political power.

Often ethnic groups (and sometimes individuals) are barred from accessing membership because they are perceived as disloyal or untrustworthy, as a result of their past or present actions, and thus as likely to jeopardize the national security of the state. The Bihari of Bangladesh, for example, were stripped of their citizenship rights by the Bangladeshi government for their perceived sympathy for Pakistan during the country's intervention in the Bengali struggle for independence in the early 1970s (Advisory Board on Human Security, 2004: 9). Even where a present danger is lacking, denial of citizenship can be a form of collective punishment dished out to ethnic groups for past actions. Russians and natives of other Soviet republics have been frozen out of citizenship in Estonia and Latvia because memories of their role in the Russian colonization of the Baltic States remain (ibid.).

Arguably, more frequent is the exclusion of specific ethnic groups from citizenship because they risk challenging the power of a state's dominant ethnic group or groups, either by claiming a share of scarce societal resources or by upsetting a fragile ethnic balance by increasing the size and influence of one of the participating (or hitherto excluded) groups. Politics is a competitive activity, and just as appeals to ethnic identity can be one way of mobilizing political support for a beleaguered regime or for political entrepreneurs keen on gaining or increasing their power, identifying some ethnic groups as undeserving of membership in the *demos* can be a way of neutralizing potential competitors for power. The use of citizenship as part of competitive electoral politics is unfortunately common. Most recently, in the Côte d'Ivoire, a concept of the authentic community membership – *Ivoirité* – has been constructed by the government to justify the stripping of citizenship rights (including passport ownership, access to civil service occupations and rights to ownership of land) from residents of immigrant backgrounds (Advisory Board on Human Security, 2004: 12).

However, the *inclusion* of noncitizens can also be highly political and ethically dubious. A case in point can be seen in Sabah, Malaysia, where the dominant Malay parties have used fraudulent documentation corruptly to enfranchise illegal Filipino worker migrants. In a recent article, Kamal Sadiq (2005: 116) has argued that Malay elites have deliberately attempted to change 'the demographic and political character of Sabah so that it becomes Malay-Muslim dominated' in order to boost their political position vis-à-vis other ethnic groups.

Barriers to citizenship can also result from *ethnic and cultural understandings of national membership*. In some countries, entry to citizenship is barred by long-established ideas that link citizenship to membership in the dominant ethnic community. This is the case, for example, in Japan, Germany, and Israel, each of which has in recent years set stringent restrictions on the ability of nonethnics to access citizenship (Joppke, 2005). Exclusion in these countries is, however, not necessarily driven by the kind of short-term political interests resulting from the play of domestic politics discussed above. Instead, exclusion is the product of long-held ideas of national self-determination or habits of national chauvinism. Typically, such countries make it equally difficult for members of *all* other ethnic or national groups to access citizenship. Of course, the fact that this type of exclusion is not the same as exclusion driven by short-term political goals, or applies only to disfavoured ethnic groups, does not make its effects any more pleasant for those residents denied citizenship.

A final set of obstacles is *economic*. Exclusion from citizenship may not only weaken the political power of noncitizens, it may also weaken their economic bargaining power. In a capitalist economy, noncitizens (especially those without any official status) may form a useful and pliable labour force because they are denied the protection of minimum wages, unions, and the courts. Many observers have argued that illegal migrants now form a large and important (though usually unrecognized) part of the workforce in many countries, including Japan, Malaysia, Thailand, the United States, and the UK (Castles and Miller, 2003). Those in business and government employing or otherwise benefiting from this workforce may have strong economic reasons to resist its transfer to the more empowered status of citizen.

The factors that reproduce *second-class citizenship* status over time are broadly similar. For example, political interests may give a group a powerful reason to limit citizenship rights to another group sharing the same state.

The defining reason for the maintenance of apartheid in South Africa, for example, was to prevent black majority rule. In this case and others, however, such as the exclusion of women from voting, the justification for exclusion typically draws upon cultural understandings of the excluded group as somehow unfit or unsuitable for full participation. These justifications include but are not limited to claims of intellectual inferiority or divinely prescribed subordination to the dominant group. Other forms of second-class citizenship, such as that generated by moving between states within Nigeria, might be considered an intrastate equivalent to the ethnic conceptions of membership recently on display in Germany and Israel.

2.5 Citizenship as a focus of concern

It is apparent from the preceding discussion that the distribution of citizenship in many states is a highly politicized matter, and one that creates and reinforces hierarchies of power between individuals and social groups and the state. I now want to consider three reasons why the exclusion of noncitizens should be of concern to those investigating horizontal inequalities and their relationship to conflict in ethnically divided societies.

First, the status of citizenship controls access to key social, economic, and political goods, and how those goods are distributed has a great impact on the well-being of individuals and groups. While what separates citizens from noncitizens varies across societies, the key benefits of citizenship (vis-à-vis noncitizens) can be generally categorized in terms of access to *privileges*, *voice*, and *security*.

The privileges associated with citizenship may involve favoured or exclusive access to public goods (such as housing, welfare, state-provided healthcare, education, and so on); government (public service) positions and membership of the military, and thus access to key elevators for social advancement; and the right to own land, other forms of property, and businesses. Voice (Shachar, 2007), on the other hand, involves the right to air in public *fora* views about the use and abuse of government power and the direction of society, and to participate in (or to be elected to) political organizations that fashion society's direction and government policy. The *sine qua non* of citizenship is often thus seen as embodied in key rights associated with voice, namely rights 'to vote, hold elected and appointed government offices, to sit on various sorts of juries, and generally to participate in debates as equal community members' (Smith, 2002: 105). Finally, citizenship typically offers a unique level of security of residence or presence in a state. Citizens, unlike noncitizens, typically cannot be deported or expelled, thus their access to other goods is uniquely secure (Gibney and Hansen, 2003).

If we accept that privileges, voice and security involve fundamentally important human goods, then who has access to citizenship (and thus to these goods) is also of fundamental importance. Moreover, when access to citizenship coincides with ethnic group membership, as it does in many countries, lack of or denial of citizenship can be a key factor in explaining severe inequalities between groups and their persistence over time.

Not least because of the important goods associated with its provision, citizenship is also important because it may itself be a product or a source of conflict and tension in ethnically divided societies. Stripping minority ethnic groups of citizenship or denying them access to it can, as I have shown, be a result of deliberate efforts by dominant groups to disempower or marginalize competitor ethnic groups. The revocation or withholding of citizenship can be a tool of war, or a symbol of ongoing repression that substitutes for or complements physical violence.

From the perspective of the excluded, lack of citizenship may deprive them of key social, economic, and political goods, which they then use violent means to access. A lack of citizenship may also be experienced more deeply, as a humiliation, as something that brands the excluded as not good enough for membership in the society (Margalit, 1996). This sense of humiliation may exist even if members of the excluded group would not take up citizenship if they could: 'the humiliation', as Margalit (ibid.: 112) observes, 'comes from the sense that you do not want the humiliator to define you. You do not want them to say you are not worthy of belonging to society'. This type of humiliation can become potent fuel for violent conflict, especially when the basis of exclusion is connected to ethnicity. This shared humiliation may facilitate collective action amongst members of the ethnic group concerned to strike back at those who have humiliated them. At the very least, it is likely to make the excluded less loyal to the society in question and less committed to its social and economic development.

A final reason for examining citizenship is that even the most perfectly designed political institutions are likely to be ineffective in preventing ethnic conflict if significant groups are excluded from participating in them. The best political systems for divided societies encourage participants to learn the virtues of compromise, cooperation, and 'loyal opposition' to the legitimate government of the day. Yet the distribution of citizenship (and the rights associated with it) may freeze out just those groups that most need to acquire these virtues. If resident noncitizens are capable of disrupting social order and peace (and, for reasons stated above, this often appears to be the case), then there are powerful reasons for encouraging their participation in political institutions designed to offer an alternative to violence. Admittedly, the basis on which they should be included in the political process raises difficult and contentious issues about membership that I have not yet begun to discuss. But the best starting point for exploring these questions is by asking whether some noncitizens may have a just claim to inclusion as full citizens.

2.6   Just principles for accessing citizenship

So far I have suggested the following: that the distribution of citizenship is in many countries a highly politicized activity, closely linked to ethnic group competition; that citizenship confers control over key social, economic, and political goods that impact heavily on individual life chances and group well-being; and that those concerned with horizontal inequalities have good reason to look closely at how citizenship is distributed.

In this section of the chapter, I want to concentrate exclusively on the situation of those without citizenship. I will consider (in a rudimentary way) principles for the incorporation of noncitizens. If some current practices are rightly perceived as unfair, what would a superior basis for determining who amongst noncitizens should be included in the *demos*? In order to answer this question, I will sketch out three different responses to this question, each more inclusive than the other: the *lack of alternative political membership* principle; the *informal membership* principle; and the *democratic inclusion* principle.

2.6.1   Lack of alternative political membership

The first and least inclusive basis for a right to citizenship would derive from the fact that every individual in the world has a right to citizenship somewhere and, if they cannot claim this right anywhere else, they should be able to claim it where they are currently living. In its strictest version, this principle would apply only to those that are legally stateless, groups like the Palestinians, for example, or the Kurds in Syria, or the Bihari in Bangladesh. But it might be extended to apply to those that are 'effectively' stateless, to include refugees expelled or forced to leave their country of citizenship because of persecution or conflict. If the conditions making return impossible continue over a long time period, these people might be considered *effectively* to have lost access to their citizenship and the rights associated with it.

The idea at work in the lack of alternative political membership principle is that everyone should have citizenship somewhere. It is an idea that chimes well with a long strand of thinking in natural law (from which modern human rights thinking emerged) that everyone is entitled to a place to live. Kant, for example, wrote in 1795, that

> all men are entitled to present themselves in the society of others by virtue of communal possession of the earth's surface. Since the earth is a globe, they cannot disperse over an infinite area, but must necessarily tolerate one another's company. And no one originally has any greater right than anyone else to occupy any particular portion of the earth. (Kant, 1991: 106)

Indeed, international law recognizes the importance of dealing with the problem of the stateless and those deprived of effective citizenship. The 1951 UN Refugee Convention, under article 34, commits states to facilitating the naturalization of refugees; the Convention on the Reduction of Statelessness aims to help avoid statelessness. As a general principle, a duty to incorporate the stateless is far from radical, even if many states currently deny the existence of any such obligation. But the widespread recognition and implementation of this principle would make a substantial difference to the situation of large numbers of people.

2.6.2   Informal membership

The informal membership principle is wider in its implications than the lack of alternative political membership principle. It suggests that formal membership (citizenship) should be made available to those residents of the state who are already *de facto* or, following Bauböck (1997: 210), 'societal' members.

How might one establish that an individual is a *de facto* member of the state? A number of criteria might be used. First, one might show how the individual (or the group) has contributed to society. Like citizens, noncitizens work, pay taxes, even undertake military service in ways that are indistinguishable from formal members. Second, one might argue that, also like citizens, noncitizens have powerful and enduring ties to the country in which they reside. They may have their children in school locally, be actively involved in civil society, and have established dense social networks of friends and associates. They may have come to see their host country as their home, and consequently their country of origin as a place which no longer constitutes a serious residential option. The contribution and ties of the noncitizen are likely to be even stronger when the individual in question has been living in the society for a long period of time because one can reasonably expect their connection to the state to be stronger. An 'extended period of residence' may thus constitute a third way of establishing societal membership.

Taken together, these three criteria serve to identify noncitizens with strong and deep links and connections to the society in which they are resident, which cry out for political recognition. Noncitizens of this type are deeply implicated in the fate of the society in which they reside and should therefore have a say in its direction.

The principle of integration in this approach is communitarian. States are not simply legal membership organizations: they are communities, or at least federations of communities, and membership in these communities should correspond to membership in the state. The implications of this principle are, in some respects, more radical than the preceding one. This informal membership principle would require access to citizenship for anyone who is a societal member whether or not they are stateless or *prima facie* whether their residence is legal in the eyes of the state. By contrast, the principle would not necessarily provide a basis for the inclusion of newly settled stateless people who have yet to establish social roots and connections.

2.6.3 Democratic inclusion

The democratic inclusion principle is the most radical of all. It dictates that the constitution of the *demos* (or the distribution of political rights) should be determined by all of those that are affected by political decisions in a state. Thus, rather than defining the *demos* in terms of legal citizenship or, as above, by informal membership, the right to participate politically should be determined by 'the contours of power relationships' (Shapiro, 2003: 220): those at the receiving end of a state's power should have a say in how that power is exercised. For example, decisions on state provision of education typically touch upon the interests and well-being of citizens and noncitizens alike, as both groups are likely to have children in school. Accordingly, both groups should participate in decision-making in the realm.

The principle of democratic inclusion is widely appealed to by democratic theorists, even if its implications are sometimes less than clear. Dahl (2000: 78), for example, has argued that 'the citizen body in any democratically governed state must include *all persons* subject to the laws of that state except transients and those proved to be incapable of caring for themselves' (italics added). According to Young (2000: 23), 'a democratic decision is legitimate only if all those affected by it are included in the process of discussion and decision making.'

The principle of democratic inclusion would provide a powerful basis for the inclusion of noncitizens in political decision-making. Simply by virtue of living in a state, noncitizens are heavily affected by its decisions and directions. Yet the principle of democratic inclusion does raise some thorny questions. First, given that it is not always obvious who is 'affected' by a decision, how should we determine who is to be included in decision-making? Should not the means for deciding who is to be included also be democratic? But, if so, we have a problem of infinite regress. At some point, the decision as to who to include has to be made in a way that lacks democratic justification (Smith, 2003). Second, is it realistic to imagine a state in which rights of participation in decision-making vary from decision to decision? Wouldn't this be too complicated to be feasible? Finally, if we take the democratic principle seriously, then the ranks of who should participate in decision-making run beyond resident noncitizens to those people outside the state's boundaries who may be impacted by the state's decisions (Held, 1991). Moreover, it would also seem to provide a rationale for disenfranchising citizens no longer living in the state. In an increasingly interdependent world, taking democratic inclusion seriously would challenge us profoundly to rethink who the *demos* is and the nature and form of current political institutions.

2.7   Conclusion

In conclusion, it is worth noting that all three of the principles for inclusion in democratic decision-making considered above have real force. Indeed they are not necessarily mutually exclusive. Each of them helps to clarify what we might mean when we describe some groups as *unjustly* excluded from citizenship. Yet these principles are not reducible to each other. Each has different implications for the scope and basis of inclusion and points to a different set of political arrangements. The first two can be accommodated by expanding citizenship to include some residents of the state currently excluded from formal membership. The last principle, however, suggests that voting rights (or participation in democratic processes) should be disconnected from formal membership. Noncitizens, that is, should be able to participate politically regardless of the fact that they are noncitizens (Honig, 2001).

Clearly, more thought is required as to how we might legitimately constitute the membership of democratic societies. Nonetheless, there is, I think, a powerful and immediate case for respecting the first two principles: residents of a society who are stateless or 'informal members' (in the sense I have outlined above) should have genuine pathways to citizenship in the states in which they live.

Of course, even if we recognize the desirability of expanding access to citizenship, two major problems still remain. The first is that if these principles for citizenship have force it is because they resonate with the idea that everyone living under the authority of a state should have a say – an equal say – in how that authority is exercised. In this respect, these different formulations of who should be included heavily reflect the Western idea of citizenship and its attendant idea of individual equality. But, as I have shown, many societies are characterized by formally unequal (second-class) citizenship. Gender, race, or ethnicity is and has been used as a basis for excluding some members from full membership status.

According to some observers, the idea of the pre-social rights-bearing individual that forms the basis for equal concern and respect in Western societies lacks roots in many postcolonial societies (Adejumobi, 2001; Kabeer, 2002). The development of citizenship in many countries in Africa, it is argued, has been shaped by the interests of colonizers in keeping in place traditional status and group hierarchies in order to facilitate efficient rule (Kabeer, 2002: 17–18). Moreover, these societies never experienced the kind of social and economic transformations that helped develop the conceptualization of the individual as independent of group identity in Western countries (ibid.). As a result, group memberships have proven far more significant in determining access to rights, privileges, and security than citizenship in many developing countries. One implication may be that because some countries lack the very idea of equal concern and respect for the individual *qua* individual, there may be no principled basis on which to extend citizenship to certain excluded groups. Moreover, even if citizenship was to be extended, it would not lead to equal treatment.

A second problem is simply that even if exclusion from citizenship is unjust under some circumstances, one has to confront the reality that it often serves powerful interests. Defining the *demos* in one way or another may dramatically change the balance of power in many states, empowering some actors and weakening others. It is because citizenship is linked to key political and economic resources, of course, that it raises such important and contested issues. Yet this suggests that citizenship reform is likely to be strongly resisted, especially by those benefiting under the present dispensation, making change difficult.

These are both serious problems. Yet they should not be overstated. For a start, they are obviously in tension with each other. If we accept that national citizenship is of little importance in the distribution of political and social goods (in contrast to group identities), it's difficult to explain why the expansion of citizenship is often bitterly resisted by powerful groups. In many societies the holding of citizenship does have important power and resource implications, even if it cannot completely insulate unfavoured individuals or groups from other types of informal (and even formal) exclusion. At the very least, the possession of citizenship may give the previously excluded group a status which they can use to draw attention to the social and political inequalities associated with their plight. Access to citizenship may also allow them to benefit from measures designed to alleviate other horizontal inequalities across the citizenry.

Furthermore, while changes in citizenship are likely to be resisted, it is difficult to see why this raises issues different from those associated with addressing horizontal inequalities *among* citizens. Most horizontal inequalities serve the interests of dominant groups. Attempts to reduce or eliminate them are thus likely to be contested. The real question may be whether it is possible to convince dominant groups that the grievances generated by arbitrary exclusion from citizenship lead to conflict and instability that is not in their interest. I have attempted to show in this chapter why access to citizenship is an important subject of analysis for those concerned with inequalities across groups. But a detailed empirical understanding of the relationship between conflict and exclusion from citizenship may be required if the inequalities generated by citizenship are to be addressed.

Notes

1. I thus use the term *second-class citizens* differently from many writers, who use it as a category applicable to noncitizens (for example, guestworkers in Germany during the 1950s and 1960s) as well as citizens.

2. A notable exception to this situation is, of course, the movement of citizens of member countries between the countries of the European Union.
3. F. Weir, 'Latvia gives Russians cold shoulder'. *Christian Science Monitor*, 26 November 2002. Downloaded from http://www.csmonitor.com/2002/1126/p08s01-woeu.html.

3
Cultural Status Inequalities: An Important Dimension of Group Mobilization

Arnim Langer and Graham K. Brown

3.1 Introduction

Recent research on the causes of civil wars and communal, ethnic or religious conflicts has focused predominantly on political and economic grievances, motivations and issues (for example, Collier and Hoeffler, 2004; Fearon and Laitin, 2003; Nafziger and Auvinen, 2002; Stewart, 2000a). However, in many conflicts, political and economic issues are complemented by perceptions of cultural discrimination, exclusion or inequality of treatment. As Horowitz (2002: 22) asserts cultural matters, 'such as the designation of official languages and official religions, and educational issues, such as languages of instruction, the content of curricula, and the official recognition of degrees from various educational streams associated with various ethnic or religious groups', and freedom of cultural expression more generally, often play a central role in the emergence of violent conflicts.

What, then, is the role of culture in violent conflict? On one side stand scholars who see cultural matters primarily as potential flashpoints for violence, or what Horowitz (2001) terms a 'precipitant'. For these scholars, culture is often something *manipulated* by those with a vested interest in violence or conflict. Paul Brass, for instance, emphasizes this dimension in his account of the 'production' of Hindu–Muslim violence in India, epitomized by his well-known refrain of 'the theft of an idol' (Brass, 1997, 2003). This is not to say that Brass does not accept the importance of culture to people's lives and sense of self; but he sees its role in conflict as primarily *instrumental*.

On the other side is Samuel Huntington's hypothesis of the 'clash of civilizations', which emphasizes cultural difference as the root of conflict in the post–Cold War era: 'the fundamental source of conflict in this new world will not be primarily ideological or primarily economic. The great divisions among humankind and the dominating source of conflict will be cultural' (1993: 22).

In this chapter, we take a different view and analyze the relationship between culture and conflict within the broader framework of horizontal inequalities (HIs) – that is, inequalities between culturally defined groups (Stewart, 2000a). Culture, of course, plays a fundamental role in framing socioeconomic and political HIs generally since it is a common culture or identity which binds groups together. But in this chapter we consider how the way different cultures are treated by the state (and others) itself forms an important HI, which can contribute to group mobilization, independently of political or socioeconomic HIs. We argue that an important link between culture and group mobilization, including violent conflict, is the extent to which cultural groups' practices and customs are *differentially recognized in and by the state*. Differences in the *status* afforded to different cultures by the state, whether implicitly or explicitly, and popular perceptions of and anxieties over *differences* in cultural status thus constitute a third dimension of HIs, in addition to the political and socioeconomic dimensions, which we term 'cultural status inequalities'. It is important here to distinguish this from broader concepts of state discrimination on the basis of culture, that is exclusion from access to socioeconomic or political assets on the basis of an individual's cultural identity. Our concern here is more specifically with how the state in particular, but also state-related actors and nonstate actors such as the media, treat different groups' cultural norms and practices in themselves.

In this chapter, we argue that the analysis of cultural status inequalities in plural societies is an important complement to political and economic analysis in understanding the emergence of (violent) group mobilization. The second section elucidates further the concept of cultural status inequality. The third section focuses on the three main aspects of cultural status – recognition of religion and religious observance; language rights and language recognition; and recognition of ethnocultural practices. The final section analyzes more closely the link between cultural status inequality and (violent) group mobilization.

3.2   Conceptualizing cultural status inequalities

We define cultural status inequalities as perceived or actual differences in the treatment, public recognition or status of different groups' cultural norms, practices, symbols and customs. This definition clearly covers a range of practices and intentionality on the part of the state in question. The most extreme form of cultural status inequality consists of the phenomenon, sometimes labelled 'cultural genocide' or 'ethnocide', whereby the state explicitly takes on the cultural garb of the dominant group and repudiates the expression of other cultural identities not only in the public sphere, but also in the private sphere. For instance, until 1990, the Kurds in Turkey who numbered about 10 million were not allowed to use their own language in public. The official policy of the Turkish government was to deny their existence and to refer to them, if at all, as 'Mountain Turks' (Gurr, 2000). The restrictions imposed on religious and cultural practices in Tibet by the Chinese government is another example of an attempt to deculturize a particular group. During the Cultural Revolution (1966–1976), the Chinese government 'destroyed nearly all Buddhist monasteries and religious symbols and outlawed all manifest-ations of Tibetan culture' (Khosla, 2000: 214). While restrictions on the practice of Buddhism were relaxed in the 1980s, they were tightened again from the mid-1990s. In 1994, for instance, the Chinese authorities banned the display of photographs of the Dalai Lama. In the same year, the Chinese government also denounced the Dalai Lama's choice of 'Panchem Lama', the second most senior religious position, and appointed its own successor (ibid.). The 'Stolen Generation' of Aboriginal children forcibly resettled with white parents in Australia is another example that demonstrates that such cultural genocide is not unique to undemocratic developing countries (van Krieken, 1999).

Less extreme than cultural genocide are cases where one or more particular groups are afforded an explicitly lower status in society but the state does not seek to eradicate the culture altogether. When the democratic franchise is limited to certain cultural groups – what van den Berghe terms '*Herrenvolk* democracy' – cultural status inequalities become virtually coterminous with political inequalities, in which some groups are treated 'as disenfranchised subjects with separate and inferior status as slaves, pariahs or conquered nations' (van den Berghe, 2002: 437). South Africa during the apartheid era and the pre–Civil War United States are obvious examples here. In such cases, not only is the cultural status of subordinated groups demeaned, but they are also denied the possibility of assimilation. This argument is well illustrated by the treatment of the Chinese in New Order Indonesia. Victims of some of the most blatant ethnic suppression, including the banning of Chinese names and Chinese characters, in the early years of the regime, the Chinese were held up by the New Order as a contaminating 'other' that threatened the authenticity of the nationalist project (Heryanto, 1998: 97; Rakindo, 1975). Forever subject to assimilationist policies, they were thus denied the possibility of assimilating fully – for instance, alone amongst Indonesian citizens, they were obliged to have their ethnicity marked on their identity cards – and thus remained 'second-class' citizens.

Cultural status inequality can also occur where the state is associated *primarily although not exclusively* with one cultural group. Nepal has histor-ically privileged Hindu identity over others – the country's first civil code, the 1854 *Muluki Ain*, went as far as ascribing a place in the Hindu caste hierarchy to non-Hindu groups (Höfer, 1979) and, until the restoration of parliament in 2006 and the subsequent curtailing of the King's power, Nepal was the world's only officially Hindu state. In this respect, it is noteworthy that while the recent Maoist insurgency in Nepal sought to mobilize on the basis of *caste* exclusion, it was most successful in recruiting and mobilizing among the janajati *ethnic* minorities rather than the low-caste Hindus (Lecomte-Tilouine, 2004; Schneiderman and Turin, 2004).

In other cases, the state may not explicitly align itself with specific cultural groups but nonetheless affords them a *de facto* higher status. This is arguably the case with regard to most Western European countries, where immigrant groups are faced with a *de facto* white, Christian state. As Bikhu Parekh points out, where one group has historic cultural dominance or even exclusivity, a façade of cultural neutrality is often little more than the implicit privileging of the dominant culture:

> Since it [a state] necessarily needs some conception of the good life to structure its institutions and shape its laws and policies, it unwittingly adopts, institutionalizes and enforces the categories, practices, and values of the dominant culture. In so doing, it discriminates against other cultures, and creates a climate inhospitable to their flourishing or even survival.
>
> (Parekh, 2004: 201)

Thus far, we have discussed the varying degrees to which different states have given precedence to particular cultural groups, explicitly or implicitly. In contrast, other states have implemented a variety of measures and practices aimed at ensuring that the different cultural groups within a country are given *equal* visibility and recognition. An example of such neutrality is Belgium, where the constitution entails numerous checks and balances to ensure the equal treatment and recognition of the major ethnolinguistic groups' languages and practices, in addition to a comprehensive set of rules and institutions aimed at maintaining political inclusivity and equality. For instance, all federal institutions are required to be equally accessible in any of the three official languages; parliamentarians at the federal level can address the assembly in each language; and the national anthem has a recognized version in all three languages. In addition to these more formal mechanisms, many informal and symbolic conventions and practices exist which reinforce and give public prominence to this constitutional equality, such as the convention whereby the prime minister employs the two major languages (Dutch/Flemish and French) in his addresses to parliament and the media.

In Ghana, most successive governments since that of the first president of the modern state, Kwame Nkrumah, have promoted cultural inclusiveness and status equality through a range of formal, informal and symbolic policies and practices. Thus, for instance, Nkrumah's practice of alternating between suits, *kente* cloths and northern smocks on public occasions has been continued by most heads of state, especially Jerry Rawlings. Many more examples of culturally and religiously inclusive practices and customs that are common in Ghana are discussed in Chapter 8.

However, official rhetoric of cultural inclusion may be used to mask other types of inequality – this is the 'dark side' of cultural status equality. In some cases, the official recognition of cultural status equality on the part of the state, combined with symbolic promotion of ethnic or religious diversity, has served as part of a political agenda to divert attention from underlying socioeconomic and political inequalities. Parekh (2004: 202) makes a similar point when he notes that 'the politics of recognition plays into the hands of the dominant class, which is all too happy to allow the Sikh his turban, the American Indians their peyote, the Muslims their *halal* meal, and so on, as long as the inequalities of wealth and power are left unchallenged'. An indicative case here is again the New Order period in Indonesia, where a national motto of 'Unity in Diversity' was realized through national-level celebrations of cultural diversity. Cultural projects, such as the *Taman Mini Indonesia Indah* (Beautiful Indonesia in Miniature Park), 'presented the acceptable limits of Indonesia's cultural difference' (Murray Li, 2000: 149; Pemberton, 1994); museum curators became the 'modern day palace-poets' of Indonesia (Taylor, 2003: 343). All this celebration of diversity, however, was largely a mask for the political dominance of the Javanese, many of whose cultural practices were in fact used as the basis of institutions throughout the country. This phenomenon was epitomized by the 1979 Village Law, which reorganized village administrations uniformly across the country according to the Javanese *desa* system (Antlöv, 2003).

The concept of cultural status inequality as elucidated here is clearly linked to ideas of multiculturalism and cultural discrimination, but also differs from these in important ways. The Minorities at Risk project defines groups to be subject to cultural discrimination if 'their members are *restricted* in the pursuit of their cultural interests and expression of their customs and values' (Gurr, 2000: 118, emphasis added). According to Kymlicka (2004: 2), cultural exclusion 'occurs when the culture of a group, including its language, religion, or traditional customs and lifestyles, is denigrated or suppressed by the state.' Thus the presence of cultural discrimination and exclusion points to the existence of severe cultural status inequalities. But the absence of such cultural discrimination and exclusion does not necessarily mean that there are *no* real or perceived differences in public visibility, recognition and status among different cultural groups and practices.

It is important to clarify how cultural status inequalities relate to other forms of horizontal inequality. Cultural status inequalities are likely to be associated with exclusion and inequality in the economic and political dimensions (see Chapters 8 and 12). Political and socioeconomic HIs themselves usually arise where there are cultural differences around which groups form. This in itself need not imply cultural status inequalities. However, often the presence of one form of inequality leads to others. Thus political inequalities are often responsible for cultural status inequalities; and cultural status inequalities can be a source of political or socioeconomic inequalities.

A good example here is language. The adoption of an official language not only increases the cultural status of the groups associated with that language, but it can also have direct material benefits in terms of, for instance, access to employment in the official sphere.

3.3   Three aspects of cultural status inequality

In this section, we discuss the three main aspects of cultural status inequality: recognition of religious practices and observances; language rights and language recognition; and recognition of ethnocultural practices.

3.3.1   Recognition of religious practices and observances

Religion and perceived religious insults are particularly potent for group mobilization because of their immense symbolic value for adherents. As already noted, this can take the instrumental form of deliberate 'insults' aimed at provoking conflict – 'stray pigs at a mosque, a cow's head in a temple, the alleged kicking of the Quran and Ramayana during religious processions . . . . All are a signal for riot' (Horowitz, 2001: 289). Our concern here, however, is more with the relative status afforded to different religions by the state, and its actions, which may be perceived by members of different religious groups as an indication of their group's cultural status within that society.

In multireligious societies, differing levels of formal recognition or restrictions on the observance of religious practices are often an important source of cultural status inequality. The state's relationship with religion varies from a total lack of official relationship (complete secularity) to complete integration (theocracy). Theocracies invest political legitimacy in a specific religious framework thus incorporating a strong and formal hierarchy of religious recognition. Even where states are not theocratic, cultural status inequalities in the religious dimension can take extreme forms, including banning particular religions altogether, as with both Jews and Muslims in fifteenth-century Christian Spain, or the Protestant Huguenots in sixteenth-century France. More recently, Egypt forbade the rebuilding of Coptic Christian churches in the 1990s.

In less extreme cases, states privilege one religion over others by adopting it as the 'national religion', which carries varying degrees of privilege. For example, in Malaysia, Islam is designated the official religion but the constitution guarantees freedom of religion for non-Muslims. Despite this, proselytization of Muslims by non-Muslims is forbidden and, while not technically illegal, official recognition of apostasy for ex-Muslims is in practice virtually impossible. Indonesia is an interesting example of an explicitly nonsecular state which however gave official recognition to all major religions in the country under the 'national ideology' of *Pancasila* (Ramage, 1995).

Informal practices can also privilege certain religions over others, even when the state is officially neutral and/or secular. For instance, when the then Ivorian president Félix Houphouët-Boigny ordered the construction of a Catholic Basilica in Yamoussoukro in the 1980s for the approximately $600 million, which he claimed to have paid himself, many Muslims perceived this as a clear indication of Christian supremacy in Côte d'Ivoire (Langer, 2005). Indeed, in officially secular states there is often nonetheless bias towards the majority religion. In most secular Western European countries, Christianity retains a privileged public position through, for example, the designation of public holidays and even permitted first names. Furthermore, the fact that many political parties in secular states around the world have a particular religious affiliation and world view may result in the alienation of other religious groups if these parties gain power. The association between political parties and religion can be either explicit, as with the Christian Democrats (CDU) in Germany, or associative, as with the Republican Party and the Christian Right in the United States.

3.3.2   Language rights and language recognition

The privileging of one or a few languages over others often signals, or is at least perceived by minority-language speakers as signalling, the dominance of those for whom these languages are the mother tongue. Moreover, as the UNDP Human Development Report 2004 notes, '[r]ecognizing a language means more than just the use of that language. It symbolizes respect for the people who speak it, their culture and their full inclusion in society' (UNDP, 2004: 9). At one extreme, governments may actively penalize the use of a minority language. An example is Niger, where the Tameshaq language of the Tuareg people was banned from use in public places. Beyond Africa, language restrictions remain in place in some countries, such as Syria, which limits the use of Kurdish. A more common situation is the determination of a 'national' or 'official' language. Designating a single language as the national language may be seen as a means of promoting a cohesive and overarching 'national' identity, but it can also generate resentment among minority-language speakers who may feel symbolically excluded in addition, possibly, to being materially disadvantaged.

Conflicts revolving around language have been notable in India, where a high level of linguistic diversity has created status problems since independence. Indeed, in the period after 1956, the constituent states of the Indian federation were redrawn along explicitly linguistic lines in an attempt to mitigate this problem. Most resentment revolved around the imposition of Hindi as the main national language, which was seen as a form of 'Hindi imperialism'. Violent protests resulted in a number of places, notably Madras, where the violence has been seen as a product of 'the ruling authority's failure to establish communication with the people who had intense feelings concerning the language issue' (Das Gupta, 1970: 240). The assertion of a three-language formula, which guaranteed the continued status of English as a national *lingua franca* alongside Hindi, undercut much of this tension but language recognition and language issues continue to provoke tensions that have sometimes turned violent in parts of India. For example, in 2005, activists from the United Forum for Safeguarding Manipuri Script and Language (MEELAL, or *Meetei Eron Eyek Loinasinlon Apunba Lup*) set fire to the state's Central Library, destroying around 150,000 books, protesting against the use of the Bengali script for their language (Egreteau, 2006).

3.3.3   Recognition of ethnocultural practices

The state's recognition of, and support for, the cultural practices of different groups is another important aspect of cultural status inequality. Also important in this respect are the ethnocultural practices and customs employed in the functioning of the state itself, which express the 'identity' of the state. As already argued, even when states are broadly tolerant of cultural diversity, official practices may privilege the dominant cultural group through, for instance, the incorporation of their cultural identity and practices into the rituals and symbols of governance, national holidays, naming conventions (of buildings, streets and so on) and promulgation of national 'heroes' and histories. Attempts by the state to remain 'neutral' may sometimes be interpreted negatively by minority groups who associate 'neutrality' with *de facto* dominance of the majority culture. This was arguably the case when the French government introduced a ban on the wearing of any obvious religious symbols in schools and other public spaces, which was widely interpreted by Muslims as an attack on Islamic headscarves rather than a broader secular move. Lack of recognition of different cultural practices by the state can feed into broader informal practices within the society at large – an example is the assimilationist pressure in Guatemala against indigenous school girls wearing indigenous dress. Stereotyping by the media is evidently very important here, as it plays a vital role in '(re)producing' the cultural identity of the state. In Côte d'Ivoire, for instance, some newspapers closely linked to the governing party were and still are instrumental in the promotion of the concept of *l'Ivoirité*, which was introduced around the time of the 1995 presidential elections to categorize the residents of Côte d'Ivoire into 'real' Ivorians and 'foreigners' (Langer, 2005). Although this had immediate political implications for the presidential elections, it also fed into broader processes of cultural stereotyping.

An important factor in many countries concerns the treatment of customary law practices and principles. On the one hand, lack of recognition of customary law practices can generate alienation towards the legal system as a whole among minority groups. Plural legal systems not only increase the access of these minorities to the legal system, but also their overall sense of being culturally valued. In Guatemala, for instance, the 1996 Accord on Indigenous Identity and Rights states that 'the lack of knowledge by the national legislative body of the customary norms that regulate indigenous community life as well as the lack of access that the indigenous population has to the resources of the national justice system, have caused negation of rights, discrimination and marginalization' (quoted in Buvollen, 2002: 3). In order to overcome this, both the Guatemalan government and opposition agreed to implement a range of policies 'acknowledging the distinct cultures of indigenous peoples in Guatemala', such as free interpretation services into indigenous languages for judicial proceedings, cultural sensitivity programmes for judiciary members and recognition of indigenous communities' judicial norms (UNDP, 2004: 59). At times, customary or religious legal systems may conflict with the underlying foundations of the civil legal code. Conflicts that emerge from such incompatibilities are often at the heart of the cultural status debate within multicultural and multireligious countries. The emergence of civil unrest and severe tensions and occasionally serious violent clashes between Christians and Muslims after 12 of Nigeria's 36 states decided to adopt Sharia law in the period 2000–2002, clearly points towards the divisiveness of these issues.

Beyond customary law, denigration or suppression of other cultural practices and appearances associated with particular ethnic groups are also important aspects of cultural status inequality and can contribute to grievances and group mobilization around these issues. This was the case in the southern Malay-dominated provinces of Thailand which rebelled against the ethnic Thai government in the 1940s. In 1932, the Thai government tried to integrate its Malay citizens into the mainstream Thai body politic through educational inculcation, including the teaching of the Thai language and Thai history. These moves 'had little success but also aroused little opposition' (Forbes, 1982: 1059). After 1938, however, the government stance became more aggressively assimilatory rather than integrationist, including measures discriminating against the Malay language and the abrogation of Sharia laws. More potent than these policies, however, were explicitly cultural restrictions on Malay practices. As Forbes (1982: 1059) states,

> *sarongs* [traditional Malay dress] were banned and the wearing of western style long trousers and topees was made compulsory for all men. The chewing of betel and areca nuts was prohibited, and it was even stipulated that loads should be carried on the shoulder (Thai fashion) rather than on the head (Malay fashion) . . . [These measures] contributed substantially to the emergence of a Malay separatist movement.

Table 3.1   Dimensions of cultural status inequality

Recognition of religion and religious observances	Language rights and language recognition	Recognition of ethnocultural practices
• State religion and religious 'identity' of the state • State support for different religions • Religious freedoms and rights • Religious schooling • Religious legal systems • Recognition of religious holidays and festivals	• Official and national languages • Policies towards vernacular education • Provisions for vernacular broadcast media • Support for vernacular language study	• Ethnic rituals and symbols of governance • Recognition of customary law practices and principles • Dress and appearance • Recognition of multicultural histories in educational curricula • Promotion of national 'heroes' and festivals • State recognition of ethnic holidays and festivals • Recognition of customary leadership (for example, chieftains)

Table 3.1 summarizes important elements within each of the three main aspects of cultural status inequality. Understanding differential treatment, policies and practices across these elements is necessary to gain a complete picture of a country's cultural status inequalities. The list is indicative rather than exhaustive and it is important to emphasize that state and social practices relating to these different elements may take the form of formal policies, informal policies and practices, or symbolic gestures. Clearly, not all elements will be relevant in all contexts. Further, in some cases, the prohibition of particular cultural customs, the implementation of restrictions on some cultural groups' practices, or even the special treatment of certain cultural groups in the legal sphere, might be considered as indications of the state's promotion of cultural status *equality* rather than status inequality and exclusion. Examples are the prohibition on Orange Marches passing through certain Catholic neighbourhoods in Northern Ireland, restrictions on the use of English in Quebec or the exemption of Sikhs from wearing motorcycle helmets in various Western countries. In addition to understanding cultural status inequalities as practised by the state, the media plays a vital role in representing, and to some extent shaping, cultural status inequalities and is thus also an important area for research and policy. Thus all points to the need for these issues to be analysed and studied in a country-specific context.

3.4   Status anxiety: Linking cultural status inequalities, mobilization and conflict

There are two ways in which cultural status inequalities are an important source of group mobilization and potentially violent conflict. Firstly, cultural status inequalities are often in themselves an important cause of *group griev-ances*. If the state attributes inferior status to certain cultural identities, members of these cultural groups are more likely to feel alienated from the state and to mobilize along cultural lines in order to improve their group's cultural status. For instance, in Côte d'Ivoire, while the political exclusion and relative socioeconomic deprivation of the northern ethnic groups were both essential factors contributing to the emergence of the violent conflict there, perceptions of nonrecognition and secondary status of the Muslim religion, predominant in the northern regions (including the construction of the Catholic Basilica mentioned above), also played an important role in fostering northern group grievances and the subsequent outbreak of rebellion (Langer, 2005).

Secondly, cultural status inequalities can play an important role in affecting the political *salience* of other dimensions of horizontal inequality (political and socioeconomic). While severe socioeconomic HIs can persist for decades without raising violent responses (Chapter 4), changes in cultural status inequalities, like changes in political HIs, can be important in the politicization of inequalities, and can be a factor in group mobilization for violence. Where socioeconomic inequalities combine with state policies that appear to privilege one set of cultural norms and practices above others, group mobilization along cultural lines becomes more likely. The simultan-eous presence of severe cultural status inequalities alongside political *and* socioeconomic HIs represents a particularly explosive situation, because in such a context the excluded political elites not only have strong incent-ives to mobilize their supporters for violent conflict along cultural lines, but are also likely to gain support among their cultural constituencies relatively easily (Langer, 2007).

Cultural status inequalities are particularly potent for group mobiliza-tion because of their inherent link to group *identity*. As John Sidel notes in his study of religious violence in Indonesia, identity is 'inherently incomplete, unstable, and interactive . . . at the core of any identity is always a constitutive sense of *lack*, of *inadequacy*' (2006: 13, emphasis added). Such anxieties are important for violent group mobilization because they are an important determinant of the political salience of group differentials.

Linked to this is the particular potency of incidents involving cultural status inequalities in triggering violent conflict. Symbolic events which rein-force or publicly 'perform' cultural status inequalities have an important role in triggering group violence. In some cases, this may be deliberate and cynical provocation. In other cases, ongoing contestation over cultural status can be heightened around regularly reoccuring events, such as the Orange Marches in Northern Ireland, which find their origins in celebrations of Protestant conquests over Catholic Ireland. In such circumstances, the state's response towards these contestations – for instance, whether to allow or disallow marching through Catholic areas – can affect different groups' perceptions of their respective cultural status. These cases are all the more problematic and difficult to resolve where they become embedded in the cultural practices of the groups involved. Even where direct or institutionalized 'provocation' is not present, contingent events that reveal the extent of cultural status inequalities may provoke (violent) group mobilization.

As we noted above, cultural status inequalities are an important influence in determining the political salience of socioeconomic and political HIs. As mobilizing agents in themselves, cultural status inequalities have direct resonance with people, and do not necessarily need to be 'interpreted' by leaders. Indeed, mobilization for apparently acultural motives is often given additional force when movement leaders adopt an explicitly cultural interpretive frame. Thus, for instance, Brown's (2004a) analysis of the dynamics of social mobilization in Malaysia found that contentious politics around apparently nonethnic demands such as environmentalism often drew their mobilizational force from perceptions of ethnic favouritism on the part of the government. For instance, environmental movements protesting what was seen as excessive or environmentally-destructive 'development' programmes were most successful when they drew upon issues that conflated with Chinese perceptions of cultural status inequality, such as the campaign against the development of *Bukit Cina*, an old Chinese cemetery. The point here is that the relationship between cultural status inequalities and (violent) group mobilization can be more direct than with other forms of horizontal inequality because of the inherently cultural dimension of the grievances involved.

3.5   Conclusions

In this chapter, we have argued that differential treatment and recognition of different groups' cultural practices and norms by the state constitute cultural status inequalities. While we do not contest the importance of political and socioeconomic grievances as drivers of (violent) group mobilization, we have argued that group grievances can also emerge out of the inferior treatment or status afforded different groups' cultural practices by the state. Moreover, we have argued that the most dangerous situations exist where all three dimensions of horizontal inequality – socioeconomic, political and cultural status – run in the same direction, or are consistent.

In order to assess the extent of a country's cultural status inequalities, we have categorized differential treatment in policies and practices – formal, informal, and symbolic – into three elements: religion and religious observation; language rights and language recognition; and recognition of ethnocultural practices.

Cultural status inequalities are particularly prone to group mobilization, and potentially violence, because of the inherent link with *group identity*. This can take the form both of 'entrepreneurial' mobilization by self-interested elites or grievance-based mobilization on the part of disadvantaged groups. Many scholars, for instance, see the 'language conflicts' of India as instrumental, being exploited by disaffected elites (for example Brass, 1974). Yet this does not mean that there are not 'genuine' group grievances about cultural status underlying such instrumental mobilization. Indeed, it is our contention that instrumental mobilization often draws upon issues of cultural status precisely because of the degree to which they matter to the wider population. Where groups feel their identity is accorded insufficient recognition, they are more likely to become alienated from that state and to resort to mobilization, which could turn violent.

4
Horizontal Inequalities: Explaining Persistence and Change

Frances Stewart and Arnim Langer

4.1 Introduction

In many cases horizontal inequalities persist over long periods. For example, black/white differentials in the US, or indigenous/Ladino differentials in Latin America have been in existence for centuries. Other examples include the northern peoples in Ghana and blacks in South Africa. In contrast, some immigrant groups who were initially poor relative to the national average soon achieved above-average incomes. Where horizontal inequalities (HIs) persist they are particularly deleterious as they trap people, generation after generation, in a situation of deprivation. These conditions may also give rise to greater social instability. Consequently, this chapter is devoted to understanding the determinants of socioeconomic HIs over time, why they are so persistent in some cases but prove temporary in others.

In considering this issue, we draw on previous work on the question, both theoretical and empirical. For example, Tilly (1998) has made important contributions on both fronts, mainly considering the US situation. Recent work by Mogues and Carter (2005) has considered theoretical issues, this time with a greater focus on developing countries, while there have been a number of empirical studies with bearing on the issue (for example, Adato *et al.*, 2006; Borjas, 1992, 1995; and Durlauf, 2002). These analyses have generally focussed on one or two elements accounting for HIs over time. We adopt a more comprehensive approach, aiming to incorporate the whole range of factors that are significant in explaining change in HIs over time, both economic and political. This comprehensive approach is important because of interactions among the various factors, which are relevant to persistence, and because it permits identification of a wider range of policies towards HIs.

In order to consider persistence of HIs over time, a prerequisite is that we can identify long-term cultural markers that differentiate the groups being considered. This involves not only the definitional issues discussed in

54

the first chapter about how to define the salient group boundaries necessary to identify HIs at a point in time, but also considering whether these same boundaries remain salient over time. As time proceeds, intermarriage, migration and cultural and religious changes may mean that prior group boundaries become insignificant or dissolve altogether, while new salient groups may emerge. Thus in eleventh-century Britain, the difference between Anglo-Saxons and Normans was important politically, but by the twenty-first century, differences between these groups have all but disappeared and new salient group boundaries (for example, between Muslims and Christians, or groups defined according to their migration status and country of origin) have emerged.

The issue of persistent HIs only arises where group boundaries also persist over time, that is, where the groups themselves remain a salient category. There may be some circularity here, as the persistence of the salience of an identity may itself be partly dependent on the persistence of HIs – since sharp HIs tend to stimulate group consciousness. We should note that because of this, empirical investigation will tend to overestimate the persistence of HIs, because cases where group boundaries cease to be of significance or disappear completely will not be explored, and these are the cases where it is likely that HIs did not persist. But even if the examples we find of persistence exaggerate the issue for society as a whole, they are important in themselves, perhaps especially so because in other cases catch-up occurs.

As noted in Chapter 1, HIs are multidimensional, with the main dimensions being economic, social, political and cultural, and with numerous elements within each category. This multidimensionality is particularly important in understanding persistence because interactions among the dimensions and the elements within them are an important factor determining persistent deprivation and also persistent above-average performance. For example, lack of access to education (a social inequality) may lead to low incomes (an economic one) and both may be responsible for and also caused by lack of political power. We shall elaborate on these causal interactions much more below.

Vertical inequality, or inequality among all individuals or households in a society, is also typically persistent (that is, a continuously high Gini coefficient is often observed), yet individuals or families may move in and out of poverty, in what has been defined as 'churning'. For example, one study in China found that 50 per cent of poverty in four rural provinces was transient (Jalan and Ravallion, 2000). In Uganda, a study in the Central and Western regions showed that 24 per cent of households moved out of poverty in a 25-year period (Krishna *et al.*, 2006), while 'In most European countries, the combination of modest inequality and extensive mobility among the poor enabled *virtually all* families to avoid relative deprivation at least occasionally' (Duncan *et al.*, 1993: 215).

With persistent HI, in contrast, individuals/families are 'trapped' to a greater degree because of the difficulties of moving across groups, so that a higher proportion of families in deprived groups remain deprived over time. This is confirmed by a range of studies. For instance, Duncan *et al.* (1993), Devine *et al.* (1992) and Corcoran (1995) found much greater persistence of poverty among the black population in the US than among other US groups. A similar differentiation according to race was found by a study in rural Appalachia (Blee and Billings, 1996). Moreover, evidence for Kenya and Madagascar shows that people in remote and poor agro-ecological sites show more persistent poverty than those in more favourable areas (Barrett *et al.*, 2006).

Hence taking lifetime outcomes as the area of concern, the welfare cost of inequality is likely to be higher in relation to HI than VI. Group inequality can be more damaging for individual well-being than similar inequality among a homogeneous population because people in deprived groups may feel trapped in their situation, particularly when persistence occurs across generations. Hence the importance of the question being investigated in this chapter.

The chapter is organized as follows: the next section develops a theoretical framework for understanding the evolution of HIs over time. Section 4.3 draws on empirical examples of long-run HIs to illustrate what happens to HIs in a variety of cases, and which parts of our framework seem to account for the persistence or changes. Section 4.4 concludes with some policy implications.

4.2   A framework for considering the evolution of horizontal inequalities

While HIs are multidimensional, in our framework we focus initially on income as an outcome, and we point to political and social inequalities as a *cause* of the income inequalities. We start with income because it is a fundamental dimension of economic welfare and a source of many other inequalities; and because our understanding of the determinants of income and income inequality is considerably more advanced than it is with respect to other inequalities. However, in principle we can extend the approach to encompass other inequalities, and the empirical section contains information on a much wider range of inequalities than simply income.

To start with we consider the immediate causes of economic inequality among individuals at a point in time. Incomes of an individual are a function of assets which they have and the employment and productivity of those assets. Inequality between groups is then the consequence of inequality in asset ownership between groups and inequalities in the returns to these assets. Assets include land; financial assets; education; public infrastructure; and social capital. Each of these assets is somewhat problematic to measure and quality and quantity interact. Thus land ownership can be defined in terms of acreage or value (taking into account quality, market opportunities, the nature of the property rights); financial capital measures the ability to buy productive assets, and the value of the asset depends on the nature of the financial instrument adopted; human capital may be defined as years of education and access to health services, or it may also include the quality and nature of that education and of health services. Social capital is the most difficult to define. It is intended to include all the influences on productive opportunities and productivity stemming from social interactions. The 'quantity' of social capital is normally measured by the size of the network an individual has access to, or the daily interactions a person has, but it could be defined also to include a measure of the quality of these interactions, which clearly affects the returns to any amount of social capital when defined quantitatively.

For each asset, then, there is a major problem in differentiating the quantity a group owns of each asset from the returns on the asset. This arises particularly acutely in the case of social capital. We start, however, by assuming that we can make the distinction between quantity of an asset and the returns on that asset.

To simplify matters, we assume that an individual's income depends on just three types of asset: human capital, financial capital and social capital. Then the income of the ith individual in a population is given by Equation 4.1:

$$y_i = f(h_i, p_i, s_i) \qquad (4.1)$$

where h_i, p_i, s_i, are the human, financial and social capital of individual i, respectively. Adding up the capital and income of all members of a group and dividing by a group's size, we get the average incomes of each social group.

For group 1, average income of each group member is given by Equation 4.2:

$$y_1 = f_1(h_1, p_1, s_1) \qquad (4.2)$$

where h_1, p_1, s_1 are the *average* human, financial and social capital. Assuming the returns to each type of capital are H_1, P_1, S_1 we obtain Equation 4.3:

$$y_1 = f_1(h_1^{H_1}, p_1^{P_1}, s_1^{S_1}) \qquad (4.3)$$

And with two groups, 1 and 2, income HI at time t is given by Equation 4.4:

$$HI_t = \frac{y_1^t}{y_2^t} = \frac{f_1^t(h_{1t}^{H_{1t}}, p_{1t}^{P_{1t}}, s_{1t}^{S_{1t}})}{f_2^t(h_{2t}^{H_{2t}}, p_{2t}^{P_{2t}}, s_{2t}^{S_{2t}})} \qquad (4.4)$$

We are assuming that different groups may face different production functions (that is, H_1 is not necessarily equal to H_2, P_1 to P_2, S_1 to S_2);

moreover, we are *not* assuming that the returns are constant over time or in relation to each other. This complicates our presentation as it means we cannot present a Constant Elasticity of Substitution (CES) production function, but it is important to the argument about the determinants of changing HIs over time.

In exploring group inequality at a point in time (Equation 4.4), then, we need to consider inequalities in both access to and ownership of capital and in the productivity of that capital, where the productivity of capital includes the extent of its use as well as its productivity in use. There is evidence that not only does the capital available to different groups vary, but also the returns vary. For example, poorer groups (like individuals) consistently have lower levels of human and financial capital (Barrón Ayllón, 2007) and also often secure lower returns on the capital they have. For example, African-Americans have been shown to have lower returns for a given level of human capital, while lower returns, as well as less education quantitatively, have been shown to be a feature of minorities in Vietnam (van der Walle and Gunewardena, 2001).

Moreover, social capital is not truly 'social' but is a property of groups, with networks biased towards within-group connections, and consequently less advantageous for poorer groups (see Bourdieu, 1986). This follows from the definition of social capital since it encompasses neighbourhood and group effects on behaviour, opportunities and productivity, including peer group and cultural impacts on behaviour and aspirations as well as networks which may open up or facilitate opportunities. We can then differentiate the 'quantity' of social capital of a group, defined as the number of contacts the group as a whole has, from the quality of that social capital, defined as the impact of the network (quantity of contacts) on economic achievements. A common distinction is between 'bridging' and 'bonding' social capital, sometimes defined as between-family or -group and within-family or -group contacts. In general within-group social networks exceed between-group networks in quantity. For poor groups, bonding or within-group contacts are likely to be of lower quality than bridging or between-group contacts. For rich groups, the reverse may be true. A number of studies have demonstrated the importance of 'neighbourhood', 'ethnic group' and 'social connection' effects on opportunities and incomes empirically (Borjas, 1995; Cooper *et al.*, 1993; Corcoran *et al.*, 1989; and Datcher, 1982, all for the US; Adato *et al.*, 2006, for South Africa; and Nurmela, 2006, for Finland).

Thus less capital of each kind and lower returns on that capital can explain the existence of inequality among individuals/groups at a point of time. But this does not explain what happens over time. In the second period, *t*+1, HI will be given as follows:

$$HI_{t+1} = \frac{f_1^{t+1}(h_{1(t+1)}^{H_1(t+1)}, p_{1(t+1)}^{P_1(t+1)}, s_{1(t+1)}^{S_1(t+1)})}{f_2^{t+1}(h_{2(t+1)}^{H_2(t+1)}, p_{2(t+1)}^{P_2(t+1)}, s_{2(t+1)}^{S_2(t+1)})} \qquad (4.5)$$

Changes in HI (HI_{t+1}/H_t) therefore depend on changing relative rates of accumulation of each type of capital, and changing returns to each type of capital. Thus it is possible that groups catch up over time, for example by accumulating more than the more privileged groups, or by catching up technologically and hence reducing differentials in returns. Moreover, for some of the nonincome elements of HIs, notably health and education, there are upper limits to achievements (for example, 100 per cent literacy is a maximum) so that some catching up is likely to arise from this 'boundedness'.[1] But there are other reasons why catch up does not occur and inequality persists. We identify five factors in this respect.

First, there are cumulative forces, such that deprivation/riches at one point in time make it harder/easier to accumulate assets in the future. If an individual has a higher income due to higher assets, then saving (including educating children) is easier, so we might assume that the rate of saving and accumulation is likely to be higher among richer individuals/groups. Moreover, in the case of human capital, there is a direct intergenerational impact on behaviour so that a major predictor of a child's education (and nutrition and health) is the education of her mother (Behrman, 1990; King and Hill, 1993). In theory, 'perfect' capital markets should enable people to borrow to overcome the disadvantage of not having their own savings. But in practice, banks require collateral so that borrowing too is easier for the rich than for the poor. Loury (1981) shows how family income determines mobility in the absence of a perfect capital market for educational loans, leading to poverty traps. Banerjee and Newman (1993) have developed a theoretical model showing how capital market imperfections reduce job choices of the financial-capital poor, and thus constrain earnings in subsequent periods. Extensive empirical evidence shows that poorer individuals/groups accumulate less, both with respect to human and financial capital. However, upper limits on education mean that once richer groups approach this level, their educational accumulation will be limited and a relatively faster rate of accumulation can be expected among poorer individuals/groups.

Second, there are interactions among returns to different types of capital according to the *other* types of capital a person/group has. Thus human capital permits greater earnings, which enable people to accumulate more; financial capital is more productive if people have human capital with which to use it; human capital may be more productively employed if people have financial capital; and both types of capital are likely to be better used with good networks (that is, more social capital). In addition, social capital of a group improves as people within the group become better educated and richer so that they have better-educated and richer contacts.

What this means is that the returns to one type of capital depend not only on the accumulation of that type of capital, but also on the accumulation of other types, so that, for example, P (the returns to financial capital) depend on the level of human and social capital (h and s). This is why we do not assume a CES production function and we posit different production functions for each group.

Third, HIs might persist because of persistent asymmetries in social capital which then cause the unequal returns on other types of capital just noted. While asymmetry in social capital occurs among individuals – poor people tend to have more contacts with other poor people than with richer people – it applies even more strongly among groups. Indeed, some have defined groups as being collections of individuals whose transactions/contacts within group are significantly greater than their transactions outside the group (Blau, 1977). This effect has been modelled by Lundberg and Startz (1998) and Mogues and Carter (2005), while Durlauf (2002) shows how 'neighbourhood' effects can sustain poverty, via peer group effects, social learning and social complementarities. An empirical investigation into neighbourhoods in the US found that neighbourhood effects influence intergenerational mobility, while ethnic factors play an additional role even among people who grow up in the same neighbourhood (Borjas, 1995). Borjas also showed empirically that 'the skills and labor market outcomes of today's generation depend not only on the skills and labor market experiences of their parents but also on the average skills and labor market experiences of the ethnic group in the parent's generation' (Borjas, 1992: 148). Neighbourhood effects (again in the US) have also been shown to influence the development of children and adolescents, including IQ and school leaving, with long term consequences for socioeconomic outcomes (Brooks-Gunn *et al.*, 1993). There is empirical evidence for South Africa too that asymmetries of social capital have blocked pathways of social mobility even in the post-apartheid era (Adato *et al.*, 2006). Based on panel data for 1993–1998, Adato *et al.* (2006: 244) conclude that 'social capital becomes more narrowly constructed and increasingly ineffective as a means of capital access for poor people in a country facing a legacy of horizontal inequality and social exclusion.'

A fourth reason for the persistence of group inequality is that group members are often subject to overt (or implicit) discrimination or favouritism by nongroup members in access to different types of capital and in employment, in virtue of their group (cultural) characteristics. This illustrated in Figure 4.1, which shows how returns to financial capital vary according to the level of other types of capital, and that group 1 has higher returns to financial capital, for any level of human/social capital.

We should note that historic discrimination contributes to poor returns *even where it seems there is no current discrimination*. For example, unequal endowments today may be partly a reflection of past discrimination. Effects persist even if there is no current discrimination, that is even if, for example,

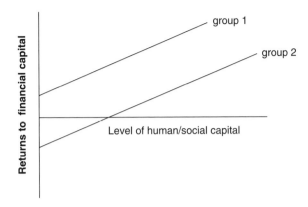

Figure 4.1   Variations in returns to financial capital according to group discrimination

there are equal employment opportunities for the same educational attainments, since past discrimination may have led to inequality in educational endowments (see, for example, M. K. Brown *et al.*, 2005). Further, Loury (2002) argues that negative stereotypes about certain groups can become self-fulfilling which amounts *de facto* to (implicit) discrimination against the stereotyped groups. Thus, for instance, the negative stereotype that black people do not work hard may result in a situation that employers with imperfect information are more likely to fire them. Consequently, black people may decide that it is not worth working hard because they are likely to get fired anyway regardless of their individual work ethic. If black people conform to a negative stereotype, their relatively poor treatment may appear to be justified and not be identified as due to discrimination, yet discrimination (via negative stereotypes) underlies the situation.

Finally, group inequalities in most cases include political inequalities in the same direction as the socioeconomic inequalities. This means those who are deprived in socioeconomic dimensions also lack political power. These political inequalities generally underpin the socioeconomic inequalities since they often lead to bias in the distribution of government resources, including access to social and economic services and government employment and contracts. Moreover, the political inequalities can prevent corrective action towards the relatively powerless group. In general, where political inequalities and socioeconomic inequalities are in the same direction, we would expect each to reinforce the other. But there are occasional cases where a majority (privileged) government takes action to help a deprived group, although this is generally not enough to eliminate the inequality (for example, affirmative action in the US or Brazil). This was the case in Northern Ireland, where government policy from the mid-1970s reduced centuries-old inequalities, as discussed further below. There are situations, in contrast, where political power and socioeconomic deprivation are in opposite directions, as in the recent history of Malaysia or South Africa. In these cases, governments are more likely to take action to correct the socioeconomic HIs so that over time they can be expected to become less marked.

Returning to the key variables determining the direction in which economic HIs move over time:

- $h_{(t+1)}/h_t$ (or the relative accumulation of human capital): this is likely to diverge in the early stages of development because of differing rates of accumulation, but may converge as the richer groups attain high levels of education. It may also converge because of government policy to spread education widely.
- $p_{(t+1)}/p_t$ (or the relative accumulation of financial capital): this may diverge because of differing rates of savings. Directed credit schemes may achieve some convergence.
- $s_{(t+1)}/s_t$ (or the relative accumulation of social capital): this might converge with the increased mobility that occurs with development as contacts increase, although richer groups may also upgrade their contacts over time (for example, internationally).
- $H_{(t+1)}/H_t$ (or the change in the relative returns to human capital): we are in somewhat uncertain territory here. Outcomes will depend on what happens to other types of capital and to discrimination.
- $P_{(t+1)}/P_t$ (or the change in the relative returns to financial capital): differences between rich and poor groups are likely to persist for reasons given above, but it is difficult to say whether these will increase or decrease over time. The normal neo-classical assumption of diminishing returns to capital accumulation may be offset by indivisibilities and technological change. Government policy is again potentially relevant here, since it can provide technological assistance targeted at deprived groups, or conversely further help the privileged groups.
- $S_{(t+1)}/S_t$ (or the change in the relative returns to social capital): this is a matter of the quality or effectiveness of social capital. As a group's education increases, the quality of the interactions within group may improve. In addition, increased cross-group interactions may occur with increased development, and in response to government/civil society policies to increase them. Equally governments and civil society sometimes follow policies to reduce cross-group interactions.

One general feature which may reduce (or increase) group inequalities is a weakening (or tightening) of group boundaries. As group boundaries weaken – for example due to education, intermarriage and so on – more people may switch groups, which would tend to reduce inequalities. Conversely, if governments or people themselves increase the tightness of group boundaries (for example, by categorizing people, preventing mixing, mobilizing on identity lines), this element of group convergence will disappear. Even the categorization of people into different groups for affirmative action purposes (for example, in the US and India), or for purposes of quota allocations (for example, in Nigeria and India), may contribute to an increase in the salience of group differences, which in turn inhibits the inequality-reducing mechanism of group-switching. It is argued, for example, that the Malaysian affirmative action policies have 'entrenched' group politics and difference, although without much supporting evidence.[2]

Migration – national and international – is another way that convergence might be achieved. In principle, migration can offer people/groups opportunities to improve their situation, thereby potentially reducing inequalities. But in practice, both formal and informal[3] limits to migration often constrain this possibility. Internal migration is especially relevant in developing countries with severe climatic and ecological differences. However, although migration might improve the socioeconomic situation of the migrants relative to their region of origin, potentially reducing spatial HIs, it may establish a new set of unequal relations and mechanisms in the recipient areas, while leaving the sending areas without their most dynamic people. In Ghana and Côte d'Ivoire, for instance, a large number of people from the poorer and less well-endowed northern regions migrated to the southern regions in order to work on the cocoa and coffee plantations there. However, restrictions on land ownership and lack of resources meant that they were primarily employed as agricultural labourers on other people's land, thereby maintaining and to some extent further engraining the inequalities between 'southern' and 'northern' people. Another reason migration does not necessarily lead to a large reduction in HIs is related to the fact that the cities or regions to which people migrate are often unable to incorporate all the additional labour supply, resulting in high unemployment and poverty rates among the migrants. The development of vast slums and shanty towns in a large number of developing countries, where migrants often live in very poor conditions, is a clear indication that migration does not necessarily improve the socioeconomic situation of the migrants. The situation of immigrant populations in Europe also shows how new HIs can arise from migration.

To summarize, there are good reasons for expecting economic HIs to persist, although there are features which might lead to convergence. If a group starts from an unequal position, stemming from unequal access to different types of capital, key features sustaining such group inequality are

1. Unequal rates of accumulation, due to inequalities in incomes and imperfect markets.
2. Dependence of the returns to one type of capital on the availability of other types.
3. Asymmetries in social capital.

4. Present and past discrimination by individuals and nongovernmental institutions.
5. Political inequalities leading to discrimination by governments.

Of the five factors, groups as such are affected by 3, 4 and 5. The other reasons (1 and 2) apply to individuals as well as groups and thus explain persistent inequality in homogeneous societies. Previous work on persistent group inequalities has focussed on different elements among these five factors. For example, Tilly's (1998) important work categorized causes of persistence into discrimination, hoarding and emulation. Discrimination is explicitly included in reason 4 above. Hoarding consists in a privileged group introducing deliberate restrictions which favour it. This amounts to intervention in the market in such a way as to alter access to and returns to capital of various types. Emulation consists in the spread of this practice. These could be thought of as an additional reason for unequal accumulation and for differential returns, and as a consequence of asymmetrical social capital. Mogues and Carter (2005) have modelled asymmetries in social capital (reason 3) as responsible for persistent group inequality. In general, the political system has not been explicitly included in most discussion. Yet governments play an important role in furthering or reducing economic inequalities, so it is important that this too enters systematically into the analysis.

Taken together, these factors lead to the possibility of virtuous and vicious cycles: those groups starting in a privileged position being able to accumulate more fall into a virtuous cycle, having higher returns to assets and thus sustaining their privilege, while those who start in an underprivileged position fall into a vicious cycle, or poverty trap (see also Galor and Zeira, 1993). This is broadly the same as the accumulation and disaccumulation analyzed by M. K. Brown *et al.* (2005) in explaining persistent racial inequality in the US. There is a parallel here with country performance, in which poor economic performance handicaps human development and accumulation and poor human development handicaps economic growth (see Ranis *et al.*, 2000).

What these five factors do not tell us is what causes the initial inequality which sets in motion the interactions leading to the persistence of HIs. An important and pervasive cause among developing countries is a foundational shock, as noted by Figueroa, which can be reinforced by climatic differences (Figueroa *et al.*, 1996). This is typically a massive political event – for example, an invasion, followed by colonialism. In the case of Northern Ireland, for instance, the initial Protestant–Catholic inequalities were the outcome of a colonial experience, followed by the division of Ireland into an independent republic and a UK-controlled Northern Ireland; in the case of the US, the slave trade provided the foundational shock and in the case of Ghana, the north–south inequalities stem from colonial policy which favoured certain ethnic groups and regions, but also reflect climatic differences.

4.3   Evidence for the persistence and change of horizontal inequalities

A full investigation of why HIs persist should explore those that do not endure, as well as those that do. In this section, therefore, we examine some evidence of very persistent HIs (in Peru, Ghana and the United States), HIs that appear to have been reduced significantly (in Northern Ireland and Malaysia) and HIs that appear to have been reversed (Filipino and Japanese immigrants in the US). In each case, we aim to explain developments according to elements in the framework advanced above.

4.3.1   Education, labour markets and persistent inequality in Peru[4]

Among heterogeneous societies in Latin America, the foundational shock of colonial invasion and settlements led to the emergence of very large HIs between indigenous peoples and the colonial settlers (Figueroa *et al.*, 1996). Large inequalities in incomes and many other socioeconomic indicators have persisted since this shock, despite an expansion (and some equalization) in educational access. In the heterogenous society of Peru – made up of indigenous people, mestizos, and whites – persistent vertical inequality is a consequence, in large part, of persistent HI.

The evidence shows persistent inequality in access to schooling. Both mean years of schooling and level of schooling show strong inequalities, with whites most favoured, followed by mestizos and then indigenous people (Table 4.1).

Evidence on the returns to education shows that wages and salaries are positively related to the level of education attained, as predicted by 'human capital' theory. But in a heterogeneous society, there may be differences in returns according to group, as argued above, because of differences in school quality, learning environment and social capital, as well as discrimination. Statistical analysis shows significant differences in the returns to education across groups in Peru (see Figure 4.2 below). Thus mean incomes for those completing primary education are 800 soles per month for whites, 700 for mestizos and 600 for indigenous. These differences in returns to education imply that even as deprived groups catch up with more privileged groups in educational access, they still fall behind in incomes. This is supported

Table 4.1   Educational inequality in Peru, 2003

	Whites	Mestizos	Indigenous
Mean years of schooling	14	11	7
Proportion with post-secondary education, %	70	36	15

Source: Figueroa (2006).

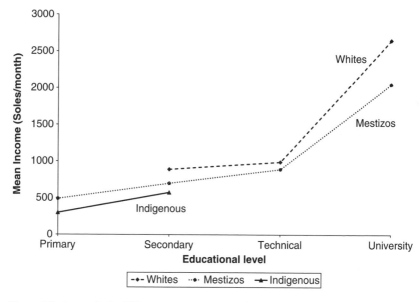

Figure 4.2   Interethnic differences in returns to education in Peru
Source: Figueroa (2006).

by data showing some educational catch-up in quantitative terms, indicated by differential across generations, but large gaps in incomes. Thus among whites, average years of education attained by people aged 25–34 in 2003 were 17 per cent higher than those aged 55–64, among mestizos years of education rose by a third, but among the indigenous group the average years of education more than doubled. The ratio of indigenous education years to whites' education years was 0.57 for all age groups in 2003. But the income gap was much higher, with a ratio of 0.28 of average indigenous incomes to whites' incomes.

Following Figueroa (2006), we hypothesize that the difference in returns to education are due to (i) persistent differences in the quality of education due to inequalities in the quality of infrastructure across locations; (ii) persistent differences in the learning achievements of children across groups due to language issues and differences in learning environments in the home; and (iii) overt or implicit discrimination. On top of the still highly unequal access to education (despite some catch-up), this leads to large inequalities in incomes.

4.3.2   North–south inequalities in Ghana

Like several other West African countries (for example, Côte d'Ivoire, Togo, Benin and Nigeria), Ghana is confronted with a severe developmental north–south gap. Regional inequalities overlap closely with ethnic differences and are also associated with religious differences. Ghana's current regional inequalities arise from a combination of circumstances and policies (see, among others, Dickson, 1975; Rimmer, 1992; Roe and Schneider, 1992; Songsore, 2003). Three important factors can be identified in this respect: First, the geographical concentration of most marketable agricultural activities/resources, particularly tree crops such as cocoa, as well as natural resources, notably minerals and forest resources, in the southern regions. Due to scant and irregular rainfall, most of the crops cultivated in the northern regions are subsistence crops.

A second reason relates to the British colonial policy of investing more heavily in those regions where exploitable resources such as gold, diamonds, manganese, timber and cocoa were available or could readily be produced, and from where they could most cheaply be exported. Consequently, in addition to the administrative core region (the Greater Accra Region), the gold-rich regions (Ashanti and Western) and the cocoa-growing regions (Eastern, Central and Ashanti) received the bulk of the capital investments made during the colonial era.

A third factor relates to postcolonial investment patterns and economic policies. The Structural Adjustment Programmes (SAPs) especially, implemented from the mid-1980s, reinforced the existing regional developmental inequalities. In particular, in line with the SAPs' objectives of restoring economic growth by rehabilitating Ghana's export economy, most external funding went to Ghana's 'industrial core region', the Greater Accra Region, as well as the cocoa, timber and mineral industries in the Western, Eastern, Ashanti and Brong Ahafo regions (Songsore, 2003). Ghana's northern regions, in contrast, benefited very little from this renewed economic stimulus. However, in order to redress the economic exclusion of the northern regions, consecutive postcolonial regimes undertook specific projects in the northern regions, including the extension of the national electricity grid, the rehabilitation of the north–south roads and greater expenditure on education.

Long-term data nonetheless (Table 4.2) show the persistence of north–south differences. Indeed, in some respects inequalities have worsened since 1931. For instance, a comparison between the infant and child mortality rates in the northern and southern regions in 1931 and 1993 shows a worsening of north–south differences in relative terms. Infant and child mortality rates in the Northern Territories in the Gold Coast were considerably closer to the national average than they were in the same area in Ghana in 1993.

Despite specific measures taken to correct north–south inequalities in recent years, Ghana's socioeconomic north–south divide remains severe – and has in some respects worsened, as illustrated by Table 4.3.

With respect to poverty incidence, the north–south divide widened during the 1990s: while the overall incidence of poverty decreased from 52 per

Table 4.2 Infant/child mortality rates for Gold Coast and Ghana in 1931 and 1993

	Absolute mortality rates, per 1000		Relative to national average	
	Infant mortality	Child mortality[a]	Infant mortality	Child mortality
Gold Coast, 1931				
Eastern Province, Colony	159	161	0.93	0.70
Central Province, Colony	171	283	1.00	1.23
Western Province, Colony	148	311	0.87	1.36
Ashanti	145	240	0.85	1.05
Northern Territories	214	248	1.26	1.09
National average	171	229	1.00	1.00
Ghana, 1993				
Western Region	76	60	1.15	1.05
Central Region	72	61	1.09	1.07
Greater Accra Region	58	44	0.88	0.77
Volta Region	79	42	1.20	0.74
Eastern Region	56	40	0.85	0.70
Ashanti Region	65	34	0.98	0.60
Brong Ahafo Region	49	48	0.74	0.84
Northern Region	114	139	1.73	2.44
Upper West Region	85	113	1.29	1.98
Upper East Region	105	84	1.59	1.47
National average	66	57	1.00	1.00

Sources: Gold Coast figures are calculated from the 1931 Census. The 1993 mortality rates are drawn from the 1997 Ghana Human Development Report.
[a] The child mortality rate for 1931 differs somewhat from the conventional definition as it is based on the number of children that died before reaching puberty rather than under the age of five.

cent to 40 per cent in the period 1992–1999, two of three northern regions (the Northern and Upper East regions) actually witnessed an increase in the incidence of poverty, although it appears that the northern regions were able to catch up slightly with the southern regions on literacy.

The theoretical insights developed earlier prove helpful for understanding the emergence and persistence of the socioeconomic inequalities between Ghana's northern and southern regions. Thus the initial north–south inequalities emerged as a result of the combined effect of the colonial 'shock' and prevailing climatic/ecological differences. Despite the

Table 4.3 Socioeconomic inequalities across Ghana's regions in the 1990s

Region	Incidence of poverty (%)[a]		Literacy (% of literate)[b]		Access to health services (%)[c]	Primary school enrolment (%)[c]
	1992	1999	1993	1998	1997	1997
Western	60	27	37	54	28	75
Central	44	48	43	55	36	72
Greater Accra	26	5	60	76	78	70
Volta	57	38	46	58	42	70
Eastern	48	44	46	66	33	78
Ashanti	41	28	31	64	43	72
Brong Ahafo	65	36	30	53	32	72
Northern	63	69	8	13	18	40
Upper West	88	84	12	20	8	45
Upper East	67	88	8	20	20	36
National average	52	40	34	51	37	67

[a] Data drawn from Songsore (2003). The poverty line was the same in both years, that is ¢ 900,000 per adult per year.
[b] Authors' calculations based on data from the 1993 and 1998 Demographic and Health Surveys.
[c] Data drawn from the 1997 Ghana Core Welfare Indicators Survey.

educational programmes in the northern regions, undertaken by consecutive Ghanaian governments since independence in 1957, income inequality has persisted, supporting the view that increases in human capital alone, without corresponding increases in financial and social capital, are insufficient to kick-start development and reduce HIs. In the case of Ghana, the impact of adjustment policies was to reinforce the advantage of the south as against the north, making it especially difficult for the educated to find good productive opportunities and leading to an out-migration to the south.

Migration from the northern regions to the southern regions improved the socioeconomic situation of some migrants, but it did not lead to a significant reduction in north–south inequalities, partly because most northern migrants are among the poorest section of the population in the southern regions.

4.3.3 Black/white inequalities in the United States

The racial inequalities in the United States have their origins in 300 years of economic, physical, legal, cultural and political discrimination based on race, with slavery as the foundational shock which initiated the persistent inequalities.

Although some progress has been made in reducing racial economic inequalities, there is an abundance of evidence showing persistently large income and wealth gaps between blacks and whites. In 2001, for instance, 'the real median income of black families was only about 62 per cent of that of Whites, only 10 per cent higher than it was in 1947 when the ratio was 52 per cent' (M. K. Brown *et al.*, 2005: 13). In *absolute* terms, the black–white real median income gap doubled from $10,386 to $20,469 in the period from 1947 to 2001 (p. 13).

Racial inequalities in wealth and financial assets are even more pronounced than inequalities in family incomes. According to Shapiro and Kenty-Drane (2005), in 1999, the black–white wealth gap ratio was 0.10, with typical white households having an overall median net worth of nearly $81,450 and blacks a median of just $8000. The black–white financial assets gap ratio was even lower, at 0.09. While the median net financial assets of white families in 1999 was $33,500, the median black family possessed just $3000. This severe wealth disparity exists even between blacks and whites in the top 20 per cent category of income earners (see Table 4.4). While the 1968 Fair Housing Act outlawed housing discrimination, blacks are far more likely to live in segregated neighbourhoods than either Asian Americans or Latinos (Massey and Denton, 1993).

Another important factor affecting racial income and wealth inequalities is differences in educational opportunities (see, for example, Keister, 2000).

The average educational attainment of black and white persons aged between 25 and 29 did converge significantly between 1940–1982: while blacks completed around three and a half fewer years of school than whites in 1940, the difference had decreased to about two years in 1960 and to about half a year in 1982 (Farley, 1984). Nonetheless, racial disparities persist at the highest level of educational attainment in modern-day US. Although the black–white gap in college attendance (Table 4.5) narrowed in the period 1960–1995, there continues to be a significant difference in the proportion of blacks and whites with a college degree.

The persistence of black inequality in the US exemplifies several of the factors identified in the theoretical framework. In the US, slavery was the

Table 4.4   Wealth by income and race ($)

	White		Black		Black/White ratio[a]	
	NW	NFA	NW	NFA	NW	NFA
Highest fifth median	133,607	40,465	43,806	7,448	0.33	0.18
Second-highest median	65,998	13,362	29,851	2,699	0.45	0.20
Middle fifth median	50,350	6,800	14,902	800	0.30	0.12
Second-lowest median	39,908	3,599	6,879	249	0.17	0.07
Lowest fifth median	17,066	7,400	2,400	100	0.14	0.01

Source: Shapiro and Kenty-Drane (2005: 177).
Note: NW = net worth; NFA = net financial assets.
[a] Our calculation based on Shapiro and Kenty-Drane's (2005) data.

Table 4.5 College attendance and completion by race, persons aged 25 or older, 1960–1995

Year	Black	White	Black/White ratio
	Percentage who attended college		
1960	7.2	17.4	0.41
1970	10.3	22.4	0.46
1980	21.9	33.1	0.66
1995	37.5	49.0	0.76
	Percentage with four or more years of college		
1960	3.1	8.1	0.38
1970	4.4	11.3	0.39
1980	8.4	17.1	0.49
1995	13.2	24.0	0.55

Sources: Figures for 1940–1980 from Bogue (1985: 413); 1995 figures from Bureau of the Census (1996: Tables 1 and 18). Cited in Thernstrom and Thernstrom (1997: 192).

obvious foundational shock which lies at the heart of the racial inequalities. The period of slavery, followed by institutionalized racial discrimination and oppression, lasting until the emergence of the civil rights movement in the 1960s, caused severe educational, income, wealth and health disadvantages for the black population. Despite 30 years of affirmative action programmes which followed and which contributed to a significant reduction in racial inequalities in education, persistently large gaps between blacks and whites have continued in almost all economic, social and health indicators. Inequalities in some health indicators (for example, infant mortality rates) have even widened during the last two decades. This persistence in inequality arose because historic discrimination and disadvantages not only resulted in lower levels of human, financial and social capital for the black population, but also (indirectly) in lower returns to these different types of capital. For example, poor black families are currently either unable to secure a mortgage loan because they cannot contribute funds of their own, or, if they do get a mortgage, they are charged higher interest rates, which means lower returns to their investment, while neighbourhood effects have been shown to handicap blacks in educational and employment opportunities. Achieving a significant reduction in racial wealth inequalities is therefore proving extremely difficult, even though affirmative action programmes have contributed to increasing the human capital stock of the black population.

4.3.4 Protestant/Catholic inequalities in Northern Ireland

The origins of economic inequality lie in the seventeenth century when it was created as a matter of government policy. . . . Protestants were in firm control of Northern Ireland's economic resources from partition [1921] until the 1960s. They were dominant at all levels of the private sector including the crucial areas of industry and finance . . .

(Ruane and Todd, 1996: 153, 171)

The evidence shows that systematic inequalities persisted for the first three-quarters of the twentieth century. For example, a study of occupational mobility in Belfast between 1901 and 1951 shows no narrowing of the gap, with the Catholics disfavoured at every level (Hepburn, 1983), with fewer Catholics moving upwards from manual to nonmanual occupations from 1901 to 1951 than Protestants, and more Catholics than Protestants moving downwards. For the 1970s, Miller (1983) found that the initial disadvantage of Catholics worsened further across generations. The unemployment rate among Catholics remained consistently above that of Protestants during most of the twentieth century.

The Catholics were consistently underrepresented in the higher echelons of the civil service. In 1927, 6 per cent of 'staff officers' were Catholic (while the Catholic share of the population was about 30 per cent); in 1959, the proportion was still 6 per cent; in 1943 it was 5.8 per cent; and in 1971, 11 per cent of senior public officials were Catholic (while their share of population was then 31 per cent) (Whyte, 1983). Catholics were also severely underrepresented in the police force (the Royal Ulster Constabulary-RUC), accounting for only 17 per cent of the police force in 1936, 12 per cent in 1961 and 11 per cent in 1969.

In education, Protestant English-speaking schools were established in the sixteenth century and Catholic and vernacular ones prohibited. Catholic schools were allowed from 1812. However, data shows Catholic disadvantage in admission to grammar schools and O- and A-level achievements up to the mid-1970s. Other indicators of inequality were the higher proportion of Catholics on income support (37 per cent compared with 20 per cent among Protestants in the mid-1980s), and poorer housing conditions. In 1971, for example, 29.3 per cent of Catholics had a housing density of more than one person per room compared with 9.8 per cent of Protestants.

There were also sharp political inequalities. One of the first changes made after partition was to abolish the proportional representation system, followed by the redrawing of boundaries. Buckland (1979: 233) shows that the 'sole concern' of the Ministry of Home Affairs was 'how to give effect to the views of the Unionist [Protestant] rank and file' (quoted in Whyte, 1983). Given the numerical majority of the Protestants, the majoritarian voting system and redrawn boundaries assured the Protestant community permanent power.

The disadvantage of the Catholics again illustrates many of the factors identified in the earlier theoretical discussion. First, there was a foundational shock, represented by the British assumption of power and the immigration of people from Britain who took the best land and dominated official employment. Secondly, severe educational disadvantage followed. Thirdly, there was sustained discrimination in employment, with cumulative impact via informal networks: 'The informal networks which are still so powerful in Northern Ireland and through which so much employment is found, operate to maintain and reinforce employment patterns already established' (Murray and Darby, 1980: 5). This illustrates the importance of asymmetrical social capital. Because of this discrimination and other handicaps, Catholics attained lower returns to education, an estimated increase in incomes of $159 for each extra year of schooling, compared with $254 for Protestants (Covello and Ashby, 1980), and Catholics were less likely to find jobs than Protestants for any given level of education (Cormack *et al.*, 1980). An investigation into Catholic–Protestant differences in mean income for 1989 and 1990 among employees found that this 'could entirely be explained in terms of different rates of reward attached to a given set of labour market characteristics' (Borooah *et al.*, 1995: 41).

From the mid-1970s, however, UK and EU policy aimed to eliminate these inequalities, and they succeeded to a remarkable extent (see Figure 4.3). For

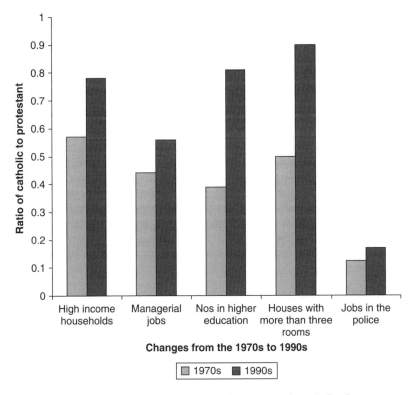

Figure 4.3 The evolution of horizontal inequalities in Northern Ireland
Source: Authors' calculations, derived from Gallagher (1995); Melaugh (1994); Fair Employment Commission (1998); and PPRU (1993).

instance, Catholics caught up significantly with Protestants in university education and the share of managerial positions, so that very little disadvantage remained. Catholic housing conditions also improved considerably so that they were almost equivalent to Protestant conditions. There was a much diminished net advantage of Protestants in employment over the period 1973–1996 (Breen, 2000).

However, some disadvantage remained. For example, Protestants were still overrepresented in the 40 largest companies (with 1.6 times the employment, while being 1.2 times the population size, in 1997) and a higher proportion of Catholics remained on income support. Further, a government survey in 2004 on inequality in health and social care found that Catholics were significantly disadvantaged in each area reported on (McWhirter, 2004).

4.3.5   Malay/Chinese inequalities in Malaysia

In Malaysia, the *bumiputera* (an umbrella term for indigenous groups), who account for the majority of Malaysia's population, were at a severe economic disadvantage vis-à-vis the Chinese when the country became independent in 1957, leading to a potentially explosive situation. But systematic affirmative action has lowered this tension. A total of 62 per cent of Malaysians are *bumiputera*, 30 per cent are ethnic Chinese and 8 per cent are Indians. At independence, economic and social HIs systematically favoured the Chinese: for example, *bumiputera* household incomes were less than half those of the Chinese, they accounted for only 8 per cent of registered professionals, less than 2 per cent of ownership of capital on the stock exchange and their educational enrolment rates were lower at each level of education (see Figure 4.4).

The economic disadvantage of the Malay community, who form the majority of the *bumiputera*, has its origins in the colonial period. Under British colonial rule, the method of production was organized into two distinct and parallel types which was complemented by an 'ethnic division of labour' (see Abraham, 1997; Brown, 1997; and Faaland *et al.*, 2003). By the mid-twentieth century, the Chinese dominated the economy, while the numerically dominant Malay community was severely economically disadvantaged. In 1967, for instance, the average income in absolute terms was approximately $3000 for non-Malays compared to about $1750 for Malays (Faaland *et al.*, 2003: 62).

After the May 1969 general election descended into ethnic rioting, the government identified the severe economic inequalities between the Malays and Chinese as the major cause of the emergence of ethnic violence and introduced an ambitious and comprehensive redistribution policy, the New Economic Policy (NEP). The NEP was aimed at creating 'the socioeconomic conditions for national unity through reducing poverty and interethnic economic disparities, especially between the indigenous Bumiputeras (mainly Malays, especially in peninsular Malaysia) and non-Bumiputeras (mainly Chinese and Indian Malaysians)' (Jomo, 1990: 469).

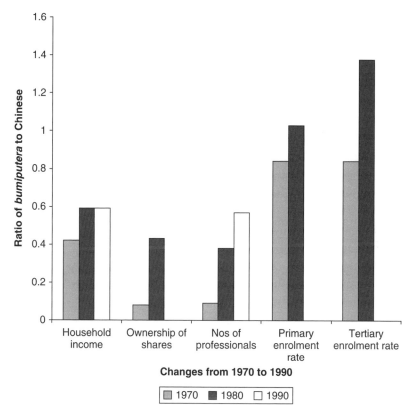

Figure 4.4 The evolution of different horizontal inequality indicators in Malaysia, 1970–1990
Source: Stewart (2002).

The NEP is arguably the most successful ethnic-inequality-reducing programme implemented by a developing country. Policies that followed included quotas, targets and affirmative action with respect to education, land ownership, public service employment and ownership of quoted companies. The policies were undoubtedly successful. The proportion of *bumiputera* professionals rose from 8 per cent to 54 per cent; *bumiputera* students in tertiary education increased from 43 per cent to 54 per cent of the total, and there was a similar improvement at other levels of education. The share of corporate stock ownership rose from 1.5 per cent in 1969 to 20.6 per cent in 1995 (see Figure 4.4 above). While *bumiputeras* retained their dominant position in agriculture, there was an economy-wide switch out of agriculture into manufacturing and services, and the *bumiputera* position in these sectors improved significantly.

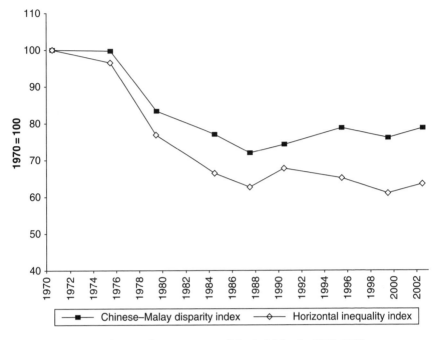

Figure 4.5   The evolution of income inequalities in Malaysia, 1970–2002
Source: Brown (2005a: 2).

Although the NEP led to a drastic reduction in the Malay–Chinese income inequalities, severe income differences persist. This point is illustrated by Figure 4.5, which depicts the evolution of two measures of HI in Malaysia over the period since the inception of the NEP in 1970 (Brown, 2005a).[5] Both measures show substantial reductions in inequality.

4.3.6   Japanese, Chinese and Filipino immigrants in the United States

The Chinese were the first to move from Asia to the United States, especially California, between 1850 and 1882. From the early 1880s, Japanese immigrants started arriving and around the turn of the century a large wave of Filipino immigrants migrated, initially to Hawaii and later to the American mainland. However, as a result of government restrictions on Asian immigration, the proportion of Asian Americans in the US population remained insignificant in relation to the rest of the population until the late 1960s. However, following the introduction of the Immigration and Nationality Act of 1965, which abolished discrimination in immigration on the basis of national origin, Asian immigration increased dramatically. In particular, in the period

1965–2002, about 8.3 million Asian immigrants were admitted to the US, increasing their number from approximately 1.5 million or 1 per cent of the US population in 1970 to approximately 12 million or 4.2 per cent of the population in 2000.[6] Acknowledging the very substantial differences in the socioeconomic progress of different Asian American communities, we focus here on arguably the three most successful Asian immigrant groups to date: Japanese, Chinese and Filipino.

Most Asian immigrants arriving from the late 1960s onwards tended to be highly educated due to the selective stipulations of the 1965 Immigration Act (Sakamoto and Xie, 2006). Moreover, there were known vacancies for the skills such migrants brought. Consequently, it is hardly surprising that their experience was much more successful than many other deprived or immigrant groups. Table 4.6 illustrates this point. All three Asian immigrant groups discussed here significantly improved their educational attainment position relative to the whites from 1960 to 1970, particularly with regard to the proportion of people of 25 years or older who had attended four or more years of college. From 1970 to 2000 they improved, or at least maintained, their higher levels of educational attainment relative to the US white population further. This contrasts with the evolution of the educational position of the black population, discussed earlier, which also got better, but started at much lower levels and improved less at the higher education levels, despite benefiting from affirmative action.

Table 4.6 The evolution of educational differences between whites, blacks and three Asian immigrant groups in the US, 1940–1990

Groups	1940	1950	1960[a]	1970	1980	1990	2000[b]
	People of 25 years or older who completed at least 4 years of high school (proportion relative to the whites)						
Blacks	0.28	0.35	0.46	0.58	0.74	0.81	0.89
Japanese	1.26	1.54	1.24	1.26	1.19	1.12	1.11
Chinese	0.46	0.79	1.02	1.06	1.04	0.94	1.10
Filipino	0.71	0.60	0.72	1.00	1.08	1.06	1.05
	People of 25 years or older who completed 4 or more years of college (proportion relative to the whites)						
Blacks	0.24	0.33	0.33	0.39	0.49	0.53	0.52
Japanese	1.02	0.98	1.16	1.41	1.54	1.60	1.79
Chinese	0.61	1.41	1.96	2.27	2.14	1.89	2.31
Filipino	0.55	0.53	0.95	1.99	2.16	1.83	1.24

Source: Authors' calculation based on data drawn from various US censuses.
[a] The 1960 figures are based on people of 14 years and older.
[b] Data drawn from Sakamoto and Xie (2006).

In addition to the positive impact of the high initial levels of education of the Asian immigrants as 'the offspring of more educated people tend to become more educated themselves,' group differences in norms and aspirations also appear to have played an important role. In particular, Asian Americans are often argued to have 'high aspirations and expectations for their children's economic success' (Sakamoto and Xie, 2006: 56). Correspondingly, '. . . , Asian American parents expect their children to achieve higher education than the parents of other racial groups' (ibid.: 58). It is reported that 'in order to achieve the goals that parents set for them and they set for themselves, Asian American children report doing, on average, close to one hour more of homework per week than do white children' (p. 58).

Many of the highly educated Asian Americans who arrived after the 1965 Immigration Act also appear to have been able to convert their high levels of education into high-status occupations and jobs. While during the first half of the century, 'Asians were concentrated at the bottom of the economic ladder, restricted to retailing, food service, menial service, and agricultural occupations', in modern-day America they are well represented in the 'well-paid, educated, white-collar sector of the workforce' (Espiritu, 1996: 65). For instance, Sakamoto and Xie (2006) show that 33 per cent of male Asian Americans are employed as 'professionals' ('highly skilled occupations that typically require specialized training or licensed accreditation'), compared to 21 per cent of whites and only 13 per cent of African Americans.

Income differentials between Asian Americans and whites have almost completely disappeared: in 2000, the average earnings of white individuals were approximately $46,000, while native-born Asian Americans earned on average $43,000. The average earnings of African Americans were substantially lower at only $30,000. These aggregate figures for 'Asian Americans', however, disguise substantial differences in earnings between the different Asian American immigrant communities (see Table 4.7). For instance, while Korean ($40,000) and Vietnamese ($24,000) Americans earned on average considerably less than white Americans ($46,000), the Chinese ($56,000) and Japanese ($53,000) Americans earned substantially more than the whites.

The example of Asian immigrants to the US shows that HIs do *not* necessarily persist. The factors that seem to explain Asian immigrant groups' ability to 'catch up', as, indeed, European immigrants had earlier (Alba *et al.*, 2001), are (i) their initially high levels of education; (ii) their group values, perhaps associated with these education levels, which led to high aspirations and strong group pressure for achievement in education and work – social capital and other group pressures were thus asymmetrically *advantageous*, rather than disadvantageous for these groups – and (iii) the fact that the selective immigration policies ensured that relatively highly paid jobs were available for most migrants.

Table 4.7 Average wages and earnings of male workers, 2000

Race/ethnicity	Wages ($/hour)	Earnings ($)
Whites	23	46,000
Blacks	18	30,000
Native-born Asians		
All	22	43,000
Chinese	28	56,000
Japanese	26	53,000
Filipino	19	33,000
Korean	21	40,000
Asian Indian	22	39,000
Vietnamese	15	24,000
Other Asian	17	30,000

Source: Sakamoto and Xie (2006: 61).

4.4 Conclusions and policy implications

This chapter has presented theoretical reasons and some empirical evidence to suggest that socioeconomic HIs can be very persistent over time, in some cases lasting not just decades but centuries, often initiated by a foundational shock. In developing countries, colonialism and associated movements of people – not only from the imperial power, but also the movement of indentured labour from one part of the world to another – is the most important form of inequality-creating shock. Against the predictions of equilibrium neo-classical economics, where diminishing returns should equalize incomes over time, these initial inequalities have frequently persisted, sometimes narrowing but often remaining very large. This inequality is undesirable – because it traps people of certain ethnicities or races in relative poverty and powerlessness – and because it threatens political stability, since cultural difference provides a powerful potential mechanism of political mobilization. For both these reasons, HIs have a more adverse impact than VI, of which they are one cause. Moreover, in some cases it is extremely difficult to reduce poverty without reducing HIs, since general anti-poverty measures will fail to take into account the special circumstances of deprived groups.

Our analysis suggests that group inequalities in various types of capital and in the returns to this capital initiate HI, but this is often perpetuated by inequality of accumulation and by differential returns across groups, because the returns to any one type of capital are kept low by deficiencies in quantity and quality of other types of capital, as well as by past and current discrimination. The political system plays a central part because government policies can reinforce or offset other sources of inequality.

However, sometimes groups do succeed in catching up – in the cases of Malaysia and Northern Ireland strongly supported by policy, and in the case of some Asian immigrant groups to the US through their own efforts assisted by selective immigration policies. These 'success' stories provide insights on how HIs can be reduced over time.

Adopting the framework and using the examples discussed above, factors that help prevent persistent HIs are the following:

- Processes that reduce the tightness of group boundaries, so that the salience of group membership falls and people can switch to more privileged groups, moving towards an equilibrium in which either group boundaries become invisible, or of no significance, or group inequalities are gradually eliminated.
- Processes that reduce inequalities in capital accumulation. Here policies towards reducing inequalities need to ensure that discrimination in loans, education admissions and so on is prohibited. But more is needed if past discrimination is to be offset. For example, unequal accumulation in the past will mean that any loan allocations requiring collateral discriminate against poor applicants. Similarly, educational admission policies based on competitive examination, or 'merit', will discriminate against children from uneducated backgrounds, those that do not speak the dominant language and so on. Hence it is usually necessary to go beyond out-ruling existing discriminatory practices to positive current discrimination (or affirmative action) in order to offset the disadvantages incurred by past discrimination.
- Processes to improve the returns to different types of capital. One requirement is to give simultaneous support to different types of capital accumulation in the deprived group, since investment in one type of capital alone may have little impact: for example, policies to extend education in northern Ghana have little impact on the incomes of those who attend schools because they lack financial and social capital. A second requirement is to outlaw discrimination in employment, and, as in the allocation of capital, to practise affirmative action as an offset to past discrimination, in employment. Thus fair employment legislation – which can make a substantial difference – may not be enough, and positive discrimination may be needed.
- One important subset of policies to correct HIs over time are those directed at offsetting asymmetries in the quality of social capital. To do this, it is necessary to promote 'bridging' social capital for poorer groups so that more of their contacts are with the richer groups. However, this is not a matter of promoting any old contact; contacts which involve hierarchy (as in servant/master relationships) are not likely to generate effective social capital – people need to meet on roughly equal terms. There are a variety of ways that such bridging might be achieved: these include promoting

mixed schools (for example, boarding schools containing members of all groups where groups are scattered regionally) and comprehensive schools plus bussing in areas where different groups live fairly close together; housing policies to promote mixed neighbourhoods; and encouragement of mixed civil society organizations.

The examples of Northern Ireland and Malaysia, given above, show that policies can be effective in reducing long-term HIs substantially in a fairly short period. In both cases, the policies placed prime emphasis on human capital (improving the quantity and returns), but supported them by measures to improve the equity of economic opportunities. In contrast, some efforts were made to correct HIs in the cases of northern Ghanaians and blacks in the US, but they had a rather marginal impact, probably because they were not comprehensive enough – in each case focussing mainly on education, in a way that was insufficient to offset the legacy of previous discrimination and the handicaps imposed by deficiencies in other types of capital.

The role of politics is critical in explaining failures to combat socioeconomic HIs. The concerted efforts needed mean that the political system has to back the policy fully. This is likely to be the case where political HIs favour the deprived group, which happens in a democracy where this group forms the majority of the population, as in Malaysia. But where the political system is dominated by the more privileged group, as in Ghana and the US, then strong and comprehensive redistributory policies are less likely. Northern Ireland in the 1980s and 1990s was a special case, where the UK and EU determined policy, not the majority (privileged) Protestant population. But even where the deprived group forms the majority, it is difficult to combat high HIs in the context of strong opposition from the privileged groups. As some members of the deprived group gain elite positions (generally the potential leaders of the group), they too may be content to live with the HIs. The prevailing market philosophy also presents an obstacle since, while it favours less current discrimination, it disfavours affirmative action to offset the effects of past discrimination. Hence there are cases, like Nigeria and South Africa, where politics is dominated by the poorer group(s), but there is limited and ineffective action to correct the socioeconomic HIs.

Notes

1. Empirical work on intercountry inequality shows much more convergence of human indicators than economic, probably for this reason.
2. 'The racialisation of state initiatives like the New Economic Policy (NEP) have institutionalized race and made it part of an effective political system' (Mandal, 2004: 58).
3. Informal constraints include language and financial requirements for migration.

4. This section is taken from Figueroa (2006), which provides a much richer and fuller analysis.
5. The first measure is a simple unweighted ratio of Chinese to Malay average household income and the second measure is a population-weighted standard deviation of group incomes from the national mean. Both measures are indexed to 1970.
6. This paragraph is based on Pyong (2006).

Part II

Measurement and Statistical Analysis

5
Approaches to the Measurement of Horizontal Inequalities

Luca Mancini, Frances Stewart, and Graham K. Brown

5.1 Introduction

Most measures of inequality concern vertical inequality (VI), or inequality among individuals, and are generally confined to a few economic variables such as income, consumption, and sometimes assets. In this arena, Lorenz curves and the Gini coefficient have been extensively and powerfully used as measures of inequality. Much less attention has been paid to measuring inequalities between groups (or horizontal inequalities (HIs)). Although some measures of VI are decomposable into groups, these can be hard to interpret and, moreover, measure the *contribution* of group inequalities to *overall* VI rather than group inequality as such. This chapter considers alternative ways of measuring HIs and provides some empirical applications of different measures, showing how far the different measures correlate with one another.

The next section discusses some general issues concerning concepts and measurement. Section 5.3 is devoted to aggregate measures of HIs which are not sensitive to distribution *within* each group; this is followed by applications of alternative measures in a few empirical cases in Section 5.4; Section 5.5 considers measures which do allow one to look at HIs for different segments of the distribution, together with an empirical illustration; Section 5.6 presents conclusions.

5.2 Problems of measuring horizontal inequalities

The first step in understanding the status and dynamics of HIs in a country is to classify the relevant identity groups: the group boundaries that people mind about, and the boundaries on the basis of which discrimination or favouritism occurs. This raises many problems since as explored in Chapter 1, given multiple identities and their social construction, there are very few groups for which boundaries are clear cut.

An initial in-depth investigation of the history and political economy of the country in question will suggest important group distinctions. Where surveys of people's own perceptions of identity distinctions are available, or such a survey can be carried out, this can provide valuable further insights. (See, for instance, Chapter 10.) Such surveys ask people which groups they feel are privileged or deprived, and which are favoured or disfavoured by the government. They can also ask about the importance of different aspects of identity to the people themselves. Often it can be useful to consider alternative group classifications (for example, ethnic, regional, and religious), and see where the main inequalities emerge. The categorization should, in so far as is possible, be sensitive to people's self-positioning (and how others in society position them). It is also desirable to explore whether adopting different categorization criteria changes the results. In practice, data deficiencies mean that only rather crude classifications are typically available. But once the importance of the issue is acknowledged, multiple classifications may emerge, as they have, for instance, in terms of ethnic classification in the UK census.

5.2.1   Differences in measuring inequalities between individuals and between groups

We now come to the issue of constructing an indicator of HI. This is similar to the issue of identifying a single measure of VI, but there are some important differences, however. One is that by definition there are fewer groups in a society than individuals – in fact for many countries there could be rather few salient ethnic or religious groups. With so few observations, it is possible to look at the dyadic differences separately and aggregation into a single measure is not only less needed but may actually conceal important information. In contrast, when we are dealing with a large population of individuals in a society, it is essential to find aggregate measures of inequality to be able to comprehend the mass of information available.

Secondly, the number of individuals in each group is likely to differ. Hence the option of group weighting arises. With an unweighted measure, the relative position of small groups would get the same weight as those of large groups. Yet from a well-being and a political perspective, this represents a different situation in that very different numbers of individuals are affected. Therefore, a population-weighted index is generally desirable.

A third difference between group and individual inequality is that each group is made up of a number of individuals – so the intra-group distribution may be of interest as well as the intergroup. It is possible to include a measure of within-group inequality in the measure of each group's performance. However, this would in effect conflate two separate issues – inter-group and intra-group disparities. Hence, initially, in Sections 5.3 and 5.4, we discuss how to measure HIs without consideration of the distributional issues. In Section 5.5 we turn to issues of intra-group distribution.

Finally, because of the essentially multidimensional nature of HIs, the question arises of whether and how to amalgamate each dimension into a single index. This issue also arises for measures of VI, and a number of methods for developing multidimensional indices have been employed (Bourguignon and Chakravarty, 2003; Deutsch and Silber, 2005). However, in this chapter we put this difficult question aside, and consider how to develop an index for each dimension separately.

5.3 Measuring horizontal inequalities at an aggregate level

5.3.1 Some principles of measurement

Three well-established general principles of a good measure of inequality have been developed for VI, which may be helpful in thinking about a good measure of HI:

1. independence of the distribution from the mean;
2. the principle of transfers (Pigou-Dalton): transfers from a richer person to a poorer person reduce inequality; and
3. the transfer of an equal amount from rich to poor counts for more than one from rich to less rich.

However, it is arguable that the same principles need not apply in relation to HI (Subramanian, 2006). In particular, there does not seem to be good reason to accept the third principle. The reason we wish to find a group inequality measure is primarily to explore how far group inequality affects other variables such as growth, happiness, or conflict. Given this objective, in addition to the first two principles, which it seems reasonable to adopt for group measures too, two further requirements are

4. in so far as possible, to find a measure which is descriptive, not evaluative. This is not perfectly achievable since any measure involves some implicit valuation, but we aim to minimize this and hence will discard measures which have explicit inequality aversion built in; and
5. to measure group inequality as such, not the contribution of group inequality to either social welfare as a whole (like the gender-weighted Human Development Index (HDI)) or to income distribution as a whole.

Ratios of average performance of pertinent groups are the most straightforward and intuitively appealing measure of group inequality (for example, the ratio of black to white per capita incomes in South Africa). However, such ratios apply only to two groups, and other measures are needed where there are a larger number. Østby (2003, Chapter 7) deals with this problem by choosing the two largest groups and calculating the ratios for these groups.

Another possibility would be to choose the two groups that seem to be politically competitive (not necessarily the two largest in population size) in the particular context. However, this would impart a large element of political judgement to the choice. In general, both to assess how fair a society is and to test how far group inequality affects various objectives, there is a need for a synthetic measure which incorporates *all* group inequalities into a single measure of HI. However, we should bear in mind the possibility that the synthetic aggregate measure may be influenced by 'irrelevant' alternatives. Hence for some purposes, especially when the number of relevant groups is small, it may be helpful to look at simple ratios of each group to the mean, and/or ratios of major groups to each other, as well as the synthetic measures to be discussed below.

5.3.2   Possible aggregate measures of horizontal inequalities

Common measures of inequality devised to measure VI, that in principle could be used for HI, are the following:

a. The coefficient of variation, that is, the variance divided by the mean (COV: Appendix 5A, Equation A1). This is a common measure of regional disparities (for example, Quah, 1996; Williamson, 1965). While it does achieve independence from the mean, it attaches equal weight to redistributions at different income levels. However, we do not think this is important for a measure of HI, given our objective of arriving at a descriptive measure. The COV involves squaring the deviations from the mean, thus giving more weight to the extremes, in a somewhat arbitrary fashion (Sen, 1997: 28). This measures differences from the mean, not each groups' difference with every other group. When adapted to measure group inequality (GCOV), this measure could be unweighted (Appendix 5A, Equation A6a), or weighted by the size of the population in each group (Appendix 5A, EquationA6b). Without population weighting, change in the position of a very small group (say accounting for 0.1 per cent of the population) would have the same effect as one involving a large group (accounting for, say, 60 per cent of the population). These issues will be explored further in Section 5.3;

b. The Gini coefficient of group incomes (GINI: Appendix 5A, Equation A2). This has the advantage that it compares every group with every other group. The aim of the Gini is to measure variance in individual performance, although observations are often grouped according to achievement on the variable of interest. For our purpose, we wish to group people by 'noneconomic' characteristics (religion, ethnicity, race, and so on) and not by the variable for which the inequality is being calculated. We shall define such a Gini as a group Gini (GGINI: Appendix 5A, Equation A7);

c. The Theil index (THEIL: Appendix 5A, Equation A3). This is especially sensitive to the lower end of the distribution. The Theil compares each group with the mean (like the GCOV) in contrast to the group Gini. Unlike the Gini coefficient, the Theil is always precisely decomposable and it has often been used to divide overall VI into inequality due to within-group (WG) and that due to between-group (BG) (Anand, 1983; Heshmati, 2004). However, we are not interested in using the decomposed measure since we are seeking an independent measure of HI. Some researchers have questioned the intuitive appeal of the Theil inequality index (Sen, 1992). However, as far as group inequality is concerned, no intuitive understanding has built up of the group Gini either, because of the lack of experience in interpreting it. The group Theil (GTHEIL: Appendix 5A, Equation A8) represents a reasonable alternative to the two previous measures for measuring group inequality;

d. Utility-based indices, including Dalton's (DALTON: Appendix 5A, Equation A4) and Atkinson's index (A(ε): Appendix 5A, Equation A5) (Atkinson, 1970; Dalton, 1920). Dalton's measure compares actual aggregate utility with the total level of utility if income were equally divided, assuming diminishing marginal utility. Atkinson criticized it for changing according to linear transformations of the utility function and developed his own equally distributed equivalent measure. Both are explicitly normative measures; Atkinson's measure varies according to the value assumed for inequality aversion, to be derived from a Social Welfare Function (SWF). The well-known problems in arriving at an SWF for individuals are multiplied where groups are concerned, which makes this difficult if not impossible, though some value for inequality aversion could be introduced without basing it on an SWF. However, the normative basis of these measures makes them inappropriate for a group inequality measure intended to be primarily descriptive.

Other measures have been specifically designed to explore aspects of group inequality:

e. The Esteban/Ray (ER) polarization index (ER(1.5): Appendix 5A, Equation A9) (Duclos *et al.*, 2004; Esteban and Ray, 1994). The ER index is similar to a group Gini,[1] weighted by population, but includes an index $(1 + \alpha,$ where $1 \leq \alpha < 1.6$) which is higher the greater the weight attached to the share of group population. A common value for α is 1.5 (Kanbur and Zhang, 1999). This index is not decomposable. The point of α is to increase the weight given to large groups, so that the index rises as the population is distributed among fewer and more equally sized groups. Consequently, two populations might have the same value of the index, despite one having less variance in resource access or incomes between the groups than the other, so long as the one with less variance had a smaller number of larger groups than the other. Esteban and Ray do not intend the index to be a measure of group inequality but of societal polarization. The disadvantage of the measure from our perspective is first, that it includes two elements that we wish to explore separately – the demographic polarization of the groups and the extent of inequality among them; and second, that there is an arbitrariness about the choice of α. The ER measure also violates the Pigou–Dalton condition because increased demographic polarization can offset a given income transfer from a richer to a poorer group;

f. The Zhang/Kanbur (ZK: Appendix 5A, Equation A10) index is the ratio of BG/WG, using Theil to measure BG and WG (Zhang and Kanbur, 2003). This is higher the more HIs contribute to overall inequality. The problem with this, from our perspective, is that the size of the measure will vary according to within-group variance. Thus the same between-group variance will lead to different measures according to WG. We wish to separate our measure of HIs from what is happening within the group;

g. The odds ratio suggested by Chakrabarty (2001). This measure calculates the odds of individuals in a particular group falling into a particular category (for example, rich or poor), and then expresses the group differences as the ratio of these odds. This basically resembles the method of using simple ratios of performance, except that the performance of each group is not the average but the odds of being poor, calculated as a proportion of the poor to the total population in each group. Hence it requires somewhat more data than the ratios of average proportion. Since it is designed to measure differences between two groups, some other method would need to be introduced to generalize to many groups (for example, by adopting a Gini of the odds).

Work in this area has tended to be less interested in measuring group inequality as such, and more interested in devising a measure of general welfare that allows for group inequality – for example, Anand and Sen (1995) in their gender-weighted HDI (the Gender Development Index or GDI). This is a social welfare evaluation, which weights trade-offs between higher average achievement and more inequality between genders. Similarly, Majumdar and Subramanian (2001) adjust a measure of deprivation, or capability failure, by a group deprivation index. The capability index is a weighted index of several deprivations. The index is adjusted by a formula for the deprivation of the particular group. Again the aim is to adjust aggregate welfare by some valuation of group disparities rather than to describe group inequality.

5.3.3 Conclusions on approaches to measuring group inequality

The first consideration is that we aim, as far as possible, to get a descriptive measure of HIs – hence we reject those measures which involve a strong explicitly evaluative element, that is, the Dalton/Atkinson measures. This is also a problem with the ER polarization index. Nonetheless, the other measures also, unavoidably, contain some element of valuation – for example, the GCOV by squaring the observations gives more weight to observations further from the mean and the Gini gives relatively more weight to the middle of the distribution.

Secondly, we are keen to have a measure of HI which is distinct from other influences such as VI and population distribution. This is a problem with both the ER index and the ZK index. The ER index combines two elements: inequality and population polarization. Hence the same distance between groups would get greater weight the more the population is demographically polarized. The ZK index incorporates both BG and WG inequality into the index. Thus the same HIs would get different values according to the extent of WG. From our perspective this is not desirable, as in empirical work we wish to describe the extent of between-group inequality, and to test what impact this has on various outcomes. While the impact of HIs may vary according to the extent of heterogeneity within the group or the extent of demographic polarization, we wish to test both these elements separately, which is not possible if they are incorporated in a single index. Third, we need a measure which captures inequality among more than two groups. Hence the odds ratio by itself is insufficient, though it could provide the inputs into another measure, such as a group Gini, which aggregates across a number of groups.

This leaves us with three measures of those discussed above, each of which can be weighted according to the size of the population in each group:

1. The coefficient of variation among groups (GCOV);
2. The group Gini (GGINI) coefficient; and
3. The group Theil (GTHEIL).

5.4   Applications of the aggregate measures: South Africa, the United States, and Indonesia

This section explores whether selected measures of VI and HI in practice move together on the basis of data from South Africa, the US and Indonesia. This gives insight, first, into how far it matters which measure we use; and, second, which measure seems to fit our intuitive understanding of the situation.

Longitudinal income data from South Africa (Figure 5.1) shows that measures used for HI over time can produce divergent trends: in particular an unweighted GCOV among racial groups shows a rise in HI since 1975, while the population-weighted GCOV and the GGINI each show a trend fall. The surprising rising trend in the unweighted GCOV can be attributed to a particular feature of the overall inequality trends in these data.

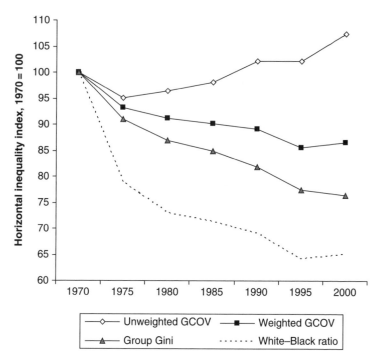

Figure 5.1 South Africa – Aggregate measures of horizontal inequality in *per capita* income by ethnic group, 1970–2000
Source: Calculated from data in van der Berg and Louw (1994).
Note: van der Berg and Louw give two separate estimates for the year 2000 – one 'optimistic', the other 'pessimistic'. For our purposes here, the mid-way point between the two estimates was taken.

Over the period, the mean income of all four population groups increased at a faster rate than the mean of the population as a whole, due to the concomitant increase in population share of the poorest group, black South Africans, which effectively dragged down the rate of increase in the overall mean. While the various weighted measures compensate for this unusual trend precisely because they incorporate a degree of population weighting, the unweighted GCOV treats every group as static over time in terms of size. The increase in the unweighted GCOV is counterintuitive: the ratio of black/white income *per capita* fell significantly.

Similarly, we find conflicting trends for the US from 1967 to 2001 for black/white/other inequality (Figure 5.2). The population unweighted GCOV shows fluctuations but little change, while there appears to be a slightly rising trend for the population weighted GCOV and a bigger rise for the group Gini. As in the South African data all groups improved their position relative to the mean over the period, although only by a tiny amount for

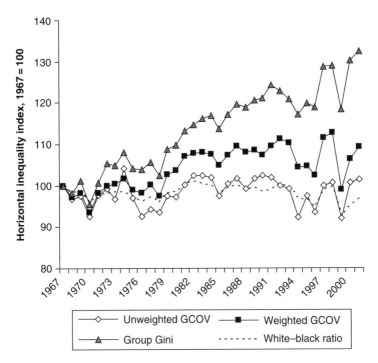

Figure 5.2 United States – Aggregate measures of horizontal inequality in *per capita* income by ethnic group, 1967–2001
Source: Calculated from US Census Bureau data.

the white population. The increase in inequality shown in the weighted GCOV and the group Gini is largely due to the changes in the 'Others' category, which increased both in relative income (from 2.5 per cent above the overall mean average income to 14.1 per cent above) and in population share (from 1.5 per cent to 4.8 per cent). Hence, the impact of their increasing distance from the overall mean was amplified in the weighted GCOV by their increasing population share. These contrasts indicate that the appropriate measure depends on what we are concerned with: the weighted GCOV and Group Gini measures indicate overall changes in HIs, but may actually conceal the changes in the black/white performance which could be the variable of most interest.

We explore these relationships further using cross-sectional data from Indonesian censal data in 1990 and 1995 at the district level.[2] Table 5.1 shows the correlation between measures of VI and HI based on years of education for 88 *religiously diverse* districts in Indonesia.[3] The numbers on the diagonal (in bold) show the correlation of each indicator with its own

Table 5.1 Correlation matrix between inequality measures based on years of education in Indonesia, 1990 and 1995

	Year	Vertical inequality			Population-weighted horizontal inequality					Demographic fragmentation
		GINI	THEIL	COV	GGINI	GTHEIL	ER(1.5)	GCOV	ZK	ERF
GINI		**0.87** ***								
THEIL	1995	0.99 ***	**0.83** ***							
	1990	0.98 ***								
COV	1995	0.99 ***	0.99 ***	**0.86** ***						
	1990	0.99 ***	0.99 ***							
GGINI	1995	0.40 ***	0.42 ***	0.40 ***	**0.81** ***					
	1990	0.41 ***	0.36 ***	0.39 ***						
GTHEIL	1995	0.52 ***	0.54 ***	0.52 ***	0.91 ***	**0.77** ***				
	1990	0.43 ***	0.39 ***	0.41 ***	0.91 ***					
ER(1.5)	1995	0.29 ***	0.30 ***	0.28 ***	0.91 ***	0.79 ***	**0.64** ***			
	1990	0.33 ***	0.29 ***	0.32 ***	0.88 ***	0.76 ***				
GCOV	1995	0.46 ***	0.47 ***	0.45 ***	0.93 ***	0.91 ***	0.92 ***	**0.74** ***		
	1990	0.47 ***	0.42 ***	0.44 ***	0.95 ***	0.91 ***	0.92 ***			
ZK	1995	0.16	0.17	0.15	0.87 ***	0.84 ***	0.87 ***	0.88 ***	**0.69** ***	
	1990	0.21 **	0.18 *	0.20 *	0.90 ***	0.92 ***	0.84 ***	0.90 ***		
ERF	1995	0.13	0.15	0.13	0.58 ***	0.39 ***	0.35 ***	0.35 ***	0.36 ***	**0.78** ***
	1990	0.15	0.13	0.14	0.58 ***	0.40 ***	0.29 ***	0.38 ***	0.37 ***	

Sources: Authors' calculation from random sample of the Indonesian Census 1990 and the complete sample of the Indonesian Inter-censal Survey 1995.
Notes: 88 religiously diverse districts are considered (ERF>=0.1).
***, **, * indicate significance at 1%, 5%, and 10% level, respectively.
The diagonal elements shown in bold for each index are the correlation coefficients between 1990 and 1995.

value in the two years. The following are the interesting results that emerge from the data:

- The indices of VI – Gini, Theil, and the coefficient of variation (COV) – are nearly perfectly correlated in both years, indicating that for this dataset it is not important which measure is selected;
- HI measures are also highly correlated with each other in both years, with coefficients ranging between 0.76 and 0.96 – again suggesting that the choice of group inequality indicator may not be important;
- The correlations between measures of VI and HI are much smaller than the correlations within either the VI or HI measures. In Table 5.1, there is generally a positive correlation between the VI and HI measures (apart from the ZK measure which has been constructed to eliminate the element of VI accounted for by HI). Table 5.1, however, excludes ethnically/religiously homogeneous districts. When these are included (not shown here) the correlation between each measure of HI and VI is negative, and generally statistically nonsignificant at standard levels. It is relevant to include homogeneous districts if one wants to explore how far a measure of VI can proxy for HI in society as a whole. However, given our main purpose is to contrast measures of HIs, it seems more relevant to explore multigroup districts.
- HI measures are positively correlated with ethnoreligious (demographic) fragmentation (ERF: Appendix 5A, Equation A12). The GGINI measure appears to be significantly more sensitive to fragmentation than other HI indicators; and
- HI measures tend to be less correlated over time than VI indicators, although all show a quite high correlation over time. The ER(1.5) measure shows the lowest correlation over time, confirming that it is not an appropriate measure of HI. The difference in correlations over time between VI and HI measures implies that HI and VI dynamics differed across Indonesian districts over the five-year period. From one perspective this is surprising – if group inequality stemmed from discrimination or asset inequality one would not expect this to change quickly while individuals might move more readily up or down the income scale. However, the very large numbers involved in VI mean that upward and downward changes are more likely to offset each other than in the case of HI which is based on small numbers of groups. The data on South African white/black income ratios shown above (Figure 5.1) similarly shows much more change than VI in South Africa over the same period.

Carrying out a similar exercise with income data for 154 religiously diverse districts (Table 5.2) in 1995 broadly confirms the results of Table 5.1. Again, there are quite high correlations among alternative measures of HI, but much lower correlations between HI and VI.

Table 5.2 Correlation matrix between inequality measures in *per capita* income in Indonesia, 1995

	Vertical inequality			Population-weighted horizontal inequality					Demographic fragmentation
	GINI	THEIL	COV	GGINI	GTHEIL	ER1.5	GCOV	ZK	ERF
GINI	1.00								
THEIL	0.94 ***	1.00							
COV	0.81 ***	0.94 ***	1.00						
GGINI	0.25 ***	0.34 ***	0.40 ***	1.00					
GTHEIL	0.36 ***	0.49 ***	0.56 ***	0.80 ***	1.00				
GCOV	0.37 ***	0.46 ***	0.52 ***	0.86 ***	0.84 ***	1.00			
ER1.5	0.32 ***	0.41 ***	0.47 ***	0.95 ***	0.85 ***	0.92 ***	1.00		
ZK	0.01	0.10	0.17 *	0.80 ***	0.65 ***	0.84 ***	0.81 ***	1.00	
ERF	-0.19 **	-0.19 **	-0.17 **	0.17 **	-0.09	-0.09	-0.17 ***	-0.05	1.00

Source: Authors' calculations from the 1995 Indonesian Inter-censal Survey data
Notes: 154 religiously diverse districts are considered (ERF>=0.1).
***, **, * indicate significance at 1%, 5%, and 10% level, respectively.

5.5   Measuring horizontal inequalities in different segments of the income distribution

So far, we have taken group performance as equivalent to the average *per capita* performance of the group. But within-group distributions can vary from one another. Both the political and the welfare significance of HIs may alter according to the distribution within each group. There are good reasons to think that the impact of HIs on violent mobilization will differ according to whether the main differences are at the upper or the lower end of the distribution or both. For example, if the difference is more or less constant throughout the income distribution, then both the 'elites' and 'masses' of the deprived group will suffer deprivation and may be inclined to mobilize. If the main differences were confined to the lower end of the distribution, however, potential leaders may not themselves have an economic motive for protest. Equally, if the lower end were broadly equal and the differences were just at the upper end, the deprived at the upper end would have a reason for protest but might not get ready support from the people. Hence it is desirable to find a way of investigating HIs at different segments of the income distribution.

Therefore using simple group (arithmetic) means may be unsatisfactory if this conceals a lot of variation in how groups compare along the respective distributions of incomes. The objective of this section is to explore HI measures that allow comparisons of the whole distribution of each group with that of other group(s). We consider four different approaches:

1. The first approach (q-means henceforth) consists of dividing the income distribution of each group into n quantiles and comparing group means for each quantile. This approach allows us to see how the richest quantile of one group compares with that of other, and similarly for the other quantiles.
2. The second approach (α-means) derived from the work of Foster[4] (α-means: Appendix 5A, Equation A11) is to calculate group means for each group at different points of the income distribution by using parametric means. The value of the parameter determines how much weight is given to different sections of the distribution. Hence the estimate of HI would vary according to the chosen value of the parameter, α.

It is easy to see that for some values of α the expression reduces to more familiar statistics such as, for instance, the arithmetic mean ($\alpha = 1$), the geometric mean ($\alpha = 0$) and the harmonic mean ($\alpha = -1$). For values of $\alpha < 1$, α-means are more sensitive to low income values and increasingly so as $\alpha \to -\infty$. Therefore, the geometric mean attaches more weight than the arithmetic mean but less weight than the harmonic mean to low incomes. The reverse is true for values of $\alpha > 1$. As $\alpha \to \infty$ α-means are increasingly more sensitive to high incomes. By the same logic where $\alpha = 1$ (the arithmetic mean) the mean value is most sensitive to median incomes. Comparing α-means for different values of α thus indicates how HIs differ in different parts of the income distributions of the two groups and thus, like the first method, allows a comparison of group means in different quantiles of each group's income distribution.

The main difference between the first and second approaches is that whereas q-means are calculated on sections of the group's income distribution, α-means are calculated over the entire range of the group's distribution but with different portions weighted differently according to the value of α. It is in principle possible to set α such that the difference between α-means and q-means becomes negligible.

3. A third approach divides the *overall* income distribution into n quantiles and, for each group, compares the proportion of people in each quantile.[5] We term this the *group population proportions* method. This approach is distinct from the other two as it does not tell us the income ratio (or HI) of the groups directly at all, but rather the distribution of the two populations in different quantiles of the overall income distribution and thus gives indirect information on HIs.

4. A fourth approach again divides the overall income distribution into n quantiles and then, for each quantile, estimates the proportion of the population in that quantile accounted for by each group. We call this the *group representation method*. This too says nothing directly about HIs. A strength of this approach is that it shows how well represented different groups are in different segments of the overall distribution. A weakness is that it can change over time due to changing numbers of the two populations without any distributional changes. Given this shortcoming we will not discuss this approach further.

To illustrate possible similarities and complementarities between these approaches, we look at income inequality between the black African and white populations in South Africa using data from the 1996 and 2001 Censuses.[6] The sample is restricted to household heads in magisterial districts which are sufficiently diverse in their racial composition in both years. This will most probably underestimate black–white HIs in South Africa as it excludes many poor black areas. However, since the purpose of this exercise is purely to compare different indicators, this is not of concern here.

Figures 5.3a and b show mean incomes for black Africans and whites at different points of their respective income distributions. We used two alternative sets of cut-off points: income quintiles and α parameters. We may broadly assume that $\alpha = -1$ (harmonic mean incomes) corresponds to the bottom or first quintile, $\alpha = 1$ (arithmetic mean incomes) to the middle or third quintile and $\alpha = 3$ to the top or fifth quintile.[7] With this assumption,

Figures 5.3a and 5.3b show that q-means and α-means are highly correlated, particularly in 1996. With the exception of the top quintile q-means are lower than the corresponding α-means in both years. The results also clearly show that in both years black Africans' incomes were much lower than whites' at any point of the income distribution.

Figures 5.4a and b show income inequality between racial groups (HI) measured as group disparity ratios of mean incomes. In 1996, whites' mean income levels are between three and five times higher than blacks' mean incomes and the gap tends to be lower at the top end of the income distribution. The values of the disparity ratio calculated using q-means and α-means for different values of α are very similar in 1996. However, with the noticeable exception of the bottom quintile ($\alpha = -1$), in 2001 disparity ratios

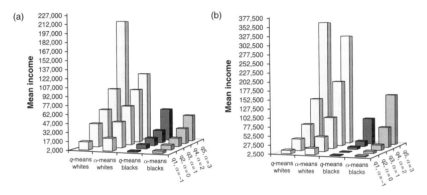

Figure 5.3 Mean incomes of black Africans and whites, by quintile and alpha, (a) 1996 and (b) 2001

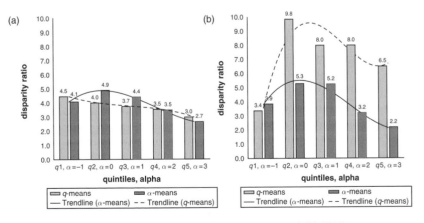

Figure 5.4 White/black income disparity ratios, (a) 1996 and (b) 2001

between q-means are significantly higher than the corresponding α-means. In 2001, there is also more variation across income quintiles/α-means compared to 1996. α-means ratios tend to be higher in the middle range of the income distribution (hump-shaped trends) in both years, while ratios between q-means are less consistent between census years. Both measures suggest that HIs broadly fall as one moves up the income distribution in 1996, while in 2001, they are lower for the bottom of the distribution, rise in the middle and then fall at the top.

The income distributions of both groups became more unequal in 2001. This can be seen comparing Figures 5.3a and 5.3b. Whereas in 1996 mean incomes increase almost linearly in α-values, in 2001 incomes grew nearly exponentially, especially for the black population. This can be shown more intuitively by plotting the percentage growth in mean incomes between the two census years (Figure 5.5). After adjusting for inflation, growth rates were actually negative for low incomes and high and positive for high incomes, particularly for blacks. This implies that intra-group VI significantly increased in both subpopulations.

Figures 5.6a and 5.6b show the third approach, the *group population proportions* method. According to this approach, there is a consistent reduction in HIs, with the proportion of the population accounted for by whites rising at the lower end of the distribution and falling at the upper end. Thus this approach gives a different perspective than the previous two. It does not tell

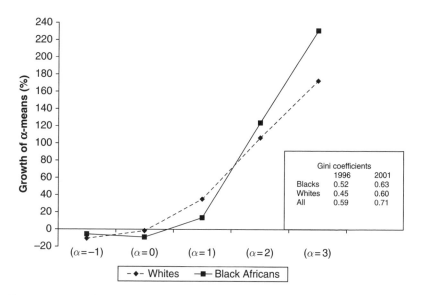

Figure 5.5   Growth in real incomes of whites and black Africans, 1996 and 2001

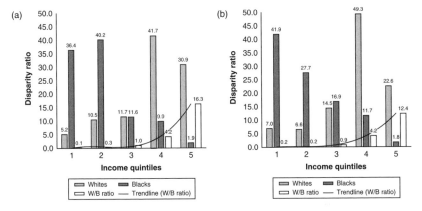

Figure 5.6 Group population proportion, by quintile of overall income distribution, (a) 1996 and (b) 2001

us, however, what has happened to the absolute ratios of incomes and thus needs to be supplemented by one or other of the first two approaches.

Our conclusion is that the α-means method is the most useful approach to summarizing HIs, while allowing for distributional considerations, since it incorporates information on the whole population while allowing one to show how giving different weights to different parts of the distribution alters HIs. The *group population proportions* approach can give interesting supplementary information. Moreover, comparing group α-means at different points of the distribution as well as their trends over time provides interesting insights into the interplay between within-group VI and HI.

5.6   Some conclusions

This chapter explored alternative approaches to the measurement of group inequality. We acknowledge the severe problem of defining group boundaries, since identities are fluid, multiple and may even be endogenous. Nonetheless, felt differences seem important enough and clear enough in many societies to make it possible to measure group performance so long as one is sensitive to the possibility and implications of alterations in group boundaries.

We reviewed alternative aggregate measures of group inequality and made comparisons using Indonesian data for two separate dates, as well as longitudinal data for South Africa and the US. The Indonesian data show that each of the measures of VI is highly correlated with every other one; the measures of group inequality are also correlated with each other but less strongly. When homogenous districts are excluded, there is a positive correlation between HI and VI for an education variable (not exceeding 0.54), but when homogeneous districts are included this correlation becomes very low. Both VI and HI show persistence over time. But for education, within districts, HI changes more over time than VI, which could be important politically as durable HI is likely to be particularly provocative. We have not been able to investigate this issue using income.

Data on South Africa and the US show that different HI measures can generate different trends. One important difference is that the population unweighted GCOV moves in a different direction from the population weighted measure and the group Gini. In the case of South Africa, the unweighted GCOV shows increasing HI, while the other measures show some decline. In the case of the US it is the other way round, with the unweighted GCOV showing little change and the other measures showing some increase. The population-weighted GCOV and the group Gini measures generally move in the same direction, with the GCOV showing the least change.

If one is particularly concerned with the position of one group, or of that group relative to one other group, the clearest way to present the data is to take the ratio of the performance of the group to the mean, or the ratio of the performance of the two groups, rather than some group measure of inequality which also introduces other groups and may thus conceal the variable of interest as indicated by both US and South African data.

We also explored alternative methods of assessing HIs at different segments of the income distribution. A number of approaches are possible, and each conveys slightly different information. We found that the α-means measure provided the most instructive summary of the way HIs alter as one alters the weights given to different parts of the distribution. However, the other measures discussed provide useful supplementary perspectives.

The value of a measure of inequality depends on the purpose for which it is needed. One purpose is to make a general statement about whether a society is getting fairer or less fair over time from a group perspective. Another objective is to identify a variable which will enable us to test whether particular inequalities are correlated with other events such as conflict, criminality, and unhappiness. For both purposes, group weighting by population would seem desirable, adopting an α-means approach. However, it could be argued that the first objective might require measures which are widely understood – which could be a problem for these measures. From the perspective of assessing how fair a society is, the measure of inequality could include some element of evaluation (as in ER where $\alpha > 0$). However, unless this valuation is widely understood and shared, it may be better to present the data without such a valuation element. From the perspective of intuitive understanding of how HIs vary across the distribution, the q-means approach could be useful, despite its disadvantages.

For the second objective – to identify a variable we can use to explore consequences of HIs – it is preferable to exclude elements of evaluation, as far as possible, and to have a separate measure of HI and VI. The ZK measure does not present separate measures of between-group and within-group inequality, and is consequently ruled out from this perspective. Hence, the population-weighted GCOV or the group Gini appear to be the preferred measures for this objective. These measures can be used in combination with the α-means measure.

Appendix 5A

Vertical inequality

$$\text{COV} = \frac{1}{\bar{y}} \left(\frac{1}{n-1} \sum_{i}^{n} (y_i - \bar{y})^2 \right)^{\frac{1}{2}} \tag{A1}$$

$$\text{GINI} = \frac{1}{2n^2\bar{y}} \sum_{i}^{n} \sum_{j}^{n} |y_i - y_j| \tag{A2}$$

$$\text{THEIL} = \frac{1}{n} \sum_{i}^{n} \frac{y_i}{\bar{y}} \log \left(\frac{y_i}{\bar{y}} \right) \tag{A3}$$

$$\text{DALTON} = \frac{\log \left(\frac{1}{n} \sum_{i=1}^{n} y_i \right)}{\frac{1}{n} \sum_{i=1}^{n} \log y_i} \tag{A4}$$

$$\text{A}(\varepsilon) = 1 - \left[\frac{1}{n} \sum_{i=1}^{n} \left(\frac{y_i}{y} \right)^{1-\varepsilon} \right]^{\frac{1}{1-\varepsilon}} \qquad \varepsilon \geq 0 \tag{A5}$$

where $\bar{y}$ is the sample mean, y_i is the number of years of education of individual i and n is the sample size.

Horizontal inequality

$$\text{Unweighted GCOV} = \frac{1}{\bar{y}} \left(\frac{1}{R-1} \sum_{r}^{R} (\bar{y}_r - \bar{y})^2 \right)^{\frac{1}{2}} \tag{A6a}$$

$$\text{Weighted GCOV} = \frac{1}{\bar{y}} \left(\sum_{r}^{R} p_r (\bar{y}_r - \bar{y})^2 \right)^{\frac{1}{2}} \tag{A6b}$$

$$\text{GGINI} = \frac{1}{2\bar{y}} \sum_r^R \sum_s^S p_r p_s \, |\bar{y}_r - \bar{y}_s| \tag{A7}$$

$$\text{GTHEIL} = \sum_r^R p_r \frac{\bar{y}_r}{\bar{y}} \log\left(\frac{\bar{y}_r}{\bar{y}}\right) \tag{A8}$$

$$\text{ER}(k, \alpha) = k \sum_r^R \sum_s^S p_r^{1+\alpha} p_s \, |\bar{y}_r - \bar{y}_s|, k = \frac{1}{\bar{y}}, \alpha = 1.5 \tag{A9}$$

$$\text{ZK} = \text{BG/WG}, \text{WG} = \sum_r^R \frac{Y_r}{Y} \left[\frac{1}{n_r} \sum_i^{n_r} \frac{y_{ir}}{\bar{y}_r} \log\left(\frac{y_{ir}}{\bar{y}_r}\right)\right], BG = THEIL - WG \tag{A10}$$

$$\alpha\text{-means} = \begin{cases} \bar{y}_{r\alpha} = \left(\sum_i^n y_{ir}^\alpha / n\right)^{\frac{1}{\alpha}} & \alpha \neq 0, \alpha \in \Re \\[2ex] \bar{y}_{r\alpha} = \exp\left(\dfrac{\sum_i^n \ln(y_{ir})}{n}\right) & \alpha = 0 \end{cases} \tag{A11}$$

where $\bar{y}_r = \frac{1}{n_r} \sum_i^{n_r} y_{ir}$ is group r mean value, p_r is group r population share, R is group r population size, y_{ir} is the value of y for the ith member of group r, Y_r is group's r total value of y, Y is the grand total value of y in the sample/population, and α is a scalar.

Demographic fragmentation

$$\text{ERF} = 1 - \sum_j^J p_r^2 \tag{A12}$$

Notes

1. Where $\alpha = 0$, this is equivalent to the group Gini.
2. The 1995 dataset contains 304 rather than 282 districts because the province of East Timor was excluded from the 1990 dataset due to undersampling.
3. Groups are defined by religion, which in both samples is categorized as Islam, Catholic, Protestant/Other Christian, Hindu, Buddhist and Other.
4. See Foster and Szekely (2006); Foster, Lopez-Calva, and Szekely (2003) for details. Foster *et al.* define these parametric means as 'general means'.
5. This approach was suggested by James Boyce, personal communication.

6. South African Census sample data taken from the Minnesota Population Center, *Integrated Public Use Microdata Series – International Version 3.0*. Minneapolis: University of Minnesota, 2007; original data collection by Statistics South Africa.

7. The values of α that minimize the differences between α-means and q-means depend on the income distribution under study. In the case of South Africa, for instance, differences over the chosen range of α values (–1 to 3) are small except for the top quintile (q5) of the whites' distribution where the q-mean is significantly higher than the α-mean at $\alpha = 3$ in both years. We find that $\alpha = 5$ must be chosen to minimize the discrepancy between α-means and q-means in the top quintile. We also find that using $\alpha = 5$ does not affect the main conclusions of this section.

6
Horizontal Inequality and Communal Violence: Evidence from Indonesian Districts

Luca Mancini

6.1 Introduction

The evidence on the inequality–political conflict nexus remains controversial. Recent cross-country econometric research shows mixed results, endorsing Lichbach's (1989) extensive review. Whereas some studies find that sociopolitical instability increases with income inequality (Alesina and Perotti, 1996; Auvinen and Nafziger, 1999), other studies find no significant relationship with civil conflict onset (Collier and Hoeffler, 1998; Fearon and Laitin, 2003).

One reason for the inconsistency of the findings lies in different definitions of violent conflict. For instance, some only include episodes of violence where the state or government is one of the factions involved (*Armed Conflict Dataset*, see Strand *et al.*, 2003), while others also consider incidents between nongovernment factions (*Minorities at Risk*, see Gurr, 1993); some account for internal displacement as well as death toll in measuring the severity of violence; some exclude genocides (Auvinen and Nafziger, 1999).

A second reason is that inequality is conventionally measured using Gini coefficients based on individual income or wealth, or vertical income inequality. This approach has been challenged on two main counts: first, it fails to capture other crucial dimensions of inequality pertaining to access to politically sensitive items such as political participation, employment, education, land, and housing; and secondly, it neglects group membership as a vital dimension of human well-being and social stability. Horizontal inequality (HI) (Stewart, 2000a and 2002), socially embedded inequality (Figueroa, 2003; Mogues and Carter, 2005), durable inequality (Tilly, 1998), and intergroup differentials (Gurr, 1993) are alternative ways to define a similar concept: culturally defined groups are central to civil strife, and it is their perceived relative deprivation in the economic, social, and political spheres that buttresses group identity and cohesion to become a powerful mobilizing agent.

Theories of civil conflict share the common conviction that ethnic identity facilitates collective action and as such it plays a key role in the understanding of civil violence. In plural societies ethnic identity is often a more accurate predictor of political behaviour than class identity. This view is supported by evidence that the large majority of intrastate violence has ethnic roots (Fearon and Laitin, 1996), with conflicts over 'identity' accounting for 70 per cent of all civil wars started between 1960 and 1999 (Sambanis, 2001). However, the channels linking ethnic diversity to conflict remain a subject of controversy.

One aim of this chapter is to bring together the empirical literature on the inequality–political violence nexus with that on ethnic diversity and intrastate violent conflict. It argues that inequality between ethnic groups represents a potentially important channel through which ethnic diversity can lead to violence. This claim is tested empirically using a comprehensive dataset which merges census data with information on ethnocommunal violence that took place in Indonesia between 1990 and 2003. In contrast to cross-country econometric analyses of political conflict, focusing on one country has the advantage of eliminating country-specific heterogeneity in political structure and history, which are likely to mediate the impact of inequality on collective violence (Barron *et al.*, 2004; Deininger, 2003; Moore *et al.*, 1995). Yet as a result of its size, geography, ethnic diversity and assortment of internecine violence, Indonesia provides more than a case study, in the sense that the findings and implications of the present analysis are likely to have relevance beyond the national boundaries.

The chapter is structured as follows: Section 6.2 surveys alternative approaches used in the empirical literature on conflict and growth to operationalize ethnicity; Section 6.3 reviews previous empirical studies on the link between HIs and conflict; Section 6.4 provides some background information on Indonesia focusing particularly on its economic performance, patterns of inequality, and conflict history; Section 6.5 illustrates the modelling strategy and discusses its limitations; Section 6.6 presents the data used in the analysis; Section 6.7 illustrates the main features of the sample; Section 6.8 presents and discusses the main findings; and Section 6.9 concludes.

6.2   Operationalizing ethnicity: Three approaches

A review of the empirical literature on civil conflict suggests three main approaches to operationalizing ethnicity: (1) ethnic diversity, (2) cultural distance, and (3) horizontal inequalities. These are discussed in turn in the rest of this section.

6.2.1   Ethnic diversity

The measurement of ethnic diversity has taken many forms: ethnic dominance (Collier, 2001), the size of the second largest group (Ellingsen, 2000), categorical indicators ranking ethnic structure from unipolar to fragmented multipolarity (Barrows, 1976; Bangura, 2001), Herfindahl-type measures of ethnic dispersion, commonly known as *ethnic fractionalization indices* (Alesina *et al.*, 2003), and median-based indicators of demographic clustering around ethnic poles, commonly known as *polarization indices* (Reynal-Querol, 2002a).[1] The choice between the last two indices – which are most commonly used – depends on what one seeks to explain. A number of authors have convincingly argued that to explain violent conflict, polarization is superior to fractionalization (Esteban and Ray, 1994 and 1998; Montalvo and Reynal-Querol, 2005) because collective action is needed for conflict and greater fragmentation makes collective action more difficult.[2] If groups are not large enough to represent viable political bases, their cultural cleavages remain unexploited (Posner, 2004a). Moreover, the tendency to polarization is particularly dangerous in ethnic politics since it is conducive to zero-sum outcomes which are less likely with greater fluidity of alignments (Horowitz, 2001). Furthermore, perceptions of identity themselves depend on numbers. Using survey data from nine African countries, Bannon *et al.* (2004) find that individuals are less likely to identify themselves first in ethnic terms as ethnic fractionalization increases, implying that in more ethnically fragmented societies the salience of ethnicity as a mobilizing agent may be weaker.

However, measures of fragmentation and demographic polarization simply record numerical composition and not the differences between groups which may give rise to conflict. The next two approaches aim to measure these differences.

6.2.2   Social (cultural) distance

This approach goes beyond purely demographic indicators of diversity to measure the depth of cultural differences between groups. Cultural difference between groups can enhance group cohesion, identity, and the salience of cleavages. Fearon (2003) proposes a measure of cultural distance between groups based on commonalities of language 'tree branches', arguing that the number of common classifications in the language tree can be used as a measure of cultural proximity. Barrows (1976) constructs a composite index of ethnic pluralism (or cultural diversity between the ethnic groups of a nation) based on 12 indicators differentiating aspects such as dependence on agriculture, family organization, settlements patterns, type of authority system, descent and inheritance system. Gurr (1993) uses an indicator of intergroup cultural differentials based on six reinforcing traits: ethnicity, language, religion, social customs, historical origins, and urban versus rural residence.

The validity of the view that cultural diversity and distance lead to conflict has, however, been seriously challenged. Fearon and Laitin (1996), for example, provide the striking estimate that in Africa there has only been one instance of ethnic violence for every 2000 cases that would have been predicted on the basis of cultural differences alone. Moreover, Brubaker and Cooper (2000: 24–25) observe that 'in much of modern Africa some of the most bitter conflicts have taken place within collectivities that are relatively uniform culturally and linguistically (Rwanda and Somalia) and between loose economic and social networks based more on patron-client relations than ethnic affiliations (Angola, Sierra Leone)'. Similarly, Gurr (1993: 57) notes that 'the global analysis show[s] that there is no strong empirical evidence whatsoever between the extent of cultural differentials [...] for ethno-classes and communal contenders'. Posner (2004a) presents an interesting natural experiment involving two ethnic groups, the Chewas and the Tumbukas, whose native territory was split between Zambia and Malawi following the arbitrary drawing of the border between the two nations. The fact that both ethnic groups have mobilized politically in Malawi, where they form a large proportion of the whole population, but not in Zambia, where their relative size is small, suggests that the salience of cultural cleavages to conflict dynamics depends on the size of the groups rather than on (or in combination with) their cultural differences.

A second way of capturing the depth of cultural differences is to consider the nature of the cleavage, on the assumption that some cleavages are intrinsically less tractable than others. For instance, it has been claimed that religious cleavages are deeper because of the exclusivity of religion. As noted by Reynal-Querol (2002a), one can speak several languages but believe in just one God. Therefore, religiously divided societies are more prone to intense conflict than multiracial monoreligious societies. However, Alesina *et al.* (2003) have challenged this view on the grounds that religion can be more easily hidden than language or race as people can conform to the state-imposed or official religion to avoid repression.

A third way of looking at cultural distance is through the nature and quantity of affiliations. When more than one marker (religion, class, ethnicity, or race) defines a group, group identity is stronger and the politicization and mobilization of grievances is more likely to occur. In contrast, crosscutting or competing social identities increase perceived intracategory differentiation and decrease perceived intercategory differences, thus reducing the salience of category distinctions (Ensari and Miller, 2001; Hewstone *et al.*, 2002). For example, Varshney (2002) stresses the importance of civic engagement defined as crosscutting affiliations in preventing Hindu–Muslim riots in India. From an empirical perspective, however, the problem with civic engagement as an effective means to defuse violence is that it itself often constitutes an outcome to be explained.

6.2.3   Horizontal inequalities

While the approaches just reviewed aim to gauge cultural differences between groups, the HI approach measures differences in access to resources and outcomes. It is argued that HIs defined as differences between culturally formed groups in political opportunities, social access, economic assets, employment and income, play an important role in determining when and where violent conflict will take place (Chapter 1). This accords with Gurr's view that relative deprivation is a necessary precondition for civil strife : 'treat a group differently by denial or privilege, and its members become more self-conscious about their common bonds and interests. Minimize differences and communal identification becomes less significant as a unifying principle' (1993: 3).

While inequality need not always cause conflict when grievances can be politicized within an ethnic framework, increased interethnic conflict may be the eventual result (Sriskandarajah, 2003). For social stability as for individual well-being, inequality of access to inputs such as political and civil rights, education, land and housing, may be at least as important as inequality of outcomes like income, consumption or wealth (Sen, 1980), particularly as the inputs are both visible (and hence widely perceived) and instrumental for inequality in outcomes. Economists tend to focus mainly on income or consumption inequality not only because they themselves constitute a concern as a measure of utility or welfare, but also because they are expected to serve as good proxies for other nonmonetary dimensions such as education and health. Yet much research has shown that it is not justified to assume that income inequality is a good proxy for other nonincome inequalities. For example, Justino *et al.* (2004), using 1996 household survey data from Brazil, find very little (and negative) correlation between the distribution of household health (health status is measured by the proportion of stillborn babies in the household) and the distribution of household income.

It has been argued that the concept of economic polarization rather than economic inequality holds the key to explaining communal conflict (Esteban and Ray, 1994 and 1998). Polarization captures the extent to which society is clustered around a small number of distant and relatively (within-group) homogeneous groupings. This means that a society is more polarized the wider the gap between groups (alienation), the closer the population structure to perfect bimodality (demographic polarization), and the more internally homogenous the group (lower intragroup inequality). A society is perfectly polarized when it is evenly divided (and perfectly stratified) into those possessing a special attribute and those not possessing it. A highly polarized society is then expected to be more conflictual than a highly unequal society (Podder, 1998). Polarization is linked to inequality in a complex, nonlinear way: it increases with the level of inequality between groups and decreases with the level of inequality within groups (Zhang and Kanbur, 2003).

In contrast to existing measures of polarization like Esteban and Ray's, which implicitly presume that only economic class shapes identity and polarization, this chapter defines groups according to some politically relevant 'noneconomic' dimensions such as language or religion rather than in terms of the same metric (for example, income or years of education) used to summarize the distance between them.[3] This reflects the view echoed by Stewart (2000a) and Figueroa (2003) that inequality is more destabilizing when it is socially embedded.[4] The concept of HI thus brings together the ethnic diversity literature with the (vertical) economic inequality literature.

6.3   Previous quantitative literature on horizontal inequality

Few studies have attempted to test the effects of HIs on collective violence using large-N econometric analysis. This is not too surprising given the difficulties of defining groups and of measuring inequality between them. In an early attempt Barrows (1976) defines HI as the degree of disproportionality between the size of groups and their respective share of certain resources or assets such as political power, wealth, and education. Results from a sample of 32 sub-Saharan countries suggest that the effect of HIs on political instability is positive and statistically robust. Barrows (1976: 66) concludes that 'intergroup disparities in access to the benefits of modernity conspire to activate the ethnic group competition that often erupts into violence'.

Gurr and Moore (1997) use the Minority at Risk (MAR) dataset on 202 politically active communal groups from the 1980s.[5] Intergroup differences in a number of political and socioeconomic dimensions are measured. Using simultaneous equation models which jointly model rebellion, mobilization, grievances, and state repression, the authors find that HIs have indirect positive effects on the likelihood of ethnopolitical rebellion through higher ethnopolitical mobilization.

In Chapter 7, of this book, Østby investigates the relationship between HIs, some political variables, and the onset of conflict using Demographic and Health Survey (DHS) data. Earlier Østby (2003) explored the relationship between HIs and conflict incidence and onset for 43 developing countries between 1986 and 2001, also on the basis of DHS data. The results of this logit analysis reveal sizeable positive effects on the likelihood of conflict onset associated with social HIs. The impact of economic HI is weaker in magnitude and statistical significance, while the effect of health HI on the probability of conflict incidence is negative (although the effect becomes insignificant statistically when the dependent variable is conflict onset). Other findings suggest no effect on conflict onset associated with vertical inequality, ethnic fractionalization, or polarization once HIs are controlled for. Interestingly, the inclusion of interaction terms between VIs and HIs suggests that the likelihood of civil conflict is highest when low intragroup inequality coexists with high between-group inequalities.

Barron *et al.* (2004) use data on 69,000 villages and neighbourhoods from the 2002 Indonesian Village Census (PODES). They measure education HIs between ethnic groups (based on years of schooling of household heads) defined as the ratio of average education attainment of the most and least educated groups.[6] Information on whether there had been conflict in the previous year was collected from village heads. The logit analysis suggests that HIs are negatively associated with conflict incidence in rural areas, although the effect disappears in urban areas.

The relationship between the total number of people killed in episodes of civil violence in a district and HIs in assets and income in the Nepal civil war is estimated by Murshed and Gates (2005). Controlling for geographical factors such as resource dependence and the extent of mountainous terrain, they find that conflict is more intense in the most disadvantaged districts in terms of human development and asset (land) holdings. In contrast, spatial differences in literacy rates, life expectancy, and road density all have negative effects on conflict intensity.

6.4   The Indonesian context

With a total population of over 200 million comprising around 1000 ethnic groups, Indonesia is one of the world's most ethnically diverse countries. The formation of ethnic identities in Indonesia has been deeply and ambivalently influenced by its colonial past. The introduction of parallel legal systems and census classifications and, above all, the promotion of the division of labour along ethnic lines by the Dutch colonial power contributed to the demarcation of ethnic boundaries in pre-Independence Indonesia. On the other hand, by fostering local ethnic and religious identities in a crude divide-and-rule strategy, colonial policies also laid down the basis for an Indonesian national identity founded on a shared experience of colonization (Brown, 2005b).

Since gaining independence in 1950, Indonesia's stability has been marred by waves of extensive internal conflict. In the late 1950s a rebellion by some of the outer islands of the 13,000-island-strong archipelago was brutally suppressed by Indonesia's first president, Sukarno. Subsequently, a failed coup by communist sympathizers in 1965 provoked a successful counter-coup, accompanied by massive killings, which paved the way for the ascent to power of Major General Suharto in 1967 and his three-decade-long presidency known as the New Order. Interestingly, the impact of the New Order on identity formation in Indonesia was also characterized by ambivalence and unintended consequences, although the outcome was the obverse of the colonial experience. Paradoxically, by privileging a discourse of national identity, which suppressed ethnicity in the public domain, the New Order's social policies helped reinforce local identities and set them against each other (Brown, 2005b).

Under Suharto, the Indonesian economy grew at an average rate of 4.5 per cent *per annum* (Smith *et al.*, 2002). During this period, Indonesia saw a decline in the incidence of poverty, and improvements in child mortality and literacy rates. However, this rapid growth was accompanied by increasing inequality, especially in urban areas. The oil boom in the 1970s had the effect of increasing spatial inequalities between urban and rural areas as a result of the real appreciation of the rupiah (Booth, 2000), although the government adopted a regionally redistributive expenditure strategy. Relative poverty measured as the proportion of the population spending below 50 per cent of average *per capita* consumption expenditure increased significantly between 1987 and 1996. According to Booth (2000), this sharp rise in the incidence of relative poverty at a time when average incomes were increasing rapidly partly explains the growing social, racial, and religious tensions which became obvious even before the full impact of the financial crisis hit in late 1997.

After nearly 30 years of uninterrupted growth, low inflation and stable currency, in 1997 Indonesia was hit by a currency crisis which rapidly spread from the financial sector to the whole economy through upward-spiralling prices and falling formal sector employment. To make things worse the currency crisis coincided with natural calamities (the 1998 drought and forest fires that raged across parts of Sumatra, Sulawesi, and Kalimantan). It also ushered in dramatic political change. The poverty rate increased from 15 per cent at the onset of the crisis in mid-1997 to a high point of 33 per cent at the end of 1998 (Suryahadi *et al.*, 2003). In 1998, real GDP fell by nearly 14 per cent, while inflation rose to 78 per cent. Moreover, this figure conceals the much higher increase in food prices (Friedman and Levinsohn, 2001).

Suharto's authoritarian, centralizing and corrupt regime and its failure to create a pluralistic society to reflect the ethnic diversity of the archipelago undoubtedly contributed to the generation of conflict across the country. The annexation and brutal occupation of West Papua, the invasion and reign of terror in East Timor, the long-term military repression in Aceh, the deleterious environmental and economic impact of the transmigration programme on many indigenous people together with its not-so-veiled goal of strengthening national defence and security and the pursuit of exclusionary policies targeted at specific ethnoreligious groups are all examples of the role played by the Indonesian central government in stirring existing animosities and interethnic hatred (Bertrand, 2004).[7] It is therefore not surprising that violence exploded in 1997 in a climate of economic uncertainty following the financial crisis, and escalated dramatically with the power vacuum left by Suharto's fall in 1998.

Ethnocommunal violence in Indonesia has been highly concentrated in time and space. According to Varshney *et al.* (2004), 14 provinces (out of 30) accounted for 96.4 per cent of all nonsecessionist communal conflict deaths between 1990 and 2002.[8] More strikingly, in 2000 15 districts alone, whose share of the national population did not exceed 7 per cent, accounted for 85.5 per cent of all deaths in group violence. This is at odds with the view that violence in Indonesia is endemic to its very social fabric, history, and culture. The highly localized pattern of violence also challenges Bertrand's (2004) view of violence as the result of the exclusionary ethnoreligious policies of Suharto's New Order. Given that Muslim–Christian, anti-Chinese and Dayak–Madurese are the three dominant types of communal conflict in Indonesia, this theory has some merits according to Varshney *et al.* since 'the exclusion of Dayaks [. . .] on grounds of lack of modernity, the Chinese for lack of indigeneity [. . .] and Islam on grounds of ideology' (2004: 19) appears to vindicate Bertrand's claim. However, the fact that the Chinese were targeted only in some parts of Indonesia and that Muslim–Christian violence mostly took place in the Malukus and parts of Central Sulawesi while much of Central Sulawesi and almost all of North Sulawesi remained quiet, poses a bit of a puzzle. In the words of Varshney *et al.* (2004: 20) this suggests that 'an emphasis on institutional factors at the level of the nation or region can constitute only part of the explanation for the highly localized concentration of group violence our database has discovered'.

6.5   Methodology

This chapter focuses on ethnocommunal violence. Following Horowitz (2001), ethnic violence is defined as violence perpetrated across ethnic lines in which at least one party is not the state and in which victims are chosen by their group membership. The distinction is relevant for a country like Indonesia where ethnocommunal violence is just one form of collective violence, though one of the deadliest. Among the main types of violence which are *not* considered in this chapter as they fall outside the Horowitz definition of ethnocommunal conflict are the secessionist civil wars in Aceh, Irian Jaya, and East Timor, mass sickle battles between communities, vigilante killings, and the burning of alleged *dukun santet* (witch doctors) in Java.

The econometric analysis uses Indonesian districts as the unit of analysis. This is partly dictated by the availability of conflict data at the district level. The district represents a good choice also because, on the one hand, given the nature of ethnocommunal violence in Indonesia, the province is too wide a geographical unit to capture the considerable variation in violence observed across districts.[9] Illuminating examples are the bordering districts of Kota Waringin Barat (KWB) and Kota Waringin Timur (KWT) in the Central Kalimantan province and the districts of Poso and Donggala in Central Sulawesi. Whereas KWB and Poso have witnessed some of the most deadly ethnocommunal riots in the whole country, KWT and Donggala have remained relatively or completely quiescent. On the other hand, any unit smaller than the district would not capture the conflict spread, since the interethnic riots witnessed between 1997 and 2001 were clashes involving large masses of coethnics which spread well beyond the borders of villages and even of subdistricts. This is one of the problems with the village-based study of Barron *et al.* (2004), cited earlier. Also, following the decentralization programme post-Suharto, a large number of central government functions have been devolved to the district government. Therefore, competition for power among ethnic and religious groups at the district level is an increasingly central issue in Indonesian politics.

The dependent variable is defined as a binary dummy taking a value of 1 if deadly ethnic violence occurred in the period 1997–2003 in district *i* and zero otherwise. The effect of HIs on the probability of deadly ethnic conflict is estimated using logit regressions. Logit models of conflict incidence and conflict outset have been widely used in the empirical literature, which makes results more readily comparable with previous findings.

HI indicators are calculated as weighted coefficients of variation (GCOV), following the conclusions of Chapter 5 – see the formula in Appendix 5A. Six different indicators were considered: five measures of socioeconomic HIs, including child mortality rates (GCOVCHM), average years of education (GCOVEDU), the proportion of landless agricultural labourers and poor farmers (GCOVLANDP), average labour income (GCOVINC), and the proportion of unemployed young males (aged 14–30) (GCOVMYUN). This last dimension of socioeconomic group inequality seems especially relevant in the case of Indonesia where youth clashes constitute the single most important trigger of group violence (Varshney *et al.*, 2004), perhaps because of the particularly harsh effect that the 1997–1998 financial crisis had on young wage workers. We also consider one measure of political HI, that is, the proportion of civil servants (GCOVPS) belonging to each group.[10] Each of these indicators was constructed for both ethnolinguistic and ethnoreligious groups (for the latter the variables take the suffix _R). This dual definition is expected to provide clues as to which type of cleavage matters more to conflict in Indonesia and serves as a sensitivity and robustness test for the effect of HIs across alternative definitions of group membership. Not all groups are included in the analysis. Very small groups are excluded mainly because for these groups sample information cannot be taken as representative. Following previous research, a cut-off point is set; here we exclude ethnic groups which represent less than 5 per cent of the district population.

Focusing on a country like Indonesia to investigate the inequality–conflict nexus offers some advantages vis-à-vis a cross-country analysis. First, as already pointed out, cross-country conflict datasets generally overlook much of the communal conflict that does not take the form of civil war but that nonetheless can involve high fatalities and much destruction. Second, an intracountry analysis can generally do away with otherwise key confounding (and often unobservable) factors such as regime repressiveness, proximity of electoral contexts to the timing of the survey, state strength, colonial heritage, political institutionalization, regime type; and devote more statistical and modelling resources to controlling other potential intervening effects such as overall inequality, level of development, and ethnic diversity. Moreover, Indonesia is such a vast and extraordinarily diverse country both in its ethnic composition and conflict history that the results of this analysis are potentially interesting beyond the national borders.

Other independent variables include the following (for a complete list of the variables and their description refer to Appendix 6A, Table 6A.1):

- The logarithm of the district population (LNPOP). A large population implies difficulties in controlling developments at the local level and increases the number of potential rebels that can be recruited by the insurgents (Fearon and Laitin, 2003).
- The overall level of violence observed in the district between 1990 and 1996 (S_PRE97). This variable is expected to capture both the proneness to violence and/or potential path dependence in violent behaviour in the period immediately preceding the explosion of interethnic riots.
- The district 1996 Human Development Index (HDI96) as a proxy for the overall level of economic development.[11]
- The district unemployment rate among young males (aged 14–30) (MYUN).
- The district degree of dependence on natural resources (NATRES). Greater funding opportunities for would-be rebels (Collier and Hoeffler, 2004), weaker state apparatuses (Fearon and Laitin, 2003), or grievances over resource revenue distribution (Ross, 2003) are alternative mechanisms which make countries whose economies are heavily reliant on natural resources more vulnerable to intrastate violence. Without investigating the transmission mechanism, this chapter aims to assess the role of natural resources measured as the proportion of the district population employed in the mining and timber industries.
- The proportion of migrants who arrived in the district during the previous five years (NEWMIG). This is an important factor to consider, given the ethnic tensions and the fears of Javanization provoked by the conspicuous fluxes of transmigrants and voluntary migrants during the 1980s and 1990s.
- The proportion of the district population living in urban areas (URBAN). This variable may partly capture the impact of the crisis on ethnic violence in Indonesia since the urban population is believed to have been worst affected. Differences in the rural/urban composition across districts

may also partially capture interdistrict differences in the level of civic engagement (Varshney, 2002).

- The district GDP growth in 1998 (GDPGR98). This is a more direct proxy for the severity with which the district was hit by the financial crisis.
- The level of vertical income inequality in the district (INCGINI). The Gini coefficient is based on monetary as well as nonmonetary (goods) labour income.
- The degree of ethnolinguistic fractionalization in the district (ELF).[12]
- The degree of demographic ethnolinguistic polarization in the district (ETHPOL).
- The degree of demographic ethnoreligious polarization in the district (RELPOL).[13]

The analysis is subject to a number of limitations. Firstly, group membership is assumed to be exogenously given. Yet the notion of endogenous ethnic identity is becoming increasingly popular among social scientists. Group boundaries are not watertight as politically salient groups can grow and shrink, emerge, and disappear. These are important but complex and contested issues which are clearly beyond the scope of the chapter. However, in spite of these acknowledged difficulties, qualitative research suggests that when it comes to actual cases, the relevant groups and boundaries are generally fairly obvious. When group markers are quite obvious there is some justification for assuming that ethnicity is 'exogenous' with respect to opportunities, access, and discrimination in the society.

Second, the choice of *which* groups to focus on could be endogenous to the outcome it is used to explain. If there are multiple plausible ways of listing a country's ethnic groups one must be careful not to choose the coding that best supports the chosen theory (Fearon, 2003). Yet, as far as HIs are concerned, there is a strong case to exclude politically irrelevant groups on the ground that their grievances may confound or divert attention from the true fault lines (Posner, 2004b; Chapter 5, this volume). There are no easy answers to these concerns or obvious empirical strategies to address them. This chapter takes the view that a good compromise between the two dangers is to proxy the political salience of a group by its population share within the relevant political arena, which in the case of ethnocommunal conflict in Indonesia is represented by the administrative district, as argued earlier. Posner's natural experiment results for Malawi and Zambia vindicate the choice of focusing on the bigger groups. However, to assess the sensitivity of the results to group selection, the analysis is replicated without the largest ethnic group, the Javanese, who, in spite of their overwhelming demographic dominance, are seldom involved in the violence either as targets or perpetrators.

Third, inequality and identity, both real and perceived, are likely to be influenced by violent conflict. As Sambanis notes, 'If people cannot escape their identity in an escalating struggle, then even if their original preferences were nonviolent war would cause a preference shock that would bring them in line with their leaders' preferences' (2001: 23). This poses serious problems for a correct assessment of the causal impact of HIs on violence, particularly when conflict and inequality information are contemporaneous.[14] The strategy adopted in this chapter to mitigate the endogeneity of HI with respect to violent ethnocommunal conflict is to measure group inequality on the basis of information that predates conflict by at least two years. In addition, the inclusion in the regressions of a variable capturing the district's proneness to violence in the period immediately preceding the explosion of interethnic riots is expected to attenuate the circularity issue.

Finally, the definition of the dependent variable as a binary outcome makes no distinction between cases with only one fatality and cases where hundreds of people were killed. The choice was justified by possible misreporting of deaths by the national and provincial newspapers, and because conflict intensity is likely to depend on a variety of factors such as the type and timing of state military intervention, the involvement of militia groups, or the role of the police. Despite these concerns, in Section 6.8 (Table 6.7, column (4)) the analysis is replicated using an ordered logit model with the dependent variable redefined as a three-way ordinal indicator (no deadly violence, low fatality violence, high fatality violence) to gauge the sensitivity of the main findings to the chosen binary specification of the dependent variable.

6.6   Data

The dataset was constructed by averaging individual-level information from the Indonesian 1995 Intercensal Population Survey (SUPAS)[15] up to the district level (rural *kabupaten* and urban *kota*). The census population is a nationally representative random sample accounting for 0.5 per cent (nearly 1 million individuals) of the total population of Indonesia in 1995. After the averaging process, aggregated census data were merged with district-wide information on ethnocommunal violence compiled by the United Nations Support Facility for Indonesian Recovery (UNSFIR) (Varshney *et al.*, 2004).

The UNSFIR Database II contains information on collective violence in 14 Indonesian provinces (12 if considering the 1995 administrative boundaries) for a total of over 3600 violent incidents (involving at least a group either as perpetrator or as target) based on news reported in both national and provincial newspapers.[16] The choice of these 14 provinces is justified on the grounds that group violence in Indonesia is highly concentrated in space.

Ethnicity information was not directly available because discussion of ethnic differences was prohibited in the public realm. Only in 2000 was an ethnicity question included in the census questionnaire. Hence, ethnic groups are defined either in terms of self-reported language information, or of religious affiliation. The use of language[17] as a proxy for ethnicity in Indonesia is not a major limitation to the analysis since a comparison between the classification of ethnic groups in this dataset and the 2002 SUSENAS dataset which includes ethnicity codes shows a close correspondence between the ranking and relative sizes of the main groups (see also Ross, 2003). This confirms that language is a good proxy for ethnicity in Indonesia.

6.7 Sample and summary statistics

From the original population of nearly 1 million Indonesians sampled in Supas 1995, the number of observations included in the sample was reduced to 352,295 individuals living in 164 districts across 19 provinces. Individuals living in the provinces of Aceh, East Timor and Irian Jaya were excluded due to the different nature of the conflict in these areas, as explained earlier. Individuals residing in the island of Java were also excluded because, with the important exception of the capital Jakarta and very few other major cities, Javanese districts are largely homogenous in both their religious and ethnic composition. Furthermore, the districts of Java have mainly witnessed incidents of collective violence of a nonethnic nature such as the killing of *dukun santet*, village brawls and episodes of 'popular justice' (for example, vigilante killings). If one excludes the bloody but very exceptional May 1998 anti-Chinese riots in Jakarta and Solo, ethnocommunal incidents represent only 2 per cent of all incidents of collective violence and account for less than 3 per cent of all fatalities recorded in Java between 1990 and 2003 (Varshney *et al.*, 2004). Sample size was further reduced through the selection of individuals aged 10–70. In addition, about 12.5 per cent of the census population provided either missing or 'unhelpful' language information[18] which fell to 8 per cent when father's language was assigned to daughters and sons living in the household who had missing language information. Summary statistics (not shown) reveal that this residual subsample of 'nonrespondents' was not significantly different from 'respondents' except for being slightly more educated and urbanized. Therefore, it was decided to exclude them from the computation of the ethnolinguistic HIs.

Conflict information based on the UNSFIR database is available for only 73 of the 164 districts included in the sample and the remaining 91 districts are treated as 'zero' conflict cases. Figure 6.1 shows that ethnocommunal clashes account for over 95 per cent of all fatalities.[19] The plots also clearly show that deadly ethnocommunal violence in Indonesia exploded dramatically in 1997, immediately preceding the fall of Suharto, and peaked in 2000 before declining steadily in the first years of the new millennium.

Of the nearly 250 ethnolanguage groups originally found in the 1995 SUPAS only the 70 major groups were included in the sample on the basis of

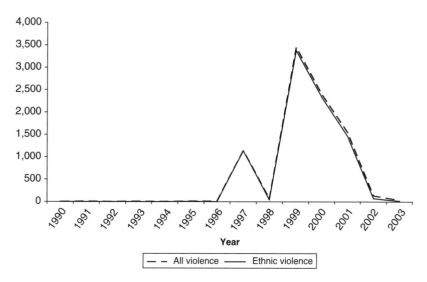

Figure 6.1   Number of fatalities
Source: UNSFIR Database.

the group size criterion discussed in Section 6.5. Table 6.1 shows the ethnic (proxied by language) and religious composition of Indonesia in 1995. For presentational purposes, only the 15 major ethnic groups are listed in the table. Many of the ethnic groups not listed are very small on the national scale but, being highly geographically concentrated, their size is significant at the district level (greater than 5 per cent of the district population). Javanese represent the dominant ethnic group accounting for 12 per cent of the sample, even after Java has been excluded from the sample. In terms of religious affiliation, Islam is by far the dominant religion, adhered to by over 73 per cent of the sample population.

Table 6.2 shows that religiously diverse districts tend to have a higher number of incidents of conflict and a higher average number of fatalities than ethnically diverse districts. A look at the HI indicators shows that group inequality in income and education is lower than group inequality in other dimensions.

Deadly ethnic conflict is concentrated almost exclusively in districts which are diverse both in terms of language and religion (Table 6.3). This is only partly implicit in the definition of the dependent variable, because the fact that conflict is hardly present in the 59 districts which are either religiously or linguistically diverse, but not both, needs explaining. In the light of this evidence, the 38 homogenous districts (both in terms of language and religion) will not be considered further in this analysis. In fact, by definition, in these districts the dependent variable and the HI measures are both zero. This means that if these homogenous districts were retained in the

Table 6.1 Sample composition of language and religious groups

Language			Religion		
Group	No.	%	Group	No.	%
Javanese	37,538	12.01	Muslim	258,513	73.38
Melayu	29,873	9.56	Protestant	43,692	12.4
Buginese	28,709	9.19	Catholic	23,660	6.72
Minang	26,913	8.61	Hindu	19,346	5.49
Banjarese	21,391	6.85	Buddhist	5,149	1.46
Balinese	18,715	5.99	Other	1,935	0.55
Batak	13,914	4.45			
Makassarese	13,542	4.33			
Dayak	8,570	2.74			
Sasak	7,940	2.54			
Chinese	6,623	2.12			
Bima	5,210	1.67			
Toraja	5,065	1.62			
Muna-Buton	4,516	1.45			
Gorontalo	4,488	1.44			
Sumba	4,141	1.33			
Mandar	3,938	1.26			
Dawan	3,905	1.25			
Palembang	3,745	1.2			
Sundanese	3,445	1.1			
Other	60,289	19.29			
All	312,470[a]			352,295	

[a] Individuals who only speak the national language are excluded.

sample then the significance and magnitude of the HI marginal effects on the likelihood of violent conflict that this chapter seeks to estimate would be inflated.

In Tables 6.4 and 6.5, ethnically and religiously diverse districts, respectively, are stratified by their violent/nonviolent status. The figures report average HI values for each stratum as well as the difference in mean HIs (with standard errors) between the two strata. The statistics are calculated for the whole sample as well as for the subsets of districts located in the islands of Kalimantan and Sulawesi. These two islands are of particular interest because they present situations of highly violent districts bordering relatively peaceful ones, often within the same province. The results suggest that, on average, HIs are generally lower in peaceful districts (negative difference), particularly with respect to education, land ownership, public sector employment, and child mortality. Not surprisingly, these HI variables are highly (positively) correlated with each other, as shown in Appendix 6A, Table 6A.2. Interestingly, the association of income HIs with the violent/peaceful status of the district is on average much weaker than for the other dimensions.

Table 6.2 Variable means

Variable	All districts	Ethnically diverse districts	Religiously diverse districts
ETHNCONF_D	0.18	0.23	0.32
KILLED	3.24	4.55	6.69
S_PRE97	0.78	0.87	1.19
LNPOP	12.47	12.55	12.51
NATRES	0.04	0.05	0.05
URBAN	0.29	0.32	0.36
NEWMIG	0.11	0.15	0.11
MYUN	0.12	0.12	0.11
HDI96	66.59	67.24	67.66
ELF	0.42	0.58	0.54
RELPOL	0.36	0.44	0.64
INCGINI	0.36	0.35	0.35
GCOVEDU	0.10	0.13	0.13
GCOVLANDP	0.34	0.47	0.46
GCOVMYUN	0.31	0.42	0.37
GCOVINC	0.13	0.17	0.16
GCOVPS	0.31	0.43	0.41
GCOVCHM	0.23	0.32	0.32
GCOVEDU_R	0.05	0.06	0.08
GCOVLANDP_R	0.15	0.19	0.30
GCOVMYUN_R	0.10	0.11	0.19
GCOVINC_R	0.06	0.08	0.10
GCOVPS_R	0.16	0.19	0.31
GCOVCHM_R	0.12	0.15	0.22
N	164	115	78

Table 6.3 Distribution of violent outcomes

Districts		Incidents			Fatalities		
Ethnically diverse	Religiously diverse	No.	No.	%	No.	%
NO	NO	38	5	0.0	2	0.0
YES	NO	48	4	1.0	140	2.0
NO	YES	11	3	1.0	27	0.0
YES	YES	67	519	98.0	8289	98.0
Total		164	531	100	8458	100

This may be partly due to well-known difficulties in measuring income in developing countries (Deaton, 1995). In light of this preliminary evidence, the econometric analysis presented in the next section will focus on those HI dimensions whose association with conflict is more statistically robust, according to this analysis.

Table 6.4 Mean differences in horizontal inequalities between ethnic groups, by violent (V)/nonviolent (NV) status (ethnically diverse districts only)

		No.	EDU	LANDP	MYUN	INC	PS	CHM
All districts	NV	88	0.121	0.418	0.38	0.162	0.393	0.266
	V	27	0.169	0.632	0.45	0.182	0.567	0.383
	difference		−0.048***	−0.213**	−0.07	−0.020	−0.175***	−0.117***
			(0.00)	(0.087)	(0.06)	(0.02)	(0.06)	(0.03)
Sulawesi	NV	15	0.117	0.511	0.347	0.145	0.275	0.289
	V	7	0.164	0.508	0.373	0.219	0.432	0.327
	difference		−0.046	0.003	−0.026	−0.074	−0.157**	−0.038
			(0.03)	(0.12)	(0.09)	(0.04)	(0.07)	(0.08)
Kalimantan	NV	16	0.145	0.558	0.418	0.154	0.446	0.264
	V	9	0.144	0.718	0.595	0.128	0.677	0.405
	difference		0.001	−0.16	−0.176	0.026	−0.231*	−0.141**
			(0.02)	(0.18)	(0.15)	(0.02)	(0.11)	(0.06)

Note: Standard errors are shown in parentheses; *** indicates significance at 1%, ** at 5% and * at 10% level, respectively.

Table 6.5 Mean differences in horizontal inequalities between religious groups, by violent (V)/nonviolent (NV) status (religiously diverse districts only)

		N	EDU	LANDP	MYUN	INC	PS	CHM
All districts	NV	53	0.074	0.294	0.257	0.104	0.285	0.201
	V	25	0.086	0.305	0.255	0.101	0.352	0.255
	difference		−0.012	−0.011	0.002	0.003	−0.067	−0.054
			(0.01)	(0.06)	(0.06)	(0.02)	(0.06)	(0.03)
Sulawesi	NV	7	0.059	0.170	0.238	0.118	0.230	0.173
	V	7	0.067	0.159	0.206	0.092	0.213	0.177
	difference		−0.008	0.011	0.032	0.026	0.017	−0.004
			(0.01)	(0.09)	(0.06)	(0.03)	(0.05)	(0.06)
Kalimantan	NV	12	0.100	0.299	0.264	0.130	0.330	0.225
	V	8	0.111	0.424	0.369	0.125	0.567	0.319
	difference		−0.011	−0.125	−0.105	0.005	−0.237*	−0.094
			(0.02)	(0.15)	(0.14)	(0.03)	(0.12)	(0.06)

Note: Standard errors are shown in parentheses; *** indicates significance at 1%, ** at 5% and * at 10% level, respectively.

6.8 Results

Table 6.6 shows the estimated coefficients (with standard errors) of the logit regressions run separately for ethnically and religiously diverse districts. Some regularities emerge across different subsamples and model specifications. Deadly ethnocommunal conflict is more likely to occur in case of the

Table 6.6 Estimation results

	Ethnically diverse districts		Religiously diverse districts	
	(1)	**(2)**	**(3)**	**(4)**
LNPOP	−0.015	0.030	0.183	0.321
	(0.23)	(0.32)	(0.34)	(0.49)
S_PRE97	0.732 **	0.779 **	0.635	0.810 *
	(0.34)	(0.31)	(0.35)	(0.36)
HDI96	−0.171 **	−0.177 *	−0.211 ***	−0.027 **
	(0.07)	(0.10)	(0.075)	(0.12)
NATRES	−2.638	−1.932	−10.346	−15.379
	(10.08)	(8.63)	(13.55)	(12.10)
MYUN	2.834	0.390	2.348	0.393
	(4.66)	(5.03)	(4.94)	(5.40)
ELF	2.694	0.282	3.880 *	5.183 *
	(2.37)	(2.96)	(2.31) *	(2.81)
RELPOL	4.009 ***	3.653 ***	2.857	3.159
	(0.79)	(1.35)	(1.94)	(2.25)
NEWMIG	4.658 *	5.275 *	7.492 **	10.394 *
	(2.82)	(2.82)	(3.84)	(6.14)
INCGINI	−1.755	−3.106	−2.832	−0.001
	(4.89)	(5.69)	(7.88)	(7.82)
GDPGR98	−0.018	0.006	0.025	0.071
	(0.07)	(0.08)	(0.09)	(0.11)
GCOVEDU		−0.179		
		(4.38)		
GCOVLANDP		−0.075		
		(1.15)		
GCOVPS		0.673		
		(1.05)		
GCOVCHM		3.563 **		
		(1.53)		
GCOVEDU_R				1.881
				(8.07)
GCOVLANDP_R				−2.704
				(1.69)
GCOVPS_R				−0.046
				(1.46)
GCOVCHM_R				9.195 **
				(3.64)
Constant	5.857	6.619	6.899	5.682
	(5.20)	(5.88)	(7.68)	(10.01)
N	115	115	78	78
LL	−42.82	−40.82	−32.42	−28.52
Pred. prob. (mean)	0.19	0.18	0.29	0.26
pseudo R^2	0.32	0.35	0.34	0.42

Note: Standard errors are shown in parentheses; *** indicates significance at 1%, ** at 5%, * at 10% level, respectively.

following four factors: (a) the higher the overall number of violent incidents recorded in the district between 1990 and 1996, (b) the lower the district's Human Development Index (HDI), (c) the higher the proportion of the district's population made up of migrants who have moved into the district since 1990, and (d) the wider the gap between groups in child mortality rates. To illustrate the impact of the child mortality HI on the likelihood of violence, Figures 6.2 and 6.3 plot the change in the predicted probability of deadly ethnocommunal violence to changes in the level of the HI in child mortality rate. The likelihood of violence clearly increases with inequality and the gradient tends to be steeper at lower levels of economic development.[20] Results suggests that, on average, a 10 per cent increase in GCOVCHM leads to a 5.3 per cent increase in the probability of observing violent conflict in the district. Despite the estimated effect of each of the four HI variables being positive and statistically significant when entered individually in the model alongside the other confounding factors (not shown), the child mortality effect is the strongest statistically. This is clearly shown in Table 6.6 where HI in child mortality is the only dimension of group inequality which has a statistically significant impact on the likelihood of communal violence when all HI variables are jointly included in the

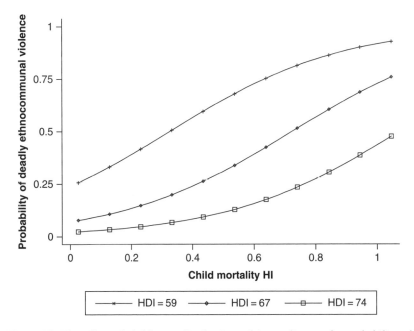

Figure 6.2 The effect of child mortality horizontal inequality on the probability of violence at different levels of economic development: Ethnic groups

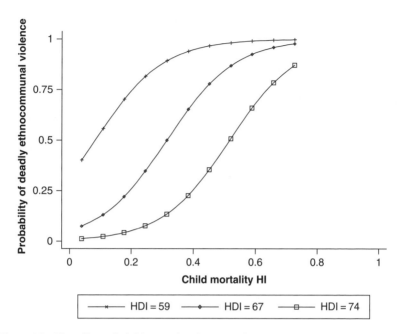

Figure 6.3   The effect of child mortality horizontal inequality on the probability of violence at different levels of economic development: Religious groups

model specification. The weak effects of the other HI variables, when all are included, can be explained by the high and positive correlation coefficients between these dimensions (see Appendix 6A, Table 6A.2). This makes intuitive sense: group differences in child mortality rates often reflect inequalities in other socioeconomic dimensions such as levels of education, family income/wealth, and housing conditions. Of all types of group inequalities considered in this chapter, child mortality is perhaps the most disturbing because it puts in the spotlight the level of destitution of the poorest groups in society. It is also a very visible type of inequality which can be used instrumentally by ethnic elites to mobilize coethnics. Table 6.6 also suggests that religious polarization in ethnically diverse districts has a significant positive effect on the likelihood of deadly ethnocommunal conflict, while ethnolinguistic fractionalization (ELF) also has a positive effect but it is statistically weaker and only significant at the 10 per cent level when estimation is restricted to religiously diverse districts.[21] Interestingly, natural resource dependence (NATRES), unemployment rates among young males (MYUN), vertical income inequality (INCGINI), and district growth rates (GDPGR98) have *no* significant impact on the dependent variable.[22]

Table 6.7 presents additional results intended to test the robustness of the findings presented in Table 6.6, particularly the HI effects. In columns

Table 6.7 Additional results

	(1)		(2)		(3)		(4)		(5)	
S_PRE97	0.710	**	0.644	**	0.770	**	0.101	***	0.595	**
	(0.34)		(0.29)		(0.38)		(0.03)		(0.30)	
HDI96	-0.163	**	-0.190	**	-0.146	*	-0.195	***	-0.192	**
	(0.07)		(0.08)		(0.07)		(0.06)		(0.08)	
ELF	1.345		3.281		1.897		2.596	*	4.146	*
	(1.88)		(2.55)		(1.91)		(1.54)		(2.52)	
RELPOL	3.809	***	2.252	***	4.055	***	4.087	***	3.539	
	(0.89)		(1.99)		(0.86)		(0.90)		(2.38)	
NEWMIG	4.871		7.080		4.618		2.637		7.724	
	(3.17)		(5.45)		(3.38)		(2.92)		(6.59)	
GCOVCHM_NJ	2.245	**								
	(1.02)									
GCOVCHM_R_NJ			4.360	**						
			(1.88)							
HI_CHM					2.597	**	2.221	*		
					(1.16)		(1.31)			
GCOVCHM_R_90									0.714	
									(4.22)	
DGCOV95_90									4.386	*
									(2.37)	
Constant	4.956		6.127		3.272				5.570	
	(4.37)		(4.64)		(4.03)				(4.74)	
N	115		78		126		126		72	
LL	-42.17		-31.98		-43.94		-67.27		-29.82	
Pred. prob. (mean)	0.184		0.29		0.162		0.22		0.25	
pseudo R2	0.33		0.35		0.34				0.33	

Note: Standard errors are shown in parentheses; *** indicates significance at 1%, ** at 5%, * at 10% level, respectively.

(1) and (2), the HI measures of child mortality between both ethnic and religious groups were recalculated excluding the Javanese. The Javanese are the largest ethnic group in Indonesia, and they are present in significant numbers in almost every district of the archipelago. Javanese have seldom been involved in ethnic violence, arguably because they constitute too size-able and powerful a group (they are seen to dominate the army and to have the backing of the central state) in the wide national political arena to become a feasible target for rival ethnic groups even in the most peripheral corners of the country. Excluding them from the computation of the HI measures is a way to check whether the impact of GCOVCHM and GCOVCHM_R is sensitive to the inclusion of potentially 'irrelevant' groups. Table 6.7 shows that this is not the case and that the estimated HI coefficients remain large, positive, and statistically significant after excluding the Javanese.

Column (3) includes all 126 districts which are either ethnically or religiously diverse. The child mortality HI variable is redefined as the larger value between the measure based on language groups and the measure based on religious groups.[23] The logic behind this is that the larger the grievance, the stronger is group cohesion and the sense of identity. The results confirm that child mortality HIs have a positive and statistically significant influence on the likelihood that deadly ethnocommunal violence breaks out in a given district.

The definition of the dependent variable used so far makes no distinction between cases with only one fatality and cases where hundreds of people were killed. To test the sensitivity of the main findings to the definition of the dependent variable as a binary outcome, column (4) in Table 6.7 presents the results from an ordered logit regression where the dependent variable takes value 0 if no deadly violence occurred in the district between 1997 and 2003, 1 if the number of fatalities from interethnic violence ranged between 1 and 24 and 2 if the death toll was 25 or higher. The 25-death-toll threshold is a standard value used in the literature on civil war. The evidence suggests that when the dependent variable takes some account of the severity of the violence, the sign, magnitude and statistical significance of the HI effect (as well as the other main effects such as religious polarization and economic development) remain largely unaffected.

Finally, an interesting extension to the analysis is to explore whether ethnocommunal conflict is associated not only with absolute levels of socioeconomic inequalities between ethnic and religious groups, but also with their change over time. Although group inequalities are expected to change slowly because they tend to be durable and socially embedded, even relatively small changes may be perceived by people as being very significant, which in turn may heavily influence group mobilization and conflict dynamics. To this end, the same measure of child mortality HI is constructed from a nationally representative random sample of the 1990 Indonesian

Table 6.8 Child mortality ('000) and child mortality horizontal inequality by year and violent (V)/nonviolent (NV) status

Year	1990			1995		
	NV	**V**	**diff**	**NV**	**V**	**diff**
Child mortality (%)	109.1	107.8	2.3 (7.7)	63.8	67.9	−4.1 (5.7)
GCOVCHM_R	0.119	0.204	−0.084*** (0.03)	0.129	0.235	−0.106*** (0.03)
No.	89	25		89	25	

Note: Standard errors are shown in parentheses; *** indicates significance at 1%, ** at 5%, * at 10% level, respectively.

Population Census which contains roughly the same number of observations as the 1995 SUPAS. The variable is calculated between ethnoreligious groups only, owing to the lack of consistency in the definition of language groups between the two datasets, and to the concern that in some districts the salient groups may have changed between the two years thus making comparisons over time more difficult. These issues are less of a concern with ethnoreligious groups which are much larger and stable over time. Table 6.8 shows that although child mortality rates on average nearly halved between 1990 and 1995 across the 114 religiously diverse districts for which data were available in both years, the level of inequality has slightly increased on average, particularly in those districts which turned violent from 1997. This suggests that it may be not only absolute levels but also differences over time in child mortality rates between groups that discriminate between violent and nonviolent districts. Table 6.7 column (5) shows the effect of a change in HI (constructed as the difference between the 1995 and 1990 values) on the likelihood of ethnocommunal conflict is positive and statistically significant, which confirms that variation in HI over time could also play an important role in predicting ethnocommunal violence.

6.9 Conclusions

Existing research in experimental psychology, sociology, and economic theory points to the importance of intergroup bias in access to inputs and outcomes to explain group behaviour, group mobilization and, ultimately, social unrest. However, intergroup inequalities or HIs have received little attention in the lively empirical literature on civil conflict. To an extent, this is not surprising given the daunting task of measuring distances between groups whose boundaries are typically based on noneconomic dimensions. The chapter relies on a comprehensive dataset of Indonesian districts where detailed conflict data between 1990 and 2003 was merged with a wealth of socioeconomic characteristics obtained by averaging up to the district level individual and household information from the 1990 to 1995 population census data. Unlike cross-country econometric analyses of political conflict, focusing on a large and diverse country like Indonesia offers the advantage of doing away with country-specific heterogeneity. In line with earlier studies, the results from a cross-district logistic analysis suggest that less developed districts (lower HDI) were more likely to experience deadly ethnocommunal conflict between 1997 and 2003. This suggests that the financial crisis and the ensuing economic crisis that hit Indonesia in 1998 may have fuelled simmering tensions and contributed to precipitating violent events in many parts of the country. Interestingly, of the traditional proxies of ethnic diversity, the degree of religious polarization in the district has the greater impact on the likelihood of ethnocommunal violence. Also, in line with previous evidence, (vertical) income inequality plays no significant role in predicting the occurrence of violence.

A key result of the chapter is that HIs seem to matter to violent conflict. A number of different dimensions were considered capturing various social and economic aspects of inequality. The results suggest that districts with larger intergroup differentials in child mortality rates in 1995 as well as districts where these inequalities widened between 1990 and 1995 tend to be those where deadly conflict occurred. The effect is both consistent across a number of different model specifications and robust to alternative ways of defining and measuring group inequality. It also survives the inclusion of purely demographic measures of ethnic diversity as well as variables capturing the (economic) opportunity cost of taking up arms such as youth unemployment and level of economic development. Inequality in child mortality is strongly correlated with other dimensions of socioeconomic inequality like education, employment and income as the data clearly show. However the latter are found to have no significant direct impact on the likelihood of violent conflict once child mortality HI was controlled for. We suggest that this is the case because HI in child mortality truly is a type of inequality which not only stands out under statistical scrutiny but is also highly visible to the population generally and can be used instrumentally by ethnic elites to mobilize coethnics. It is also a particularly disturbing type of inequality because it exposes the relative destitution of the poorest groups in society. Moreover, because of its high correlation with other variables (such as education), its effects in part represent the impact of HIs in these dimensions. Arguably, monitoring the level of these inequalities as well as their change over time may provide some useful clues as to where destructive ethnocommunal violence is likely to erupt.

Appendix 6A

Table 6A.1 Variable definition

Variable	Definition
ETHNCONF_D	Dummy: 1 if district had deadly ethnocommunal conflict, 0 otherwise
S_PRE97	Number of incidents of communal violence in the district between 1990 and 1996 (ethnic and nonethnic)
LNPOP	Logarithm of district population
NATRES	Proportion of district active workforce employed in oil and gas and timber industries
RURAL	Dummy: 1 if district is classified as rural (*kabupaten*), 0 if district is classified as urban (*kota*)
URBAN	Proportion of district population living in urban areas
NEWMIG	Proportion of district population born in a different province and resident in current district for less than five years.
MYUN	District proportion of unemployed young males (aged 14–30)
HDI96	UNDP 1996 Human Development Index
ELF	Ethnolinguistic fractionalization index
ETHPOL	Ethnolinguistic polarization index
RELPOL	Religious polarization index
INCGINI	Gini coefficient of vertical income inequality based on labour income (monetary and nonmonetary)
GDPGR98	The district GDP growth in 1998
GCOVEDU	Weighted coefficient of variation in average years of education between ethnolinguistic groups from district overall mean
GCOVLANDP	As above, but variation is the proportion of people employed in agriculture who are either landless or own less than 0.5 ha of land.
GCOVMYUN	As above, but variation is in proportion of young male unemployed
GCOVPS	As above, but variation is in proportion of civil servants
GCOVCHM	As above, but variation is in child mortality rates
GCOVINC	As above, but variation is in labour income (monetary and nonmonetary)
GCOVEDU_R	As GCOVEDU, but between religious groups
GCOVLANDP_R	As GCOVLANDP, but between religious groups
GCOVMYUN_R	As GCOMYUN, but between religious groups
GCOVPS_R	As GCOVPS, but between religious groups
GCOVCHM_R	As GCOVCHM, but between religious groups
GCOVINC_R	As GCOVINC, but between religious groups
HI_CHM	Max (GCOVCHM,GCOVCHM_R)
GCOVCHM_NJ	As GCOVCHM, but without the Javanese
GCOVCHM_R_NJ	As GCOVCHM_NJ, but between religious groups
GCOVCHM_R_90	As GCOVCHM_R, 1990 value calculated from 1990 Indonesian Census
DGCOV95_90	(GCOVCHM_R - GCOVCHM_R_90)

Table 6A.2 Correlation matrix

		lnpop	S_pre97	natres	urban	myun	elf	relpol	newmig	hdi96	incgini
s_pre97	coeff	0.158**	1								
	N	126	126								
natres	coeff	-0.235	-0.036	1							
	N	126	126	126							
urban	coeff	-0.101	0.197***	0.138	1						
	N	126	126	126	126						
myun	coeff	0.053	0.228***	0.063	0.749***	1					
	N	126	126	126	126	126					
elf	coeff	0.170**	0.069	0.180**	0.293***	0.417***	1				
	N	126	126	126	126	126	126				
relpol	coeff	-0.089	0.064	0.059	0.269***	0.078	0.132	1			
	N	126	126	126	126	126	126	126			
newmig	coeff	0.191***	-0.041	0.156*	0.204***	0.198***	0.523***	-0.208***	1		
	N	126	126	126	126	126	126	126	126		
hdi96	coeff	0.003	0.083	0.179**	0.672***	0.594***	0.372***	0.239***	0.317***	1	
	N	126	126	126	126	126	126	126	126	126	
incgini	coeff	0.094	0.056	-0.092	-0.067	0.013	0.024	-0.190	0.047	-0.193	1
	N	126	126	126	126	126	126	126	126	126	126
gcovedu	coeff	0.056	0.209***	0.103	0.409***	0.44***	0.643***	0.319***	0.376***	0.260***	0.054
	N	115	115	115	115	115	115	115	115	115	115
gcovlandp	coeff	0.013	0.002	0.095	-0.037	-0.066	0.461***	0.312***	0.20***	0.009	0.002
	N	115	115	115	115	115	115	115	115	115	115
gcovmyun	coeff	0.104	-0.096	0.07	-0.181***	-0.193***	0.365***	0.105	0.176***	-0.146	0.029
	N	115	115	115	115	115	115	115	115	115	115
gcovps	coeff	0.201***	0.035	0.031	0.2***	0.259***	0.515***	0.262***	0.337***	0.12	-0.039
	N	115	115	115	115	115	115	115	115	115	115
gcovchm	coeff	-0.004	-0.016	0.052	0.364***	0.406***	0.599***	0.375***	0.128	0.363***	-0.006
	N	115	115	115	115	115	115	115	115	115	115
gcovinc	coeff	0.122	0.034	-0.034	0.227***	0.323***	0.634***	0.149	0.275***	0.258***	0.398***
	N	115	115	115	115	115	115	115	115	115	115
gcovedu_r	coeff	-0.136	0.012	0.184	0.006	-0.106	0.112	0.342***	0.141	-0.183	-0.079
	N	78	78	78	78	78	78	78	78	78	78
gcovlandp_r	coeff	-0.098	-0.140	0.14	-0.199*	-0.219*	-0.091	0.425***	-0.023	-0.194*	-0.143
	N	78	78	78	78	78	78	78	78	78	78
gcovmyun_r	coeff	-0.066	-0.109	-0.061	-0.362***	-0.460***	-0.291***	0.256***	-0.268***	-0.449***	-0.055
	N	78	78	78	78	78	78	78	78	78	78
gcovps_r	coeff	-0.037	-0.029	-0.106	-0.103	-0.159	0.046	0.308***	-0.019	-0.214***	-0.182
	N	78	78	78	78	78	78	78	78	78	78
gcovchm_r	coeff	-0.084	0.062	0.163	0.144	0.094	0.113	0.394***	-0.133	0.031	-0.359***
	N	78	78	78	78	78	78	78	78	78	78
gcovinc_r	coeff	0.004	-0.041	0.126	-0.112	-0.176	0.121	0.307***	0.092	-0.129	0.103
	N	78	78	78	78	78	78	78	78	78	78

		gcovedu	gcovlandp	gcovmyun	gcovps	gcovchm	gcovinc	gcovedu_r	gcovlandp_r	gcovmyun_r	gcovps_r	gcovchm_r
s_pre97	coeff											
	N											
natres	coeff											
	N											
urban	coeff											
	N											
myun	coeff											
	N											
elf	coeff												
	N											
relpol	coeff												
	N											
newmig	coeff												
	N											
hdi96	coeff												
	N											
incgini	coeff												
	N											
gcovedu	coeff	1										
	N	115										
gcovlandp	coeff	0.385***										
	N	115										
gcovmyun	coeff	0.287***	0.442***	1								
	N	115	115	115								
gcovps	coeff	0.528***	0.389***	0.372***	1							
	N	115	115	115	115							
gcovchm	coeff	0.489***	0.470***	0.273***	0.477***	1						
	N	115	115	115	115	115						
gcovinc	coeff	0.630***	0.315***	0.262***	0.409***	0.508***	1					
	N	115	115	115	115	115						
gcovedu_r	coeff	0.298***	0.265***	0.088	0.212***	0.078	0.043	1				
	N	115	115	78	78	78	78	78				
gcovlandp_r	coeff	0.15	0.548***	0.357***	0.243**	0.184	0.04	0.266**	1			
	N	78	115	78	78	78	78	78	78			
gcovmyun_r	coeff	-0.092	0.322***	0.099	0.001	-0.124	-0.194***	0.382***	0.375***	1		
	N	78	115	78	78	78	78	78	78	78		
gcovps_r	coeff	0.147	0.329***	0.08	0.263***	0.136	-0.021	0.577***	0.327***	0.487***	1	
	N	126	115	78	78	78	78	78	78	78	78	
gcovchm_r	coeff	0.192***	0.297***	0.081	0.220***	0.294***	-0.016	0.133	0.289***	0.105	0.278***	1
	N	78	115	78	78	78	78	78	78	78	78	78
gcovinc_r	coeff	0.221***	0.310***	0.151	0.195***	0.049	0.121	0.666***	0.216*	0.363***	0.445***	0.084
	N	78	115	78	78	78	78	78	78	78	78	78

Note: *** indicates significance at 1% ** at 5%, * at 10% level, respectively.

Notes

1. Ethnic dominance is a binary dummy which equals 1 if one single ethnic group makes up 45 to 90 per cent of the total population and zero otherwise.
2. There is a clear inverted U-shaped relationship between polarization and fractionalization (Montalvo and Reynal-Querol, 2005).
3. The polarization index proposed by Esteban and Ray is a parametric version of the Gini coefficient of inequality between groups. See Chapter 5.
4. Mogues and Carter (2005) derive a socioeconomic polarization index which combines economic and noneconomic dimensions of an individual's identity.
5. To qualify as minorities at risk, groups must have experienced political or economic discrimination and have taken political action to protect their group's interests, implying that these groups are mostly mobilized with significant cohesion.
6. HI indicators are calculated for subdistricts rather than villages.
7. The transmigration programme was a geopolitical cornerstone of the New Order, which was officially terminated in 2000. It inflamed ethnic tensions. For example, in Western and Central Kalimantan thousands of ethnic Madurese were killed or forced to flee by the indigenous Dayak communities.
8. This excludes conflicts in Irian Jaya, East Timor and particularly in Aceh where, between 1998 and 2003, 4300 people, mostly civilians, were killed (Ross, 2003).
9. Nonetheless, the model controls for the fact that observations may not necessarily be independent within provinces. Corrected standard errors are calculated.
10. Data limitations prevented the construction of additional dimensions of political HIs such as employment in local government, police and army forces.
11. From the 2001 Human Development Report for Indonesia.
12. This is measured as, $ELF = 1 - \sum_{r=1}^{R} p_j^2$, where p_j is group j's population share. The equivalent measure for ethnoreligious groups was dropped from the analysis because of its high correlation (over 95 per cent) with the religious polarization variable.
13. The ETHPOL and RELPOL measures are based on the Reynal-Querol index.

$$RELPOL = 1 - \sum_{r=1}^{R} \left(\frac{0.5 - p_r}{0.5} \right)^2 p_j.$$

14. This simultaneity problem is for instance an issue in the study by Barron *et al.* (2004).
15. Survei Penduduk Antar Sensus.
16. At the time of survey the provinces of Banten and North Maluku were still part of West Java and Maluku, respectively.
17. Language here means mother tongue. When such information was unavailable, language spoken daily at home was used instead.
18. Strictly speaking the nonresponse rate is about 1 per cent. The remaining 11.5 per cent is made up of individuals who indicated Bahasa Indonesia (the national language) as their mother tongue or daily spoken language.
19. As noted above, separatist violence in Aceh, Irian Jaya and East Timor are excluded from these calculations.
20. Models with interaction terms between the HI indicators and religious polarization, income inequality and the Human Development Index were also estimated but results were not statistically significant at conventional levels and therefore results were not reported.

21. Ethnolinguistic polarization was never statistically significant and it was therefore excluded from the final specifications.
22. The impact of natural resource dependence on the probability of violence remained elusive even when alternative measures of the district's dependence on natural resources were used, such as the proportion of the district's 1998 real *per capita* GDP accounted for by oil and gas revenues.
23. This also prevents the relationship between the two HI variables and the dependent variable being inflated by the inclusion of ethnically and religiously homogenous districts.

7
Inequalities, the Political Environment and Civil Conflict: Evidence from 55 Developing Countries

*Gudrun Østby**

7.1 Introduction

This chapter addresses the interplay between socioeconomic and identity-related factors in civil conflict, guided by the concept of horizontal inequalities (HIs). In a series of case studies, Stewart (2002) found that various dimensions of HIs provoked some kind of conflict, ranging from a high level of criminality in Brazil to civil war in Uganda and Sri Lanka. In order to test whether these findings can be generalized beyond the particular case studies, there is a need for large-N investigations. Drawing on national survey data, Østby (2008) provided quantitative evidence that Stewart's findings hold when socioeconomic inequalities between ethnic groups are tested systematically across 36 developing countries. Moreover, I found similar effects for horizontal inequalities at the regional level with a larger sample (Østby, 2005).

An important issue that has not been systematically addressed to date is whether horizontal inequalities are especially conflict provoking under certain political conditions. There has been little systematic theorization of the role of political institutions (such as regime type and electoral system) in ameliorating (or exacerbating) the conflict potential of horizontal inequalities. This chapter examines the independent and interactive effects of socioeconomic horizontal inequalities and regime type, electoral system and

*I am indebted to Scott Gates, Håvard Hegre, Arnim Langer, Luca Mancini, Eric Neumayer, Frances Stewart, Håvard Strand, and Martha Reynal–Querol for many insightful comments on earlier versions of this chapter. Results, claims and remaining errors are solely my responsibility.

actual political exclusion of minority groups. I put forward specific hypotheses as to how the political environment interacts with socioeconomic horizontal inequalities. For instance, I expect that horizontal inequalities may be particularly explosive in democratic and semidemocratic regimes because the relatively deprived groups have both a strong motive and an opportunity for violent mobilization. In order to test these hypotheses, I conduct a large-N analysis of civil conflict in up to 55[1] developing countries in the period 1986–2003.

The chapter is organized as follows: Section 7.2 provides a theoretical framework for the relationship between horizontal inequalities and conflict. Section 7.3 discusses the possible impact of regime type, electoral system, and political exclusion of minority groups in influencing the nexus between socioeconomic horizontal inequalities and conflict. Section 7.4 presents the data and research design. Section 7.5 provides the results from the empirical tests, revealing that the positive effect of horizontal inequalities on conflict onset is influenced by regime type and electoral system. The last section concludes.

7.2 Horizontal inequalities and civil conflict

A shared cultural identity may be a powerful organizing principle for a group. First, it overcomes the collective action problem (Olson, 1965) whereby people are unable to cooperate because of mutual suspicions. However, there is reason to believe that a shared identity is not a sufficient factor to produce conflict, but that some well-defined grievances are required for identity-based conflict (Murshed and Gates, 2005).

Given that groups are the central units in conflicts, the question then is how they are mobilized. Different identity bases have been the source of group differentiation and mobilization: for example, in central Africa, ethnicity has been the major basis of group categorization; while in Central America, group identification and organization has developed along social class lines, with some overlapping ethnic dimensions; and in the Balkans and Northern Ireland, religion has been the primary feature of categorization. However, regional location is also a source of group differentiation, which often coincides with ethnic or linguistic cleavages, as for example in Uganda (Minority Rights Group International, 1997) and Zambia (Posner, 2004a). The question of regional, or spatial, inequality has begun to attract significant interest among scholars and policy makers. In most developing countries, there is a sense that regional inequalities within countries in economic activities and social indicators are rising (Kanbur and Venables, 2005). Moreover, data on group inequalities is far more accessible for regional than ethnic or religious groups, since questions concerning ethnic affiliation are often not included in national surveys and censuses. Regional groups may also be important in their own right: in a natural field experiment among the Chewa and Tumbuka groups in Zambia, Posner (2004a: 543) found that regional cohesion seemed to be stronger than the claims of ethnic affiliation.[2]

Why should horizontal inequalities be relevant for conflict? The most obvious answer relates to the effect of collective grievances. Members of disadvantaged groups are likely to feel frustration and antagonism, especially when their relative deprivation is the result of actual exploitation and discrimination, which is apparently often the case (for example in Senegal and Uganda). Despite the intuitive logic of this argument, one cannot assume that it is only resentment on the part of the disadvantaged groups that may cause political instability. When people in rich regions perceive the central government's policies as unfair and authoritarian, they may see greater autonomy, or even secession, as a better alternative than the status quo. As Aristotle said, 'Inferiors revolt in order that they may be equal, and equals that they may be superior' (quoted in Sigelman and Simpson, 1977: 106). In line with this logic, the initiative for conflict may come from the richest and most privileged groups as well as the poorest and most deprived groups. For example, privileged groups that are geographically concentrated may demand independence, such as the Basques in Spain or the Biafrans in Nigeria in the 1960s. According to Tadjoeddin (2003) this has occured in Indonesia, where some conflicts stem from confrontations between the central authorities and provinces which are richer in terms of natural resources (although poorer in terms of welfare indicators) whose people are upset by the centre's use of their region's wealth to subsidize poorer regions.

Both types of reactions point to the conclusion that a society with large horizontal inequalities has a higher risk of civil war than societies without such inequalities. While it is easier to maintain group cohesiveness and motivation for rebellion if the elite can draw on ethnic, religious, or regional differences to construct a well-defined identity group with a common enemy, what may matter more than the identity differences which form the basis for the cleavage is whether the groups are systematically different in terms of economic and social welfare. This leads to my first hypothesis:

> H1: *Countries with severe socioeconomic horizontal inequalities are particularly likely to experience civil conflict.*

7.3 Mediating effects of the political environment on the horizontal inequality–conflict nexus

A plausible, but so far unexplored, issue is whether political institutions and practice can affect the degree to which horizontal inequalities can translate into conflict propensity. Consequently, this chapter aims to investigate how the political environment in a country may influence the relationship between horizontal inequalities and civil conflict onset.

7.3.1 The impact of regime type

According to Rothchild (1983: 172), '[G]roup disparities and unequal exchange are, in and of themselves, insufficient to explain the course of interethnic conflict.' In line with this, Stewart (2000: 11) argues that the sheer existence of objective horizontal inequalities may not spur conflict 'if there is a strong state which suppresses it or if ideological elements are such that the inequalities are not widely perceived.' If this is the case, the emergence of violent group mobilization in countries with sharp horizontal inequalities may depend on the characteristics of the political regime.

The relationship between regime type and civil conflict has been widely studied. Hegre *et al.* (2001) have demonstrated empirically an inversed U-shaped relation between the level of democracy and the incidence of civil war over time, concluding that semidemocracies are indeed the most prone to civil strife. At both extremes, in autocracies and democracies, civil wars are rare – and even rarer under a democracy than under an autocracy. However, in a semidemocracy, they argue, the combination of both grievances and the opportunity to rebel is at its peak. In a democracy, grievances are generally less common and more moderate while there are plenty of possibilities to express these grievances and to secure change through channels other than violence. In an autocracy, on the other hand, grievances are likely to be great and frequent but state repression may prevent them from being openly expressed.

Regime characteristics may provide the incentives for deprived groups to riot against the government, as autocratic regimes are likely to have a very restricted recruitment process for both political and economic positions (Goldstone, 2001). In general, autocracies have a tendency to exacerbate inequality (Rogowski and MacRae, 2004). Consequently, one could reason that when horizontal inequalities are pervasive, autocracies are likely to be more at risk of conflict than democracies. This chapter, however, turns this reasoning upside down arguing rather that it is democratic regimes that suffer from the most serious effects of horizontal inequalities. The rationale for this is elaborated below.

The theory of democratic peace makes a heroic assumption: that democracies are actually responsive and do address group grievances. Intuitively, this makes perfect sense. Democracies are by definition expected to be more responsive than autocracies, if for no other reason than that they usually entertain a free press, which makes it harder to ignore petitions from below, and because governments can be voted out. However, the fact that it is more responsive than an ideal autocracy is not sufficient reason to argue that a democracy is able to avoid all potential conflicts. If, for various reasons, a democracy is unable to satisfy basic needs universally and ensure a certain level of group equity, a whole set of new dynamics may appear. The opportunity to rebel is still present, but it is now combined with the presence of strong group grievances, or motives. In other words, in a country with both a suppressive regime *and* persistent horizontal inequalities, there will be very little opportunity to mobilize, although grievances among the disadvantaged groups are likely to be very strong. In a democracy with sharp horizontal inequalities, on the other hand, opportunities and grievances are both present. A democracy, however, is expected to host moderate inequalities and consequently less severe grievances between identity groups. This is due to the existence of several peaceful channels through which relatively deprived groups may express their potential grievances and try to influence the process of redistribution through democratic means. However, if these efforts do not reduce the gap between the expected and actual outcomes for the relatively disadvantaged groups, it may cause frustration and facilitate the mobilization of people to engage in conflict. This argument was originally expressed by Davies (1962) as the J-curve of need satisfaction and revolution. In line with this reasoning one should expect the most conflict-prone societies to be democracies with sharp horizontal inequalities. Hence, I propose the following hypothesis:

H2: *The conflict potential of socioeconomic horizontal inequalities is stronger for democracies and semidemocracies than for autocracies.*

By 'semidemocracies' I refer to regimes which are neither fully democratic nor fully autocratic. Such regimes are often also transitional polities. Political change is complicated, and democratization can be marked by increased risk of internal conflict (Hegre *et al.*, 2001). For example, voting may threaten the power of particular groups, which may use violence during elections or immediately post election. This may be so because, while willing to accept democratic institutions in principle, these groups may not be willing to accept the transfer of power that is involved. In line with this, Horowitz (1993) found that political change is particularly likely to be accompanied by civil conflict in countries with ethnic minorities.

Hegre *et al.* (2001: 33) conclude that 'intermediate regimes', or semidemocracies, are most prone to civil war, even when they have had time to stabilize from a regime change. However, the authors also note that in order to assess whether intermediate regime or regime transition (or both) is significant, one needs to control for each factor. Following this advice, I control for the time since regime change when testing H2.

7.3.2   The impact of electoral system

Political inclusion of minority groups is necessary to avoid the monopolization of political power by one ethnic group or another. Inclusion, however, does not follow automatically from all forms of democratic institutions (Rogowski and MacRae, 2004). Reynal-Querol (2002a, b) shows that what matters for conflict is not simply the degree of political freedom (or democracy), but rather the combination of this and the system of representation of the voters. Specifically, she found that proportional voting systems have a lower risk of conflict than majoritarian systems. Her explanation is that the opportunity cost of rebellion is higher under proportional systems because such systems are likely to be more inclusive and hence curb grievances. Reynal-Querol's results corroborate Binningsbø (2005), who in a large-N study of 118 post-conflict societies between 1985 and 2002 found that power-sharing institutions as recommended by Lijphart (for example, 1999) were positively associated with lasting peace. Despite such findings, Lijphart's theory about consociational democracy in plural societies has also met scepticism. For example, van den Berghe (2002) argues that the institutional model of consociational democracy mostly benefits the ruling elites.[3] Furthermore, Horowitz (1985) has criticized Lijphart on the grounds that the heterogeneous countries in Europe which form the basis of Lijphart's theory are not sufficiently comparable to deeply divided countries in Africa and Asia. In fact, Horowitz argues that a proportional representation system does not necessarily create compromise or moderate attitudes, but may actually fuel such differences, as it can encourage ethnic or religious political parties. Lebanon would be a good example of this.

Based on case studies of Kenya, Uganda, and Sri Lanka, Stewart and O'Sullivan (1999) argue that democratic institutions are not sufficient to prevent conflict in strongly divided societies, and that redesigning democratic institutions in order to reduce conflict can fail, or even accentuate conflict, as in Sri Lanka. They conclude that in order to prevent conflict there is a need for inclusive government – economically as well as politically. This entails not only political participation by all major groups, but also a spread of economic benefits throughout society.

In countries with strong socioeconomic horizontal inequalities but inclusive electoral systems, Stewart and O'Sullivan (1999) note that political parties and leaders tend to accentuate ethnic divisions in order to gain support from their kinsmen. This in turn can provoke violence. Hence, I expect that the levels of frustration among those who are relatively deprived economically will be particularly high in democracies with highly inclusive electoral systems which, despite this institutional arrangement, fail to even out, or at least reduce, systematic socioeconomic inequalities between identity groups:

H3: *The conflict potential of socioeconomic horizontal inequalities increases with more inclusive electoral systems.*

7.3.3 The impact of political exclusion of minorities

Regime type and formal political institutions, such as the electoral system, do not necessarily reflect the distributional politics in a society.[4] There are examples of democratic countries with rather inclusive electoral systems which nonetheless restrict the political participation of certain minority groups, notably several Latin American countries. Stewart (2000) holds that countries in which horizontal inequalities are consistent across different dimensions of inequality have a greater risk of conflict than countries in which horizontal inequalities are nonexistent or inconsistent. This implies that one can expect particularly negative consequences where horizontal inequalities are inconsistent across dimensions (for example, where one group is favoured in terms of economic assets, but relatively deprived concerning access to the political system).

Langer (2005) further develops this argument in a study of violent group mobilization and conflict in Côte d'Ivoire. He focuses on socioeconomic horizontal inequalities at the mass level and political horizontal inequalities at the elite level, arguing that the simultaneous presence of these phenomena can be especially explosive for two reasons: first, in such situations the excluded political elites have strong incentives to mobilize their supporters for violent conflict along group lines, and second, with widespread socioeconomic inequalities, the elites are likely to gain support among their ethnic constituencies fairly easily. According to Langer (2005), the absence of political horizontal inequalities among the elites reduces the risk of violent group mobilization because group leaders hence lack the incentives to mobilize their constituents for violent conflict. My final hypothesis tests Langer's argument with a cross-national sample:

H4: *The conflict potential of socioeconomic horizontal inequalities increases with the level of political exclusion of minority groups in a country.*

7.4 Data and research design

A statistical analysis of onsets of civil conflicts in a sample of developing countries serves as the empirical test of the hypotheses outlined. I include all developing countries where at least one Demographic and Health Survey (DHS) was conducted from 1986 to 2003, and for which the relevant data were available. This amounts to 123 national surveys in 61 countries. The total number of observations in the dataset adds up to 1160 country years. However, when consecutive years of conflict are removed from the analysis, a maximum of 806 country years remains. Appendix 7A, Table 7A.1 provides summary statistics of all the variables used in the analyses.

7.4.1 The dependent variable: Conflict onset

The conflict data is derived from the Uppsala/PRIO Armed Conflict Dataset (ACD), which includes every armed conflict between a state government and an organized opposition group that caused at least 25 battle-related deaths per year (Gleditsch *et al.*, 2002). My definition of conflict applies the 'two-year rule' (see, for example, Buhaug and Gates, 2002): if a conflict falls below the casualty threshold for at least two consecutive calendar years, the next observation is coded as a separate onset. I merge subconflicts that only differ in type (internal vs. internationalized internal conflict), and censor consecutive years of conflict.

7.4.2   Core variables: Horizontal inequalities and political environment

The DHS project provides a rich set of large, representative surveys with nearly identical questionnaires, presenting an excellent opportunity for generating objective measures of inequalities across identity groups.[5] However, a challenge is that the DHS generally lack information on income or consumption expenditures. I overcome this by using two indicators of socioeconomic welfare to calculate the inequality measures and evaluate the hypotheses: a household asset index and a variable measuring the years of education for each respondent.[6]

The household asset index was generated by using dummies for whether or not each household has electricity, a radio, a television, a refrigerator, a bicycle, a motorcycle, and/or a car. The second indicator, schooling inequality, uses the years of education completed.

Horizontal inequalities in household assets and educational level are measured by three different group identifiers: ethnicity, religion, and region of residence. First, I calculate the socioeconomic divisions (HIs) between the two largest ethnic groups in each country. Secondly, I do the same for the two largest religious groups.[7] Finally, I examine HI as ratios of welfare scores between the region in which the capital is located and the rest of the country. This measure is calculated on the basis of the formula introduced by Østby (2008):

$$HI = 1 - \exp\left[-\left|\ln\left(\sum_{i=1}^{M} \frac{A_{i1}/A_{i2}}{M}\right)\right|\right]$$ (7.1)

where M is the maximum number of household assets; A_1 refers to mean asset score of group 1 (the capital region) and A_2 is the corresponding mean score of group 2 (the rest of the country). This provides a continuous variable potentially ranging from 0 (the lowest level of asset inequality between capital region and the rest of the country) to 1 (the highest level of such inequality). The measure of educational inequality is generated along the same lines. For countries with multiple surveys, I interpolate values for intervening years and copy the value from the survey nearest in time for previous and subsequent years within the period 1986–2003 in order to increase the sample size. In countries with only one survey, I use that value for all years within the period. This could imply a problem of endogeneity (that is, HI could result from former conflict instead of vice versa), and it would, of course, be preferable to have yearly data on group inequalities for each country. However, as stated earlier, group inequalities tend to be quite stable

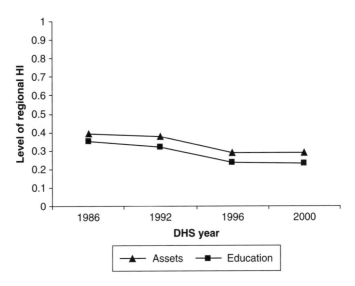

Figure 7.1 Regional horizontal inequalities in Peru, various years
Source: Author's calculation based on DHS.

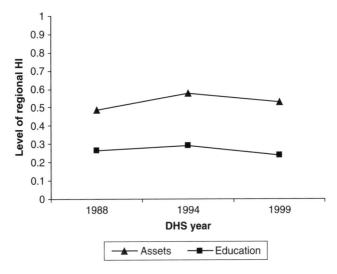

Figure 7.2 Regional horizontal inequalities in Zimbabwe, various years
Source: Author's calculation based on DHS.

over time, which is also evident from the data for some of the countries which have had several surveys during the period 1986–2003. Figures 7.1 and 7.2 depict the level of inequality in terms of average household assets and years of education for the capital region and the rest of the country in Peru and Zimbabwe, respectively, for various survey years. In both countries, the level of inequality has remained relatively stable over the entire period.

To measure political regime type, I use data on regime type from the Polity IV data (Marshall and Jaggers, 2003). Like Jaggers and Gurr (1995), I compute one single regime indicator, subtracting the score of autocracy from that of democracy, ranging from –10 (most autocratic) to 10 (most democratic). In order to test the curvilinear relationship between regime type and civil conflict, I include a squared term for regime type. Finally, to assess whether horizontal inequalities are more dangerous in certain regime types, I split the polity term into three categories: democracies (6 to 10), semidemocracies (–5 to 5), and autocracies (–10 to –6), following Ellingsen (2000) and others. I include the dummies for semidemocracies and autocracies in the analysis, with democracies as the reference category.

In order to test my hypotheses with an alternative operationalization of regime type, I also include the term 'Scalar Index of Polities' (SIP) proposed by Gates *et al.* (2006). This measure is the average of the scores on three dimensions. The first dimension is the regulation of Executive Recruitment, based on three indicators from the Polity IV dataset: 'Regulation of Chief Executive Recruitment', 'Competitiveness of Executive Recruitment', and 'Openness of Executive Recruitment'. The second dimension characterizes the constraints on the executive and is based on a single indicator 'Decision Constraints on the Chief Executive' from Polity IV. The third dimension concerns political participation, and is based on a slightly modified version of the Polity Participation index from Vanhanen's (2000) Polyarchy dataset. The SIP measure ranges from 0 to 1. Finally, in order to test H2, I include interaction terms multiplying regime type and regional HIs.

As stated earlier, semidemocracies are found to be the most conflict-prone (Ellingsen, 2000; Hegre *et al.*, 2001). This category includes both regimes in transition and institutionally inconsistent regimes. In order to control for whether transitions might make up parts of this relationship as opposed to institutionally inconsistent regimes, as suggested by Hegre *et al.* (2001), I introduce a variable measuring the time since regime transition when evaluating H2. Polity IV includes a variable which measures regime durability (that is, years since regime transition) as a function of the number of years since the most recent regime change, or the end of transition period, defined by the lack of stable political institutions (denoted by a standardized authority score). Following Hegre *et al.* (2001), I then code Proximity of Regime Transition as $2^{(-\text{ years since regime transition}/X)}$. I chose 1 as the value of X, which assumes that the impact of a regime transition on the probability of domestic-armed conflict is initially high and then falls at a constant rate with a half-life of one year.

A term measuring the inclusiveness of electoral systems is constructed on the basis of data from Golder (2005). I basically adopt the idea presented in Reynal-Querol (2002a, b), constructing an ordinal variable ranging four dummies with respect to electoral inclusiveness. However, I base my measure on Golder's definition of the electoral system followed in the assembly and type of the executive: The variable takes the value '0' if the system is not free (that is, if it has a Polity score of −6 or less or is coded as an autocracy by Golder (2005)), '1' if it has a majoritarian system, '2' if it has a mixed system, and '3' if it has a proportional system. As noted by Reynal-Querol (2002a: 45), the election of a president is by definition by majority rule, and what can differ is the voting rule followed for electing the assembly. Hence, presidential systems which use a proportional or mixed voting rule in the election of the assembly are coded as '2' in my variable for inclusive electoral system. Otherwise, they are coded as '1'. Since the codings of electoral and institutional systems are from the end of each year, the variable is lagged one year to help determine causality. About 15 per cent of observations are missing, most due to the fact that the voting data only go to 2000 (or 2001 when lagged). In order to test whether electoral inclusiveness influences the relationship between HI and civil conflict, I also include an interaction term multiplying electoral inclusiveness and regional HIs.

I also include a term for political exclusion of minority groups in a given year, drawing on the Discrimination Dataset of the Minorities at Risk (MAR) Project (Davenport, 2003), The variable POLDIS was originally coded for each minority group as an ordinal variable ranging from 0 (no discrimination) to 4 (exclusion/repressive policy: public policies substantially restrict the group's political participation by comparison with other groups). Aggregating this information to the country level, I multiply the discrimination index with the population share of the minority discriminated against. In case of several minorities, the sum of all population-weighted discrimination indices is taken.[8] For my sample, the new continuous variable ranges from 0 (for example, Tanzania, various years) to 3.56 (Rwanda, 1994). I also include interaction terms multiplying the political exclusion and regional HIs.

7.4.3   Control variables and statistical model

While I do not adhere to Achen's (2002) 'Rule of Three', which states that every analysis with more than three variables on the right-hand side will invariably be invalidated by serious problems of multicollinearity, I do aim to keep the control variables to a minimum, especially given the limited sample size under study.

I include the three core variables which are almost always included in models of civil war onset: the natural log of population, the natural log of per capita GDP, and the time since the last conflict (Hegre and Sambanis, 2006). Data on population size stem from the WDI (World Bank, 2004). The variable is interpolated and log-transformed. To proxy economic development, I use log-transformed GDP *per capita* measured in constant 1995 US$, also from the WDI (ibid.). The variable is lagged by one year.

As suggested by Beck *et al.* (1998), I control for temporal dependence through a variable measuring time since the last conflict and three cubic splines that approximate the discrete time hazard rates for conflict. Time since the last conflict counts the number of whole years since the end of the last conflict (peaceyears). The statistical tests were conducted using STATA, Version 8.2 (StataCorp., 2003), and all models were estimated by logit regressions with robust standard errors clustered by countries.

7.5 Results

The findings from the empirical tests of the hypotheses are presented in Tables 7.1–7.4. All models include the base variables: the terms for population size, GDP *per capita*, and controls for conflict history (peaceyears and cubic splines). To these I add my various terms for horizontal inequalities and interactions of these with the terms for political institutions in order to evaluate Hypotheses 1–4.

7.5.1 Do horizontal inequalities matter for conflict across different group identifiers?

Models 1–6 in Table 7.1 report the effects of socioeconomic horizontal inequalities (measured in terms of household assets and education years) with regard to conflict onset. I test the impact of HIs between ethnic, religious, and regional groups respectively. For the control variables, the results are inconsistent. I fail to find the positive relationship between population size and conflict reported by most other studies of civil war (see, for example, Collier and Hoeffler, 2004; Fearon and Laitin, 2003). In Model 1 the effect is in fact negative at the 10 per cent level, but in Model 2 the effect drops below significance. In Models 3–6 the effect is positive but never reaches significance. Similarly, the term for GDP yields inconclusive results, and is only negative and significant in Models 1 and 2, while the sign switches in the rest of the models. However, these results are perhaps not so surprising, given that the sample is restricted to low- and medium-income countries.[9] Finally, the term for years of peace never reaches significance in any model, but that may be due to the short time period (1986–2003).[10]

In contrast to the control variables, the HI terms reveal some interesting results. My first hypothesis (H1), assuming a higher risk of conflict for countries with severe socioeconomic horizontal inequalities, is quite well supported in Table 7.1. All the terms show positive significant effects. Models 1 and 2 report the effects of HIs between the two largest ethnic groups in a country, Models 3 and 4 report the effects of HIs between the two largest religious groups in each country, and Models 5 and 6 report the effects of HIs between the capital region and the rest of the country. The reason for the

Table 7.1 Logit regression of civil war onset and horizontal inequalities, 1986–2003

	Model 1 (Ethnic gr.)	Model 2 (Ethnic gr.)	Model 3 (Rel. gr.)	Model 4 (Rel gr.)	Model 5 (Regions)	Model 6 (Regions)
HI_Asset (Ethnic gr.)	3.39* (1.82)					
HI_Educ. (Ethnic gr.)		1.96** (2.02)				
HI_Asset (Religious gr.)			3.67** (2.52)			
HI_Educ. (Religious gr.)				1.84** (2.51)		
HI_Asset (Regions)					2.70*** (3.15)	
HI_Educ. (Regions)						2.18*** (3.04)
Population (ln)	-0.59* (-1.74)	-0.46 (-1.50)	0.053 (0.18)	0.13 (0.43)	0.22 (0.78)	0.17 (0.63)
GDP per capita $(\ln)_{t-1}$	-0.81** (-2.27)	-0.67* (-1.83)	0.14 (0.41)	0.28 (0.78)	0.027 (0.10)	0.051 (0.20)
Peaceyears	0.42 (1.10)	0.39 (1.15)	-0.012 (-0.05)	0.0057 (0.02)	-0.069 (-0.37)	-0.11 (-0.58)
Constant	11.33* (1.71)	8.37 (1.32)	-4.82 (-0.74)	-7.11 (-1.04)	-7.26 (-1.25)	-6.37 (-1.21)
LL	-73.57	-73.69	-93.39	-93.34	-136.88	-137.13
Pseudo R^2	0.112	0.110	0.088	0.089	0.061	0.059
# Conflicts	20	20	25	25	36	36
# Countries	35	35	41	41	55	55
N	473	473	566	566	777	777

Note: Logit regression coefficients, z-values are in parentheses. Estimates for three natural cubic splines not shown in table. *$p < 0.10$; **$p \leq 0.05$; ***$p \leq 0.01$.

differences in N is the different availability of data. All the DHS include questions regarding regional affiliation, but several surveys exclude questions about ethnic and religious affiliations.

As expected, the term for horizontal asset inequality between ethnic groups shows a positive significant effect in Model 1. Although only significant at the 10 per cent level, the marginal effect is quite strong. For a country with mean values on all the explanatory factors, the probability of onset of civil conflict in any given year is 2.3 per cent. If we increase the level of horizontal asset inequality to the 95th percentile while maintaining the other variables at their mean, the probability of a conflict onset increases to 6.1 per cent.[11] The effect for educational HI between ethnic groups (Model 2) is also positive, with the probability of conflict increasing to 5.4 per cent. Focusing on HIs between religious rather than ethnic groups in Model 3 and 4, the effects seem quite similar.[12] Models 5 and 6 both provide strong support for H1, showing that interregional horizontal inequalities increase the risk of conflict both with regard to assets and education level. Both coefficients are positive at the 1 per cent significance level, and their effects are very similar: If we increase the level of inter-regional HI to the 95th percentile while maintaining the other variables at their mean, the probability of conflict increases from about 3.8 per cent to 9.5 per cent.[13] This finding corresponds well to related investigations, such as Murshed and Gates (2005), who find that Nepalese districts with severe gaps relative to Kathmandu in terms of schooling are associated with higher conflict intensity.

The data material presented here might be too restricted to conclude convincingly that regional inequalities matter more for conflict than HIs between ethnic or religious groups. However, since there are more data for regional HIs than ethnic or religious HIs, I conduct the rest of the analyses only with the former terms in order to maximize the size of the sample (and number of conflicts) when testing the effects of interactions with the institutional variables. Ideally, we should know which groups are salient with regard to welfare distribution and conflict potential in each society (Stewart, 2000). Some studies measure inequalities between ethnic groups (Østby, 2008), some focus on inequalities between religious groups (Brown, 2005c), while others investigate inequalities between regions (Østby, 2005). One solution could be to calculate group inequalities between all these groups and then simply investigate the conflict potential of the most severe variants of intergroup inequalities in each country. However, there are potential problems with such an approach as well. First of all the reason some states choose to exclude information about ethnicity and religion could be because these group factors may be particularly explosive (see Strand and Urdal, 2005), and hence the missing information on horizontal inequalities between these groups could very well be biased. Nevertheless, I calculated such terms of maximum HIs for both asset and educational inequality and, among the three different group-identifiers, HIs between regions is the term that correlates most strongly with the term for maximum HIs: $r = 0.93$ for asset HI and $r = 0.79$ for educational HI. The corresponding values for ethnic HIs are 0.63 and 0.25, and for religious HIs, 0.51 and 0.26.

7.5.2   Are horizontal inequalities more likely to lead to conflict in democracies?

Can we expect the effect of horizontal inequalities to be contingent on regime type as indicated by H2? This hypothesis is tested in Table 7.2. First of all, the effect of regional asset HI seems to be independent of regime type (Model 7). The positive effect is robust to the inclusion of the dummies for autocracy and semidemocracy, but there is no significant interaction effect with either of the terms. However, the hypothesis is supported in Models 9–12, which include the interaction terms of regional educational HI and the various regime variables. First of all, the positive effect of horizontal educational inequality is significantly weaker for autocracies than for democracies and semidemocracies (Model 9). Although not significantly different from each other, the effect also seems to be weaker in semidemocracies than in fully fledged democracies. In sum, horizontal inequalities seem to be less likely to cause conflict in autocracies.

Figure 7.3 visualizes the association between interregional educational inequality and the estimated probability of conflict onset for the three different regime types: democracies (solid line), semidemocracies (dashed line) and autocracies (thin line). The figure shows that for relatively low levels of horizontal inequalities (0–0.3) the risk of conflict seems to be lowest for the democracies and highest for the autocracies. However, with increasing levels of horizontal educational inequality the picture changes quite dramatically: A democracy with strong horizontal educational inequality between regions (95th percentile = 0.8) is in fact about twice as likely (approximately 14 per cent) to face a conflict onset as an autocracy with the same level of HI (approximately 7 per cent).[14] In a semidemocracy with severe HIs, the risk of conflict is about 11 per cent, but this is not significantly different from democracies. This finding corroborates Acemoglu and Robinson (2006), who argue that the risk of conflict is likely to be high if civil society is well developed, inequality is substantial and the people find it easy to organize.

The relationships between HIs, regime type, and conflict onset also hold when I include the term for proximity to regime change in Model 10, with the coefficients remaining largely similar. However, as the model demonstrates, proximity to regime change seems to be strongly and positively associated with conflict for the developing countries in my sample.[15]

Furthermore, H2 gains further support in Models 11 and 12 where I include the two different continuous regime measures, Polity and SIP. The more democratic the regime, the stronger the positive effect of horizontal inequalities for conflict onset.

Table 7.2 Logit regression of civil war onset, horizontal inequalities and regime type, 1986–2003

	Model 7	Model 8	Model 9	Model 10	Model 11	Model 12
HI_Asset (Regions)	3.11**					
	(2.35)					
HI_Educ. (Regions)		2.046***	2.50***	2.59***	2.64***	2.89***
		(2.98)	(2.82)	(2.82)	(3.19)	(2.84)
Semidemocracy $_{t-1}$ (ref.c.: Democracy)	0.79	0.67	0.89	0.66		
	(1.34)	(1.28)	(1.46)	(1.13)		
Autocracy $_{t-1}$ (ref.c.: Democracy)	0.65	0.73	1.07	1.01		
	(0.94)	(1.20)	(1.63)	(1.53)		
HI_Asset*Semidem	−1.36					
	(−0.43)					
HI_Asset*Autocracy	−0.89					
	(−0.27)					
HI_Educ.*Semidem			−2.53	−1.89		
			(−1.31)	(−1.04)		
HI_Educ.*Autocracy			−4.11**	−4.56**		
			(−1.99)	(−2.06)		
Polity $_{t-1}$					−0.038	
					(−1.06)	
HI_Educ.*Polity					0.27**	
					(2.47)	
SIP $_{t-1}$						−1.25
						(−1.44)
HI_Educ.*SIP						6.70**
						(2.26)
Proximity of Transition				1.45***		
				(3.30)		
Population (ln)	0.26	0.16	0.14	0.20	0.17	0.21
	(0.83)	(0.62)	(0.52)	(0.81)	(0.63)	(0.73)
GDP pcr capita (ln)$_{t-1}$	0.044	0.037	0.19	0.23	0.20	0.29
	(0.16)	(0.14)	(0.69)	(0.86)	(0.71)	(0.96)
Peaceyears	−0.068	−0.11	−0.14	−0.060	−0.15	−0.044
	(−0.37)	(−0.62)	(−0.79)	(−0.35)	(−0.89)	(−0.24)
Constant	−7.075	−6.54	−6.24	−8.14*	−6.80	−8.20
	(−1.22)	(−1.30)	(−1.27)	(−1.76)	(−1.26)	(−1.44)
LL	−130.63	−131.56	−129.59	−125.10	−130.34	−113.85
Pseudo R²	0.077	0.070	0.084	0.116	0.079	0.085
# Conflicts	35	35	35	35	35	31
# Countries	55	55	55	55	55	53
N	752	752	752	752	752	648

Note: Logit regression coefficients, z-values are in parentheses. Estimates for three natural cubic splines not shown in table. *$p < 0.10$; **$p \leq 0.05$; ***$p \leq 0.01$.

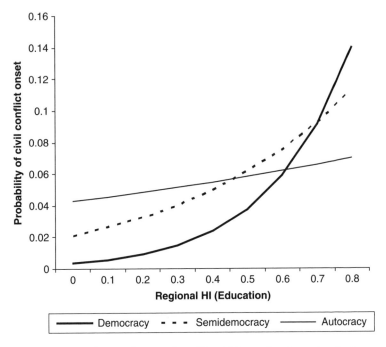

Figure 7.3   Horizontal inequalities and conflict risk by regime type, developing countries, 1986–2003

Note: Figure 7.3 is generated on the basis of Model 9 in Table 7.2.

7.5.3   Is the horizontal inequality–conflict nexus affected by the electoral system?

Are certain unequal democracies more at risk of conflict than others? In Models 13–16 in Table 7.3, I test the interaction effects of socioeconomic inequalities between regions and electoral inclusiveness. Again, both the terms for HI remain strongly positively significant regardless of the inclusion of the term for electoral inclusiveness. The single effect of the latter is negative, indicating that conflict risk decreases with increased electoral inclusiveness, but this effect is not significant even at the 10 per cent level. Although with a positive sign, the interaction effect of asset HI and electoral inclusiveness is not significant, as shown in Model 13. However, the effect of educational HIs is positively affected with increased electoral inclusiveness (Model 15). This also holds when I control for political regime type. Hence, the results in Table 7.3 partly support H3, which stated that the conflict potential of HIs actually increases with more inclusive electoral systems.

Table 7.3 Logit regression of civil war onset, horizontal inequalities and electoral system, 1986–2003

	Model 13	Model 14	Model 15	Model 16
HI_Asset (Regions)	3.34**			
	(2.43)			
HI_Educ. (Regions)		1.98**	2.90***	2.98***
		(2.51)	(2.78)	(3.13)
Inclusive Electoral Syst.	–0.51	–0.46	–0.75**	–1.30***
(IES) $_{t-1}$	(–1.58)	(–1.27)	(–2.02)	(–2.72)
HI Asset*IES	1.40			
	(0.81)			
HI_Educ*IES			2.68*	2.78*
			(1.85)	(1.72)
Polity $_{t-1}$				0.066
				(1.25)
Polity2 $_{t-1}$				0.0091
				(1.19)
Population (ln)	0.21	0.12	0.12	0.12
	(0.67)	(0.43)	(0.42)	(0.40)
GDP per capita (ln) $_{t-1}$	0.18	0.10	0.17	0.12
	(0.65)	(0.40)	(0.70)	(0.44)
Peaceyears	0.021	–0.0092	–0.017	–0.056
	(0.11)	(–0.05)	(–0.09)	(–0.31)
Constant	–7.50	–5.67	–6.035	–5.90
	(–1.22)	(–1.05)	(–1.12)	(–1.08)
LL	–120.58	–122.31	–120.10	–114.91
Pseudo R^2	0.080	0.067	0.084	0.096
# Conflicts	33	33	33	32
# Countries	53	53	53	53
N	661	661	661	640

Note: Logit regression coefficients, z-values are in parentheses. Estimates for three natural cubic splines not shown in table. *$p < 0.10$; **$p \leq 0.05$; ***$p \leq 0.01$.

7.5.4 Socioeconomic horizontal inequality and political exclusion – A dangerous mix?

Finally, I set out to test Langer's (2005) argument that the simultaneous presence of socioeconomic horizontal inequalities between the masses and political exclusion (implying horizontal inequalities among the elites) can be especially explosive. In Table 7.4, I include interaction terms between the two kinds of interregional HI in order to investigate whether the effect of socioeconomic horizontal inequalities increases with higher levels of political exclusion of minority group elites.

Table 7.4 reveals that the term for political exclusion never has a separate significant effect, and the sign is even negative. However, the variable has a

Table 7.4 Logit regression of civil war onset, horizontal inequalities and political exclusion, 1986–2003

	Model 17	Model 18	Model 19	Model 20
HI_Asset (Regions)	3.78**	4.37**		
	(2.19)	(2.08)		
HI_Educ. (Regions)			2.75**	2.91**
			(2.54)	(2.27)
Political Exclusion $_{t-1}$	–0.088	–0.79	–0.050	–0.53
	(–0.24)	(–1.59)	(–0.11)	(–0.72)
HI_Asset*Pol_Excl		3.50***		
		(2.59)		
HI_Educ.*Pol_Excl				2.48
				(1.51)
Population (ln)	0.59	0.68	0.436	0.48
	(1.56)	(1.95)	(1.34)	(1.48)
GDP per capita (ln)$_{t-1}$	0.11	0.12	–0.027	–0.087
	(0.29)	(0.29)	(–0.08)	(–0.28)
Peaceyears	0.083	0.15	0.032	0.083
	(0.43)	(0.73)	(0.14)	(0.38)
Constant	–14.56*	–15.20**	–10.63	–10.031
	(–1.79)	(–2.12)	(–1.60)	(–1.61)
LL	–88.87	–86.38	–88.78	–87.24
Pseudo R^2	0.098	0.123	0.099	0.114
# Conflicts	24	24	24	24
# Countries	41	41	41	41
N	547	547	547	547

Note: Logit regression coefficients, z-values are in parentheses. Estimates for three natural cubic splines not shown in table. $*p < 0.10$; $**p \leq 0.05$; $***p \leq 0.01$.

very strong impact on the relationship between interregional asset inequality and conflict, as demonstrated by the interaction term regional asset HI and political exclusion in Model 18. This relationship is graphed in Figure 7.4.

The figure shows that the effect of regional asset HI is positive for all levels of political exclusion, but drastically increases with severe political exclusion. The peak for the two curves is extremely high – indicating that the risk of a conflict onset in a given year is close to 24 per cent. However, few observations are found within this range of the variables. An example is Burundi in the 1990s, with the values 2.55 on political exclusion and 0.74 on interregional asset inequality.

The interaction term for political exclusion and regional educational HI (Model 20) is also strongly positive, but not significantly so. In sum, Table 7.4 provides some empirical support for H4. However, it should be noted that the measure for political exclusion is rather crude. It could be worth retesting the hypothesis with disaggregated data at the subnational level.

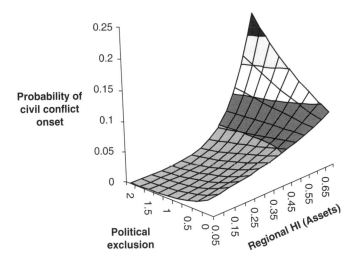

Figure 7.4 Regional horizontal inequalities (assets) and political exclusion, developing countries, 1986–2003
Note: Figure 7.4 is generated on the basis of Model 18 in Table 7.4.

7.6 Concluding remarks

This chapter represents a first effort at systematically measuring the impact of the political environment on the relationship between socioeconomic horizontal inequalities and civil conflict onset. The main finding is that socioeconomic horizontal inequalities seem to be positively related with conflict for all the three kinds of group identifiers suggested here (ethnic, religious, and regional groups). Furthermore, the relationship between regional (educational) HIs and conflict seems to be affected by regime type and electoral system, as well as the level of political exclusion in society. In fact horizontal inequalities seem to be particularly conflict provoking in democratic regimes with inclusive electoral systems. This is of course not to say that democracy and/or an inclusive electoral system as such breed conflict – in fact, as demonstrated in Figure 7.3, the countries with the lowest risk of conflict onset seem to be democracies with low levels of horizontal inequalities. Nevertheless, countries with sharp socioeconomic HIs, despite democratic rule and a seemingly politically inclusive system, may be particularly at risk of conflict. Furthermore, I find a strong interaction effect between regional asset HI and the level of *de facto* political exclusion of certain minorities. In sum, these results provide some support to all the Hypotheses 1–4, but the estimates are sensitive to what indicator of inequality is used. Sometimes it is the household asset indicator which shows a significant effect, and at other times it is the education indicator. These two indicators of social well-being are quite interrelated both in theory and statistical correlation, so it would be risky to speculate too much about their potential different effects.

Despite some interesting findings, several factors call for caution when interpreting the results reported here. First, the sample is limited to developing countries which have hosted DHS in the period 1986–2003, which calls into question the degree to which the results can be generalized. Also, within this sample the intra- and extrapolations of inequality values could be problematic. However, this should not be too huge a problem, since horizontal inequalities seem to remain quite stable over time, as noted above.[16]

Second, there is always a potential problem of producing misleading findings due to poor operationalizations of certain variables. Generating summary measures of horizontal inequalities at the national level is a challenging task. There is a need to define the relevant groups, calculate their respective mean welfare scores, and then measure inequalities based on these scores. Most empirical work on group differences, including the tests presented here, uses simple measures of differences in performance between the major groups in society, aggregating these for cross-country comparisons. The advantage of such an approach is that the measure is very simple and makes sense intuitively. However, it is potentially problematic since it may ignore certain politically relevant groups in society (see Chapter 5). Following, for example, Mancini (Chapter 6), I reran all the models with an alternative measure of horizontal inequalities, the group-based coefficient of variation (GCOV),[17] weighted by group size for all the groups consisting of more than 1 per cent of the population in each country (results not reported here). Most of the effects remained quite similar, but dropped below significance in many models. It is hard to say whether this means that horizontal inequalities may be less important than suggested here, or if it just signals that HIs are extremely complex phenomena and very sensitive to different measurement techniques. The implication of the latter seems to be that whenever possible, horizontal inequalities should be measured and analyzed at the subnational level. A handful of quantitative case studies of particular countries have done exactly this (see, for example, Mancini, Chapter 6, this volume; Murshed and Gates, 2005; Tadjoeddin, 2003), but this of course requires disaggregation of the dependent variable and preferably the other independent variables (see also Østby *et al.*, 2006 for a preliminary disaggregated analysis of inter- and intraregional inequalities and civil conflict in 21 African countries). Despite the advantage of disaggregated studies of conflict, political variables such as regime type and electoral system (which are important indicators in this chapter) are by definition country-level variables. Testing the combined effects of subnational and national variables could be carried out in a multilevel model, though (see, for example, Goldstein, 1995).

The main policy implication that can be drawn from the results reported in this chapter is the importance of addressing horizontal inequalities. Political institutions are not sufficient to ensure peace. The findings of this chapter support Stewart and O'Sullivan's (1999) conclusion drawn from case studies: the combination of two factors seems to be of utmost importance in mitigating conflict. The first factor is the establishment of politically inclusive government which incorporates representatives from all the major identity groups at the political level. The second factor is the realization of a social system which widely spreads the benefits of progress, providing socioeconomic growth among all the significant regional, religious and ethnic groups in society. In other words, what seems to be required in order to ensure peace in developing countries is the combination of politically *and* economically inclusive government.

Appendix 7A

Table 7A.1 Summary statistics of all variables

Variable	N	Mean	Std. Dev.	Min	Max
Conflict onset	806	0.048	0.215	0	1
HI_Asset (Ethnic group)	702	0.238	0.174	0.004	0.710
HI_Educ. (Ethnic group)	702	0.331	0.251	0.002	0.875
HI_Asset (Religious group)	828	0.148	0.120	0.002	0.490
HI_Educ. (Religious group)	828	0.259	0.235	0.000	0.858
HI_Asset (Regions)	1098	0.326	0.218	0.010	0.801
HI_Educ. (Regions)	1098	0.354	0.242	0.001	0.850
Population (ln)	1069	16.501	1.366	12.845	20.771
GDP per capita (ln) $_{t-1}$	1036	7.522	0.780	6.084	9.166
Polity $_{t-1}$	1028	0.369	6.299	−9	10
Polity2 $_{t-1}$	1028	39.779	24.944	0	100
Semidemocracy $_{t-1}$	1028	0.353	0.478	0	1
Autocracy $_{t-1}$	1028	0.292	0.455	0	1
SIP $_{t-1}$	893	0.460	0.349	0	0.955
Proximity to Transition	1074	0.193	0.337	2.47e-32	1
Inclusive Electoral System $_{t-1}$	919	0.600	0.870	0	3
Political Exclusion $_{t-1}$	809	0.619	0.662	0	3.56
Peaceyears	1074	12.953	14.740	0	57
_spline1	1074	−1678.040	2617.469	−12320	0
_spline2	1074	−6179.320	10518.610	−52118	0
_spline3	1074	−6858.145	12994.400	−71200	0

Notes

1. Although the DHS allowed calculations of HIs for 61 countries, six disappeared from the regression analysis either because there was a conflict going on during the entire period 1986–2003, implying that all conflict years were deleted, or due to missing observations on certain of the other variables for the entire 1986–2003 period (the six were India, Myanmar, Liberia, Philippines, Sudan, and Turkey).

2. Nevertheless, it should not be ignored that some of the worst forms of ethnic attack have been nonregional, such as the conflict between Hutus and Tutsis in Rwanda.

3. However, this could be true and yet also be conducive to peace.

4. In fact, the correlation between regime type and political discrimination is –0.09 in my dataset.

5. For more information about the surveys, see the DHS webpage: http://www.measuredhs.com/

6. An online appendix, Appendix 7B, provides a complete list of all the DHS (countries and survey years) used in this analysis to generate the HI variables (see http://folk.uio.no/gudruno/).

7. The group sizes are based on weighted measures of ethnic and religious groups (see Rutstein and Rojas (2003) for details on DHS weighting procedures).

8. See Neumayer (2003) for a similar application of the MAR data with regard to economic group discrimination at the country level.

9. When I ran the baseline model (that is, excluding any term for HIs) on a more inclusive sample (up to 147 countries) for the same period, both the terms for population size and GDP per capita showed the expected effects. Furthermore, when I reran the model with the same sample as in Model 6, but no term for HI, the effects of population size and GDP per capita dropped to insignificant levels (results reported in online Appendix 7C: http://folk.uio.no/gudruno/).

10. It is always possible that conflict history (peaceyears) may be explained by other independent variables. Hence, I also ran Models 1–19 without the terms for peaceyears and splines (regressions not shown here), but there were no substantial changes in the results.

11. Marginal effects were calculated with the aid of CLARIFY software in Stata 8.2 (see Tomz *et al.*, 2003).

12. Increasing the inter-religious HI term for assets and education respectively, the conflict risk increases from 2.9 per cent to 7.2 per cent and 7.1 per cent.

13. When I ran Models 5 and 6 with the same sample as Models 1 and 2 ($n=473$) the results for the interregional HIs largely hold, although the effects are slightly weaker.

14. Not surprisingly, there are not many examples of countries in my sample which are democracies that host severe inequalities and conflict onset in a given year. One example is the conflict onset in Niger in 1994, corresponding with a lagged polity score of 8 and an HI (education) score of approximately 0.80.

15. I also ran all the subsequent models including the term for proximity to transition. The term turned out positive and significant in all models, but the other regression results did not change substantively (results not shown here).

16. Even so, I reran all the models without allowing for any backward extrapolation of the inequality values. Most of the results remained similar, but some effects

dropped below significance (results not reported here). This procedure radically decreases the sample to less than half and the number of conflicts drops to very low figures in many of the models.

17. The weighted group coefficient of variation was also proposed by Williamson (1965).

Part III

Horizontal Inequalities and Conflict in Three Regions

8
When do Horizontal Inequalities Lead to Conflict? Lessons from a Comparative Study of Ghana and Côte d'Ivoire

Arnim Langer

8.1 Introduction

In order to unravel the linkages between the presence of severe horizontal inequalities and the outbreak of violent conflict in plural societies, this chapter compares the experiences of Ghana and Côte d'Ivoire. Despite some differences, a Ghana/Côte d'Ivoire study has a strong foundation for comparison because of the large number of structural similarities between these two countries – including population size, location, geography and climate, variety and distribution of ethnic groups, regional developmental inequalities, economic structure and level of development. Yet, while both countries were and are confronted with severe socioeconomic inequalities between their northern and southern regions, only Côte d'Ivoire has experienced a violent national conflict with a clear north–south dimension. Ghana has remained relatively stable and peaceful at the national level since the Fourth Republic came into existence in January 1993. And even though Ghana's political history before 1993 was rather turbulent with several coup d'états and prolonged periods of military rule, no serious ethnic or religious violence has taken place at the national level.[1] By analyzing why a north–south conflict has emerged in Côte d'Ivoire, and not in Ghana, this chapter aims to contribute to enhancing our understanding of the circumstances in which horizontal inequalities are likely to provoke violent conflict.

While I start from the hypothesis that the presence of severe horizontal inequalities puts a country at greater risk of having a violent conflict, it is important to recognize that 'group disparities and unequal exchange are, in and of themselves, insufficient to explain the course of interethnic conflict' (Rothchild, 1983: 172). Whether group grievances and discontent actually become an issue in the national political sphere largely depends on whether or not political elites decide to organize the process of grievance formation and/or (violent) group mobilization. Hence, if the political elite at the centre is satisfied with the distribution of political and economic power, severe socioeconomic inequalities are less likely to result in group violence. Other things being equal, I hypothesize that the *simultaneous* presence of severe political, socioeconomic and cultural status inequalities is likely to form an extremely explosive sociopolitical situation because in this situation the excluded political elites not only have strong incentives to mobilize their supporters for violent conflict along 'cultural' group lines, but are also likely to gain support among group members relatively easily.

Conversely, the emergence of violent conflict becomes less likely if a country's political, socioeconomic and cultural status inequalities do not coincide. For instance, a situation where an ethnoregional or religious group is economically deprived or disadvantaged yet at the same time its leaders are politically included and its cultural practices are recognized *in* and *by* the state is less prone to widespread political instability and violent group mobilization because not only do the political leaders lack strong incentives to mobilize their group members for violent action, but also the access to political power provides peaceful ways of addressing their group's socioeconomic underdevelopment and grievances. An important objective of this comparative study between Ghana and Côte d'Ivoire is to 'test' these hypotheses.

8.2   From Ivorian 'miracle' to violent conflict[2]

Côte d'Ivoire is a multiethnic country with approximately 40 different ethnic groups which can be grouped into five larger sociocultural or ethnolinguistic groups: Akan, Krou, Northern Mandé, Southern Mandé and Voltaic. While the largest ethnic group is the Akan, with approximately 42 per cent of the population, the two northern ethnic groups, Northern Mandé and Voltaic, together constitute about 34 per cent of the population (see Table 8.1). Although the latter two ethnic groups originate from Côte d'Ivoire's northern regions, due to extensive north–south migration both in the colonial and postcolonial period, many people belonging to these groups now live in the southern regions. In addition to internal migration, Côte d'Ivoire has also received a very large number of international migrants initiated by the French colonial administration which brought forced labour from the Upper Volta, today's Burkina Faso, to the cocoa and coffee plantations in the southern parts of Côte d'Ivoire.

Although forced labour was abolished by the French Assembly in 1946, Côte d'Ivoire continued to attract large numbers of migrants from neighbouring countries. The country's first president, Félix Houphouët-Boigny, promoted the influx of foreign workers by introducing liberal land-ownership laws, under the slogan 'the land belongs to those that develop it' (Gonin, 1998: 174). As a result, the origin of a large proportion of the people in Côte d'Ivoire, in both the current and previous generations, is from outside the country. In 1998, such 'foreigners' accounted for over

Table 8.1   Ethnic and religious composition of Côte d'Ivoire in 1998

	Ethnic composition (%)				
	Akan	**Krou**	**Southern Mandé**	**Northern Mandé**	**Voltaic**
North	22.9	1.8	2.3	26.6	45.6
South	49.0	16.7	12.9	12.8	7.4
Total Ivorian population	42.1	12.7	10.0	16.5	17.6
	Religious composition (%)				
	Christian	**Muslim**	**Traditionalist**	**Other religions**	**No religion**
North	17.2	49.6	17.8	0.7	13.7
South	34.0	35.4	10.2	2.1	17.6
Total Ivorian population	33.9	27.4	15.3	2.0	20.7
Total resident population	30.3	38.6	11.9	1.7	16.7

Source: Author's calculations based on the 1998 Côte d'Ivoire population census (see République de Côte d'Ivoire, 2001).

Notes: The 'South' comprises the following regions: Montagnes, Moyen-Cavally, Haut-Sassandra, Bas-Sassandra, Marahoué, Fromager, Sud-Bandama, N'Zi Comoé, Moyen-Comoé, Agnéby, Lagunes, Sud-Comoé and Lacs. The 'North' comprises the following regions: Denguélé, Savanes, Zanzan, Bafing, Worodougou and Vallée du Bandama.

As the 1998 population census did not provide the ethnic background of the foreign nationals, the ethnic composition is based on Ivorian nationals only.

The religious composition of the 'north' and 'south' is based on the *resident* population (that is, it includes foreign nationals).

4 million people or roughly 25 per cent of the population (République de Côte d'Ivoire, 2001). About 50 per cent of these 'foreigners' or 'non-Ivorians' were born in Côte d'Ivoire. Significantly the ethnocultural and religious background of these non-Ivorians is very similar to that of the northern ethnic groups.

Religion significantly reinforces the ethnoregional north–south differences. While the Akan and Krou are predominantly Christians, the dominant religion among the northern ethnic groups is Islam. As shown in Table 8.1, almost 50 per cent of the people in the north are Muslim. Islam is therefore a strong unifying factor among the two northern ethnic groups. As the vast majority of non-Ivorians (about 70 per cent) is Muslim, their presence in Côte d'Ivoire tilts the religious balance in favour of Islam at the national level.

When Côte d'Ivoire became independent in August 1960, a one-party system was adopted. The *Parti Démocratique de la Côte d'Ivoire* (PDCI) was founded by the Baoulé tribal chief Houphouët-Boigny in 1946 and *de facto* controlled the Ivorian political system between 1960 and 1999. Houphouët-Boigny was elected the first president of Côte d'Ivoire and he remained in power until his death in December 1993. During the first 20 years of his presidency, Côte d'Ivoire achieved remarkable economic growth with real annual GDP growth rates of more than 7 per cent. In addition to its strong economic progress, Côte d'Ivoire also benefited from a relatively stable political environment in these years. In the light of these economic and political achievements, international observers often referred to Côte d'Ivoire as *Le Miracle Africain*.

While the favourable economic environment contributed heavily to Côte d'Ivoire's relatively stable political environment, other factors also played a crucial role. Some scholars have stressed the importance of Houphouët-Boigny's approach to politics which was characterized by a culture of dialogue, compromise, rewards, punishment, forgiveness and reintegration (see, for example, Akindès, 2004). A crucial aspect of *Le modèle Houphouétiste* was his use of economic incentives to co-opt individuals who might consider challenging the system (Zartman and Delgado, 1984). The robustness of the economy provided sufficient resources for Houphouët-Boigny's patronage system effectively to neutralize most sources of dissatisfaction (Gyimah-Boadi and Daddieh, 1999). Houphouët-Boigny was, however, uncompromising about the need to maintain order and stability in order to secure national economic development (ibid.). His willingness to use considerable force in order to secure such order and stability was demonstrated on several occasions, most notably during the secessionist revolt of the Sanwi king in December 1969 as well as during the Guébié crisis in November 1970.

Another factor which contributed to maintaining political stability was Houphouët-Boigny's 'system of ethnic quotas', which was aimed at establishing a balance between different regions and ethnic groups within the main state institutions (Bakery, 1984: 35). Table 8.2 illustrates Houphouët-Boigny's 'balancing' policy, showing the relative proportion of the different ethnic groups in the major political institutions for the period 1959–1980. Although the Akan dominated the political scene, all major ethnic groups (including the northern ethnic groups, Malinké and Voltaic) were reasonably well represented in Côte d'Ivoire's main political institutions.

While Côte d'Ivoire's outward-oriented agricultural development strategy produced impressive economic results, the concentration of investment, jobs and wealth in the southern parts of the country, especially in Abidjan and the cocoa area known as the *Boucle du Cacao*, exacerbated the socioeconomic disparities between the north and south. In 1974, for instance, the income *per capita* of the four northern departments Boundiali (CFAF28,480), Ferkéssédougou (CFAF49,554), Korhogo (CFAF45,041) and Odienné (CFAF29,034) was significantly below Côte d'Ivoire's national average (CFAF67,679) and was 65–80 per cent lower than that of the richest department, Abidjan

Table 8.2 Elite by ethnic group, 1959–1980

Ethnic group	Total political elite		Minister		Deputy		Economic and social councillors		PDCI Politburo		Total population in 1975
	No.	%	No.	%	No.	%	No.	%	No.	%	%
Akan	163	50.9	39	53.4	100	50.0	50	56.1	43	55.1	41.4
Krou	33	19.6	15	20.5	41	20.5	13	14.6	10	12.8	16.7
Malinké	33	10.3	7	9.5	19	9.0	10	11.2	8	10.25	14.8
S. Mandé	17	5.3	2	2.7	13	6.5	4	4.4	4	5.1	10.2
Voltaic	29	9.06	6	8.2	9	4.5	4	4.4	7	8.9	15.7
Others	13	4.06	4	5.4	6	3.0	7	7.8	5	6.4	1.2
Unknown	1	0.3	–	–	1	0.5	–	–	–	–	–

Source: Bakery (1984: 36).

(CFAF142,895) (Den Tuinder, 1978).[3] The accumulation of these inequalities increasingly began to threaten Côte d'Ivoire's ethnoregional harmony (Gyimah-Boadi and Daddieh, 1999).

In response to the increasing discontent of the people in the northern regions regarding their relative socioeconomic situation, Houphouët-Boigny made several highly publicized visits to the north in 1974. During these visits, he promised the local population increased public investment in order to attain equality with the south. The president fulfilled his promise by initiating the *Programme du Nord*, which allocated about CFAF20 billion to investment programmes in the northern and central regions (Den Tuinder, 1978). The increase in public investment in the north after 1974 is shown in Table 8.3. Another measure to mitigate the ethnoregional imbalances in the distribution of social services was 'to alternate Ivorian independence festivities between Abidjan and the different prefecture capitals' (Gyimah-Boadi and Daddieh, 1999: 137). The massive facelifts that these capitals would undergo in preparation for this event created a considerable number of jobs.

However, the increase in public investment in the northern regions quickly dried up with the deteriorating economic environment at the end of the 1970s. The sharp decline in the commodity prices of coffee and cocoa clearly exposed Côte d'Ivoire's vulnerability to international commodity markets. Throughout the 1980s, the economy was stagnant and the socioeconomic north–south divide remained as severe in the mid-1980s as it had been in the mid-1970s (Table 8.4).

The negative economic environment in the 1980s not only reduced the standard of living, but also exacerbated tensions between locals and foreign migrants, as well as between internal migrants from the north and locals in the southern regions. As most migrants (both internal and foreign) belonged to the northern ethnic groups, the communal tensions were increasingly perceived as a conflict between north and south. As Dembélé (2003: 36, my translation) argues, 'The communal conflict between north and south was mainly related to land issues and the presence of too many migrants from the centre and north in the rural economy in the southwestern regions and the urban economy in the south.'

In April 1990, the economic crisis resulted in major demonstrations by the still officially illegal political opposition. In an attempt to restore social and political stability, in May 1990 Houphouët-Boigny decided to abandon one-party rule and legalize opposition parties. The first competitive presidential elections took place in October 1990. Houphouët-Boigny won the elections with a considerable margin against the main opposition party candidate, Laurent Gbagbo. However, the most significant aspect of these elections was the introduction of ethnonationalism and xenophobia into Côte d'Ivoire's electoral politics. In particular, during the 1990 elections, Côte d'Ivoire's main opposition party, *Front Populaire Ivoirien* (FPI – Ivorian Popular Front), initiated a political campaign around the message that 'the PDCI was a

Table 8.3 Public investment *per capita* by region, 1971–1977 (CFAF thousands)

Region	1971	1972	1973	1974	1975[a]	1976[a]	1977[a]	1971–1977	1973 Population[b]
North	1.3	10.8	21.3	18.4	27.0	28.8	29.4	137.0	554.6
East	5.3	0.4	0.4	1.1	1.5	1.1	1.5	11.3	266.5
South	6.5	7.7	6.3	8.2	12.3	13.2	13.6	67.9	1,193.6
West	0.3	3.4	2.3	3.7	4.6	2.8	3.1	20.2	701.9
Centre West	0.3	0.1	0.1	0.7	2.5	3.2	0.6	7.6	712.0
Centre	10.8	11.5	9.2	11.0	13.5	10.4	4.3	70.7	1,490.4
Southwest	49.4	17.9	13.5	33.3	60.3	75.0	102.6	351.9	156.0
Abidjan	11.7	14.5	23.0	31.1	41.4	33.0	22.4	177.0	840.0
Nonallocated	2.3	2.8	3.0	4.2	6.2	6.8	6.9	32.2	n.a.[c]
Total	9.6	11.0	12.4	16.1	22.9	22.1	19.8	113.8	5,910.0

Source: Den Tuinder (1978: 151).

Notes: [a] Projected

[b] In thousands. The 1973 population was used for all years. Thus, figures for the later years are biased upward in comparison with earlier years.

[c] Not applicable

Table 8.4   Some socioeconomic indicators for different regions and ethnic groups in Côte d'Ivoire in 1985

	Mean expenditure *per capita* (CFAF x 1000 yr.)	Distribution of poverty		
		Poorest 10%	Poorest 30%	All Ivorians
Region				
Abidjan	633.8	2.0	3.5	18.8
Other Urban	412.7	2.0	10.8	22.4
West Forest	296.0	8.1	11.2	15.2
East Forest	246.2	31.1	34.4	24.7
Savannah	177.7	56.8	40.1	18.9
Côte d'Ivoire	350.9	–	–	–
Ethnic group				
Akan	354.6	34.0	38.4	38.1
Krou	367.5	5.2	9.9	13.9
Southern Mandé	388.9	4.8	7.6	11.2
Northern Mandé	338.5	22.3	15.4	13.0
Voltaic	244.7	26.5	16.8	9.5
Non-Ivorian	377.2	6.5	11.6	14.1
Côte d'Ivoire	350.9	–	–	–

Source: Glewwe (1988: 11, 38–39).

Notes: The Savannah region depicts the situation of the northern regions; and the Northern Mandé and Voltaic ethnic groups are illustrative for the northern ethnic groups.

partial regime which had systematically favoured the interests of particular Ivorian ethnic groups – Baoulé and groups from the north – and of foreigners' (Crook, 1997: 222).

In an important change, Alassane Ouattara – a Malinké, a subgroup of the Northern Mandé ethnic group – was appointed to the newly created position of prime minister following the elections. As a former African director at the International Monetary Fund (IMF) and governor of the Central Bank for West African States (BCEAO), Ouattara was chosen mainly for his economic management skills and international reputation. However, by appointing Ouattara as prime minister, 'the conflicts between the forest people from the south and the northerners in the land and economic sphere shifted to the political sphere' (Dembélé, 2003: 36, my translation). When Houphouët-Boigny died on 7 December 1993, Henri Konan Bédié, also a Baoulé, succeeded him for the remainder of the presidential term.

Although the combination of several years of structural reforms and the 1994 CFA franc devaluation led to a significant recovery in economic growth, most people did not benefit from the economic recovery (see, for example, Azam, 2004). Côte d'Ivoire also continued to experience serious political confrontations and ethnic tensions, particularly in the lead-up to the October 1995 presidential elections. Growing northern conscious-ness was an important change that contributed to the escalation of ethnic tensions at the beginning of the 1990s. The distribution of an anonymous document called *Le Charte du Grand Nord* (Charter of the North) in 1992 illustrated the changed attitudes of the northerners regarding the sociopol-itical system in general and the Baoulé group in particular. The Charter 'called for fuller recognition of the Muslim religion [. . .], more efforts to reduce regional inequalities, greater political recognition of the north's polit-ical loyalty during the upheavals of the 1980s and [. . .] an end to Baoulé nepotism in recruitment to public jobs' (Crook, 1997: 226). Northern griev-ances and dissatisfaction were not limited to the economic and political sphere, but also had a 'cultural status' dimension. The call for greater recogni-tion of the Muslim religion in Côte d'Ivoire clearly illustrates this. While Côte d'Ivoire's 1960 constitution had a secular character, a direct consequence of Houphouët-Boigny's long stay in power as head of state was a growing blurring in perceptions of the separation of religion and state. Though the political inclusion of the northerners/Muslims in various state institutions helped to counter this impression, the creation of an immense Basilica in Yamoussoukro by Houphouët-Boigny in the late 1980s was perceived by many Muslims as a clear indication of the superior position given to Chris-tianity in Côte d'Ivoire.

The emergence of a new opposition party, *Rassemblement des républicains* (RDR), in 1994, reflected a further split among Côte d'Ivoire's political elite. The RDR aimed to draw support from people with a northern and/or Muslim background, predominantly found among the Voltaic and Northern Mandé ethnic groups. Alassane Ouattara – in 1994 again working in Washington – would soon become their political leader. The emergence of this new party confronted Bédié with a serious challenge because the RDR was likely to reduce PDCI's electoral support in the northern regions (Crook, 1997). In response, as Crook (ibid.: 227) states, 'Bédié's initial strategy was familiar to any student of electoral politics: he stole the opposition's clothes, and adopted a policy of Ivorian nationalism, under the slogan of the promotion of *Ivoirité* (Ivorianness).'

Although Bédié claimed that the concept of *Ivoirité* was solely aimed at creating a sense of cultural unity among all the people living in the territory of Côte d'Ivoire, it is widely recognized that it was introduced for a specific political reason: to prevent Ouattara from participating in the presidential elections in 1995. *Ivoirité* changed the electoral code, requiring both parents of a presidential candidate to be Ivorian. The new 1995 electoral code further stipulated that the candidate himself must have lived in the country for the past five years. Consequently, Ouattara was effectively excluded from participating in the October 1995 presidential elections, which in turn disen-franchised an important part of the northern population. The introduction of the ideology of *Ivoirité* had however an impact far beyond the political sphere because it led to a general erosion of northern Ivorians' social standing and cultural status, *de facto* making them secondary citizens in Côte d'Ivoire. As a result of Ouattara's exclusion, the RDR boycotted the October 1995 presidential elections. The leader of the FPI Laurent Gbagbo also decided to boycott the elections, claiming that the electoral process had been manipulated. Due to the absence of his main rivals, Bédié won the October 1995 elections with a landslide. Until the coup d'état in December 1999, the two opposition parties RDR and FPI together formed the *Front républicain*. In sharp contrast to Houphouët-Boigny, Bédié almost completely stopped the efforts to balance the different ethnoregional interests and parties, and started a process of *'baoulisation'* of state institutions (Dozon, 2000), which was attacked by the *Front républicain*. Table 8.5, showing the ethnic representation of government for the period 1980–2003, illustrates this. Each ethnic group's *relative representation* (RR) is calculated by dividing an ethnic group's relative proportion in government (in per cent) by its relative size in the entire population. Consequently, 1 means proportional representation; figures higher than 1 point to overrepresentation and less than 1 to underrepresentation.

As shown in Table 8.5, Houphouët-Boigny's governments of the 1980s were reasonably well balanced in ethnic terms. His government of July 1986, in particular, had an ethnically balanced outlook, with only the Southern Mandé and the northern ethnic group, Voltaic, somewhat underrepresented in relation to their demographic size. Moreover, the 'northerners' – defined here as individuals belonging to the Voltaic and Northern Mandé ethnic groups – were overall reasonably well represented in the 1980s. While the northerners were around 40 per cent underrepresented in relation to their demographic size in Houphouët-Boigny's last government of November 1991, it is important to remember that Alassane Ouattara, a 'northerner', was prime minister and *de facto* head of the government as Houphouët-Boigny was increasingly incapacitated by illness. While the Baoulé were almost proportionately represented in Houphouët-Boigny's government of November 1991, under Bédié, they became increasingly overrepresented in relation to their demographic size; amounting to 1.86 times their demographic size in the August 1998 government.

In addition to the *baoulisation* of the political-administrative sector, Bédié also began to change the ethnic composition of the military forces in favour of his own ethnic group (Contamin and Losch, 2000). The ethnic tensions that stemmed from favouritism towards the Baoulé were compounded by general discontent in the armed forces due to a gradual decline in their status during the 1990s, mainly arising from reduced expenditures following from the precarious financial and economic situation (Kieffer, 2000).

The grievances within the armed forces triggered a coup d'état in December 1999, initiated by a group of noncommissioned officers who claimed they were owed financial compensation for their participation in an international

Table 8.5 Ethnic composition of government, 1980–2003

	Felix Houphouët-Boigny								Henri Konan Bédié						Robert Gueï				Laurent Gbagbo			
	Nov-1980		Jul-1986		Oct-1989		Nov-1991		Dec-1993		Jan-1996		Aug-1998		Jan-2000		May-2000		Jan-2001		Aug-2002	
	%	RRᵃ	%	RR	%	RR	%	RR	%	RR	%	RR	%	RR	%	RR	%	RR	%	RR	%	RR
Akan	0.49	1.15	0.41	0.96	0.47	1.11	0.61	1.44	0.52	1.24	0.52	1.23	0.59	1.41	0.50	1.19	0.30	0.72	0.46	1.10	0.52	1.23
Baoulé	0.22	1.33	0.24	1.45	0.2	1.21	0.17	1.03	0.24	1.43	0.28	1.64	0.31	1.86	0.13	0.74	0.04	0.26	0.11	0.64	0.13	0.77
Krou	0.19	1.19	0.2	1.26	0.2	1.26	0.17	1.07	0.24	1.89	0.21	1.63	0.16	1.23	0.13	0.98	0.22	1.71	0.29	2.25	0.19	1.52
S. Mandé	0.05	0.42	0.1	0.83	0.13	1.08	0.04	0.33	0.04	0.40	0.10	1.03	0.06	0.63	0.08	0.83	0.17	1.73	0.18	1.79	0.16	1.61
N. Mandé	0.08	0.59	0.17	1.25	0.13	0.96	0.09	0.66	0.08	0.48	0.07	0.42	0.03	0.19	0.17	1.01	0.17	1.05	0.07	0.43	0.13	0.78
Voltaic	0.14	0.91	0.1	0.65	0.03	0.19	0.09	0.58	0.12	0.68	0.10	0.59	0.13	0.71	0.13	0.71	0.08	0.47	0.00	0.00	0.00	0.00
Southerners	0.73	1.04	0.71	1.01	0.8	1.14	0.82	1.16	0.8	1.23	0.83	1.28	0.81	1.25	0.71	1.10	0.69	1.06	0.93	1.44	0.87	1.34
Northerners	0.22	0.76	0.27	0.93	0.16	0.55	0.18	0.62	0.2	0.59	0.17	0.50	0.16	0.47	0.3	0.88	0.25	0.73	0.07	0.21	0.13	0.38
No.	N=37		N=41		N=30		N=23		N=25		N=29		N=32		N=24		N=23		N=28		N=31	

Notes: To compile this table, the ethnic background of government ministers was inferred on the basis of name recognition. In this regard, I would like to thank Professor Francis Akindès and his doctoral students Moustapha Touré and Kouamé Severin for taking the time to fill in my questionnaires. While the relative representation (RR) figures for the period 1980–1991 are based on the ethnic composition data from the 1988 population census, those from the December 1993 government onwards are based on the ethnic composition data from the 1998 population census. Southerners include the Akan, Southern Mandé and Krou ethnic groups; Northerners are comprised of the Northern Mandé and Voltaic ethnic groups.
ᵃRR=relative representation.

peacekeeping mission in Central Africa (Kieffer, 2000). This protest movement quickly developed into a large-scale mutiny, at which stage more senior
officers got involved. Although the coup d'état appears to have originated
initially from individual grievances, these grievances and fears of exclusion cannot be separated from what was happening in the rest of society.
As Kieffer argues, the opposition parties' discourse of exclusion and Baoulé
domination of the Ivorian state is likely to have had an important impact on
the attitudes of the young noncommissioned officers involved in the coup
d'état. Significantly, at the time of the coup d'état in December 1999, both
the Baoulé overrepresentation and the underrepresentation of the northerners in government were at their most severe in Côte d'Ivoire's postcolonial
history up to that point.

Following Bédié's removal from power, the military forces established the
Comité national de salut public (CNSP), headed by General Gueï who was a
Yacouba, one of the ethnic groups belonging to the Southern Mandé ethnic
group. In line with *Le modèle Houphouétiste*, Gueï initially promoted the ideals
of national integration and reconciliation, and openly opposed the ideology
of *Ivoirité* (Akindès, 2004). After negotiations between the various political
parties and the military junta, a transitional government was installed on 4
January 2000. This transitional government was one of the most inclusive
governments of the period 1980–2003 (see Table 8.5). However, after several
months in office, Gueï's political objectives and strategy changed drastically.
In contrast to his earlier statements, Gueï decided after all to participate in
the next presidential elections. Further, without explicitly using the term,
he also began to use the ideology of *Ivoirité* in order to gain political support
and exclude political opponents, in particular Alassane Ouattara and his
RDR party (ibid.).

The presidential elections of October 2000 were marked by chaos and
violence. When the minister of interior Grena Mouassi proclaimed that Gueï
had won the elections, this sparked off massive street demonstrations by
FPI supporters as well as members of the security forces. The military forces
supporting these demonstrations, which eventually forced Gueï to leave the
country, were mainly of northern origin (Banégas and Losch, 2002). The
official results proclaimed by the national electoral commission stated that
Laurent Gbagbo had won the elections with 59.4 per cent of the votes (Le
Pape, 2002). Following the exclusion of their presidential candidate Alassane
Ouattara for *nationalité douteuse* (nationality in doubt), the RDR refused to
recognize the legality of the results and demanded new elections. To support
their demands, RDR supporters started to organize large-scale street protests
which led to violent confrontations with both the FPI supporters and security
forces.

Gbagbo originates from the western town of Gagnoa. He is a Bété, one of
the ethnic groups of the Krou family. In line with his anti-Ouattara and anti-
RDR and therefore *de facto* anti-northern rhetoric, Gbagbo allocated most

government positions in the January 2001 government to his own party, the FPI. Northerners were largely excluded from his January 2001 government. Indeed, the northern underrepresentation in his first government was considerably worse than in any government of Bédié (see Table 8.5). This obviously aggravated the feelings of political exclusion among the RDR supporters. Paradoxically, the same military forces that had chased Gueï away, and thereby helped Gbagbo become president of Côte d'Ivoire, attempted to overthrow Gbagbo's regime in January 2001 (Banégas and Losch, 2002). However, the coup d'état failed and the military forces involved were forced into exile.

Like his two predecessors, Bédié and Gueï, Gbagbo wanted to change the ethnic composition of the military forces to favour his own ethnic group. In order to achieve this, Gbagbo planned to demobilize two contingents that predominantly consisted of soldiers who had been recruited during the brief reign of Gueï (Banégas and Losch, 2002). In response to the planned demobilization, however, these soldiers supported a mutiny which quickly turned into a more organized rebellion, led by officers who had gone into exile either because of the military purges during the Gueï regime or because of their involvement in the failed coup d'état in January 2001 (ibid.). It seems, therefore, likely that the military mutiny of 19 September 2002 was part of a larger plan to overthrow Gbagbo's regime.

The serious violent conflict in Côte d'Ivoire started with simultaneous attacks against the military installations of Abidjan, Bouaké and Korhogo on 19 September 2002. By the end of September, the rebels firmly controlled the northern part of the country and were referring to themselves as the *Mouvement Patriotique pour la Côte d'Ivoire* (MPCI). The main grievances put forward by the insurgents related to the land ownership laws, the criteria of eligibility for presidential elections, the question of identity cards and the political domination of the northerners by southerners (Dembélé, 2003). Although the majority of its forces had a northern background, the MPCI claimed to have no specific ethnic, regional or religious affiliation. Overall, it is estimated that up to 2007 around 10,000 people had been killed in the Ivorian conflict and approximately 1 million persons displaced (Chirot, 2006).

Since the Côte d'Ivoire descended into turmoil the conflict parties have signed a string of peace agreements, none of which has been fully implemented, and Côte d'Ivoire has therefore remained stuck in a 'no peace, no war' situation. The Ouagadougou Agreement, signed in March 2007, is the latest attempt to revive Côte d'Ivoire's stalled peace process up to the time of writing. The main provisions of the agreement include the formation of a new power-sharing government, the creation of a joint army command, and a timetable for disarmament, voter identification and elections. It is as yet uncertain whether this will result in a lasting peace or again fail.

8.3   The peaceful management of the north–south divide in Ghana

Like Côte d'Ivoire, Ghana is a multiethnic country with around 60 different ethnic groups. The four main groups, comprising together around 86 per cent of the population, are the Akan, Mole-Dagbani, Ewe and Ga-Dangme (see Table 8.6). The Akans are by far the largest ethnic group with approximately 49 per cent of the population. They are however a potpourri of around 20 smaller ethnic groups of which the Ashantis (roughly 30 per cent of the Akans) and Fantis (roughly 20 per cent of the Akans) are demographically the most important.

The main ethnic group in the northern regions and the second largest in the country as a whole are the Mole-Dagbanis. It is of significance however that the Mole-Dagbanis are a very loose ethnocultural grouping consisting of about 15 relatively small ethnic subgroups, which have very different histories, customs and traditions (Brukum, 1995). Moreover, different Mole-Dagbani subgroups have repeatedly had violent clashes and conflicts with one and other.[4] These ethnic conflicts 'arise from several years of relegation of certain ethnic groups, so-called "minority" groups, to "second-rate citizens" in the traditional and political administration of the region' (ibid.: 138). When one includes the smaller ethnic groups from the north, such as the Gurma and Grusi, the northern ethnic groups together comprise about 23 per cent of Ghana's population. The Ewes are the third largest ethnic

Table 8.6   Ethnic and religious composition of Ghana in 2000

	Ethnic composition (%)				
	Akan	**Ewe**	**Ga-Dangme**	**Mole-Dagbani**	**Others**
North	6.7	1.2	0.5	62.4	29.3
South	58.4	15.2	9.6	6.5	10.3
Total population	49.1	12.7	16.5	8.0	13.7
	Religious composition (%)				
	Christian	**Muslim**	**Traditionalist**	**Other religions**	**No religion**
North	24.6	42.7	29.6	0.6	2.5
South	78.2	10.2	4.0	0.7	6.9
Total population	68.8	15.9	8.5	0.7	6.1

Source: Author's calculations based on the 2000 Ghana Housing and Population Census.
Notes: The 'south' comprises the following regions: Greater Accra, Ashanti, Brong Ahafo, Western, Eastern, Volta and Central. The 'north' comprises the following regions: Upper East, Upper West and Northern.

group in Ghana and are predominantly found in the eastern part of the country in the Volta Region. The Ga-Dangmes are the fourth largest ethnic group and originate from the Accra region where Ghana's capital is located.

Table 8.6 also shows the religious composition of Ghana. While Ghana is a predominantly Christian country, Muslims constitute around 16 per cent of the population. As in Côte d'Ivoire, Muslims form a particularly important part of the population in the northern regions. Indeed, in the largest of the three northern regions (itself called the 'Northern Region'), the majority of the population is Muslim. Ghana's religious north–south divide is however much less pronounced than in Côte d'Ivoire because Christians and Traditionalists together constitute the majority of the population (about 54 per cent) in the three northern regions (that is, Northern, Upper East and Upper West).

Like Côte d'Ivoire, Ghana's ethnoreligious north–south cleavage is complemented by a serious developmental divide between its northern and southern regions. In this context, scholars such as Smock and Smock (1975: 251) and Ladouceur (1979) argued in the 1970s that a north–south conflict in Ghana was 'latent' and could escalate at any time. However, despite the coincidence of economic, social and cultural north–south cleavages, there has been 'no development of "Northernness" as a basis of political cohesion, and no north versus south patterning of political alignments' (Brown, 1982: 42). While the north–south divide has had 'a surprisingly limited influence upon Ghanaian politics' (Lentz and Nugent, 2000: 22), Ghana's postcolonial political history is nonetheless characterized by political instability and repeated nonconstitutional regime changes as well as serious (nonviolent) ethnic tensions at times. These ethnic tensions were mainly stirred up by 'the perceived competition between Ewe and Ashanti political elites, whose constituencies are not noticeably different in terms of access to education and amenities' (ibid.: 13).

The first time that ethnoregional mobilization and tensions had a serious impact on Ghanaian politics was around the time of Independence in 1957. Ghana became independent under the leadership of the then Prime Minister Kwame Nkrumah. Nkrumah and his Convention People's Party (CPP) had been in power since the British colonial ruler granted self-governance to the Gold Coast in 1951. In the immediate pre-Independence period ethnoregional political parties emerged, including the Gurma/Mole-Dagbani-based Northern People's Party, the Ashanti-based National Liberation Movement and the Ewe-based Togoland Congress Party.

The ethnoregional tensions and mobilization around the time of Independence were followed by a period of comparative ethnic quiet in Ghana's First Republic (1960–1966) (Lentz and Nugent, 2000). Nkrumah not only took an ethnically blind stance himself in public policy matters, but also made national unity a major objective. In February 1966, however, Ghana's First Republic came to an end with the overthrow of Nkrumah's regime by the military and police. A National Liberation Council (NLC), headed by Lt General Joseph Arthur Ankrah, took control of the state institutions. An important feature of the NLC period was the re-emergence of ethnic tensions, in particular between the Akans (especially the Ashantis) and the Ewes. These ethnic tensions are usually argued to have started with the killing of an Ewe member of the NLC, Colonel Kotoka, during an attempted coup d'état by Akan junior officers in 1967 (Frempong, 2001). The ethnoregional tensions and perceived competition for power between these two groups were not only transferred into Ghana's Second Republic (1969–1972), but remained an important issue in Ghanaian politics (Agyeman, 1998; Frempong, 2001; Gyimah-Boadi, 2003; Gyimah-Boadi and Asante, 2006).

In 1969, the NLC government handed over power to the democratically elected government of Abrefa Busia, an Akan from the Brong Ahafo Region, who was the leader of the Progress Party (PP). In order to gain political support, the PP manipulated the growing Akan hostility towards the Ewes to its own advantage (Smock and Smock, 1975). While the National Alliance of Liberals (NAL), the main opposition party, won almost all the seats in the largely Ewe-speaking Volta Region, they won no seats in the predominantly Akan regions. In contrast, the PP won most of the seats in the Akan dominated regions, and only two seats in the Volta region (Gyimah-Boadi and Asante, 2006).

Ghana's Second Republic was, however, very short lived and came to an end through a coup d'état by a military colonel, Ignatius Kutu Acheampong, in 1972. This administration became known as the National Redemption Council (NRC). While Ghana's economy prospered in the initial years of this regime, from 1975 the economic and financial situation started to deteriorate rapidly. In response to the ensuing tensions, Acheampong established the Supreme Military Council (SMC) consisting entirely of service commanders (Frimpong-Ansah, 1991). This reshuffle had, however, no real positive impact on the Ghanaian economy which remained in dire straits. Two coups d'état followed, one in July 1978 and another in June 1979 led by Flight Lt Jerry Rawlings.

Although Rawlings handed over power to the democratically elected government of the People's National Party (PNP) in September 1979, he returned to power again through another coup d'état in December 1981. Rawlings' second coming was 'particularly noteworthy for the manner in which ethnic claims were subordinated to the language of class interest' (Lentz and Nugent, 2000: 22). In fact, the main disputes within the Provisional National Defence Council (PNDC), the new governing body after the 1981 coup d'état, had an ideological rather than an ethnic character, and related to the fundamental change in the economic ideology of the Rawlings regime from a radical Marxist–Leninist approach to a neo-liberal capitalist approach (Gyimah-Boadi and Asante, 2006).

In May 1992, in response to increasing domestic demands and pressures from Western donors for a return to multiparty democracy, the PNDC lifted the ban on party political activity. Presidential elections were held in October 1992. Ethnic sentiments played a major role during these elections. The continuation of the Ewe-Ashanti/Akan rivalry is indicated both by the fact that the New Patriotic Party (NPP) leader, Adu Boahen (half-Ashanti), and the National Democratic Congress (NDC) leader, Jerry Rawlings (half-Ewe), emerged as the two main contenders in these elections, as well as the voting patterns in the two candidates' home regions (Frempong, 2001). To illustrate, while Adu Boahen won a significant majority (60.5 per cent) of the votes in his home region (the Ashanti Region), he only received 3.6 per cent of the votes in the Ewe-dominated Volta Region. For Rawlings the situation was the reverse: he won 93.2 per cent of the votes in the Volta Region and only obtained 32.9 per cent of the votes in the Ashanti Region (ibid.).

While Ghana successfully consolidated its democracy after the reintroduction of multiparty elections in 1992, regional voting patterns seem to suggest that ethnicity, while not the only factor, remains important for determining political allegiances and election results in the Fourth Republic, particularly in the Ashanti and Volta regions. Further, even though the higher echelons of both the NDC and the NPP showed a high degree of ethnic mix towards the end of the 1990s, and Rawlings' successor as leader of the NDC, John Atta Mills, was a Fanti (one of the Akan subgroups), the perception of the NDC and NPP as largely Ewe and Ashanti/Akan-based parties respectively persisted into the 2000 and 2004 elections (Gyimah-Boadi and Asante, 2006). Thus the main divide from this perspective is not north–south, in line with the socioeconomic inequalities, but rather between two southern ethnic groups with a broadly similar socioeconomic position.[5]

The fact that the north–south cleavage has not become politically more salient is all the more intriguing if one considers that the socioeconomic north–south divide has hardly been reduced since Ghana gained independence in 1957. Like Côte d'Ivoire, the north–south disparities in development have their origins in differences in natural conditions and resources between the north and south, reinforced and exacerbated by 'the locating of human and physical capital in response to the economic opportunities available' (Rimmer, 1992: 98). Like the colonial economy, Ghana's postcolonial economy had an 'endogenous' tendency to favour the south over the north in terms of the location of economic activities. As shown in Table 8.7, the spatial distribution of economic activities in the colonial era resulted in a situation in which the gross value added *per capita* of the northern regions in 1960 was less than half what it was in the three main cocoa-producing regions in the south (Ashanti, Western and Brong Ahafo) and only about 20 per cent of the level of the Greater Accra Region, where the capital is located.

Nkrumah aimed to mitigate the north–south divide by undertaking specific programmes in the historically disadvantaged northern regions, often at great expense and against economic rationality. For instance, the Nkrumah regime set up a tomato-canning facility in Tamale in the Northern

Table 8.7   Regional distribution of gross value added *per capita*, 1960

Region	Gross value added *per capita*
Greater Accra	176
Western	68
Eastern	53
Volta	43
Ashanti	68
Brong Ahafo	61
Northern	30
All regions	63

Source: Szereszewski (1966: 92).

Region, even though the production of tomatoes and the main consumer markets were located in the south (Gyimah-Boadi and Daddieh, 1999). Another example is the construction of a $30 million international airport in Tamale in the Northern Region (Smock and Smock, 1975). This policy of regional redistribution, in which specific development programmes were undertaken in the relatively deprived northern regions, has been emulated by most governments since Nkrumah. However, arguably only the state-led development approaches of Kwame Nkrumah and his Convention People's Party (CPP) in Ghana's First Republic (1960–1966) and of Colonel Acheampong and his National Redemption Council/Supreme Military Council (1972–1978) included a truly 'positive vision for the development of the north' and its integration in Ghana's economy (Shepherd *et al.*, 2005: 13).

Despite Nkrumah and Acheampong's efforts to reduce the north–south divide and integrate the northern regions into Ghana's economy, at the end of the 1970s generally the north remained much poorer, in terms, for example, of income, infrastructure, education and medical services. According to Kodwo Ewusi's composite measure of development (based on a wide range of socioeconomic indicators), the Northern and Upper regions had levels of development equivalent to only 11 per cent and 7 per cent respectively of the level found in the Greater Accra Region in the mid-1970s, and 25–35 per cent of those in the main cocoa-producing regions in the south (Table 8.8).

In the 1950s, Ghana's economic success, achieving an average annual real growth rate of well over 5 per cent, was based on an open economy with the private sector as the main source of growth (particularly small-scale cocoa farming), but from 1957 Nkrumah changed this to a state-led modernization strategy based on import-substitution industrialization. The main source of funding for Ghana's industrialization came from the cocoa sector, which provided about 70 per cent of Ghana's export earnings, and foreign borrowing (Dordunoo and Nyanteng, 1997). However, from 1959, as a consequence of a sharp decline in the world market prices of cocoa,

Table 8.8 Regional developmental inequalities in 1970–1975

Region	Measure of development[a]
Greater Accra	1.000
Central	0.398
Western	0.392
Eastern	0.355
Ashanti	0.340
Volta	0.306
Brong Ahafo	0.265
Northern	0.110
Upper	0.071

Source: Ewusi (1976: 89).
Notes: Kodwo Ewusi developed his composite index of development by applying the Wroclow Taxonomic Technique to the following ten socioeconomic indicators: (1) crude participation rate, (2) *per capita* energy consumption, (3) proportion of population in nonagricultural sectors, (4) rate of urbanization, (5) literacy rate, (6) population density per sq. mile, (7) earning per worker, (8) accessibility index, (9) number of doctors per 100,000 persons, and (10) number of hospital beds per 1000 persons (for more details, see Ewusi, 1976).
[a] Measure of development for the regions with Greater Accra as base and ranked from best developed to least developed.

Ghana was forced to draw heavily on its foreign exchange reserves to carry on its 'modernization' process. Due to the rapid depletion of its foreign exchange reserves and large debt burden, Ghana was soon unable to import essential goods and services in adequate quantities needed for its economic development (ibid.).

Following some liberalization of the economy after Nkrumah, Acheampong returned to Nkrumah's policies of statism and controls (Dordunoo and Nyanteng, 1997). This approach to development had disastrous consequences for Ghana's economy. During the first 25 years after Independence in 1957, Ghana's real income *per capita* fell by more than one-third (Van Buren, 2005). After taking over power in 1981, Rawlings and his PNDC regime initially responded to the prevailing economic problems in much the same way as previous governments had (that is, they established a state monopoly on export–import trade and tried to eliminate corruption in the allocation of import licenses), but in 1983 they reversed their economic course dramatically and started implementing an extensive economic reform programme with the support of the International Monetary Fund (IMF) and the World Bank (Herbst, 1993).

Ghana's economic performance recovered after 1983, and a period of sustained growth followed (see Table 8.9). Although Ghana's structural adjustment process contributed to restoring economic growth and macroeconomic stability, different regions benefited in different degrees from the recovery (Songsore, 2003). In line with the structural adjustment

Table 8.9 Evolution of macroeconomic indicators in Ghana (in percentages)

Period	Avg. GDP growth per annum	Avg. consumer price inflation per annum	Avg. exports earnings growth per annum	Avg. gross capital formation growth per annum	Avg. GDP per capita growth per annum
1975–1981	−1.5	70.9	−7.2	−5.3	−3.8
1982–1992	3.2	34.7	5.4	3.7	0.1
1993–2000	4.2	29.5	10.6	1.9	1.7
2001–2004	4.8	21.8	1.2	23.0	2.9

Source: Author's calculations based on the World Bank's World Development Indicators database (2006).

programmes' objective to restore economic growth by rehabilitating Ghana's export economy, most external funding went to the Greater Accra Region and the cocoa, timber and mineral industries in the Akan-dominated Western, Eastern, Ashanti and Brong Ahafo Regions (ibid.). Ghana's northern regions largely failed to benefit from the ERP's economic stimulus.

Like Nkrumah, however, the Rawlings regime undertook specific investment projects in the northern regions, including the extension of the national electricity grid, the rehabilitation of the north–south roads and greater expenditure on education, aimed at mitigating the developmental north–south divide. Notwithstanding these and other measures, Ghana's socioeconomic north–south divide actually worsened in the 1990s with regard to certain socioeconomic indicators – for example the incidence of poverty (see Table 8.10). While the overall incidence of poverty decreased from 52 per cent to 40 per cent in the period 1992–1999, two of the three northern regions (the Northern and Upper East regions) actually witnessed an increase in the incidence of poverty.

Soon after taking over from Rawlings in January 2001, the Kufuor government made the reduction of regional inequalities a key policy objective (see Government of Ghana, 2003) and consequently introduced several mechanisms to redress the adverse conditions in the northern regions, particularly relating to health, social infrastructure, education and economic infrastructure. For instance, the funds that were freed up as part of the Highly Indebted Poor Country (HIPC) initiative were earmarked to benefit the north disproportionately (Shepherd *et al.*, 2005). But evidence available up to April 2007 does not show any significant narrowing of horizontal inequalities.

Despite the limited success of successive strategies of economic redistribution over the decades in closing the north–south gap, it is important to emphasize that the impact on reducing the political *salience* of the north–south divide is likely to have been much more substantial.

In addition to attempting to reduce the developmental north–south divide, consecutive Ghanaian regimes employed certain strategies in the

Table 8.10 Socioeconomic inequalities across Ghana's regions in the 1990s

Region	Incidence of poverty (%)[a]		Literacy(% of literate)[b]		Access to health services (%)[c]	Primary school enrolment (%)[c]
	1992	1999	1993	1998	1997	1997
Western	60	27	37	54	28	75
Central	44	48	43	55	36	72
Greater Accra	26	5	60	76	78	70
Volta	57	38	46	58	42	70
Eastern	48	44	46	66	33	78
Ashanti	41	28	31	64	43	72
Brong Ahafo	65	36	30	53	32	72
Northern	63	69	8	13	18	40
Upper West	88	84	12	20	8	45
Upper East	67	88	8	20	20	36
National	52	40	34	51	37	67

Source: [a] Data drawn from Songsore (2003). The poverty line was the same in both years, that is, ¢900,000 per adult per year.
[b] Author's calculations based on data from the 1994 and 1998 Demographic and Health Surveys. The standard *DHS* survey consists of a household and women's questionnaire for which a nationally representative sample of women is interviewed. In addition to asking an elaborate range of questions regarding issues such as family planning, maternal and child health, contraception, and nutrition, the surveys also asked questions regarding a respondent's ethnic background, place of birth and socio-economic situation. Macro International Inc. provides free of charge access to the DHS-data. For more information see http://www.measuredhs.com/.
[c] Data drawn from the 1997 Ghana Core Welfare Indicators Survey (see Ghana Statistical Service, 1998).

political sphere which contributed to diminishing the political salience of the north–south cleavage and helped to contain ethnoregional political mobilization more generally. As noted earlier, Nkrumah was the first Ghanaian leader to be confronted with ethnoregional tensions in the immediate pre-Independence period. His strategies to contain these divisive ethnoregional forces and promote national integration have to some extent become institutionalized, both formally and informally. In particular, against the backdrop of the emergence of ethnoregional political parties, Nkrumah introduced the Avoidance of Discrimination Act in December 1957 which prohibited the formation of political parties on ethnic, regional or religious lines. While the Avoidance of Discrimination Act was strongly opposed by the opposition at the time, since then successive Ghanaian political elites have also recognized the centrifugal potential of ethnic, religious or regional political parties. Consequently, the 1969, 1979 and 1992 Constitutions and the 2000 Political Parties Act all contain provisions aimed at curbing ethnic electoral politics and ensuring that political parties are national in character (Gyimah-Boadi and Asante, 2006).

In addition to the formal banning of ethnic, religious or regional political parties, arguably even more important for mitigating the north–south cleavage was (and still is) the largely informal 'policy' or convention among Ghana's political elites of maintaining ethnoregional balance in the political sphere. This convention ensured that political horizontal inequalities and exclusion at the elite level were generally very moderate, which in turn meant that the northern political elites had few incentives to mobilize their constituents along ethnoregional lines. Table 8.11 shows the ethnic composition of selected Ghanaian governments in the period 1954–2005 and also the representation of different ethnic groups in relation to their demographic size in the population as a whole.

Table 8.11 shows not only that the Akans were continuously the largest ethnic group in government, but also that throughout the post-Independence period the southerners persistently controlled most of the ministerial positions and were as a group somewhat overrepresented in relation to their relative demographic size. Nonetheless, most Ghanaian governments (both civilian and military) had a reasonable representation of northerners. Only on two occasions were there no northerners present in government. Excluding Nkrumah's 1960 government and Acheampong's 1975 Supreme Military Council (SMC), the relative representation in government of the northern ethnic groups ranged between 0.51 and 0.84 in the period 1954–1979. Under Rawlings, who was (*de facto*) head of state from 1981 to 2001, they were slightly overrepresented in relation to their relative demographic size for almost the entire period.

Since Kufuor assumed power in January 2001, the northerners have again become somewhat underrepresented in relation to demographic size among government ministers. However, Kufuor appears to have compensated for this underrepresentation by appointing a more than proportionate number of deputy ministers from among the northern ethnic groups (Langer, 2007). Indeed, including the deputy ministers, the northern ethnic groups were moderately overrepresented in Kufuor's January 2002 government. The political salience of the underrepresentation of the northerners among government ministers is further mitigated by the fact that the position of vice president, the second most important position in Ghana's 1992 Constitution, was occupied by a northerner, Alhaji Aliu Mahama.

Another important strategy which also contributed to mitigating the north–south cleavage relates to the culturally inclusive character of the Ghanaian state. Indeed, most successive governments since Nkrumah have promoted cultural inclusiveness and status equality through a range of formal, informal and symbolic policies and practices. Thus, for instance, Nkrumah's practice of alternating between suits, typically Ashanti *kente* cloths and northern smocks on public occasions was continued by most heads of state. Other measures and practices that illustrate the culturally inclusive and neutral character of the Ghanaian state are, for example, the

Table 8.11 Ethnic composition of government, 1954–2005

	Nkrumah-CPP								Ankrah-NLC		Busia-PP				Acheampong-NRC	
	1954		1956		1960		1965		1966		1969		1971		1972	
	%	RR[a]	%	RR	%	RR	%	RR	%	RR	%	RR	%	RR	%	RR
Akan	0.55	1.24	0.62	1.40	0.62	1.40	0.64	1.46	0.33	0.76	0.74	1.67	0.76	1.73	0.50	1.13
Ewe	0.09	0.70	0.08	0.59	0.23	1.78	0.07	0.55	0.33	2.56	0.00	0.00	0.00	0.00	0.29	2.20
Ga-Dangme	0.09	1.10	0.08	0.93	0.15	1.85	0.14	1.72	0.22	2.68	0.05	0.63	0.06	0.71	0.07	0.86
Southerners[2]	0.73	1.11	0.77	1.18	1.00	1.53	0.86	1.31	0.89	1.36	0.79	1.21	0.82	1.26	0.86	1.31
Northerners[3]	0.18	0.84	0.15	0.71	0.00	0.00	0.14	0.66	0.11	0.51	0.16	0.73	0.18	0.82	0.14	0.66
No.	N=11		N=13		N=13		N=14		N=9		N=19		N=17		N=14	

	Acheampong-SMC		Limann-PNP		Rawlings-PNDC				Rawlings-NDC				Kufuor-NPP			
	1975		1979		1981		1988		1993		1997		2002		2005	
	%	RR	%	RR	%	RR	%	RR	%	RR	%	RR	%	RR	%	RR
Akan	0.50	1.13	0.57	1.30	0.43	0.87	0.50	1.02	0.51	1.05	0.52	1.06	0.66	1.34	0.67	1.36
Ewe	0.38	2.88	0.14	1.10	0.14	1.12	0.30	2.36	0.11	0.85	0.11	0.87	0.07	0.58	0.08	0.61
Ga-Dangme	0.13	1.51	0.14	1.72	0.14	1.79	0.10	1.25	0.08	1.01	0.11	1.39	0.10	1.22	0.10	1.28
Southerners	1.00	1.53	0.86	1.31	0.71	1.02	0.90	1.29	0.70	1.01	0.74	1.06	0.83	1.19	0.85	1.21
Northerners	0.00	0.00	0.14	0.66	0.29	1.23	0.10	0.43	0.30	1.28	0.26	1.12	0.17	0.74	0.15	0.66
No.	N=8		N=14		N=7		N=10		N=37		N=27		N=41		N=39	

Sources: Gyimah-Boadi (2003), Gyimah-Boadi and Asante (2006) and Langer (2007).

Notes: While the relative representation (RR) figures for the period 1954–1979 are based on the ethnic composition data from the 1960 population census, those from the 1981 government onwards are based on the ethnic composition data from the 2000 Ghana Housing and Population Census.

Southerners are comprised of the Akan. Ewe and Ga-Dangme. The Guan, Mandé-Busanga and all other smaller ethnic groups are excluded from these calculations. Northerners include Mole-Dagbani, Gurma and Grusi ethnic groups.

[a] RR=relative representation.

persistent refusal by consecutive Ghanaian governments to promote a particular local language (especially that of the largest ethnic group, the Akan) as
Ghana's national language; active state support for the study and teaching
of Ghana's major local languages; the incorporation by institutions such as
the Ghana Dance Ensemble of songs and dances from all major ethnic groups
(Lentz and Nugent, 2000); the conscious effort to broadcast radio and television programmes in all major languages (ibid.); and the custom that representatives from the government attend the most important ethnic and/or
traditional festivals throughout the country on a regular basis. Similarly,
some (symbolic) actions and practices which demonstrate the commitment
of the political elites to promoting and sustaining religious status equality
and inclusiveness are, for instance, the practice that representatives from
all major religions are present at official state functions; the state's active
organizational support for the annual Hajj pilgrimage to the Muslim holy
sites in Saudi Arabia; and the introduction of a new public holiday on the
Muslim festival of *Eid-al-Adha* in 1996 (Langer, 2007).

8.4   Conclusions

Ever since Nkrumah and Houphouët-Boigny made their famous wager in
1960 about which country's development and modernization approach
would outperform the other, Ghana and Côte d'Ivoire's economic and political evolutions appeared to have taken opposite trajectories. While during
its 'miracle' years (1960–1978), Côte d'Ivoire clearly outperformed Ghana
in terms of economic progress and political stability (but not in socioeconomic development), from the mid-1980s the political and economic
'success' pendulum started moving slowly, but steadily, towards Ghana.
The economic decline of Côte d'Ivoire in the 1980s, coupled with the
pervasive ethnicization of its sociopolitical climate in the 1990s, formed
the precursor to the emergence of the violent conflict of September 2002.
Ghana's successful democratic consolidation in the Fourth Republic could
hardly be more different.

   The comparative study of Ghana and Côte d'Ivoire provides evidence
for the hypothesized relationship between the configuration of horizontal
inequalities and the emergence or nonemergence of violent conflict. First,
the peaceful management of the developmental north–south inequalities
in Ghana throughout the postcolonial period, and in Côte d'Ivoire under
Houphouët-Boigny, demonstrates that socioeconomic horizontal inequalities in and by themselves are not sufficient to produce violent conflict. In
fact in Ghana's case, political mobilization has been within the south, among
groups with broadly similar socioeconomic status, which may explain why
the mobilisation has remained nonviolent. In the case of Côte d'Ivoire, the
strong economic progress in the first two decades after Independence in 1960
and the specific economic 'model' on which it was based, were important

factors in reducing the political salience of the north–south divide. The inclusion of the northern migrants (and foreign migrants) in the southern economy was not only crucial for achieving the impressive economic growth in the first two decades, but it also enabled the northern migrants to improve their relative socioeconomic position. In addition to this *private* redistribution mechanism, Houphouët-Boigny's *public* redistribution efforts also contributed to reducing the political salience of the north–south divide. It seems important that while the actual redistribution effect of the increased public investment in the northern regions appeared to have been rather limited (particularly because the extra investment dried up quickly due to the decline of the Ivorian economy at the end of the 1970s), the symbolic impact appeared to have been much more substantial.

While the inclusion of the northerners in Côte d'Ivoire's cocoa and coffee economy of the south and the (limited) public redistribution efforts were important in diffusing the socioeconomic grievances among the general population as well as among northern elites (both in the northern regions and among the northerners in the south), Houphouët-Boigny's policy of ethnic quotas was a crucial complementary strategy to diffuse ethnoregional mobilization. In particular, his ethnoregional balancing policy ensured that political horizontal inequality and exclusion at the elite level was relatively small, which in turn meant that the political elites had less incentive to mobilize their constituents along ethnoregional lines.

While successive Ghanaian regimes employed very similar strategies in order to diffuse the north–south cleavage (and ethnoregional mobilization more generally for that matter), there were and are certain (structural) factors and idiosyncratic events which make a north–south conflict considerably less likely in Ghana compared to Côte d'Ivoire. For instance, while the northern ethnic groups constitute around 34 per cent of the population in Côte d'Ivoire, they constitute only about 23 per cent of the population in Ghana and are therefore less of a factor in Ghana's national political economy. Another factor that makes the mobilization of the 'north' as a group less likely in Ghana has to do with the more ethnically and religiously diverse composition of the northern regions. While the Muslim religion could be an important unifying factor among the northern ethnic groups in Côte d'Ivoire, this is much less so in Ghana since 24 per cent of the northern people are Christian and 30 per cent adhere to a traditional religion. An additional factor inhibiting northern mobilization as a group was the occurrence in the 1990s of several violent conflicts among the northern ethnic groups themselves.

In addition to these differences between Ghana and Côte d'Ivoire which made northern mobilization against the south intrinsically less likely, successive Ghanaian regimes employed similar strategies to those used by Houphouët-Boigny in order to diffuse the salience of any north–south cleavage. In addition to the policies of including different ethnoregional groups and interests in the main political institutions and of undertaking (symbolic) economic redistribution towards the deprived northern regions, successive Ghanaian regimes also furthered national unity by promoting norms and practices of cultural equality and inclusiveness.

Secondly, Côte d'Ivoire's violent disintegration at the end of the 1990s demonstrates the conflict potential of a sociopolitical situation characterized by the simultaneous presence of severe political, developmental and cultural status inequalities. When the Ivorian economy started to deteriorate in the 1980s, socioeconomic grievances became more salient and provoked serious conflicts between locals and northern as well as foreign migrants in the southern parts of the country. The emergence of these localized north–south conflicts coincided with the cessation of economic redistribution by the state in the form of increased public investment in the northern regions, thereby increasing the northern socioeconomic grievances.

The divisions in the economic sphere were transmitted to the political sphere with the arrival of Alassane Ouattara and the introduction of competitive elections at the beginning of the 1990s. The new political leaders increasingly used a discourse of ethnic exclusion and grievances as a way of building electoral support as well as challenging the supremacy and legitimacy of the PDCI. Due to the precarious financial and economic situation in the 1980s, the Houphouët-Boigny regime lacked the resources to co-opt these new elites and subelites into the political-economic system. In an electoral environment characterized by new players and 'democratic' rules, the prevailing political and economic horizontal inequalities, injustices and grievances became increasingly politicized. All three presidents who came after Houphouët-Boigny – Konan Bédié, Robert Gueï and Laurent Gbagbo – adopted strategies of political monopolization by and favouritism towards their own group. The *winner takes all* nature of politics turned the 'politics of bargaining' into the 'politics of war' (Satori, 1987, quoted in Case, 1996: 14). The main losers in this 'politics of war' were the northerners who were increasingly excluded politically, and eventually disenfranchised, in addition to being socioeconomically disadvantaged. The grievances among the northerners were, however, not limited to the economic and political sphere, as the call for a fuller recognition of the Muslim religion in *Le Charte du Grand Nord* illustrates.

Considering the configuration of horizontal inequalities in Côte d'Ivoire around the turn of the century, the emergence of the violent conflict in September 2002 should not have come as a surprise. While the Ivorian north–south conflict constitutes a stark reminder for other countries, particularly in West Africa, of the inherent conflict *potential* of severe socioeconomic horizontal inequalities, Ghana demonstrates that marked developmental inequalities can be 'neutralized' by the institutionalization of politically and culturally inclusive policies and customs.

Notes

1. While Ghana has experienced several serious ethnic violent conflicts in its northern regions, these ethnic conflicts were only significant at the local level and did not have any far-reaching consequences at the national level (Agyeman, 1998).
2. This section draws on Langer (2005).
3. The West African CFA franc (ISO Currency Code XAF) is the common currency of the following eight countries: Benin, Burkina, Côte d'Ivoire, Guinea Bissau, Mali, Niger, Senegal and Togo. These countries form the West African Economic and Monetary Union (WAEMU) whose common central bank is the Central Bank of West African States (BCEAO) (For more information on the CFA franc, see: http://www.bceao.int).
4. The most serious episode of interethnic violence occurred in 1994 between the Nanumba and Kokomba and resulted in approximately 2000 casualties.
5. For a more detailed analysis of the origins and sociopolitical relevance of the Ewe-Ashanti/Akan cleavage in Ghanaian politics, see Langer (2007).

9
Horizontal Inequalities and Ethnic Violence: Evidence from Calabar and Warri, Nigeria

Ukoha Ukiwo

9.1 Introduction

This chapter explores fundamental factors underpinning conflict through a comparison of two cities in the Delta region of Nigeria. Unlike most cities in Nigeria, which are made up of an indigenous ethnic group and migrants from other ethnic groups, both Calabar and Warri have three indigenous ethnic groups which compete for dominance. These are the Efik, Efut and Qua in Calabar and the Ijaw, Itsekiri and Urhobo in Warri. While all three ethnic groups are only indigenous to Calabar, only the Itsekiri are indigenous to Warri alone. The Ijaw and Urhobo indigenes of Warri constitute a very small proportion of the larger Ijaw and Urhobo ethnic groups. Relations between the ethnic groups in each city have been characterized by conflict. However, Calabar has managed to avoid the recurrent interethnic violence that has occurred in Warri. This chapter seeks to explain the different outcomes in ethnic relations using the horizontal inequalities framework.

9.2 Same starting line: The origins of horizontal inequalities

Both Calabar and Warri attained prominence from the sixteenth century as ports for the export of slaves. After the abolition of the slave trade in the early nineteenth century, the two cities remained important as centres of trade for oil palm. Calabar became a centre for missionary activities and the headquarters of the first British consul appointed for the Bights of Benin and Biafra. After formal colonization, Calabar was chosen as headquarters of the Southern Protectorate. Warri was not a centre of missionary activities and Western education but it served as the headquarters of trading companies and the Central Province of Southern Nigeria.

Another feature shared by Calabar and Warri was the intermediary role played by a single ethnic group, in each case, in external contacts. As a result of their settlements along the coasts, Itsekiri and Efik merchants dominated trade and consigned their neighbours to subsidiary roles. In Warri, the Urhobo acted as sources of slaves and oil palm for export and as markets for imported European goods, the same function that the Efut and Qua served in Calabar. In Warri, however, migrant Ijaw fishing communities, which were totally marginalized from the trade, turned to piracy (see Ikime, 1967).

The intermediary roles played by the Efik and Itsekiri merchant class positioned them to become the points of contact for missionaries. The missionaries initiated discussions with Efik and Itsekiri merchants and chieftains with a view to involving them in the evangelization of the hinterland. By the mid-nineteenth century, Efik merchants and chieftains had begun to embrace Christianity and Western education. The Itsekiri merchants and chieftains were, however, initially reluctant to do the same, based on the fear that to do so would precipitate a decay of the social order in Warri as it had done in Calabar. Only in the early twentieth century did the Itsekiri embraced both Christianity and Western education (see Ikime, 1967). The context for this was the employment opportunities to be found in the fledging colonial state and in foreign firms, which led to competition among different groups for education.

Since the Efik had accepted Western education about two decades before colonization, Efik catechists and teachers played crucial roles in the conversion and education of their Efut and Qua neighbours and other hinterland peoples at a time when Western education was in high demand throughout Southern Nigeria. This resulted in the spread of Efik language, culture and influence since the missionaries had translated the Bible into Efik language and preferred that both Christian and secular education should be conducted in the Efik language.

The Efik and the Itsekiri became the preferred political agents, clerks and assistants in the colonial administration. Whereas the prominence of the Efik elites in the early colonial administration stemmed from their early exposure to Western education and ways of life, the prominence of Itsekiri notables derived from the role that an Itsekiri merchant played in overcoming resistance to colonization in the Western Niger Delta. Dore Numa, who facilitated the defeat of Nana Olomu, Governor of the Benin River and the Oba of Benin, was rewarded with the post of pre-eminent paramount ruler in Warri province. He used this position to orchestrate the Itsekiri dominance of the native administration (Sagay, n.d.). Consequently, out of the 16 members in the Warri Native Court, which was constituted in 1896, 15 were Itsekiri and 1 Ijaw (Ikime, 1969). Dore was subsequently appointed to the Nigerian Council established to advise the Governor of Nigeria in 1914.

The fact that Dore was the only person appointed from Benin and Warri Provinces was evidence of the desire of colonial officers to reward elites who collaborated in the pacification project. Not surprisingly, the only person appointed to the Council from Eastern Nigeria was an Efik British political agent, Chief Richard Henshaw. As in Warri, the British emphasized Efik primacy in the constitution of the Native Administration in Calabar. For instance, before 1933 the body was virtually an Efik affair. When it was enlarged in 1933, it had 135 Efik members, 21 Qua members and 11 Efut members (Alderton, 1947). This was justified on the basis of the estimated population of each of the ethnic groups. For instance, the Senior Resident of Calabar Province reported that 'the administration is that of the Efik people with whom the Quas and the Efuts have thrown in their lot. It is a federation in which the Efik are the predominant factor' (Findlay, 1933).

Where such demographic rationalization could not be adduced, as in the case of the Itsekiri in Warri, British colonial officers deployed a 'civilizing mission' argument to justify Itsekiri dominance as illustrated in the report on Warri Division in 1925:

> When the Native Courts were being established in the outlying districts of the Division, leading Jekris with trading interests in these parts were given warrants in order to show the Sobos and other less enlightened tribes how the working of the courts should be carried on.[1]

This classification of some groups as 'enlightened' and 'progressive' and others as 'backward' and 'primitive' was also common in Calabar where the Efik were regarded as 'civilized' while the Efut and the Qua were 'primitive'. These colonially inspired categories became the basis for the uneven recognition of different groups: for instance, while the colonial administration codified the Efik paramount chieftaincy through the Old Calabar Native Rule No. 4 of 1902 and recognized pan-Efik rulers, namely the Obong of Calabar and Obong of Creek Town, it continued to address Efut and Qua traditional rulers as 'headmen'.

After the death of Dore Numa, paramount ruler in Warri, the colonial administration acceded to the request of the Itsekiri for the restoration of the precolonial Itsekiri monarchy. Although Ginuwa II, the Itsekiri monarch, did not enjoy the powers given to Dore Numa, he was undoubtedly the pre-eminent traditional ruler in Warri Division. But no recognition was accorded to Urhobo traditional rulers in Warri Division. What is more, whereas the Native Administration in Calabar was called 'Obio Efik Council', that in Warri was called the 'Itsekiri Native Administration'. These appellations offended the Efut, Qua, Ijaw and Urhobo, as they suggested that the Efik and Itsekiri respectively owned Calabar and Warri. It was for this reason that the title of 'Obong of Calabar' given to the Efik paramount ruler and that of the 'Olu of Warri' which was desired by the Itsekiri for their monarchy became seemingly intractable bones of contention.

9.3 All roads do not lead to Rome: Different conflict pathways

The cumulative effect of these external contacts was the emergence of political and social horizontal inequalities shaped by the privileged position of the Efik and Itsekiri, on the one hand, and the subaltern status of the Efut, Qua, Ijaw and Urhobo, on the other. This, however, cannot explain the different conflict outcomes in the two cities. It is to this and the implications for ethnic relations in Calabar and Warri that we now turn.

9.3.1 Between inclusive and exclusive politics

A major explanation of the different conflict outcomes in Calabar and Warri lies in the ways in which horizontal inequalities have evolved in the two cities. Whereas Calabar moved towards a more inclusive politics, Warri seemed attracted to a destructive, exclusive politics. During the crucial colonial period, Efik dominance in Calabar was mitigated by the opportunities that both the Efut and Qua had to lead the native administration and the native courts. For instance, in 1940, Ntoe Ika Ika Oqua of Big Qua was elected president of the Calabar Native Authority. The colonial administration acceded to the demand of the Efut and Qua by expunging the title 'Obio Efik Council'. It also ignored persistent pressures by the numerically dominant Efik for the adoption of a permanent Efik presidency of the native administration. Nor did it accept the position of the Efik elites that the Efik paramount ruler was superior to the traditional rulers of Efut and Qua.

The politics of inclusion in Calabar survived the advent of party politics, which was characterized by the alignment of ethnic groups with political parties. This is because, while the Efik produced the two members of parliament for the regional legislature, the government of Eastern Region officially recognized the Ntoe of Big Qua as First Class Chief, the same status accorded the Obong of Calabar. The appointment was against the spirit of the recommendation of a government commission on chieftaincy in Eastern Nigeria that population should be the yardstick for ranking chiefs. The Big Qua monarch was nominated to represent the Calabar community at a reception organized in honour of the Queen of England in 1956, and was nominated to the 1959 London Constitutional Conference.

Whereas party politics contributed to inclusive politics in Calabar since the recognition and appointment of Qua and Efut monarchs compensated for Efik dominance of elective positions, Warri drifted towards exclusionary politics in the 1950s. The Western Region Government, which now had Nigerian ministers, abandoned the caution exercised by the colonial administration previously by acceding to the Itsekiri demand for the recognition of the title of 'Olu of Warri'. This volte-face, which Ijaw and Urhobo elites construed as a restoration of the paramount status of Dore, was the trigger for the first incident of violent ethnic conflict in Warri. Aggrieved Urhobo communities attacked Itsekiri residents (Ikime, 1969; Lloyd, 1974). The reaction of the Ijaw and Urhobo to the change from 'Olu of Itsekiri' to 'Olu of Warri' should be understood in relation to the fact that the Itsekiri had also produced the two members of parliament for Warri Division.

Moreover, although Ijaw and Urhobo were elected to represent Western Ijaw and Urhobo and Western Urhobo Divisions respectively, there was no Ijaw or Urhobo member of the executive council. The only minister appointed from Warri Province (renamed Delta Province after the violence of 1951) was an Itsekiri. This generated resentment among the more populous Urhobo and Ijaw. Furthermore, Erejuwa II, the Olu of Warri, was subsequently appointed as minister without portfolio in the regional government. He was undoubtedly the most pre-eminent traditional ruler in the province. In addition, the Olu of Warri was appointed permanent president of the Warri Divisional Traditional Council. The appointment of an Itsekiri-dominated traditional council was intended to counterbalance the majority of Urhobo elected members of the municipal council, who owed their election to the preponderance of Urhobo residents in Warri Township.

The politics of exclusion was carried over into the postcolonial period. During the First Republic, an Itsekiri was one of the most powerful politicians in the country, controlling the strategic finance portfolio. Itsekiri politicians also dominated all elected positions for Warri Division. This stranglehold was consolidated with the enactment of the 1964 Midwest Region Constitution which recognized Warri as one of four special minority areas where nonindigenes were not eligible to contest elections. Warri was officially recognized as an Itsekiri 'homeland' and both Ijaw and Urhobo were barred from contesting elections there. What is more, the Olu of Warri continued to occupy pre-eminent status with his appointment as one of the few permanent members of the House of Chiefs.

In Calabar, however, the fact that the NCNC government continued to patronize Qua and Efut chieftains helped to mitigate the effects of the Efik dominance of elective positions. Even with the advent of military rule and the creation of South Eastern State in 1967, Efut and Qua elites benefited from concessionary appointments and recognition by aligning themselves with the dominant Ibibio ethnic group. During this period, Efut and Qua paramount chiefs were given official recognition and accorded the same status as the Obong of Calabar. Efut and Qua politicians also occupied various political positions even though the Efik remained dominant due to demographic factors. For instance, the Qua have produced a senator, head of service, some commissioners and local government chairmen, as well as State Assembly and Federal House of Representatives members. A Qua paramount ruler has also headed the State Council of Traditional Rulers.

Recognition in the public sphere of the kind that the Efut and Qua have enjoyed despite Efik dominance eluded the Ijaw and Urhobo of Warri, where the Itsekiri virtually monopolized all political appointments. For instance, between 1976 and 2003, all elected chairmen of local government areas in Warri were Itsekiri. The Itsekiri have also produced most of the legislators and commissioners and ministers from Warri. Between 1999 and 2003, for example, all three legislators for Warri were Itsekiri. The insistence of the Urhobo on producing one legislator, as they did in the Second Republic during the 2003 elections, led to another bout of ethnic violence. In addition, the Olu of Warri was permanent deputy president of the State Council of Traditional Rulers and permanent president of the Warri Traditional Council. It was only in 1991 that the government gave recognition to Urhobo traditional rulers in Warri. However, the Itsekiri leadership objected to the recognition of these 'fabricated' traditional rulers.

9.3.2   The role of homeland and indigeneity discourses

At the root of the Itsekiri dominance of Warri political space is the strong objection by the Itsekiri leadership to the inclusion of the Ijaw and Urhobo in Warri, a place they regard as their 'homeland'. The long-standing claim that Ijaw and Urhobo are 'settlers' in Warri was partly responsible for the colonial administration's rejection of demands made by the Ijaw for a separate native administration. It was also the basis for the enactment of the Itsekiri Communal Land Trust in 1958 which vested ownership and control of land in Warri Township in the Itsekiri traditional leadership institution, as well as sections of the 1964 Midwest Region Constitution, which excluded non-Itsekiri from contesting elections in Warri Division. It also explains why historically the Itsekiri have objected to the creation of local government areas along ethnic lines in Warri, as Ijaw and Urhobo leaders have demanded.

Consequently, successive local government creation exercises favoured the Itsekiri, with local government headquarters located in Itsekiri communities. For instance, in 1991, the headquarters of Warri North LGA were located in Koko, an Itsekiri town. The Ijaw had asked for the establishment of a Nein-Ibe LGA with headquarters at Oporoza, an Ijaw town. The trigger for the protracted violence in Warri between 1997 and 2003 was the decision of the federal government to transfer the headquarters of Warri South West LGA, earlier based at Ogbe-Ijoh, an Ijaw town, to Ogidigben, an Itsekiri town, after a period of six months. Aggrieved Ijaw youths attacked and occupied Itsekiri villages leading to intermittent outbursts of violence which lasted from 1997 to 2003. The violence ended after the state government returned the headquarters of the LGA to Ogbe-Ijoh, proactively appointed Ijaw and Urhobo from Warri to political positions and introduced development committees to Warri LGAs, actions which were expected to result in the devolution of control over LGA funds to the ethnic communities.

The Itsekiri leaders rejected these concessions, made to assuage Urhobo and Ijaw communities in Warri, on the grounds that both Urhobo and Ijaw were nonindigenes in Warri. As Chief Allison Ayida, an Itsekiri put it,

I personally find it difficult to contemplate a day when my children will wake up and try to claim Victoria Island as their native place or traditional home just because I have settled in Lagos and own property there. They will not be true Nigerians or Africans for that matter. It is no longer tenable to regard Lagos as no man's land. By the same token, Warri cannot be treated as no man's land.[2]

The Itsekiri leadership consequently reject the claim made by Urhobo and Ijaw leaders that the Itsekiri have been favoured in political appointments. Itsekiri elites claim that the Ijaw and Urhobo are not discriminated against since they are represented by their fellow Ijaw and Urhobo holding offices in Ijaw and Urhobo constituencies. The Ijaw and Urhobo have dominated the governorship positions of Bayelsa State and Delta State respectively since their inception. The Itsekiri resent the political ambitions of Ijaw and Urhobo in Warri, the more so because Itsekiri residents cannot win elections in Sapele (Urhoboland) and Bomadi (Ijawland), where they are nonindigenes (see Omatete, 2003). However, Urhobo and Ijaw leaders reject the Itsekiri position, claiming that it has no basis in the Nigerian constitution, which stipulates that local government and state of origin, not ethnic identity, are the constitutive elements of the Nigerian federation.

Itsekiri leaders regard the inclusion of the Ijaw and Urhobo in Warri as an encroachment on Itsekiri patrimony foisted upon 'minority minorities' by 'major minority' ethnic groups. To protect the rights of 'minority minority' ethnic groups, the Itsekiri leadership has canvassed for the redefinition of the basis of representation in the Nigerian state. In their view, the present framework where states and LGAs are the component units of the Nigerian federation favours major ethnic groups who dominate more states and is a travesty of the 'pact' that brought nationalities together to form Nigeria (see Itsekiri Ethnic Nationality, 2005).

The deployment of discourses centred on notions of homeland and indigeneity was the context for the zero-sum politics that evolved in Warri. This is because a 'homeland' is inherently indivisible. 'Sons of the soil' seldom accept any arrangement which could be interpreted to mean ceding to 'outsiders' an inch of territory containing the graves of their ancestors. It is for this reason that violence tends to occur in contestations over homeland (see Toft, 2003). Calabar has avoided this path due to the absence of a homeland discourse. None of the ethnic groups contests the indigeneity of the other. The bone of contention is the controversy over first settlement. The Efut and Qua claim they arrived and settled in Calabar before the Efik. However, the Efik dispute this claim, arguing that Efik historical numerical dominance suggests that the Efik were the first group to settle in Calabar (see Efik Eburutu Consultative Assembly, 2003; Efut Combined Assembly, 2003; Qua Clans Constituted Assembly, 2003).

The absence of homeland and indigeneity discourses in Calabar has facilitated the evolution of a politics of inclusion. The greatest concern of the leaders of each group has been to maximize the relative share accruing to its group from the common wealth, but not to such an extent as to exclude other groups from also partaking. This fact is exemplified by the legitimating discourse for Efik dominance deployed by Efik leaders – that of the Efik as the 'senior brother' of the Efut and Qua. Brotherhood signifies an acknowledgement of the existence of a common patrimony, as well as a claim, on the basis of the rules of primogeniture, to the largest share.

Therefore, it was possible to divide Calabar territory in such a way that leaders of each ethnic group could exercise both symbolic and political control in their spheres of influence. For instance, the creation of Calabar South LGA in 1996 enabled the paramount rulers of Efut and Qua to realize their long-standing desire of linking their traditional titles to Calabar territory. The paramount rulers are addressed as 'Muri Munene of Calabar South and Paramount Ruler of the Efut' and 'Ndidem of Calabar Municipality and Paramount Ruler of the Qua'. The Efik monarch, however, retained his title of 'Obong of Calabar'. Such opportunities for recognition helped to stop conflicts from degenerating into violence, since there is no incentive for ethnic leaders to embark on violent group mobilization.

9.3.3 An imagined community of the deprived

Even if such incentives were available, ethnic elites would still have found it difficult to incite their respective groups to violent action. This is because the populace does not feel excluded or discriminated against, which is essentially due to the absence of any discourse concerning indigeneity. Efut and Qua youth do not face any discrimination in the award of bursaries, in employment or in any other opportunities for empowerment because they are considered *bona fide* members of the Calabar political community. There is also no allegation that social amenities have been concentrated in Efik areas. If anything, to justify their claim to large portions of Calabar territory, the paramount rulers of Efut and Qua have declared themselves 'titular landlords' of most of the government and private sector establishments in Calabar. Consequently, Efut and Qua chieftaincies have been able to garner employment and contract opportunities for their people.

It is the inability of Ijaw and Urhobo traditional rulers to play similar roles in Warri that accounts for the violence there. Since exclusion in Warri is based on indigeneity, both elite and nonelite groups are deprived. The general perception that there are horizontal inequalities in political appointments, the location of social amenities and public institutions and opportunities for employment in public service and oil companies implies that all social strata in the three ethnic groups are directly affected. Because both elite and nonelite groups are directly affected it has been possible to imagine and reify a *community of the deprived*. The incentive to fight is strong when a deprived community believes it has been marginalized in all sectors. It is this convergence of interests between ambitious elites and unemployed and

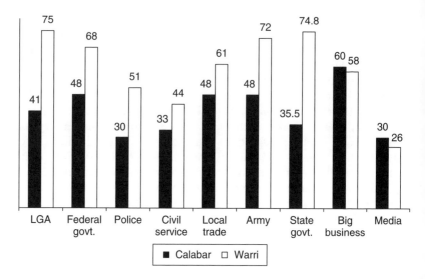

Figure 9.1 Survey respondents' perceptions of institutional domination, Warri and Calabar, Nigeria
Source: Author's fieldwork.

disenchanted youth that accounts for the recurrent outbreaks of violence in Warri (see Imobighe *et al.*, 2002; Ukiwo, 2006).

The fact that this was more the case in Warri than in Calabar is evident in the responses of randomly selected participants in a survey to the question of whether particular groups dominate specific public and organized private sector institution.[3]

As Figure 9.1 shows, while 75 per cent of Warri respondents felt particular groups dominated the LGA, the figure for Calabar was 41 per cent. A total of 68 per cent of Warri respondents and 48 per cent of Calabar respondents felt that certain groups dominated the federal government. Warri respondents consistently exhibited a stronger sense of ethnic domination of public institutions than Calabar respondents except in big business and media, where slightly more Calabar respondents felt some groups dominated. The higher figures for Warri suggest that there are stronger perceptions of inequalities in Warri than in Calabar.

The import of these findings is further substantiated by answers to the question of which group dominates various institutions. Respondents were asked to list two groups that dominated local government, the local trade sector and the state government. As shown in Figure 9.2, while 95 per cent of Warri respondents said indigenous ethnic groups dominated the local government, only 16 per cent of Calabar respondents felt likewise. More respondents from Warri (30.5 per cent) than Calabar (7 per cent) also listed indigenous groups as dominating the local trade sector. Almost all

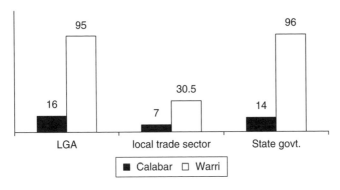

Figure 9.2 Survey respondents' perceptions of indigenous domination, Warri and Calabar, Nigeria
Source: Author's fieldwork.

Warri respondents (96 per cent) said indigenous groups dominated the state government whereas only 14 per cent of Calabar respondents listed indigenous groups as dominating it. More notably, among Warri respondents, 57 per cent said the Itsekiri dominated local government while 68 per cent said the Urhobo dominated the state government. Moreover, 24 per cent of Warri respondents said the Urhobo dominated the local trade sector. The Ijaw appear marginalized in all three areas. No indigenous group in Calabar was believed to have overwhelmingly dominated the LGA and local trade sector.

The strong perception of Itsekiri dominance of the local government in Warri is in fact a reflection of the actual situation. A Federal Character Commission fact-finding mission reported that all 413 staff members of Warri North LGA, which includes both Ijaw and Itsekiri communities, were Itsekiri.[4]

The results of the survey suggest that perceptions of horizontal inequality were more consistent in Warri than in Calabar. There were stronger perceptions of the existence of both political and economic inequalities as well as of cultural discrimination in Warri than in Calabar. This convergence of the different dimensions of horizontal inequality contributed to the emergence of imagined deprived communities in Warri and ultimately to their resort to violence.

Violent group mobilization was also made more likely by the exclusion or obliteration of the cultural symbols of particular groups in the public sphere, which was facilitated by discourses centred around notions of indigeneity and homeland. Thus, whereas Efut and Qua symbols are visible in Calabar, the Ijaw and Urhobo allege that there is a conspiracy by the Itsekiri to erase all trace of Ijaw and Urhobo identities from the Warri politico-cultural sphere. One of the complaints of the Federated Niger Delta Ijaw

Communities (FNDIC), which mobilized the Ijaw to attack the Itsekiri in 1997, was that the Itsekiri had renamed many Ijaw villages and erected Itsekiri cultural monuments all over Warri metropolis. Both Urhobo and Ijaw elites also decried the exclusive teaching of Itsekiri language in primary schools in Warri and the use of Itsekiri as the official language of the Warri Traditional Council.

Against the backdrop of complaints about the Itsekiri domination in the political, economic and educational spheres, the alleged marginalization of Ijaw and Urhobo cultural symbols in Warri made both elite and nonelite groups increasingly see marginalization as their *common fate* and conceive of themselves as *deprived communities*. Little wonder, therefore, that along with elections and the struggles over oil-bearing land and the placement of local government headquarters, a recurrent trigger of violence in Warri is the annual coronation anniversary procession of the Olu of Warri. The Ijaw and Urhobo oppose what they regard as cultural trespass on their territory in the same way that Northern Ireland Catholics reject what they regard as triumphalist Orange Order marches through Catholic communities.

9.3.4 The role of the state and powerful third-party actors

Group anxiety over ethnic domination of state institutions derives from the perceived role of the state in the creation, termination and reversal of horizontal inequalities. Violence occurs when some groups lose confidence in the state as a neutral arbiter. This was the case when the Urhobo attacked the Itsekiri after the government approved the title of Olu of Warri. The Urhobo, Ijaw and other ethnic groups in the province believed the change occurred at the behest of Chief Arthur Prest, an Itsekiri politician who was central minister for communications.

Since this first incident of ethnic violence, virtually all major government interventions have been interpreted as serving the interest of one group or the other. The Special Minority Areas Clause in the 1964 Midwest Constitution was said to have been the handiwork of Chief Festus Okotie-Eboh, an Itsekiri who was federal minister of finance at the time. When Egbeoma, an Ijaw clan in Warri, was transferred from Bendel State to Ondo State in 1977, Ijaw and Urhobo elites alleged that the transfer was masterminded by the secretary to the state government and the commissioner for local government and chieftaincy affairs, who were both Itsekiri, in order to prepare the way for the election of an Itsekiri LGA chairman. The Itsekiri principal officers were also alleged to have frustrated a move by the state government to recognize Urhobo traditional rulers in Warri in 1978 (Urhobo Indigenes of Warri, 1997).

When the newly created Delta State government finally recognized the Urhobo traditional rulers in 1991, Itsekiri elites attributed the decision to the emergence of an Urhobo as governor of the state (see The Committee of Concerned Itsekiri, 1998). The group also blamed the announcement of Ogbe-Ijoh as the headquarters of the newly created Warri South-West Government on the machinations of Ijaw generals and their 'lackey', the military administrator of Delta State. It was, of course, the turn of Ijaw elites to attack the Itsekiri in the federal bureaucracy for the relocation of the headquarters to Ogidigben. Itsekiri elites have also rejected the Warri 'Road Map for Peace' of the Delta State Government, alleging that the state governor, an Urhobo, is prosecuting the agenda of the Ijaw and Urhobo to take over Warri.

A lack of confidence in potential mediators in Warri is aggravated by the perception that oil companies and security agencies have intervened in a partisan manner. For instance, Ijaw and Urhobo elites have accused Chevron Texaco, which has an Itsekiri on its Board of Directors, of favouring the Itsekiri in its employment and corporate social responsibility programmes. On their part, Itsekiri elites have alleged that Shell, the Oil Minerals Producing Areas Development Commission (OMPADEC) and the Niger Delta Development Commission (NDDC), have concentrated most of their community development programmes in Ijaw and Urhobo communities (see Fregene, 1997; Gbaramatu Clan Communities, 1997; Urhobo Indigenes of Warri, 1997). Moreover, as violence raged in Warri between 1997 and 2003, Ijaw militia groups claimed that Nigerian soldiers fought on the side of the Itsekiri. Chief Bello Oboko, president of FNDIC, claimed an Itsekiri was appointed as junior minister in the Ministry of Defence between 1999 and 2003 to facilitate deployment of troops and weapons in favour of the Itsekiri. As a result of such allegations and counter allegations, the military authorities moved soldiers with affinity to any of the Warri ethnic groups from the combat areas.

Although there were misgivings about some of its decisions, especially in the colonial period and the eras of Igbo domination and Ibibio domination, the state government in Calabar is regarded as relatively fair to all groups. This is because it did not take any drastic decisions to perpetuate or reverse horizontal inequalities. For instance, Igbo- and Ibibio-dominated governments of Eastern Region and South Eastern State (later renamed Cross Rivers State), alleged to be sympathetic to Efut and Qua interests, did not abrogate the title of 'Obong of Calabar' or recognize the title of 'Ndidem of Calabar' and 'Muri Munene of Calabar'. Even when a government commission of enquiry recommended that the Efik monarch should be stripped of the title of 'Edidem', the military administrator, whom the Efik had accused of orchestrating a politics of 'divide and rule' in Calabar, rejected the recommendation (see South-Eastern State of Nigeria, 1972). In another notable example of relative autonomy, the Governor of Cross Rivers State, an Efik, rejected the recommendation of a judicial panel of enquiry that the Efik monarch should be recognized as paramount ruler of five local government councils and permanent president of the state council of chiefs (see Cross Rivers State of Nigeria, 2000). Such effective and overtly nonpartisan state intervention has helped to prevent conflicts from degenerating into violence.

State intervention and the responses to it were influenced by the stakes involved. In Calabar the state was able to mediate because the stakes were lower. This is principally because initiatives aimed at enhancing the inclusion of Efut and Qua interests did not pose significant threats to Efik dominance.

9.3.5   The role of history and memory in ethnic identity mobilization

In contrast to the situation in Warri, indigeneity discourses were deplored by the Efik leadership as a way of legitimating the exclusion of Igbo and Ibibio from effective political participation in Calabar. The dynamics of the conflicts between the Efik and the Ibibio, and the Efik and the Igbo, were initially that between 'natives' and 'strangers' in Calabar; and later that between 'minority' and 'major' ethnic groups in the Eastern Region and South Eastern State. Consequently, Efik identity was mobilized in a context where the Ibibio and Igbo were the ethnic 'others'. This is because it was the Igbo and Ibibio and not the indigenous Efut and Qua who threatened Efik pre-eminence. In Warri each ethnic group defined itself against its neighbour, who became the ethnic 'other'. Urhobo and Ijaw consciousness was aroused by and mobilized against perceived Itsekiri domination and vice versa. Moreover, the phenomenon of 'cultural imperialism' that prevailed in Calabar was not common in Warri. The Urhobo and Ijaw people have memories only of Itsekiri slave and oil palm traders and court clerks. They do not have memories of Itsekiri teachers and catechists. This is explained by the chequered history of Christianity in the Western Niger Delta. In Gramscian terminology, the Itsekiri did not exert hegemony over the Ijaw and Urhobo. It is not surprising that Itsekiri dominion, which was only perceived in the form of raw power, was fiercely resisted.

The different outcomes in ethnic relations could also be explained by the differences in the histories of kingship and colonization in Warri and Calabar. British colonial officers did not meet a king in Warri as they did in Calabar. The colonial administration did not begin in Ode-Itsekiri, the traditional capital of the Itsekiri Kingdom as it did in Duke Town, Calabar. Thus, when the Itsekiri monarchy was restored after almost four decades of colonial rule, Urhobo and Ijaw elites suspected it was intended to consolidate Itsekiri dominion. This suspicion was reinforced when the Itsekiri monarch relocated from Ode-Itsekiri to Warri. Doubtless, if the British had met an Itsekiri king in 1900 and recognized him as Olu of Warri, the Urhobo and Ijaw would not have resisted the recognition as fiercely as they did in 1936 and 1951. Since the change to the Olu of Warri occurred at a time that the Urhobo had reversed Itsekiri domination, it was construed as an attempt by the government to restore waning Itsekiri influence.

9.3.6 Civil societies and ethnic peace

In Calabar, it was the Igbo and Ibibio that were able to reverse historical Efik dominance. The Efik resented the fact that the more populous Igbo and Ibibio had taken control of the Calabar economy and threatened to dominate Calabar politics as they dominated the regional and state government. This led to incidents of violent confrontation as the Efik attacked migrant Ibibio and Igbo in Calabar. Resentment towards Igbo and Ibibio advancement and encroachment also motivated the Efik to spearhead the establishment of pan-Calabar organizations, such as the Calabar Youth Movement, Nka Ekpenyong Nnuk and Nka Nkaiso, whose membership cut across the three indigenous ethnic groups. Such organizations attracted membership from some Qua and Efut elements who also resented Igbo and Ibibio domination. It was thus a convergence of interests – of the Efik, the Qua and the Efut against domination by the nonindigenous Igbo and Ibibio – that gave birth to interethnic civic associations that ultimately worked in favour of ethnic peace in both colonial and postcolonial Calabar.

The absence of such a convergence of interests against an external threat precluded the emergence of similar interethnic civic associations in Warri. Rather, the different ethnic groups maintained separate associational platforms that promoted mutually conflicting interests. Since the Ijaw and the Urhobo resented Itsekiri domination of the LGA, while the Ijaw and the Itsekiri resented Urhobo domination of the state, only *ad hoc* dyadic platforms emerged. Having been contrived to counter the interests of one or the other ethnic groups, such platforms aggravated ethnic suspicions and rivalry. The perception of horizontal inequalities, exclusion and domination and the absence of a shared interest against a common external threat undermined the emergence of interethnic civic associations. This suggests that the variables determining whether there is ethnic peace are also the factors underlying the emergence of interethnic civic associations rather than these associations being the independent factors explaining ethnic peace, as has been suggested (see Varshney, 2002).

9.4 Concluding remarks

This chapter has advanced the position that the presence and perception of horizontal inequality is crucial to understanding why conflicting relations turn violent by exploring the comparative experiences of Calabar and Warri. According to the histories of these two towns, violent group mobilization occur when feelings of alienation and inequality cut across social classes and generational groups because they are perceived as affecting all members of a particular deprived community; when exclusion and inequalities are legitimated by the discourse of indigeneity; when state intervention is perceived as geared towards perpetuating or terminating horizontal inequalities in favour of one group against the other; and when there are prospects of reverse domination in which historically dominant groups feel endangered by the advancement or agitations of hitherto disadvantaged groups. Horizontal inequalities therefore need to be tackled not just because of their direct effects on conflict but also because of their long-term impact on interethnic cooperation.

Notes

1. Nigeria National Archives, Ibadan, Ughelli Papers, File No. 25, 1925.
2. *Vanguard*, 'The Itsekiri and the nation', 15 May 1992.
3. This formed part of the CRISE survey of perceptions (see Introduction).
4. *The Guardian*, 'Federal Character seeks balanced Itsekiri-Ijaw representation', 24 August 2005.

10
Ethnicity, Religion and the State in Ghana and Nigeria: Perceptions from the Street

Arnim Langer and Ukoha Ukiwo

10.1 Introduction

Objectively speaking, both Ghana and Nigeria are characterized by severe socioeconomic inequalities among their regions, ethnic groups and religions. Yet, as ultimately collective action depends on how social groups *perceive* the world in which they live and act, unravelling such perceptions must be a critical element in any investigation of group behaviour, including violent group mobilization. Consequently, this chapter presents and analyzes survey data, drawn from perceptions surveys conducted in Ghana and Nigeria, on how people see their own identities and their perceptions of the extent of domination of state institutions by particular ethnic or religious groups. The surveys consisted principally of a set of structured questionnaires in which respondents answered closed questions.[1]

It is important to emphasize that the perceptions surveys conducted in Ghana and Nigeria were not nationally representative. The results are therefore only *statistically* representative for the selected survey locations, but we can draw wider inferences based on the assumption that the surveyed areas are *qualitatively* representative of a larger part of society. In the Ghana survey, 608 randomly selected individuals of 18 years and above were interviewed in three urban settings in the southern part of the country, namely, Accra in the Greater Accra Region, Ho in the Volta Region and Kumasi in the Ashanti Region. While Accra – Ghana's capital – is ethnically diverse, Ho and Kumasi are both much more ethnically homogenous (Ghana's 2000 Population and Housing Census). In selecting these three survey areas, we aimed to explore whether the ethnic heterogeneity of communities affected people's attitudes. To reflect differences in the size of each city, 306 interviews were conducted in Accra, 61 in Ho and 241 in Kumasi.

In the Nigerian case, we selected Lagos, Nigeria's economic capital and most populous city, and Kukawa, Borno State, in the northeastern part of the

205

country. Kukawa was the capital of the Kanem Bornu Empire and is a semi-urban area, attracting traders and artisans from different parts of the country as a result of its proximity to Lake Chad and the Nigeria, Niger and Cameroon borders. In Lagos, two sites were selected: Ajegunle, a lower-class area of high population density, and Lagos Island, the central business district with middle-class residential neighbourhoods. Out of a sample population of 597, 397 questionnaires were administered in Lagos, 199 in Ajegunle and 198 in Lagos Island and 200 in Kukawa. The rationale for the choice of survey locations was to maximize social, political, geographic and economic contrasts. Lack of census data on the ethnic composition of Nigerian cities prevented a strategy similar to that adopted in Ghana. However, as will be shown, the three survey locations in Nigeria (Ajegunle, Lagos Island and Kukawa) also differed significantly with regard to their ethnic composition. We are therefore able to explore whether the ethnic heterogeneity of the location affected perceptions. Again, respondents in the Nigerian survey had to be at least 18 years old.[2]

The chapter proceeds as follows: the next section provides a brief overview of the 'objective' socioeconomic and political horizontal inequalities in both Ghana and Nigeria. It is not only important to understand the context in which the two surveys were conducted, but it is also relevant to compare these 'objective' inequalities with respondents' perceptions. The third section summarizes the composition of the survey samples in both countries. Section 10.4 analyzes the data on the salience of different identities. Section 10.5 explores the perceived impact of ethnicity and religion on access to different public opportunities and services, while Section 10.6 focuses on the political-administrative sphere. Section 10.7 discusses respondents' perceptions of government favouritism and discrimination. Finally, Section 10.8 draws some conclusions.

10.2   'Objective' socioeconomic and political inequalities in Ghana and Nigeria

Ghana and Nigeria are both ethnically diverse. While there are 60 different ethnic groups in Ghana, Nigeria is substantially more fragmented with 374 ethnic groups (see Otite, 1990). In Ghana, the four main ethnolinguistic groups, together constituting 86 per cent of the population, are the Akan (49.1 per cent), Ewe (12.7 per cent), Ga-Dangme (8.0 per cent) and Mole-Dagbani (16.5 per cent).[3] The Mole-Dagbani is the main ethnic group in the northern regions and most are Muslims. In Nigeria, the three largest ethnic groups (based on the 1963 Census) are the Hausa/Fulani, Igbo and Yoruba, indigenous to the north, east and west of the country, respectively. Precise figures for the size of these ethnic groups are unavailable because of the omission of ethnicity in population censuses. There is an important overlap between ethnicity and religion in Nigeria: the Hausa/Fulani and

Kanuri are predominantly Muslims, the Igbo and Southern minorities are predominantly Christians and the Yoruba and Northern minorities have an almost equal number of adherents of each religion.

The most marked socioeconomic inequalities in both Ghana and Nigeria, illustrated in Tables 8.10 and 10.1, relate to the sharp developmental divide between their northern and southern regions, and consequently between their northern and southern ethnic groups as well as between Muslims and Christians. The origins of these socioeconomic inequalities are diverse and relate to such factors as ecological and climatic differences, and the differential impact of both colonial and postcolonial economic development policies.

Ghana's three northern regions (Upper East, Upper West and Northern) lag severely behind on all the socioeconomic indicators investigated compared to the Greater Accra Region and to the other regions in the South. Despite the increased public expenditure in the north in recent years, the socioeconomic north–south divide has not been reduced much and remains very severe.

In Nigeria a similar picture emerges. The two northernmost zones, Northwest and Northeast, are the least developed in socioeconomic terms (see Table 10.1). And while the third northern zone, Northcentral, has done considerably better in socioeconomic terms – because it includes Abuja, Nigeria's federal capital – it is still significantly less developed than the relatively most developed zones, Southwest and Southeast, although similar in performance to the Southsouth zone.

The socioeconomic 'backwardness' of the northern regions in Ghana and Nigeria, however, has not been paralleled by exclusion of northerners from political power. Indeed, in both countries, northern political elites have generally been included in successive governments in the post-Independence

Table 10.1   Various socioeconomic indicators across Nigeria's zones in 1995/1996

Zone	Households without electricity (%)	Children 6–11 yrs in school (%)	Children 12+ in school (%)	Literate adults, 15+ (%)	Pregnant women using clinics (%)	New born children NOT immunized (%)
Northwest	79.8	34.2	35.2	20.7	25.3	65.9
Northeast	78.3	42.3	47.6	25	39.4	60.7
Northcentral	61.2	69.8	73.7	44.7	66.8	54
Southwest	30.4	94.6	88.9	68.9	74.7	29.1
Southeast	47.7	88.3	89.6	75.8	84.8	29
Southsouth	55.7	90.9	87.6	77.2	60.7	56.9

Source: Mustapha (2005: 8). Adapted from Federal Office of Statistics (FOS), 1995/1996, General Household Survey 1995/1996 National report.

Table 10.2 Ethnoregional composition of various Ghanaian governments, 1993–2005

Ethnic group	Government ministers								Population (%)
	1993		1997		2002		2005		
	No.	%	No.	%	No.	%	No.	%	
Akan	19	51.4	14	51.9	27	65.9	26	66.7	49.1
Ewe	4	10.8	3	11.1	3	7.3	3	7.7	12.7
Ga-Dangmes	3	8.1	3	11.1	4	9.8	4	10.3	8.0
Northern ethnic groups[a]	11	29.7	7	25.9	7	17.1	6	15.4	24.4
Total[b]	37	100.0	27	100.0	41	100.1	39	100.1	94.2
Government including deputy ministers									
Akan	36	48.0	36	46.2	40	56.3	60	69.0	49.1
Ewe	10	13.3	10	12.8	4	5.6	3	3.4	12.7
Ga-Dangmes	7	9.3	8	10.3	8	11.3	9	10.3	8.0
Northern ethnic groups	22	29.3	24	30.8	19	26.8	15	17.2	24.4
Total	75	99.9	78	100.1	71	100.0	87	99.9	94.2

[a] Northern ethnic groups consist of the Mole-Dagbani, Gurma and Grusi ethnic groups.
Sources: Authors' research; Population data from 2000 Ghana Population and Housing Census.
[b] Percentages greater or less than 100 are due to rounding effects.

period (see Chapter 8 for a more detailed discussion of Ghana's post-Independence national governments; for Nigeria see Mustapha, 2005). Table 10.2, which shows the composition of four Ghanaian governments, illustrates this for Ghana's Fourth Republic, established in January 1993. The Rawlings governments of April 1993 and October 1997 were exceptionally well balanced in ethnic terms. Northern ethnic groups were actually slightly overrepresented in relation to their demographic size in Ghana's population as a whole. Under Kufuor, the ethnic composition of the government became somewhat less balanced, with more than proportionate representation of Akan among ministers and deputy ministers and a marginalization of the Ewes. The northern ethnic groups were noticeably underrepresented among government ministers but accounted for a more than proportionate number of deputy ministers and the vice president has been a northerner from January 2001 (Chapter 8).

Due to their demographic significance in Nigeria, 'northerners' have generally been very well represented in various federal governments since independence in 1960. Table 10.3, showing the composition of four Nigerian governments in the period 1985–2004, illustrates this. In all four governments, the 'northerners' were moderately overrepresented in relation to their

Table 10.3 Zonal composition of various Nigerian cabinets, 1985–2004

Zone	1985		1986		1990		1993		2004		Popula-tion (%)
	No.	%	No.	%	No.	%	No.	%	No.	%	
Northwest	6	27.3	5	22.7	6	33.3	5	22.7	7	21.2	25.8
Northeast	2	9.1	2	9.1	3	16.7	3	13.6	5	15.1	13.4
Northcentral	4	18.2	5	22.7	2	11.1	4	18.2	6	18.2	13.6
Southwest	5	22.7	5	22.7	3	16.7	4	18.2	5	15.1	19.6
Southeast	2	9.1	2	9.1	3	16.7	2	9.1	4	12.1	12.1
Southsouth	3	13.6	3	13.6	1	5.5	4	18.2	6	18.2	15.1
Total[a]	22	100.0	22	99.9	18	100.0	22	100.0	33	99.9	99.6

Source: Langer *et al.* (2007: 32) and Mustapha (2005: 7).
[a] Percentages greater or less than 100 are due to rounding effects

demographic size in Nigeria's population as a whole. Indeed, it is sometimes argued that the northerners have dominated political power at the federal level because 10 of the 13 Nigerian heads of state had northern origins.[4]

10.3   Ethnic and religious composition of the survey samples

Given the centrality of ethnicity and religion to our analysis, it is apposite briefly to discuss the ethnic and religious composition of our survey samples. Tables 10.4 and 10.5 show the ethnic composition of the Ghanaian and Nigerian survey sites according to self-identification, that is, the preferred identification of each respondent. In the Ghanaian case, Accra was, as expected, the most ethnically heterogeneous city surveyed. The largest ethnic group in the Accra sample were the Ga-Dangmes, who are indigenous to Accra; the second largest were the Akans who are the largest ethnic group in Ghana as a whole, accounting for about half the population. However, the Akan group consists of an amalgamation of around 20 smaller ethnic groups, with the Ashanti (roughly 30 per cent of the Akan) and Fanti (roughly 20 per cent of the Akan), the largest subgroups. The third largest group in the Accra sample were the Ewe, who originate from the Volta Region in the eastern part of the country, with 13.4 per cent and the fourth largest were the Mole-Dagbani, constituting only 2 per cent of the respondents. Although the Mole-Dagbani are the second largest ethnic group in Ghana, with about 16.5 per cent of the population, their relatively small representation in the Accra sample is due to the fact that they predominantly live in the three northern regions, as mentioned earlier.

The second Ghanianan city surveyed was Ho, the regional capital and largest city of the Volta Region. About 80 per cent of the respondents in the Ho sample were Ewe, and the Akan constituted 8 per cent. The reverse

Table 10.4   Ethnic composition of the Ghanaian survey (percentages)

Region	Akan	Ewe	Ga-Dangme	Mole-Dagbani	Other
Accra	36.3	13.4	36.9	2.0	11.1
Ho	8.2	80.3	1.6	3.3	6.5
Kumasi	78.4	5.4	0.4	11.2	4.6

Table 10.5   Ethnic composition of the Nigerian survey (percentages)

Region	Yoruba	Igbo	Hausa/Fulani	Kanuri	Southern minorities	Northern minorities
Ajegunle Lagos	34.8	34.3	0.5	19.2	11.1	0.0
Lagos Island	87.4	6.5	2.0	0.5	2.0	0.0
Kukawa	0.5	0.0	48.5	42.5	0.0	8.5

situation occurred in the third city surveyed, Kumasi, the regional capital of the Ashanti Region. The Akan accounted for 78 per cent of the Kumasi sample, and the Ewe constituted a small minority of 5.4 per cent. The Mole-Dagbani formed 11 per cent of the Kumasi sample. Thus, in accordance with our sampling objectives, Ho and Kumasi were indeed much more ethnically homogenous than Accra.

Given the high level of ethnic fragmentation in Nigeria, the ethnic identities mentioned in the survey were aggregated on the basis of the major ethnoregional identities in the country, namely, Hausa/Fulani, Kanuri, Northern minorities, Yoruba, Igbo and Southern minorities. As shown in Table 10.5, the Nigerian survey included respondents belonging to all six of these ethnoregional groupings. Ajegunle was the ethnically most diverse survey location, while Lagos Island was the most homogeneous. Kukawa fell somewhere in between these two. In Ajegunle, the Yoruba were the largest ethnic group, although only marginally larger than the Igbo. The Yoruba originate from southwestern Nigeria and are therefore demographically dominant in Lagos which is evident in the Lagos Island sample where they constituted over 87 per cent of the respondents. The Igbo, who originate from southeastern Nigeria, were the second largest ethnic group in the Lagos sample with 34 per cent of the respondents. In the Kukawa sample, the Kanuri with 42.5 per cent and Hausa/Fulani with 48.5 per cent of the respondents, formed the two largest groups, while 8.5 per cent belonged to a Northern minority ethnic group.

Tables 10.6 and 10.7 show the religious composition of the Ghanaian and Nigerian sampled sites. In the Ghanaian survey, the three survey locations were predominantly Christians, with over 80 per cent of the respondents in each site, reflecting the predominance of the Christians in Ghana's population as a whole. Islam was the largest minority religion both in

Table 10.6 Religious composition of the Ghanaian survey (percentages)

Region	Catholic	Protestant	Pentecostal/ Charismatic	Other Christian	Islam	No religion/ Traditional
Accra	8.8	24.5	46.4	8.2	9.5	2.3
Ho	16.4	36.1	36.1	4.9	1.6	3.3
Kumasi	15.4	15.4	41.1	10.0	14.1	3.7

Table 10.7 Religious composition of the Nigerian survey (percentages)

Region	Catholic	Protestant	Pentecostal/ Charismatic	Other Christian	Islam	No religion/ Traditional
Ajegunle Lagos	21.7	6.6	36.4	15.2	15.2	5.1
Lagos Island	8.5	10.6	12.1	6.5	60.8	1.5
Kukawa	0.0	0.0	0.0	0.0	99.5	0.5

Accra (9.5 per cent) and Kumasi (14.1 per cent). In Ho only 1.6 per cent of the respondents were Muslim, below the 3.3 per cent of the respondents who said they adhered to a traditional religion or no specific religion whatsoever. Although Muslims are a minority in the southern regions of Ghana, in two of the three northern regions (Northern and Upper East regions), Islam is the largest religion. Ghana's religious north–south divide should, however, not be exaggerated because Christians and Traditionalists together constitute the majority of the population in the three northern regions.

In Nigeria, the Kukawa sample, with a vast majority of Kanuri and Hausa/Fulani respondents, was dominated by Muslims, while, conversely, Christian respondents were by far the largest religious group in the Ajegunle sample (80 per cent). In the Lagos Island sample, the largest religious group was the Muslims (60 per cent). Christians constituted about 30 per cent of respondents in Lagos Island.

10.4   The salience of different identities

A central focus of investigation was how much the ethnic and religious identities matter to people. Respondents were asked to choose three identities (from among a list of nine possible categories) which they considered most important for the way they thought about themselves – see Figures 10.1 and 10.2. Overall, Ghanaian respondents had very similar views regarding the relative importance of different identities, regardless of survey location and therefore the extent of ethnic heterogeneity of the place in which they lived. Only with regard to the proportion of respondents who

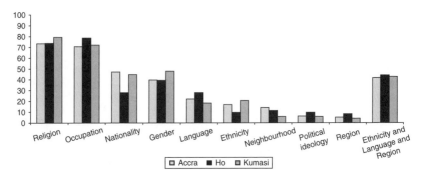

Figure 10.1   Three most important forms of self-identification in Ghana according to survey location

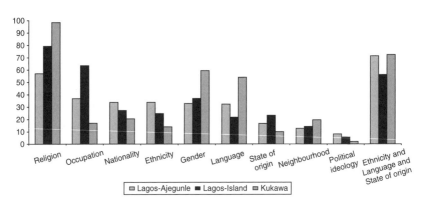

Figure 10.2   Three most important forms of self-identification in Nigeria according to survey location

mentioned nationality was there a significant difference in the three survey locations.

Over 70 per cent of the respondents in Accra, Ho and Kumasi considered both religion and occupation to be among their three most important aspects of identity. In all three survey locations, a noticeably smaller proportion of respondents (varying between 28 and 48 per cent) considered nationality or gender to be one of their three most important identities. Interestingly, only a minority (less than 20 per cent) of the respondents mentioned ethnicity in this respect. However, the latter finding might be due to the fact that ethnicity, language and region of origin are sometimes used interchangeably in the Ghanaian context. Ethnicity and language are particularly closely related as many ethnic groups are named after the language they speak (for example, Ewe and Akan). Consequently, respondents who mentioned any one of these three aspects might actually have been referring to the other two. In order to get an indication of the salience of this broadly defined 'ethnic' identity, we aggregated respondents who mentioned *either* ethnicity *or* language *or* region of origin (see the set of bars furthest to the right in Figure 10.1).[5] This reveals that about 40 per cent of the respondents considered this ethnoregional/linguistic identity to be one of their three most important identities. While this is comparable to the proportion of respondents who considered nationality and gender to be among their three most important identities, it was considerably lower than the proportion who mentioned religion or occupation.

In contrast to Ghana, there were significant variations across the three survey locations in Nigeria with regard to the salience of the different identities. These differences not only related to the proportions of respondents who considered a particular identity as one of their three most important identities, but also included a different ranking of the different identities in the three survey locations. To illustrate the first point, while 56 per cent of the respondents in Ajegunle considered religion as one of their three most important identities, in Lagos Island, this was 79 per cent, and in Kukawa nearly every respondent mentioned religion (see Figure 10.2). With regard to the ranking differences, it is noteworthy that while the two most important identities in Ajegunle and Lagos Island were the same (religion and occupation), the third one differed in both locations (nationality in Ajegunle and gender in Lagos Island). Compared to the two survey locations in Lagos, Kukawa showed a very different ranking. In particular, the three most important identities in Kukawa turned out to be (in descending order of importance) religion, gender and language. Thus, while religion once more emerged as the most important identity, the second and third most important identities in Kukawa differed from the survey locations in Lagos. A possible reason for the relative importance of occupation in Lagos (particularly in Lagos Island), but not in Kukawa, and of language in Kukawa but not in Lagos, might be the different nature of these survey locations. While Kukawa is still largely a traditional society, Lagos is a modern metropolis.

As in Ghana, ethnicity as such did not emerge as a particularly important factor in the way Nigerian respondents perceived themselves. Yet, in Nigeria, even more so than in Ghana, ethnicity, language and state of origin are often used interchangeably and tend to refer to a similar kind of identity. Figure 10.2 shows that when this broader usage of ethnicity is considered through the aggregation of the three aspects, more than 70 per cent of the respondents in Ajegunle and Kukawa considered ethnicity as one of their three most important identities. In Lagos Island, the ethnically most homogenous survey location, the proportion of respondents who mentioned this broadly defined ethnic identity was somewhat lower, but still around 56 per cent of the respondents mentioned it. Therefore, Nigerian respondents (regardless of the ethnic heterogeneity of their place of living) appeared to attach considerably more importance to ethnic background than the Ghanaian respondents, suggesting that ethnicity is more salient in Nigerian society.

This is further substantiated by the finding that ethnicity was also *relatively* more important (that is, in relation to other identities) in Nigeria than in Ghana. While in the Ghanaian survey, the proportion of respondents who mentioned ethnicity as defined in broad terms was comparable to those who mentioned nationality and gender this was, nonetheless, considerably smaller than the proportion who considered religion and occupation to be among their three most important identities (see Figure 10.1). In the Nigerian survey, in contrast, ethnicity (again broadly defined) emerged as the second and third most important identity in Kukawa and Lagos Island respectively, and the most important identity in Ajegunle (see Figure 10.2). In contrast, the respondents in the two countries had very similar perceptions with regard to religion. In all locations in Ghana and Nigeria, respondents considered religion as one of their two most important identities.

10.5   The *perceived* impact of ethnicity and religion in the public sphere

In order to assess the perceived impact of ethnicity and religion in the public sphere, the questionnaire asked respondents whether they thought ethnic or religious background affected a person's chances of getting government jobs, government contracts, public housing, preuniversity and university education. The answers are shown in Tables 10.8 and 10.9. In the Ghanaian survey, the proportion of respondents who thought that ethnic background affected a person's chances of getting government jobs, government contracts and public housing was considerably larger than the proportion of respondents who perceived this to be the case with regard to education. But there were some significant differences across locations. The proportion of respondents in Ho who perceived that ethnic background affected the chance of getting government jobs, government contracts, public housing and educational opportunities was consistently the largest of the three survey locations, while the proportion of respondents in Kumasi who perceived this to be the case was consistently the lowest and replies from Accra were between those from Ho and Kumasi. The respondents in Ho and Kumasi differed most when it came to the perceived impact of ethnicity on gaining access to government employment and contracts. In particular, while about 25 per cent of the respondents in Kumasi thought that ethnicity affected a person's chances of getting government employment and contracts, between 50 and 54 per cent of the respondents in Ho had this perception.

Kumasi is predominantly inhabited by Akan, while Ho is dominated by Ewe. Therefore, the differences between Ho and Kumasi also tell us something about the differences in perceptions between these two groups. Interestingly, the Akan and Ewe respondents in the Accra sample also had

Table 10.8 The proportion of Ghanaian respondents according to survey location who thought that ethnicity affected a person's chances of getting access to public opportunities and services (%)

Region	Government jobs	Government contracts	Public housing	Pre-university education	University education
Accra	39.5	38.6	39.5	18.6	16.0
Ho	54.1	50.8	42.6	26.2	27.9
Kumasi	24.9	24.9	35.7	11.2	9.1

Table 10.9 The proportion of Nigerian respondents according to survey location who thought that ethnicity affected a person's chances of getting access to public opportunities and services (%)

Region	Government jobs	Government contracts	Public housing	Pre-university education	University education
Ajegunle	58.6	60.1	42.4	37.4	46.0
Lagos Island	57.2	56.7	28.9	44.8	43.3
Kukawa	35.5	32.0	30.5	22.0	22.0

different perceptions on the same issue: while 38 per cent and 34 per cent of the Akan respondents in the Accra sample considered that ethnicity affected a person's chances of getting government jobs and contracts respectively, for the Ewe respondents, the figures were 44 per cent and 46 per cent. The proportion of Ga-Dangmes who perceived that ethnicity affected a person's chances of getting government employment and contracts was somewhere in between that of the Akan and Ewe respondents. Although the Akan and Ewe respondents in Accra had different views regarding the impact of ethnicity in the public sphere, they appeared to be less at odds than their ethnic counterparts in Ho and Kumasi. The views of the Mole-Dagbani respondents in the Kumasi sample, which we take here as an approximation of the views of the 'northerners', since we did not survey a northern site, also proved interesting. Not only were they less concerned about the impact of ethnicity on getting access to government jobs, contracts and public housing than the Akan respondents in Kumasi (only about 22 per cent of the Mole-Dagbani respondents thought that ethnic background affected a person's chances in this respect), but also a considerably smaller proportion of them (in fact 3.7 per cent, or one out of 27 respondents) thought that ethnic background affected a person's chances of getting educational opportunities. This is all the more interesting if one considers the severe educational inequalities between the northern and southern regions.

Differences in perceptions between the Akan and Ewe regarding access to government jobs and contracts are likely to be influenced and to some extent provoked by the fact that the current New Patriotic Party (NPP) government, led by President John Agyekum Kufuor (an Ashanti from the Ashanti Region where he has royal ancestry), is widely regarded as a pro-Ashanti/Akan government. Since its inception in 1992 the NPP has generally been perceived to be a largely Akan-based party, despite the fact that NPP's hierarchy has been multiethnic (Gyimah-Boadi and Asante, 2006). A probable reason for the persistence of this perception under Kufuor is the relative overpresentation of the Akan in government since he came to power in January 2001 (see Table 10.2).

The proportion of Nigerian respondents who perceived ethnic background as affecting a person's chances of getting access to the different public amenities and services was considerably larger (particularly in Lagos) than in the Ghanaian survey (see Tables 10.8 and 10.9). And while, as in Ghana, the proportion of respondents who thought that ethnic background affected a person's chances of accessing educational opportunities was noticeably smaller than in relation to government jobs and contracts, in the two survey locations in Lagos between 37 and 46 per cent of the respondents nonetheless perceived ethnicity as affecting a person's chances of accessing preuniversity and university education. Interestingly, in Kukawa, the location with the lowest enrolment and literacy rates, only about 22 per cent of the respondents thought that a person's chances of getting preuniversity and university education were affected by ethnic background. Arguably, a major reason why considerably more respondents in the Nigerian survey perceived ethnic background as affecting chances of gaining access to the different public amenities and services is the presence of 'affirmative action' programmes, such as the Federal Character Principle with regard to employment in state institutions and the use of quotas in university admissions.

As in the Ghanaian survey, Table 10.9 shows significant differences between the three survey locations in Nigeria. It is clear that the southern (that is, the Yoruba, Igbo and Southern minorities) and northern ethnic groups (the Hausa/Fulani, Kanuri and Northern minorities) had very different perceptions regarding the impact of ethnicity in the public sphere. The southern ethnic groups (almost all interviewed in Lagos) were much more concerned about the impact of ethnicity on access to the different public amenities and services than the northern ethnic groups (predominantly interviewed in Kukawa). Moreover, from a comparative perspective, it is striking that both in the Ghanaian and Nigerian surveys, the ethnoregional groups (the Ewe in Ghana and the southern ethnic groups in Nigeria), who feel either presently and/or historically excluded from political power, were the ones most concerned about the impact of ethnicity in the public sphere.

It is sometimes argued that increased levels of education are likely to reduce people's ethnic loyalty, for example by those who adopt a modernization perspective towards ethnicity and national integration (see Deutsch, 1961). In order to explore the validity of the modernization thesis in the Ghanaian and Nigerian contexts, we cross-tabulate respondents' level of education with perceptions of the importance of ethnic background on access to the different public goods in Tables 10.10 and 10.11.

A consistent pattern is discernible in both countries. We find that the higher the level of education of a respondent, the more likely he/she is to think that

Table 10.10 The proportion of Ghanaian respondents according to educational background and survey location who thought that ethnicity affected a person's chances of getting access to public opportunities and services (%)

Region	Government jobs	Government contracts	Public housing	Pre-university education	University education
Accra					
Primary completed	28.8	30.8	34.6	13.5	13.5
Secondary completed	39.5	38.5	41.5	20.0	16.5
Post-secondary qualific-ations and higher	50.0	46.3	37.0	18.5	16.7
Ho					
Primary completed	40.0	20.0	20.0	20.0	20.0
Secondary completed	45.2	41.9	29.0	25.8	25.8
Post-secondary qualific-ations and higher	68.0	68.0	64.0	28.0	32.0
Kumasi					
Primary completed	11.1	11.1	27.8	7.4	5.6
Secondary completed	26.3	26.3	37.5	11.3	8.8
Post-secondary qualific-ations and higher	46.2	46.2	42.3	19.2	19.2

Table 10.11   The proportion of Nigerian respondents according to educational background and survey location who thought that ethnicity affected a person's chances of getting access to public opportunities and services (%)

Region	Government jobs	Government contracts	Public housing	Pre-university education	University education
Ajegunle Lagos					
Primary completed	53.3	53.3	46.7	43.3	46.7
Secondary completed	52.6	52.6	40.2	33.0	42.3
Post-secondary qualifications and higher	68.2	72.7	42.4	37.9	48.5
Lagos Island					
Primary completed	48.1	37.0	7.4	29.6	33.3
Secondary completed	53.1	59.2	29.6	43.9	40.8
Post-secondary qualifications and higher	67.7	63.1	38.5	55.4	53.8
Kukawa					
Primary completed	35.5	32.3	31.0	22.6	22.6
Secondary completed	36.8	36.8	36.8	26.3	26.3
Post-secondary qualifications and higher	43.8	37.5	31.3	25.0	25.0

ethnic background affected a person's chances of getting government jobs and contracts. This pattern was consistent across all survey locations and levels of education, except for the second highest educational group in the Ajegunle site. A possible reason why highly educated people are more likely to think that ethnicity affects someone's chances of getting government employment and contracts is that educated people, who mainly make up the technocracy, bureaucracy and business class, are more directly engaged in the competition for these public goods.

In contrast, religion was considered to be a less influential factor in getting access to the different public amenities and services than ethnicity in *all* survey locations in both Ghana and Nigeria (see Tables 10.12 and 10.13). This is particularly noteworthy in the Nigerian context where there is often an overlap between religious and ethnic identities. In the Ghanaian survey, only Kumasi and Accra had enough Muslim respondents to allow for a direct comparison between Muslims and Christians. Two important findings emerged: first, both the Muslim and Christian respondents in Kumasi were significantly less concerned about the impact of religion in the public sphere than their religious counterparts in Accra. Second, while the proportion of Muslim respondents in both Accra and Kumasi who perceived religion as affecting a person's chances of getting government jobs, government contracts and public housing was consistently larger than that of the Christian respondents, with regard to getting access to preuniversity and university education, the proportion of Christian respondents was larger than that of Muslim respondents.

In Nigeria, an important finding was that the smaller the proportion of Muslims in the population of a survey location, the larger the proportion of Muslim respondents who perceived religion to affect a person's chances of getting the different public amenities and services. Thus 24 per cent, 31 per cent and 38 per cent of the Muslim respondents in Kukawa, Lagos Island and Ajegunle respectively thought that religion affected a person's chances

Table 10.12   The proportion of Ghanaian respondents according to survey location who thought that religion affected a person's chances of getting access to public opportunities and services (%)

Region	Government jobs	Government contracts	Public housing	Pre-university education	University education
Accra	27.8	27.8	39.5	18.6	15.4
Ho	24.6	23.0	27.9	19.7	14.8
Kumasi	15.8	14.9	30.7	10.0	7.1

Table 10.13   The proportion of Nigerian respondents according to survey location who thought that religion affected a person's chances of getting access to public opportunities and services (%)

Region	Government jobs	Government contracts	Public housing	Pre-university education	University education
Ajegunle Lagos	28.4	30.3	26.8	27.3	29.8
Lagos Island	33.0	28.4	18.0	22.7	23.7
Kukawa	24.0	23.0	21.5	18.5	18.5

of getting government employment, while virtually everyone was Muslim in Kukawa, 60 per cent was Muslim in Lagos Island and only 15 per cent in Ajegunle. This pattern emerged not only in relation to government employment, but also to government contracts, public housing and educational opportunities.

Another interesting finding in the Nigerian survey was that the Christian respondents were more concerned about the impact of religion than the Muslim respondents in the Lagos Island sample, while the Muslim respondents were more concerned than the Christian respondents in the Ajegunle sample. Bearing in mind that the Ajegunle sample had a Christian majority, while the Lagos Island sample was dominated by Muslims, this finding (like the first one) suggests that the religious composition of an area influences people's perceptions of the impact of religion in the public sphere.

10.6   Perceptions of political horizontal inequalities

In this section, we aim to assess the perceived horizontal inequalities in the political-administrative sphere by analyzing respondents' perceptions of which groups dominate the national/federal government, the top level of the police, the top level of the civil service, the top level of the armed forces and the judiciary. The relevant question in the perceptions questionnaire was two-pronged. Respondents were asked whether they thought a certain group of people (without mentioning any particular group) dominated a particular state institution; if respondents answered 'yes' to this, they were asked to name the dominant group(s) of people. The results are shown in Tables 10.14 and 10.15.

In the Ghanaian survey, there were significant differences between the three survey locations (Table 10.14). While the respondents in Accra and Kumasi had very similar perceptions regarding the alleged domination of the main state institutions, a considerably higher proportion of the respondents in Ho perceived the different state institutions to be dominated by particular groups. Nonetheless, with the exception of the national government, the

Table 10.14   The proportion of Ghanaian respondents according to survey location who considered a specific state institution to be dominated by a particular group (%)

Region	National government	Top level of the police	Top level of civil service	Top level of the armed forces	Judiciary
Accra	39.5	29.1	23.9	24.2	19.3
Ho	65.6	41.0	31.1	41.0	24.6
Kumasi	38.2	31.5	20.7	25.7	22.8

Table 10.15 The proportion of Nigerian respondents according to survey location who considered a specific state institution to be dominated by a particular group (%)

Region	Federal government	Top level of the police	Top level of civil service	Top level of the armed forces	Judiciary
Ajegunle Lagos	52.0	34.5	37.9	56.1	25.5
Lagos Island	64.2	41.6	37.2	62.2	40.9
Kukawa	24.5	22.5	21.5	18.0	29.0

proportion was relatively low, particularly in Accra and Kumasi. Moreover, the groups perceived to dominate the national government were extremely diverse, including 'lawyers', 'NPP party members', 'president's relatives' and 'Christians'. But more respondents in Ho perceived ethnic domination of the national government. About 51 per cent of them mentioned the Akan or a subgroup thereof (particularly the Ashanti) as the dominant group in the national government. Although the Akan were also the most frequently mentioned group in the other two cities too, overall only 28 per cent of the respondents in Accra and 25 per cent in Kumasi perceived this group as dominating the national government. Interestingly, the proportion of the Mole-Dagbani respondents in the Kumasi sample, used here as our 'northern' proxy, who perceived these five state institutions to be dominated by a particular group was consistently smaller than that of the Akan respondents in Kumasi. Twenty-six per cent of the Mole-Dagbani respondents perceived the national government to be dominated by a particular group, with regard to the police and armed forces it was 22 per cent and with regard to the civil service and judiciary only 19 per cent.

A significantly larger proportion of respondents in the Lagos survey locations perceived the different state institutions to be dominated by certain groups (see Table 10.15). The federal government ranked first and the top level of the armed forces second as state institutions perceived to be dominated by particular groups by a large proportion of Nigerian respondents. But a relatively high number of respondents answered that they did not know whether or not a particular group dominated the different state institutions; as many as 61 per cent of the respondents in Kukawa answered that they did not know whether a particular group of people dominated the federal government (and 33 per cent in Ajegunle and 26 per cent in Lagos Island). In the Ghanaian survey, the proportion of respondents who answered 'Don't know' when they were asked whether the national government was dominated by a particular group, was considerably smaller (between 12 and 15 per cent). It is difficult to determine whether the high proportion of respondents who answered 'Don't know' in the Nigerian survey was the result of lack of knowledge, or whether respondents were reluctant to answer the question because of the sensitive nature of the issues involved. But the fact that the largest percentage of 'Don't know' responses was recorded in Kukawa which had the lowest proportion of educated respondents may indicate that lack of knowledge was important.

Notwithstanding the high proportion of 'Don't know' responses, the vast majority of respondents who perceived the federal government and the top level of the armed forces to be dominated by a certain group mentioned either the Yoruba or the Hausa-Fulani. In the two survey locations in Lagos, the most frequently mentioned group was the Hausa-Fulani; in Ajegunle 29 per cent of the respondents perceived the Hausa-Fulani as the dominant group in the federal government and 47 per cent in Lagos Island. Twenty-three and 26 per cent of the respondents in Ajegunle and Lagos Island respectively perceived the Yoruba as dominating the federal government. The finding that a relatively higher proportion of respondents perceived the Hausa-Fulani as dominating the federal government in both the ethnically diverse survey location of Ajegunle and the Yoruba-dominated survey location of Lagos Island is particularly intriguing considering that the president of Nigeria at the time the survey was conducted, Olusegun Obasanjo, was a Yoruba. In contrast, in Kukawa, the Yoruba were indeed the most frequently mentioned ethnic group perceived as dominating the federal government.

Forty-eight per cent and 62 per cent of the respondents in Ajegunle and Lagos Island respectively perceived that the Hausa-Fulani dominated the top level of the armed forces. In Kukawa, which has a large Hausa-Fulani population, only 3 per cent of the respondents perceived the armed forces to be dominated by the Hausa-Fulani, while 14 per cent of the respondents again mentioned the Yoruba. A relatively higher proportion of respondents in the Nigerian survey perceived the most important state institutions to be dominated by certain ethnic groups than in the Ghanaian survey although again there were more 'Don't knows'. This could be taken as further evidence of the more politicized nature of ethnicity in Nigeria than in Ghana.

10.7   Perceptions of government favouritism and discrimination

A final issue concerns respondents' perceptions of government favouritism and discrimination. Respondents were asked whether or not they thought that certain groups of people were favoured or discriminated against by the government. If they answered 'Yes' to this, they were asked to name the groups of people thought to be favoured or discriminated against. Tables 10.16 and 10.17 show the results.

Table 10.16 Perceptions of government favouritism and discrimination in Ghana according to survey location (%)

Region	Favouritism	Discrimination
Accra	31.4	20.6
Ho	47.5	45.9
Kumasi	19.5	13.7

Table 10.17 Perceptions of government favouritism and discrimination in Nigeria according to survey location (%)

Region	Favouritism	Discrimination
Ajegunle Lagos	48.0	34.8
Lagos Island	51.5	35.1
Kukawa	29.5	21.0

In the Ghanaian survey, there were significant differences between the three survey locations regarding the extent of perceived favouritism or discrimination by the government. In all three survey locations, however, the proportion of respondents who perceived the government to favour certain groups was noticeably higher than the proportion of respondents who perceived certain groups to be discriminated against by the government. Again respondents in Ho and Kumasi appeared to have the most divergent perceptions regarding these issues, while respondents in Accra had views that once more fell somewhere between these two. Although respondents' perceptions of the particular groups favoured or discriminated against by the government were again extremely diverse, including such categories as 'the young and wise', 'relatives and friends of government officials', 'the rich' and 'students', most respondents who thought there was government favouritism and/or discrimination mentioned a particular ethnic group. The respondents in Ho had the largest proportion claiming there was favouritism and discrimination by the government on ethnic grounds, with 33 per cent of the Ho respondents saying that the Akan or a subgroup thereof (particularly the Ashanti) were favoured by the government, and 19 per cent of them perceived the Ewe to be discriminated against by the government. The proportion of respondents in the other two cities saying that the Akan were favoured by the government were significantly lower; 8 per cent and 17 per cent of the respondents in Kumasi and Accra respectively. Only one respondent in the whole survey perceived the Akan to be discriminated against by the Kufuor government.

As already mentioned, the differences between the respondents in Ho and Kumasi also tell us something about the differences in perceptions between the Ewe and Akan respondents. Since the emergence of Ghana's Fourth Republic in January 1993, the Ewe and Akan, particularly the Ashanti, have persistently supported opposing political parties. While the Ewe generally support the National Democratic Congress (NDC), which was founded by former military dictator and civilian president Jerry Rawlings (who is half-Ewe himself), the Ashanti/Akan have given most support to the NPP. The voting patterns in both ethnic groups' home regions (the Ashanti and Volta regions) illustrate this political divide strikingly. In particular, the NPP won by a huge majority in the Ashanti Region, while the NDC took most of the votes in the Volta Region in all four general elections during Ghana's Fourth Republic (see Chapter 8). The persistence of differences in Ewe-Ashanti/Akan voting patterns has contributed to the view that the NPP and NDC are largely Akan-based and Ewe-based political parties. Considering that the NPP is currently in power, it should not come as a surprise that a significant minority of the Ewe/Ho respondents perceived the Kufuor government to favour the Akan.

With regard to the extent of government favouritism and discrimination in Nigeria, there was again a clear north–south divide. Perceptions of government favouritism and discrimination were considerably more widespread among respondents in the two Lagos survey locations than in Kukawa. The most frequently mentioned group perceived to be favoured by the government were the Hausa-Fulani: 28 per cent of the respondents in Ajegunle and 38 per cent in Lagos Island perceived this ethnic group to be favoured by the government, while only 18 to 19 per cent of the respondents in the Lagos survey locations mentioned the Yoruba in this respect. In Kukawa, an even smaller proportion of respondents (around 9 per cent) perceived there to be Yoruba favouritism.

As in Ghana, the proportion of respondents in all survey locations who perceived there to be government favouritism was considerably higher than those who thought that the government discriminated against particular groups. Only a very small proportion of respondents in the Nigerian survey perceived that the Yoruba or Hausa-Fulani were discriminated against by the government. The most frequently mentioned group in both Ajegunle and Lagos Island perceived to be discriminated against by the government was the Igbo (mentioned by about 14 per cent of the respondents). Most of the respondents who perceived the Igbo to be discriminated against were Igbo themselves. Historical factors may account for this. While the Igbos dominated the civil service in the early years of independence, following the Nigerian civil war they became marginalized in Nigeria's main state institutions. Moreover, although they constitute one of the three major ethnic groups, they have produced the head of government for a period of only six months, whereas the Hausa/Fulani and Yoruba have produced long-serving heads of government. These factors are likely to have contributed to feelings of government discrimination among a significant proportion of the Igbo (Mustapha, 2005).

10.8   Conclusions

The surveys showed quite marked differences between Ghana and Nigeria, although we must exercise caution in making generalizations based on the limited sample and different selection strategies. We found that while more Nigerian than Ghanaian respondents perceived religious and ethnoregional/linguistic identities to be among their three most important identities, the reverse was the case with regard to occupation and nationality. Ghanaian respondents generally tended to value their national and occupational identities more than Nigerian respondents did. Moreover, more respondents in Nigeria than in Ghana believed that ethnicity affected access to public goods and that the government shows favouritism and discrimination.

Interestingly, contrary to the modernization perspective on ethnicity and national integration, attainment of higher levels of education did not diminish the tendency for people to think in ethnic terms. On the contrary, both the Ghanaian and Nigerian survey reaffirmed Melson and Wolpe's (1971) findings that educational attainment and other attributes of modernization are *positively* correlated with greater salience of ethnic identities and perceptions of favouritism on ethnic grounds. As we have argued, this is probably because it is those with higher educational attainments who compete for the most lucrative jobs and business opportunities and therefore 'know where the shoes pinch'.

Both Ghana and Nigeria have had turbulent political histories characterized by frequent military coups. However, while Nigeria has gone through a civil war and has been confronted by recurrent ethnic and religious violence, especially since the late 1980s, so far Ghana has, with the exception of communal conflicts in its northern regions, avoided serious interethnic and religious violence. The differences in comparative perceptions of identities and of perceptions of the state in Ghana and Nigeria may help explain why Nigeria has been more prone to violent conflict than Ghana. But we should note that the causality could also go the other way, from a more violent environment to greater perceptions of ethnic salience and discrimination. In addition, there are other reasons for the difference in the political salience of ethnic identities in the two countries such as the adoption of quotas for jobs according to regional origin in Nigeria. Such quotas and the related practice of the federal character principle, which also involves ensuring that different major ethnic groups are represented at many levels in the political system and the bureaucracy, may explain why ethnolinguistic and regional identities remain strong in Nigeria. At the same time, however, these policies were introduced precisely because ethnicity appeared to be so politically salient (Mustapha, 2005).

A comparison of the 'objective', socioeconomic and political horizontal inequalities in both countries (see Tables 8.10 and 10.1–10.3) with respondents' perceptions of the impact of ethnic or religious identities on getting access to educational opportunities (see Tables 10.8, 10.9, 10.12 and 10.13) as well as the extent of domination of different state institutions by particular groups (see Tables 10.14 and 10.15), proves interesting in two respects. Firstly, in Nigeria, even though the school enrolment rates are drastically lower in the Northeastern zone (where Kukawa is located), paradoxically, respondents in the two Lagos survey sites were much more concerned about the impact of ethnicity and religion on getting educational opportunities. In the Ghanaian survey, when using the Mole-Dagbani respondents in the Kumasi sample as a proxy for the perceptions of the northerners, a similar finding emerged. A possible explanation for this apparent paradox could be that respondents' perceptions of the impact of ethnic or religious background on educational opportunities are based on experiences within the region or locality in which they live, while the recorded educational differences were between regions.

Secondly, the comparison of the 'objective' and perceived political horizontal inequalities in the Ghanaian case shows that respondents belonging to the politically dominant ethnic group in objective terms (the Akan) were much less likely to perceive this political reality than the objectively underrepresented ethnic group(s) (the Ewe) to perceive themselves as underrepresented. In Nigeria, a somewhat different but related finding emerges: respondents of the two major ethnic groups in terms of objective political representation, the Hausa-Fulani and Yoruba, tended to perceive the other group as the dominant one. Both cases illustrate the finding that where you stand determines what you see.

Notes

1. The Ghanaian perceptions survey was conducted in July 2005, while the Nigerian one took place in a four-week period in August and September 2005.
2. A more extensive discussion of the survey methodology and selection strategy in both Ghana and Nigeria is provided in Guichaoua *et al.* (2006). This report is available upon request from the authors.
3. The ethnic categorization discussed here is based on the classification used by the Ghana Statistical Service (see, for example, the 2000 Ghana Population and Housing Census).
4. This includes the military leaders who seized power by nonconstitutional means.
5. Respondents who mentioned more than one of these identity aspects (that is, ethnicity, language and region of origin) among their three most important ones, were only counted once.

11
Inequality, Ethnicity and Political Violence in Latin America: The Cases of Bolivia, Guatemala and Peru

*Corinne Caumartin, George Gray Molina and Rosemary Thorp**

11.1 Introduction

This chapter provides a review of the interface between ethnicity, political violence and horizontal inequalities (HIs) in three countries: Peru, Bolivia and Guatemala. The cases chosen to develop insights from Latin America on the. relationship between HIs and conflict are the three countries with the largest indigenous populations in proportionate terms (see Table 11.1). All have a serious degree of HI across ethnic divisions, which we document in Section 11.2.

It is beyond the remit of this chapter to provide an in-depth examination of ethnicity in Latin America, but we must first define the key groups we are researching as well as briefly review some of the commonalities and differences in our three case studies. We are essentially working with indigenous and nonindigenous groups. The term 'indigenous' is a highly contested one, but in essence refers to groups descended from pre-Columbian populations.[1] However, the indigenous population in fact comprises a great diversity of ethnic groups. There are, for instance, over 20 indigenous ethnolinguistic groups in Guatemala and over 30 in Bolivia. In Bolivia, the Aymaras and Quechuas constitute a majority of the indigenous population, as do the Quechuas in Peru. In Guatemala, there are four key ethnolinguistic groups: the K'iche', K'eqchi, Mam and Kakchikel groups.[2] The nonindigenous population includes *mestizos*, *criollos* or whites and a variety of

* We acknowledge significant contributions from Luca Mancini, Maritza Paredes and Andrea Portugal. An earlier version of this chapter was published in *Bulletin of Latin American Research* 25(4), October 2006, published by Blackwell Publishing.

Table 11.1   Estimates of indigenous population sizes in Latin America, (1978–1991)

Indigenous population	Estimated % of total population
Population over 10%	
Bolivia	60–70
Guatemala	45–60
Peru	38–40
Ecuador	30–38
Mexico	12–14
Population between 5% and 10%	
Belize	9
Panama	4–8
Chile	4–6
Population under 5%	
Guyana, Surinam, Honduras, Paraguay	4–2
El Salvador, Colombia, Nicaragua, Argentina, Venezuela, French Guyana, Costa Rica, Brazil and Uruguay	<2

Source: Yashar (2005)

other minority groups such as Afro groups and migrants from Asia and the Middle East. White/*criollo* refers to small elite groups who consider themselves of European or 'white' descent. The *mestizo* (or *ladino* in the case of Guatemala) category is the largest nonindigenous population group and is no less complex or contested than the indigenous category. The *mestizo/ladino* category comprises the population of mixed cultural and/or biological descent and in practice tends to include those who do not fit easily into any of the other categories. However, there are key differences in the meaning and importance of the *mestizo/ladino* categories across our cases. In the Andes (as in Mexico), the understanding and definition of *mestizo* emphasizes the encounter between different cultures and groups (Sieder, 2002). In theory, the indigenous heritage is both acknowledged and celebrated in the *mestizo* category. Between the 1952 Revolution and the early 1990s in Bolivia and since the 1940s in Peru, official discourses purporting to abolish difference and segregation between groups have heavily promoted the supposedly common mixed/*mestizo* category (for instance, prohibiting the recording of ethnicity in population censuses). There has been no such official discourse or policy in Guatemala, where, by contrast, the key attribute of the *ladino* category has been the emphasis on the nonindigenous nature of the group and the denial of the indigenous contribution to the mainstream *ladino* group (Taracena, 2002; Warren, 1998). In addition, there is a small elite group who do not self-identify as *ladinos*, emphasizing instead their 'pure-blooded' European origins, but they are usually referred to in class terms (as the oligarchy) and there is no commonly used racial or ethnic term (Caumartin, 2005).

Finally, there are new and emergent categories in the Andes, such as the *cholos*, who do not fit easily into the traditional indigenous/nonindigenous divide. The *cholos* tend to be migrants or descendants of migrants from indigenous communities who have been incorporated into large urban centres and lifestyles (typically on the outskirts of Lima or in El Alto in Bolivia). Both on the outskirts of Lima and in El Alto, the *cholos* do not self-identify as indigenous, but nor do they necessarily feel at ease with the *mestizo* label.[3]

In Latin America, as elsewhere in the world, the boundaries between groups tend to change across time and localities, but 'fluidity' in Latin America also refers to the phenomenon of individuals self-identifying with distinct categories during the course of their lives (moving from indigenous to *mestizo* or *cholo*, or from *mestizo* to 'white' for instance). Both cultural factors (notably a sense of shared history and/or customs) and physiognomic factors (such as colouring of skin, eyes and hair) tend to play an important part in the phenomenon of self-identification or ascription to certain groups.

Turning to the theme of this book, the central hypothesis put forward in Chapter 1 is that there is a link between HIs and conflict, predicting an increased likelihood of conflict whenever socioeconomic and political HIs run in the same direction. On the surface, our Latin American cases can be made to fit well with this general approach. If we make some heroic assumptions to allow ourselves to aggregate across different HIs, then the two countries with the worse combined HIs (social, economic and political) are also those which have experienced armed conflict in the recent past (Guatemala in 1960–1996 and Peru in 1980–1992). However, the extent to which these cases really support the hypotheses of Chapter 1 is more questionable when the issue of ethnicity is taken into consideration, primarily because of the general weakness over time of ethnic politics in the region.[4] Influential indigenous movements have consolidated in some countries (especially in Bolivia and Ecuador) and the 2005 election in Bolivia of Evo Morales is notable. However, if these cases suggest that ethnic politics might one day come to play an important role, thus far ethnicity has not played the decisive role in Latin America that it has in the political systems of other countries (particularly in Africa).[5]

The second section of this chapter explores and documents, as far as is possible given the limitations of space, the deep and enduring HIs in our three cases. The third section seeks to explain why ethnic politics have emerged at very different speeds in the different cases, and why the politicization of ethnicity is typically less vigorous than one might expect given the degree of HI. The fourth section uses the insights from this to analyze the form in which widespread political violence has emerged in two of the cases and the significance of this for understanding the relationship between HIs and conflict. The final section presents conclusions and some further hypotheses distilled from this work.

11.2　Horizontal inequalities: Preliminary measurements

The three countries each exhibit strong inequalities between indigenous and nonindigenous populations. A first observation is that strong HIs are relatively independent of the country's degree of development or the size of its economy. Bolivia is the poorest of our three countries with a low ranking on its human development indicator (HDI). Guatemala, with a substantially larger GDP *per capita* has an even lower HDI ranking and a much lower adult literacy rate than our other cases. Guatemala is also the least urbanized of our three countries. Finally, Peru has the largest economy of the three and its HDI ranking is substantially higher than Bolivia or Guatemala, but it claims the highest proportion of people living below the poverty line.

Indicators of HIs are shown in Table 11.2 based on the work of Manuel Barrón.[6] The findings confirm our expectations of substantial inequalities between nonindigenous and indigenous groups. Indigenous people have less access to services, they are less educated and significantly poorer than nonindigenous people.

In Table 11.3, HIs in the three countries are ranked by attributing a ranking of 1 to the country where indigenous people perform the best, relatively, and 3 to the country where indigenous people perform the worst. On the five HI indicators presented, HIs are least acute in Peru (Peru is not ranked third in any of the categories presented here). Bolivia is an intermediate performer, usually ranked in second place. Our evidence points forcefully to Guatemala as the worst performer in four of the five categories.

A different insight into the degree to which socioeconomic HIs are important and have in part at least an ethnic dimension comes from a

Table 11.2　Horizontal inequality: Per cent living in poverty

	Bolivia			Guatemala			Peru		
	Non indigenous	Indigenous	Ratio	Non indigenous	Indigenous	Ratio	Non indigenous	Indigenous	Ratio
Extreme poverty	12.8	34.4	0.37	4.9	20.1	0.24	5.5	24.1	0.23
Poverty	28.7	31.3	0.92	27.2	47.3	0.58	21.2	29.3	0.72

Source: Barrón Ayllón (2007), derived from *Mecovi 2002, Encovi 2000, Enaho 2002*.
Note: For details on how the indigenous/nonindigenous classification problem was solved, please see Barrón Ayllón (2007). The basic problem is that the Peruvian census data do not use self-identification, and language spoken does not work as a proxy for Peru, where the indigenous population in the north of the country today speaks Spanish. Barrón Ayllón has used place of birth, but has omitted large provincial cities in the Sierra from the indigenous share, as a rough way of dealing with the fact that such cities have significant nonindigenous populations. This is problematic, but works better than any alternative solution we have been able to find. It will *tend* to underestimate the degree of HI relative to other measures such as language. The latter excludes the Spanish-speaking indigenous population, which tends to be less poor than the Quechua-speaking population.

Table 11.3   Country ranking of selected horizontal inequality indicators

Country	Literacy	Health: access[a]	Share of white collar in group EAP[b]	Extreme poverty	Poverty	Most frequent ranking
Bolivia	2 (0.8)	2 (0.8)	2	3 (2.7)	1 (1.1)	2 (3 times out of 5)
Guatemala	3 (0.7)	3 (0.7)	3	2 (4.1)	3 (1.7)	3 (4 times out of 5)
Peru	1 (0.9)	1 (0.9)	1	3 (4.4)	2 (1.4)	1 (3 times out of 5)

Note: Values in parentheses indicate the ratio of indigenous to nonindigenous population.
[a] Ratio of those who received medical attention to the proportion reporting sickness or accidents in each group
[b] 1 denotes least HI.

survey of perceptions of identity.[7] Respondents were asked if someone's ethnic or racial origins[8] affected their chances of employment in the public or private sector. In Bolivia and Peru, nearly two-thirds felt that it did, while in Guatemala 44 per cent felt that it did for the public sector and 35 per cent for the private sector. The population which self-identified as indigenous consistently saw ethnic origin as more important than did the rest of the population, but not by much – the perception was widely shared, except in Guatemala. The strongest result was for Bolivia, where 76 per cent of the indigenous population in the sample felt that ethnicity affected a person's chances of working in the state sector.[9]

Our initial findings thus exhibit deep HIs. Latin America has long been infamous for its severe vertical inequalities, but our findings indicate that our Latin American cases deserve the same degree of infamy for inequalities between indigenous and nonindigenous groups.

This can be seen more sharply using Mancini's work comparing HIs across six countries in terms of women's education, child mortality and an indicator of wealth for the relevant ethnic divide in each country (Mancini, forthcoming). Some summary data are given in Table 11.4. In women's education, the HIs are slightly worse than in Ghana and Côte d'Ivoire, but lower than in Nigeria. For child mortality, Bolivia and Peru are worse placed than all three African countries. The measure of household wealth also places Latin America in the most unequal category. In Peru, compared to nonindigenous, indigenous people are more than four times more likely to be in the bottom quintile of the wealth distribution.

Our initial evaluation of the political dimension of HIs points towards a general exclusion of indigenous people from the higher echelons of state and political parties, but with important variations within and between the three countries we are researching. In Guatemala, for instance, indigenous

Table 11.4   Indicators of horizontal inequality across six countries[a]

Most recent year	HI in women's education	HI in child mortality	HI in house-hold wealth[b]
Bolivia 1998	2.7	2.0	3.5
Guatemala 1999	3.1	1.5	2.2
Peru 2000	2.3	1.9	3.6
Peru 2004	2.4	1.9	3.7
Ghana 2003	2.3	1.4	1.6
Côte d'Ivoire 1999	2.4	1.2	1.3
Nigeria 2003	3.2	1.6	2.0

Source: Calculations provided by Luca Mancini on the basis of the DHS datasets (Mancini, forthcoming). To secure comparable data over several years, Mancini uses a different data source to that used by Barrón Ayllón for Peru. The source Mancini uses takes self-reported ethnicity as the ethnic marker for Peru and Guatemala, language for Bolivia.
[a] HIs are the ratio between average group values for each country (advantaged over disadvantaged group). The higher the value the greater the inequality, with 1 implying no inequality.
[b] Based on wealth index calculated as a weighted sum of amenities owned by the person's household with weights proportional to the degree of exclusiveness of each asset in the population.

presence in the higher echelons of state and political parties is still very limited at the national level (over the past ten years, less than 12 per cent of deputies have been indigenous) but is becoming substantial at the local/municipal levels (never less than 35 per cent since 1995: Caumartin, 2006b).[10] In Bolivia, by contrast, indigenous presence in state and political institutions has increased steadily at all levels since the early 1990s, culminating with the election of Evo Morales in 2005.

As far as cultural rights are concerned, it appears that there have been some important steps taken in the recognition of indigenous cultural rights. Official policies of actively repressing indigenous dress, customs and languages are no longer the norm in any of the three countries. However, steps taken towards 'formal recognition' still appear hesitant, notably in the cases of Peru and Guatemala.[11] In the latter case, most Mayan languages are now 'recognized' by the state and bilingual education has been permitted since the late 1980s. However, whilst 'recognized' and no longer repressed, Mayan languages still have a secondary status as the sole official language remains Spanish. In Peru, there is a longer tradition of official recognition of indigenous cultural rights than in Guatemala (Quechua has been an official language since the radical military government of General Velasco in the early 1970s). However, in practice and in everyday life informal discrimination in cultural terms remains very strong.[12]

Few who know Latin America well will be surprised by these findings. It is then of particular interest to see how these deep inequalities have affected ethnic mobilization and violence. We now summarize our findings in this regard.

11.3   The history of ethnic mobilization

This chapter argues that the key to understanding how HIs have affected ethnic mobilization lies in the formation, over time, of political and social structures and the culture of identity. This process has been shaped by geography as well as by specific historical events.

11.3.1   Early rebellion and repression

In all three cases, if we look back 300 years there is clear evidence of an incipient indigenous movement, leading to major conflict and repression. But the degree of repression and its consequences were very different.

In Peru, there is evidence for such a movement from the eighteenth century, culminating in the Rebellion of Túpac Amaru in 1780, though this is far from the only significant indication of indigenous mobilization and resentment.[13] The core motivation for rebellion was resentment at the taxation imposed by the colonial authorities and other forms of exploitation. Each act of rebellion involved an incipient alliance with some *criollo* and *mestizo* populations, but this was weakened by ethnic differences within the group. Within the indigenous group, there was a significant upper and even middle class, from which the leadership came. Education and economic opportunities in a dynamic trade circuit linked to the Potosi mine were the basis for the emergence of this elite in the eighteenth century. The leadership intention was integrationist: they wished to unite *mestizo*, *criollo*, black and Indian against the colonizing power. But this goal was not fully shared by the indigenous peasantry, who often felt as much resentment against merchants and others from the *mestizo* groups as they did against whites (Flores Galindo, 1976; Walker, 1999).

What made 1780 into a 'foundational event', in the view of most analysts, was the brutal repression and eradication of the indigenous leadership class, followed by a profound cultural repression in the south, the consequences of which are still seen today. The indigenous elite lost the right to education and the use of Quechua was prohibited, along with the use of any symbols referring to their Inca past (Canepa, 2007; Flores Galindo, 1976; Walker, 1999). With the killing of the leaders, the networks which had been the heart of the movement were destroyed. In a much-used phrase from the literature, 'the Indian was colonised for a second time'.

Bolivia's equivalent to the Peruvian events of 1780 – the Katarista uprising of 1781 including the siege of La Paz – was a foundational event which, far from leading to the destruction of the incipient indigenous movement and the elimination of its leadership, provided a revolutionary tradition and inspiration. The key difference lay in the degree of repression, which was far less extreme than that carried out in the wake of the Túpac Amaru rebellion in Cusco. Fundamental to this was geography: the fact that La Paz – later to become the capital but already a prominent city at the time – is in the heart of indigenous territory in Bolivia. The rebels laid siege to La Paz and were able to cut off supplies – a pattern repeated constantly up to the present day. This geography forced a politics of accommodation radically different from the Peruvian situation, where the rebel forces could be isolated and decimated.

A further important characteristic of the early uprisings in Bolivia is that they were typically aimed at exerting control over the judicial branch of the state – contesting colonial political and administrative decisions – thus creating the terrain for multiple forms of contestation over which spheres of state-society relations were 'negotiated' and which were 'autonomous' (Hylton, 2004). They were also not monolithic, setting a pattern of fragmented and localized indigenous movements in the following 200 years. This fragmentation facilitated the evolution of a delicate balancing act, embodied in the phrase 'the politics of accommodation', which we return to below.

Guatemala's different experience begins with the nature of the Spanish conquest itself. This was a slow affair that encountered staunch resistance from the various Mayan kingdoms established there (Saenz de Tejada, 2005) and with fewer resources invested by the colonizing power. Because of its lack of mineral wealth, Guatemala remained largely a 'rural backwater', where the opportunities for the Spaniards and *criollo* elites to amass wealth were few (Dunkerley, 1988). The state remained weak and impoverished and had only a tiny bureaucracy (ibid.). Spatially, indigenous and nonindigenous peoples cohabited in certain regions of Guatemala. In the eastern regions of Guatemala indigenous people were either displaced or absorbed into 'Spanish' communities but in the western highland of the country, indigenous inhabitants were, and remain, the majority (Smith and Moors, 1990).[14]

There is little doubt that the Spanish colonial rulers had almost no tolerance for indigenous collective action, especially if it took a violent form, and Spanish reprisals tended to be thorough and pitiless. Overall, communities often preferred less overt forms of resistance to the colonial rulers, opting for instance to refuse to pay tribute when the state's demands were too excessive (CEH, 1999; Smith and Moors, 1990). However, it is important to contrast the ferocity of the colonial authorities' repression of indigenous armed protest with the weakness of everyday rule. Control over the indigenous communities of the western highlands was often tenuous, with the colonial state having limited or no presence.[15] This allowed these communities to continue as a focal point for indigenous ethnic and political identity (Grandin, 1997: 8–9). Each municipality in the indigenous highlands was politically autonomous, with complex hierarchies of civil and religious offices (ibid.). Those who were in a position to undertake a set of obligations (financial sponsorship of events and lengthy periods of community service) rose to become community leaders: elders or *principales* (Barrios,

2001; Grandin, 1997) who in turn tended to work as intermediaries with the colonial authorities.

The system was institutionalized through the *alcaldías indígenas* (indigenous municipalities). The *alcaldías indígenas* were officially recognized until 1898, but subsequently ran in parallel with official *ladino*-dominated municipal authorities – in some cases, to the present day (Barrios, 2001).[16] Important characteristics of the system were the continued role of indigenous traditional leaders and institutions and a tendency towards the linguistic and political isolation of each individual community.[17] Considering that there are over 20 major indigenous languages and over 100 dialects which are not easily mutually understood, it is not surprising that there was little sense of a common 'indigenous' or 'Mayan' identity until the isolation of individual communities began to break down.

11.3.2   The varying responses and survival strategies: Co-optation, co-operation, accommodation, autonomy

What followed from these very different beginnings were very different strategies of survival. In the case of Peru, the interweaving of various historical events pushed indigenous peoples more and more towards efforts at assimilation. As an indigenous middle class gradually re-emerged, its goal tended to be assimilation with *criollo* culture and a downplaying of indigenous kinship and culture. At a crucial point, the defining of the nation at the point of Independence in 1821, there was no Indian elite to be present at the table (Montoya, 1998). Following Independence, the exit of capital, the loss of centralized control of indigenous labour and the decay of trade circuits and regional links all led to atomization of the loyalties and perspectives of the indigenous population. For most of the Sierra, systematic exclusion followed, as the practices known as *gamonalismo* developed in the first half of the nineteenth century.[18]

The most important event of the nineteenth century was the war with Chile.[19] During this war (1879–1883) peasants were compulsorily enrolled in the Peruvian army. In the central highlands guerrillas called *montoneras* were formed from among peasant and indigenous communities that wanted to defend the *patria* against the Chilean occupation (Mallon, 1987; Manrique, 1981). At the beginning of this resistance, Andres Avelino Caceres, a high-ranking *mestizo* in the army, emerged as the symbol of national unity around which all could gather and fight, making possible an alliance between landowners and indigenous communities to fight against the foreign force. However, class and ethnic conflict were soon to undermine the alliance. From the landowners' point of view, increasing peasant mobilization and autonomy from central command represented the greatest danger from which they had to defend themselves. Landowners understood that their best solution was peace at any price (even the fragmentation of territory), and control and repression of the peasant guerrillas.

The wartime political mobilization of indigenous people in the central highlands was a major event in the formation of 'national' consciousness. Following the war, the official interpretation made the Indians responsible for the defeat, presenting them as lacking a sense of nationhood, enemies of all whites, especially those from the coast, and ignorant of what it meant to be Peruvian. In this context, the economic, territorial and cultural unification of the country was seen as a precondition for avoiding a repetition of the 1879 disaster. In addition to the construction of roads and railways that would establish a firm material base for unification, the governing elite offered aid to the various regional oligarchies to solve their most immediate problems. In the central highlands, this meant not only eliminating the remaining pockets of peasant resistance, but also providing assistance with labour control and the modernization of the local economy (Mallon, 1987; Manrique, 1988).

The resulting weakness of the indigenous movement, and with it the absence of indigenous politics, was compounded in the twentieth century by the gradual move to a language of class, which reached its apotheosis with the military government of General Velasco. In the different Andean countries the varieties of corporatist politics played out through the middle of the twentieth century gave (usually unintended) space to indigenous communities, and Peru was no exception.[20] However, elements of contradiction and conflict emerged in the Peruvian case in the Velasco regime, described below in relation to land reform. Further, the desire to control was more in evidence than the desire to empower (as seen, for instance, in the 1970 Statute on Peasant Communities).

Such control and contradictions further weakened the communities. All in all, the historical legacy of these two centuries was a lack of indigenous leadership. In the north especially there was also loss of language: today, the indigenous population there is Spanish-speaking. In some areas, there was a weakening or loss of community institutions.

The indigenous and peasant communities failed to develop a common identity; the differences were too many and the distances and physical barriers enormous. It was more profitable to suppress one's origin and work on assimilation – particularly if one had already moved to an urban area, as close to 10 million had by the late twentieth century (INEI, 1995). This migration was not to highland cities closely related culturally to their hinterland, as in Bolivia and Ecuador. In Peru those migrating to the coast were moving to an alien and isolating culture where hiding one's identity was the rational course of action (Albó, 2002) and fragmentation was a natural consequence.

For those who remained in their communities, the principal identity reference was to that community, rooted in physical space. Research on Andean culture (Ansión *et al.*, 2004) reveals that an individual community member typically does not see the members of other communities as part of a common shared identity. Even if they are Quechua-speaking, other communities speak 'other Quechuas'. This is yet one more factor explaining the failure of indigenous politics to develop at a national level.

Such a weakness of indigenous politics does not mean its total absence, however. Part of the reason for the lack of major protest and mobilization may possibly be the quite elaborate expression of identity through 'cultural politics'. Canepa (2007) finds abundant evidence of this in Lima itself. Cultural politics refers to the use of fiestas, dance, processions and song to express identity and make (low-key) political statements. In Peru this form of expression is deeply contradictory in nature. It is rooted in attempts to allow the emerging *mestizo* class a form of expression that goes beyond their class identity as an 'emerging entrepreneur', which is where the prevailing culture tries to pigeonhole them. However, the individuals in this class are divided in their own thinking on how far the emerging group is superior to, or takes its strength from, the original indigenous culture. We see again how class and ethnicity intertwine in Peru.

Turning to Bolivia, the greater degree of autonomy of, and respect towards, the indigenous communities already evidenced in the early years led gradually, as we have indicated, to what eventually became christened the 'politics of accommodation'. As in Peru, the result of war was, perversely, to awaken fear of Aymara allies; thus Indian mobilization under Zárate in 1899 in support of the Liberal elites actually led to Liberal repression of their allies. But the need for a politics of accommodation – what the literature refers to as a 'harmony of inequalities' – thereafter shapes a complex construction and deconstruction of the 'Indian question', and periods of elite accommodation and resurgence.[21] By the early twentieth century *mestizo* alliances with workers and miners became the means of accommodation. The coup d'état of 1921 symbolized a new period of elite accommodation and resurgence. President Bautista Saavedra (1921–1925) attempted to realign working-class and indigenous sympathies more directly through clientelist political means that ushered in a form of inclusion developed by both the military socialists of the 1930s and the National Revolution of 1952.

With this new form of inclusion came a new vocabulary that celebrated the *mestizo* and 'indigenous' character of the 'Bolivian nation'. This form of recognition was itself a platform for more nuanced constructions around ethnicity and class-based cleavages over the second half of the twentieth century. The 1952 National Revolution is a milestone along this historical path, sharing as it does with pre-revolutionary periods the survival of old forms of elite accommodation in key arenas of social and political life. Universal suffrage, agrarian reform and the nationalization of mining were foundational events of the National Revolution, carried out by a loose coalition of middle-class politicians with the backing of worker and *campesino* (peasant) militias. The *Movimiento Nacionalista Revolucionario* (MNR – Revolutionary Nationalist Movement), born a decade earlier, aspired to be a hegemonic party, despite its loose political leadership and social composition (Zavaleta Mercado, 1990: 47).

The development and demise of the National Revolution have been exhaustively analyzed.[22] This section will focus on a single, but important, aspect of the Revolution as it relates to ethnicity and inequality. The Revolution constructed a new vocabulary that emancipated indigenous citizens from colonial forms of labour exploitation, but pointed to a new cohesive identity linking the working classes, peasantry and a national bourgeoisie. This mirrored but was even more clear-cut than the shift to a language of class we have already noted in Peru (and indeed in many countries at this time). The *campesino* played a key role in defining the identity of the protagonists of the Revolution's most important action: the Agrarian Reform of 1953. A significant feature of the Agrarian Reform was the dissolution of all forms of agrarian labour exploitation coupled with the massive redistribution of land over a period of 30 years. The Agrarian Reform decree erased all mention of 'Indian peoples', 'Indian race' and Aymara or Quechua identity from official discourse. The *campesino* union system, created to redistribute land, was to provide a link between the MNR and the rural society and economy for nearly half a century.

The politics of land reform illustrate the complex infighting that took place between elites and indigenous and *campesino* communities. As observed during the Liberal period, elite accommodation now focused on access to the MNR and state power provided the backdrop for new forms of social and political inclusion, based on co-optation and redistribution of the spoils of power.

An important difference from our other cases is that while ethnic-based political parties never caught on in either the Bolivian highlands or lowlands, ethnic representation increased steadily, first in municipal politics and from 2002 onwards, in national politics. Today, nearly one-third of congressional districts are represented by indigenous deputies or senators, another third is represented by urban-based popular worker or informal sectors and a third by middle-class *mestizos* representative of the 'traditional' political class. However, the mainstreaming of indigenous political demands – constitutional reform, land tenure reform, bilingual education and a Constitutional Assembly – has been achieved mostly by indigenous social movements, on the streets rather than in Congress (Calla, 2003). Indigenous movements have successfully introduced a multiethnic political agenda in Bolivia since the early 1990s. (The slow pace of reforms and achievements, however, are behind the recent backlash against conciliatory and reformist proposals.)

An important question we need to consider is why episodes of ethnic politicization were not followed by the establishment of ethnic-based political parties that might 'institutionalize' ethnic differences within the formal system of democratic governance. How can we explain the poor performance of indigenous parties but the strength of indigenous social movements?

The electoral performance of the MRTK (*Movimiento Revolucionario Tupac Katari* – Revolutionary Tupac Katari Movement) and the MITKA (*Movimiento Indio Tupac Katari* – Indian Tupac Katari Movement) in the late 1980s illustrates this pattern.[23] The *katarista* movement, which attained prominent influence within the *campesino* union system, never surpassed a 3 per cent electoral threshold from 1979 to 1989. Formally, Bolivia's electoral proportional representation system would seem to favour ethnic representation, as close to two-thirds of electoral districts are made up predominantly of Quechua, Aymara or lowland indigenous populations. However, we suggest that the limited appeal of all-indigenous political parties might be explained, rather, by a system of clientelist and corporatist inclusion inherited from the early 1900s and developed by the near-hegemonic MNR in the mid-1950s.

A number of informal institutions have organized ethnic-based, local and class-based collective action around the state. These have included clientelistic relations, dual powers (*poderes duales*), comanagement (*cogestión*) and collective self-management (*autogestión*), among others.[24] The most pervasive form of inclusion is a legacy of the conservative and liberal periods at the end of the nineteenth century. Strong elite hold over political and economic power was buttressed by clientelism between the mining-based elites, urban middle classes and indigenous communities. In 1936, President David Toro consolidated his political support by introducing compulsory unionization in urban and rural producer associations under the nascent *Central Obrera Boliviana* (COB – Confederation of Bolivian Workers). However, the most significant consolidation of clientelistic relations emerged during and after the National Revolution, when *campesino* and worker unions provided critical support.

Political clienteles shifted away from the MNR in the 1960s and towards the military between 1964 and 1982. The democratic transition in 1982 was followed by a wave of decentralization reforms in the 1990s which moved patronage relations from capital cities to small towns and municipalities. Political capture by local elites accentuated a patrimonial government style and pushed political reform and disenchantment to the fore in the late 1990s. Today, political parties suffer from the lowest level of public credibility of the past 40 years. In October 2003, President Carlos Mesa appointed a nonpolitical cabinet and dismantled many of the clientelistic networks that had participated in public employment and patronage by the executive power. While clientelistic relations are an integral part of democratic politics in present-day Bolivia, there is increased pressure to open up political participation to nonclientelistic and meritocratic forms of politics.

Important to understanding this evolution is the way the National Revolution institutionalized a dual form of government that has recurred over time since the 1950s. In the early years of the revolution, one power was constituted by a worker and *campesino* militia, associated with the COB, while the other emerged from the MNR leadership that led the revolutionary government. Dual powers allowed the popular movement access to political power without loss of autonomy.

A remarkable aspect of dual powers is its persistence beyond the hegemonic period of the National Revolution. The design of the Popular Participation reform in the 1990s, for example, institutionalized dual powers at the local level, by granting veto power to a civil society oversight committee in each municipality. The oversight committee was itself constituted by grassroots organizations, most of which developed from the *campesino* and urban union movement. At a time when the union movement was at its lowest ebb, after the collapse of tin-mining and the privatization of state companies, the Popular Participation reform created a new arena for union-based collective action. Another example is the 2001 Poverty Reduction Strategy Paper (PRSP), which delegated oversight and accountability powers to a civil society organization, *Mcanismo de Control Social* (Social Control Mechanism).

Thus a genuine degree of political participation has evolved over time, in response to the weakness of the state, its need for allies and the geography of the country. But this is not formalized: checks and balances are institutionalized outside the reach of formal government bodies or powers. They allow social movements or local grassroots organizations an arms-length control over government policy decisions in a context of weak state legitimacy. This system has been remarkably effective in avoiding the level of violent political conflict seen in the other two cases. None of this, however, could be explained without considering the emergence of a distinct form of leadership, based in rural mining and agrarian union politics: *sindicalismo*. *Sindicalismo* was born in the 1930s but became the dominant form of grassroots politics during the Bolivian National Revolution.

The story of Evo Morales, the first indigenous president of Bolivia, is illustrative of the *sindicato* leadership tradition.[25] Morales was born in 1959 in the rural Aymara-speaking town of Orinoca. At the age of 22, he took his first trip to the Chapare region where he worked on a cocoa farm and became the sports secretary of the local *sindicato*. By 1985, he was the general secretary of his union and by 1988, at the age of 29, he was one of the youngest leaders of the Federation of Unions of the Chapare Tropics. Although he learnt Aymara at an early age, and Quechua in his twenties, he communicated in Spanish with his fellow *sindicato* members and leaders. Morales' political career hit a turning point in the early 1990s, as the *campesino sindicato* movement in Bolivia reassessed its political strategy in the neoliberal era. After decades of uneasy political alliances, first with the MNR, later with left and centre-left political parties, demand emerged for a 'political instrument' that could represent the voices of *campesino*-indigenous organizations without intermediaries and also win local and national elections.

In the December municipal elections of 1995, Evo Morales' 'political instrument' (under the *Izquierda Unida*, or United Left, banner) won 49 seats and gained control of ten municipalities in the department of Cochabamba. By 1999, the 'political instrument' (under the political banner of the *Movimiento al Socialismo*, MAS – Movement for Socialism) won in over 20 municipalities in the Bolivian highlands, and again positioned Evo Morales as a national leader with the capacity to unite different factions within the *campesino*-indigenous movement. In the 2002 presidential election, Morales came in second. By the December 2005 elections, Evo Morales won by a landslide vote of 53.7 per cent, with a congressional majority in both chambers. He won with massive support from urban and rural areas, mostly concentrated in the highland regions, and with inroads into the (largely nonindigenous) departments of Santa Cruz and Tarija. Middle-class, working-class and *campesino*-indigenous voters make up the core of MAS support, much as they did the core of MNR support 50 years earlier. The story of Evo Morales is not so much the story of a person, as of a form of grassroots collective action.[26] *Sindicalismo* succeeds as much in current Bolivian politics as it did 50 years ago.

Turning to our third case, Guatemala, we find a far stronger degree of exclusion of indigenous people from formal politics than in either Peru or Bolivia, but with some important caveats. First, the exclusion of indigenous people from formal politics needs to be read within the wider context of exclusionary politics. Guatemalan politics have tended to be authoritarian and have excluded the vast majority of Guatemalans, *ladinos* and indigenous alike. Thus, indigenous males gained the right to vote in Guatemala in 1944 when literacy clauses were removed (four decades before Peru and Bolivia). Yet opportunities to exercise this newly acquired right in any substantive form were limited for both *ladinos* and indigenous people between 1954 and 1985, when a handful of actors controlled formal politics. Second, as noted above, it is important to note the resilience of local indigenous institutions. Thus, whilst traditional indigenous leaders became increasingly excluded from formal participation and representation, they retained important roles in their respective communities (where their authority long remained undisputed) and as key intermediaries with official actors.[27] In short, the influence and decision-making power of traditional leaders vis-à-vis official municipal, regional or national actors became limited by the late nineteeth century, but they retained important informal status. On the one hand, it is clear that the social and cultural cohesion of individual communities was maintained, reinforcing them as a cornerstone of collective identities (Grandin, 1997). In sharp contrast to the situation in Peru, traditional leadership allowed communities to retain a strong sense of identity. On the other hand, however, political mobilization and organization of indigenous communities was kept in check by the threat of repression, the continued isolation of individual communities (that prevented the emergence of pan-indigenous consciousness) and by the fact that traditional leaders retained a stake in the system.

The penetration of roads and commercial networks across the high-lands, the gradual erosion of subsistence agriculture and the onset of mass seasonal migration to plantations on the coast all played a part in breaking down the isolation of individual communities.[28] A number of indigenous people increased their role in the nonsubsistence sector (commerce, new rural production, manufacturing and labour recruitment), thereby increasing social differentiation within communities (Grandin, 1997: 11). A corollary to this process of social change at community level was that a small but increasing number of indigenous people did gain access to education (Bastos and Camus, 2003; Cayzac, 2001; Grandin, 1997). Most of the indigenous leaders who emerged during the 1970s had gone through a path of schooling with the Catholic Church that emphasized the importance of commitment to the community (in other words, that those who gained education had a duty to give something back to their communities).[29] The combined processes of accelerating social differentiation and the opening of new hori-zons beyond the confines of individual communities provoked a questioning of traditional authority within indigenous communities (ibid.). This was actively encouraged by the powerful Catholic network *Acción Católica* (AC – Catholic Action), which took a dim view of the rituals, beliefs and influence of indigenous traditional leaders (Cayzac, 2001).

Whilst traditional forms of authority were contested within communities, new forms of political participation started to emerge. This included an increased profile in formal and national political institutions, developing ties with the Christian Democratic Party, culminating with the elections of two indigenous deputies in the 1974 elections. These deputies went on to create the first indigenous political party in Guatemala in 1976, the FIN (*Frente de Integración Nacional*, or National Integration Front), but proved unable to capitalize on their initial successes. [30] These forays into a formal polit-ical system dominated by the armed forces were, however, rather limited. Instead, indigenous mobilization grew most rapidly in social movements that focused on rural grievances. As elsewhere in Latin America, the incor-poration of indigenous people into regional or national politics was first realized through movements and organizations (rather than political parties) and centered around *campesino* (rather than citizen) identities. Overall, these organizations tended to express class rather than 'ethnic' grievances. Their demands related to improving work conditions and pay in plantations as well as land reform and were inclusive of indigenous and *ladino* rural dwellers alike. By the early 1970s, there were 109 peasant leagues registered in Guatemala with an additional 97 agrarian unions (Saenz de Tejada, 2005: 35). Indigenous people played a prominent role in these organizations not only as base members but also as leaders. These organizations clearly transcended the local level and were an essential step in the emergence of a *campesino* movement that went on to provide the bases of support of the insurgency in the late 1970s and early 1980s.

The shift from participation in peasant movements into armed conflict was a complex phenomenon that emerged in response to a general lack of responsiveness to demands on the part of the military governments, the repression of peaceful protest and a general closing down of legal avenues for political participation.[31] Guatemalan guerrilla organizations worked throughout the 1970s to establish close contact with indigenous communities. One of these, the *Ejercito Guerrillero de los Pobres* (EGP – Guerrilla Army of the Poor), also sought to gain control of and utilize peasant organizations and trade unions as political and social aspects of the revolutionary struggle (Bastos and Camus, 1993 and 2003).

In addition to the PGT (*Partido Guatemalteco del Trabajo* – Guatemalan Labour Party, 1952) and the FAR (*Fuerzas Armadas Rebeldes* – Rebel Armed Forces, 1962), new guerrilla organizations appeared in the 1970s, the EGP (1972), the ORPA (*Organización del Pueblo en Armas* – Organization of the People in Arms, 1971) as well as the short-lived indigenous armed group, the *Movimiento Indio Tojil* (Indian Tojil Movement, 1981–1983).[32] Both ORPA and the EGP had a *ladino* cadre and leadership as well as supporters amongst the poor and *ladino* middle classes of the capital city (especially the trade union and student movements). They also had important bases of support in the indigenous western highlands of Guatemala, but it was class and the logic of class war that prevailed in the discourse of the Guatemalan insurgents. Indigenous people constituted a population with huge grievances, but it is because indigenous people were poor and fixed on the bottom quintile of an extraordinarily unequal society that the guerrillas sought their support, not because they were indigenous.

11.4 The generation of political violence – or its absence

By the post–World War II period, then, we have three very different situations. In Peru, assimilation had been fostered and aspired to through diverse political climates. In Bolivia the politics of accommodation had allowed a far more vibrant indigenous movement, held in delicate equilibrium by techniques of dual powers, co-management and clientelism. In Guatemala, the indigenous sense of identity was stronger than in Peru and indigenous institutions had legitimacy, but the various groups were isolated and formal participation was limited.

The result in Bolivia is that while collective action was repeated and vigorous, major violence was avoided, held at bay by accommodation and inclusion. In Peru and Guatemala, however, events were to take a terrible and violent turn.

The Guatemalan army had already shown that it would not hesitate to resort to brutality (see the counterrevolution of 1954 and the quelling of the first wave of guerrilla uprisings in the 1960s), but what occurred in the early 1980s was unprecedented. The worst episodes of violence took place during the regimes of General Romero Lucas García (1978–1982) and his successor General Efraín Rios Montt (1982–1983). The Guatemalan security forces started to eliminate systematically the supporters and sympathizers of the insurgent and noninsurgent left in both rural and urban areas. By the mid-1980s, Guatemala's left, centre left and the social organizations that emerged in the 1970s had been decimated, their members and leadership dead, in exile or in hiding.

Whilst unchecked violence affected both rural and urban areas, in the indigenous rural areas all restraints were removed. The armed forces carried out several scorched earth campaigns, purporting to detach guerrillas from the general population. In such campaigns entire communities were massacred, leading the Guatemalan Truth Commission to accuse the security forces of having committed acts of genocide. The Commission estimated the overall number of dead during the 36-year conflict to be around 200,000. A total of 85 per cent of those killed were indigenous, with over 90 per cent of the acts of killing, torture and violence attributed to the security forces and their allies.

Peru did not experience the complex growth of organizations and resistance which we have described in Guatemala. Yet violence emerged. However, it was restricted in the territory it engulfed. The trigger was *Sendero Luminoso*, the Maoist-inspired movement which arose in the department of Ayacucho in the early 1980s and dominated Peruvian life until the capture of its leader, Abimael Guzman, in September 1992.[33] *Sendero*[34] found fertile territory in the south, where the traditional feudal system was strongest and was combined with a poorly executed land reform.[35] The latter led to an increase in conflict, as better-off peasants were able to get control of land. It was a situation of weak identity and a sense of powerlessness, combined with very weak community institutions and little presence of the state. Great divisiveness was combined with a lack of institutions (traditional or modern) to resolve conflict. The success of *Sendero* in initial recruitment drew on the sense of rootlessness and powerlessness felt acutely by young indigenous people, radicalized via the university by a doctrine that offered a strong quasi-religious identity – a sense of belonging.

Initially, *Sendero* was successful in penetrating communities themselves. However, the movement failed to understand the nature of community institutions – it took reprisals against community leaders and in other ways deeply offended the community ethos. Growing resistance was used by the police and army, and peasants were armed in *rondas*, or community self-defence groups. The result was terrible loss of life, with many peasants caught in the crossfire.[36] The dormant conflict and the lack of 'regular' means of dealing with small-scale conflict also contributed, as individuals took advantage of the growing violence to take private revenge (Tanaka, 2002).

In the north, the story was very different. In Cajamarca, the breaking up of large estates had been going on in a piecemeal fashion since the 1920s.

The earlier land reform in the 1960s had led to more small-holding. So the Velasco measures were able to build on an existing trend in restoring community land and creating small-holdings. But peasants faced a threat from cattle thieves, in the face of the weak presence of the state. In the late 1970s, the *rondas* grew in importance and evolved through the 1980s and 1990s into strong community institutions, gradually dealing with other aspects of community life such as domestic violence or disputes about access to water. They evolved into a source of identity without explicit ethnic connotation.

It is this level of community organization which is adduced throughout the literature as the reason *Sendero* failed to penetrate the north of the country. Important also has been extensive work by external agents (NGOs and church workers) with the communities to inculcate a culture of peaceful resistance – or at least, controlled violence.

The contrasting experience of political violence in the two cases thus reflects, on the one hand the different nature of indigenous identities and propensity for collective action, and on the other the different nature of macro-politics. The deeply exclusionary nature of Guatemalan politics generated a widely based *ladino*-led guerrilla movement, which was able to mobilize and interact with indigenous populations, who in their turn were beginning to develop a sense of collective grievance and identity. In addition, there are regional and international dimensions which added impetus to the Guatemalan conflict in the late 1970s and 1980s, encouraging both mobilization and repression. In Peru, while leftwing parties have not flourished, they have also not been totally excluded. The extent of options within the system meant that nothing developed to parallel the guerrilla movements we have described in Guatemala. And on the other hand, while history explains the fertile territory *Sendero* found in Ayacucho, community organization was strong enough in many places to resist a force which had little respect for indigenous culture, community structures or lives. The death toll in Peru, while large, was still significantly lower than in Guatemala, in part because of the failure of *Sendero* to mobilize large sectors of the population. In addition, a key difference in the experience of violence between Guatemala and Peru is that *Sendero* is acknowledged as one of the main perpetrators of violent acts, whereas in Guatemala the state and its allies were responsible for most acts of violence.

What the two conflicts have in common, however, is that neither can be depicted as prototypical 'ethnic' conflicts. Unlike Mozambique, the Latin American cases were not an example of conflicts presented as ideological but with a racial or ethnic base: the conflicts did not pit indigenous against nonindigenous. Instead, *both* combatant groups, guerrillas and the armed forces, were cross-ethnic organizations that tended to have indigenous troops or bases of support and *mestizo/ladino* leadership. In the case of Peru, a majority of those killed were indigenous, but the evidence points at *Sendero* as committing most of the killings. In the case of Guatemala, the armed revolutionary movements emerged in the 1960s mostly as *ladino* organizations and did not reach the indigenous regions of the country until well into the 1970s. Mobilization did not revolve around ethnicity in either Peru or Guatemala; instead, discourses were clearly delineated along class lines, and mobilization was overwhelmingly of 'poor' against 'rich' rather than of indigenous against nonindigenous (*mestizos* and *criollos*).[37]

Thus ethnicity was not a central feature of the Guatemalan or Peruvian conflicts, either in terms of ideology or in the composition of the combatant forces. It is argued here, however, that ethnicity became a prominent feature of the conflicts in both Peru and Guatemala. To begin with, our work on HIs and our survey of perceptions of identity (see above) show that ethnicity is a key factor in establishing on which side of the poor/rich divide both individuals and groups are to be found, which indicates at the very least that even in a supposedly 'rich' versus 'poor' conflict ethnicity plays a role. In addition, neither *Sendero Luminoso* nor the Guatemalan guerrillas sought to politicize or instrumentalize ethnicity (a potentially self-defeating move for the essentially *mestizo/ladino* leadership), but both understood that enlisting the support of the indigenous rural population was essential in order to reach their objectives (overthrowing the state). Both in Peru and Guatemala, widespread socioeconomic, political and cultural HIs played an important role in creating a situation in which large sectors of the population were amenable to discourses of violent mobilization. Once again, however, the role and importance of ethnicity in the conflict should not be exaggerated: it is equally clear that without the *ladino*/external leadership it appears highly unlikely that a violent conflict incorporating indigenous people would have emerged in either Peru or Guatemala.

This subtle role of ethnicity, undoubtedly present but perhaps not centre stage, is less surprising if we note the general tendency in Latin American societies to deny, if not the existence, at least the importance or relevance of ethnicity in political or economic terms. Unsurprisingly in societies where social, economic and political elites, as well as a large proportion of the middle classes (including the academic community) are nonindigenous, to suggest that ethnicity and ethnic justice do matter provokes deep anxieties.

Overall, nonindigenous people deeply concerned with issues of poverty and inequalities have tended to focus on social justice (that is, vertical inequalities), entirely bypassing the issue of ethnicity. One of the issues raised by our work is to ask whether emphasizing vertical inequalities alone may fail to address some of the important roots of societal cleavages in Latin America.

11.5   Conclusions

We have demonstrated how both the general weakness of ethnic politics and its strong variations across our case studies can be explained in historical terms.

In Peru, we have the historical decimation of the indigenous leadership at a critical juncture as the country defined itself at Independence. This destruction is greater than in our other cases. From this flows a weakness of identity, and the specific characteristics of that identity of being on the one hand very local – one's own community – and on the other hand focussed in a contradictory manner on both assimilation and denial, and channelled into nonconfrontational, cultural forms. Where we have external mobilizers to violence, much of the country is held in a crucial tension: enough organization to resist the mobilization, but not enough to manage effective change to right injustice, given the incoherence of local and national institutional structures, including party structures.

In Bolivia, the system of political accommodation allows mobilization but maintains equilibrium, with impact on political HIs but little so far on socioeconomic HIs. In explaining the relatively high degree of mobilization, and the processes of accommodation which lead to lack of violence but also to lack of progress in socioeconomic goals, we hypothesize that geography has played a key role, as has the political weakness of government and the resulting need for allies.

In Guatemala, the endurance of traditional authority and leadership is possible given the nature of the economy and geography, and this is positive for the growth of ethnic consciousness, albeit frequently in a localized form. But the history of repression works powerfully in the other direction, as does the inaccessibility of politics to all citizens after 1954. The eventual emergence of a *ladino*-led guerrilla movement draws in the indigenous population. The resulting huge repression both reduces political activism and increases ethnic awareness.

In all three cases land reform is crucial. In Bolivia, this is because it increased participation and a sense of rights gained, though it did not significantly improve socioeconomic HIs. In Peru, the importance stems from the form it took (collectives that excluded some) while the lack of supporting institutions increased conflict and fragmentation. In Guatemala, its absence is a mobilizing factor.

The different form taken by the eruption of violence in the two 'violent' cases can be explained by the different nature of *Sendero Luminoso* and the Guatemalan guerrillas in their relationship with the communities, the different previous history of indigenous politics/movements/nonmovements, and the different management of violence by the state.

What is remarkable in these stories is how little relationship there is between the evolution of collective action with ethnic roots – violent or nonviolent – and HIs. However, the nature of the failure to mobilize effectively to reduce HIs takes very different forms in the three cases, shaped by the different histories and political structures we have described. In Guatemala, there is today, and since the early 1990s, a visible indigenous movement, but it is one that lacks serious political leverage. The 'culturalist' wing is highly visible with a degree of access to state and government, but its leverage is limited by its lack of support among the wider population. The 'popular wing' on the other hand has some important bases of support in the population, but it lacks linkages with formal political actors, limiting its capacity to influence policy and decision-making processes.[38] The latter characteristic is likely to reduce the likelihood of a successful challenge to HIs.

In Peru, while the party system has never been closed in the manner of Guatemala, it has been difficult to penetrate, principally because of the lack of vitality and coherence in local politics and in political parties. The party system, quite well developed up to the 1980s (at least at the national level), entered deep crisis with the civil war, to be dealt a near-mortal blow with Fujimori's 'antipolitics' (Crabtree, 2006; Tanaka, 2002). In addition, the deeply rooted centralizing trend in the Peruvian polity and economy has been only mildly and ineffectively challenged by the various initiatives aimed at decentralization. Such efforts come up against the absence of the state at the local level, a lack of capacity in local government and a lack of trusted intermediaries, given the distrust of parties and continuing clientelism in the one party still numerically significant at the local level: the Aprista party.

In Bolivia, the significantly lesser degree of HI is clear, and clearly very important. However, for all this, as we have seen, socioeconomic inequalities have persisted and are serious. The complex system of checks and balances has provided political accommodation, but what it has not done is provide, or allow, effective policy management that delivers in terms of horizontal – or indeed vertical – inequalities. Hence the turn of events in Bolivia in 2006, the outcome of which remains unclear.

Finally, the Latin American cases point towards an interesting fact: major episodes of violence incorporating excluded ethnic groups have taken place in the absence of formal ethnic political organization. It is evident that the mere presence of ethnic politics does not automatically lead to a major outbreak of violence (a multitude of factors intervenes, not least the decisive role played by leaders in maintaining peace or in precipitating violence) but where major episodes of ethnic conflicts have taken place (in Asia and Africa), political mobilization and organization along ethnic lines are frequently identified as important contributing factors (Horowitz, 1985). However, the Latin American cases illustrate well the complexity of the relationship between HIs, ethnic politics and violent conflict. In Latin America, of the five countries with the largest proportion of indigenous inhabitants, the three which have incorporated indigenous people into violent rebellions in the past 25 years are those which had the weakest indigenous politics or movements (Mexico, Guatemala and Peru). On the other hand, the two Andean countries where ethnic/indigenous politics are most consolidated (Bolivia and Ecuador) have not experienced such violence. Some of the critics of indigenous politics argue that ethnic politics run the risk of further entrenching deep-rooted difference and separation in these societies (see Warren, 1998). Whilst these risks should not be ignored or underplayed, it is nonetheless important to note that a general absence or weakness of ethnic mobilization in the context of severe and persistent HIs is no guarantee against the emergence of violent conflicts. To date, the most formal examples of ethnic mobilization and politics in Latin America (Ecuador and Bolivia) have been largely nonviolent and have encouraged the participation and representation of indigenous people into mainstream politics. Historically, indigenous people have been poorly incorporated into the nonindigenous political system and (unsurprisingly) to this day many regard the political party system and the state with a significant degree of suspicion. In Bolivia and Ecuador, emerging ethnic politics are challenging this long-standing scenario and indigenous people are effectively becoming central to political processes. Largely as a consequence of the increased political profile of indigenous groups and people, issues of HIs and how to address them are for the first time gaining importance, most notably in Bolivia. Whilst it is far too early to gauge the long-term consequences of the ethnicization of politics in South America, so far it seems that this might constitute an important step in breaking the hitherto dominant model of vicious circles of reproduction of HIs.

Notes

1. For a good summary of the debates on ethnicity in Latin America, see Van Cott (2000) and Assies *et al.* (2000).
2. These groups account for 85 per cent of the total indigenous population, and 17 other groups for the remaining 15 per cent (Population Census, INE, 2002).
3. See Paredes (2007). In Bolivia, the population of El Alto favours instead the category 'Aymara' (Zavaleta, 2006).
4. Donald Horowitz's seminal work surveys ethnic politics throughout the world, but he is hard pressed to find illustrations of his case in Latin America (Horowitz, 1985).
5. See Horowitz (1985); see also Yashar (2005) for comments on Horowitz.
6. Barrón's paper contains a more extensive range of indicators than those presented here. However, the general trend of the indicators is reflected here.
7. This formed part of the CRISE survey of perceptions. In Latin America the survey was funded by a grant from the Ford Foundation.
8. In Peru the question was framed in terms of racial/cultural identity, as the word 'ethnic' is not commonly understood.
9. All results cited are significant at the 5 per cent level, and most at the 1 per cent level. For details, see Caumartin (2006a), Paredes (2007), Zavaleta (2006).
10. See Cojtí and Fabian (2005: 39) and Misión Indígena de Observación Electoral (2004: 151).
11. In Guatemala, official recognition of indigenous cultural rights is recent, starting with the 1985 Constitution and expanded in the 1996 peace accords.
12. Based on Paredes (2007), using the in-depth interviews which complemented the survey of perceptions of identity.

13. According to O'Phelan Godoy (1985), the rebellion of 1780 led by Túpac Amaru was only the final episode of a convulsive century.
14. The history of the population of the eastern regions of Guatemala is much more contested; see, for example, Dary (2003).
15. The present-day departments of Alta and Baja Verapaz are included in the 'western highlands' of Guatemala.
16. Nobody knows for certain how many *alcaldías indígenas* survive to this day.
17. For a review of the debates relating to the notion of the 'closed corporate communities' in Guatemala, see Smith and Moors (1990).
18. According to Larson (2002), the *gamonal*, the traditional Sierra landlord, developed from an amorphous group of landlords, including 'indigenized whites' and *mistis*, or 'whitened indigenous', who from the latter half of the nineteenth century to the early years of the twentieth century consolidated a new position of power.
19. Chile declared war in 1879. In 1881 Peru was defeated in Lima and suffered occupation for almost three years.
20. Yashar (2005) develops an interesting comparative analysis along these lines.
21. See Irurozqui (1994) and Gray Molina (2007).
22. Two recent conferences on the 50th anniversary of the National Revolution provide a retrospective assessment of its achievements (see Grindle and Domingo, 2003, and PNUD *et al.*, 2003).
23. See Calla (2003).
24. The concept of 'dual powers' in the Bolivian context was developed in Zavaleta Mercado's (1974) seminal work: *El Poder Dual En América Latina*. In this text, dual power relates to the relative weakness of state and governments, which resulted in a series of power-sharing arrangements. For instance, the MNR remained highly dependent upon powerful nonstate actors such as the mining trade unions.
25. See Stefanoni and Do Alto (2006).
26. See Molina (2006).
27. Barrios (2001) strongly emphasizes the ongoing political importance of indigenous traditional authority. See also Piel (1995).
28. Guatemala went from having 205 kilometres of paved road in 1953 to 2638 km in 1975 (Dunkerley, 1988: 174).
29. The emergence of socially committed, Christian indigenous leaders is well reported, see Bastos and Camus (2003). It also came across during interviews with prominent indigenous, such as Manuela Arevalo, Pablo Ceto and Marco Antonio de Paz.
30. Political polarization and increasing state repression deeply affected the FIN (Bastos and Camus, 2003: 49).
31. Even moderate political organizations such as the Christian Democrat party were targeted for repression with 300 prominent members assassinated in 1980 alone (CEH, 1999: Volume I).
32. The Guatemalan guerrilla organizations united in a single organization in 1982 when the URNG (*Unidad Revolucionaria Nacional Guatemalteca* – the Guatemalan National Revolutionary Unity) was formed. See CEH (1999: Volume I).
33. Active cells still exist and *Sendero* should not be written off, given that the underlying conditions which permitted its success have hardly changed. See Degregori (1992).
34. *Sendero* was not the only group mobilizing at this time. In 1984, the *Movimiento Revolucionario Tupac Amaru* (MRTA – Revolutionary Tupac Amaru Movement), a

guerrilla movement, also declared war against the state, and was responsible for 1.5 per cent of the victims reported to the CVR. This paper focuses on *Sendero* for reasons of space.
35. The radical land reform of Velasco represented a fundamental shift in the balance of power, by expropriating large estates above a certain limit (Bourque and Palmer, 1975; McClintock, 1981).
36. And others taking sides, as the CVR concludes (2003: Volume II, Chapter 1, 3).
37. Ideology played a key role in the financing, arming and training of the guerrillas who belonged to regional revolutionary networks.
38. Interview with Dr Demetrio Cojtí, prominent Mayan intellectual and former vice minister of education (2000–2004), 6 May 2005, Guatemala City.

12
Horizontal Inequalities and Separatism in Southeast Asia: A Comparative Perspective

Graham K. Brown

12.1 Introduction

This chapter explores the role of horizontal inequalities in fomenting violent separatism through a comparative investigation of four cases in Southeast Asia. As Weller (2005: 4) notes, self-determination struggles 'have been among the most damaging and protracted to have bedevilled states and the international system since 1945'. Asia, Southeast Asia in particular, has been home to many of the longest running conflicts in the post–Second World War period.

The comparative study of separatist movements in Southeast Asia is thus unsurprisingly not a new endeavour (for example Brown, 1994; Carment, 2003; Che Man, 1990). Existing studies have emphasized a variety of factors in understanding the emergence of violent separatism in the region. For David Brown (1988; 1994), the key step towards violent separatism is the emergence of ethnic nationalism predicated upon the 'monoethnic' orientation of the existing state and concomitant tendencies to assimilationist policies which disrupted 'communal authority structures', thus displacing local ethnic elites. Christie (1996) takes a more historical approach, emphasizing the process of decolonization, which gave credence to certain identity groups in the formation of new *nation* states, but alienated and undermined other peripheral identities. Focussing on separatist movements with a particularly religious dimension, both Che Man (1990) and Chalk (2001) have emphasized the role of Islam as both a unifying and a mobilizing factor. While these scholars do not dispute the existence of socioeconomic grievances among secessionist groups, the overwhelming emphasis is on the historical and political conditions which give rise to alternative nationalisms.

The comparative and econometric literature that does focus on the political economy of separatist conflicts is typically preoccupied with the question of whether it is relatively backward or relatively advantaged regions that tend to seek secession. In an early comparative study Horowitz (1981) argued that 'backward groups' in 'backward regions' are most likely to secede. Hale (2002), however, disputes how systematic Horowitz's findings are, and proposes instead a rational choice model of secession which suggests that relatively advanced regions are more likely to seek secession, and finds empirical support for this in a quantitative study of Russian regions. Hale's investigation, however, is based purely on the region *qua* region, and does not pay attention to economic disparities between identity groups, either within the region or across regions. In the Indonesian case, Tadjoeddin *et al.* (2001) identify a similar 'aspiration to inequality' at the heart of secession. Like Hale, however, they do not explicitly examine ethnic or religious differences.

This chapter combines political and economic perspectives, comparing the experiences of three separatist struggles within Southeast Asia – the Indonesian province of Aceh, southern Thailand and the Mindanao region of the southern Philippines – and a fourth nonseparatist case, the state of Sabah in Malaysia. My concern is to examine the contemporary political economy of separatism within the broader historical context outlined by scholars such as Christie. Separatist conflict in Southeast Asia, I argue, takes the form of variations on a theme. Similar historical 'preconditions' and processes of demographic and socioeconomic marginalization created conditions of severe grievance among nationally peripheral ethnic groups in all three separatist cases. These ethnic groups typically experienced a 'double whammy' of horizontal inequalities, experiencing both relative disadvantage vis-à-vis the dominant ethnic or religious group and broader regional socioeconomic decline relative to the rest of the country. Yet all these conditions also obtain in the nonseparatist comparator of Sabah. What drove the turn to violence in Aceh, southern Thailand and Mindanao, I suggest, was the politicization of these grievances through state actions at periods of heightened tensions, actions which were perceived as directly discriminatory against the marginalized groups. In contrast, when a similar juncture arose in Sabah with violence looming, the central government in Malaysia chose to make substantial political concessions to the marginalized group.

The chapter is organized as follows. The next section provides a brief overview of the four cases. Subsequent sections examine, in turn, the demographic, socioeconomic and political determinants of separatism.

12.2 The cases

Like the rest of the Dutch East Indies, the end of the colonial era in Aceh came with the end of the Second World War and the surrender of Japan, which had occupied the archipelago from 1941. After the fall of Japan, however, Aceh was the one area of the archipelago that the Dutch did not even attempt to reoccupy (Reid, 2006) and the end of colonialism thus allowed the space for an extensive social as well as political revolution, with the annihilation of the unpopular precolonial *ulèëbalang* aristocracy that had served as colonial intermediaries during the years of Dutch rule and Japanese occupation. In their place, Islamic leaders and *ulama* came to prominence under the umbrella All-Aceh Ulama Union (PUSA, *Persatuan Ulama Seluruh Aceh*) led by Daud Beureu'eh (Reid, 1979). This new leadership actively promoted the concept of Indonesia, and Aceh's place within that 'imagined' nation, and its status as not reoccupied meant that Aceh became central to the anticolonial war.

Following the final capitulation of the Dutch and the formation of Indonesia, however, Beureu'eh and other Acehnese leaders soon despaired of the secular nature of the new republic and joined with groups from other provinces in the *Darul Islam* rebellion that sought to transform Indonesia into an Islamic state. Beureu'eh and his followers held out in rebellion against Jakarta longer than the Darul Islam movement in other provinces. Importantly, however, the Darul Islam movement was not fighting for separation from the Indonesian state, but rather its transformation into an Islamic state, although Acehnese discontent at the province being subsumed within a larger North Sumatra province was also a motivating factor. Beureu'eh's rebellion lasted until 1959, when he agreed the first 'special autonomy' package for Aceh, which saw Aceh regain provincial status as a 'special region' (*daereh istimewa*), with control over fields such as education, and the right to develop a *shari'a* court system. This special autonomy did not last long, however, and was effectively revoked by Suharto, shortly after he came to power in 1965.

In 1971, the discovery of oil and natural gas in Aceh drastically increased the significance of the province to the national economy. Five years later, rebellion re-emerged, this time in the specifically separatist form of the Free Acheh Movement (GAM, or *Gerakan Acheh Merdeka*) and its political wing, the Acheh-Sumatra National Liberation Front (ASNLF).[1]

Led by Hasan di Tiro, GAM was initially a fairly ragtag affair that posed little threat to the Indonesian state. By 1982, the movement appeared to have been beaten; and di Tiro and the ASNLF leadership fled into exile. In 1989, however, GAM re-emerged, instigating a new period of rebellion that lasted for more than a decade, with increasing accusations of human rights atrocities on both sides (Kell, 1995; Schulze, 2004). After the collapse of Suharto's New Order regime, successive democratic governments made efforts to find a solution to the Aceh problem and a Cessation of Hostilities Agreement was signed in 2002. The subsequent negotiations quickly collapsed, and Aceh was placed under martial law in 2003. The 2004 Indian Ocean tsunami that killed over 100,000 people in Aceh radically altered the political and military setting, however, eventually leading an agreed peace settlement between GAM and the Indonesian government in August 2005, which granted Aceh considerable autonomy.

The second separatist case to be explored is that of the Malay-Muslim areas of southern Thailand. Compared with Indonesia, Thailand is a largely homogenous country consisting mostly of Buddhist ethnic Thai and largely assimilated Chinese. Its Southern Region, however, also encompasses a population of ethnic Malay Muslims, particularly concentrated in the three southernmost provinces of Narathiwat, Pattani and Yala, which border Malaya. These provinces, which were integrated into Thailand (then Siam) in the early twentieth century, have been home to a long-running though intermittent rebellion since the end of the Second World War. The first surge of violence in 1947–1948 was, as in Aceh, linked to the rise of an organization of Islamic leaders, the Patani People's Movement (PPM), around a charismatic *ulama*, Haji Sulong bin Abdul Kadir. In this phase, the rebellion was more irredentist than separatist, seeking union with Malaya rather than the formation of a separate state. While these demands found some sympathy among the Malay elites in Malaya, Britain – at that stage still the colonial master in Malaya – was less receptive. Hamstrung by a Communist insurgency in Malaya and not wishing to upset the Thai government, Britain signed an agreement with Thailand assuring joint control of the border area. With this and the arrest of Haji Sulong and other leaders, the irredentist movement was 'effectively neutralized' (Suhrke, 1975: 197). Muslim resentment remained strong in southern Thailand, however, and sporadic anti-Thai violence continued over the ensuing decades. During the 1970s, an explicitly separatist, not irredentist, movement emerged, but this never reached the mobilizational levels of the earlier episode, and largely fizzled out under an amnesty announced in 1980. Since 2001, however, the region has seen a return to severe violence, which intensified in 2003.

The third separatist movement I consider is the *Bangsamoro* rebellion in the southern Philippines. The Muslim 'Moros' of Mindanao and the Sulu archipelago of the southern Philippines have long been a 'problem' for the various outside powers that controlled, or sought to control, the region – Spain from the sixteenth to late nineteenth centuries, then the United States until the mid-twentieth century and finally the independent, predominantly Christian, Philippine state.

Despite many attempts, the Spanish never gained more than a foothold in Mindanao and it was only after the islands passed to American possession in 1899, following their victory in the Spanish–American war, that a concrete colonial presence was exerted over Mindanao. Even then martial law remained in place throughout much of American occupation. Nonetheless, by the time America came to grant independence to the Philippines, a new generation of Moro leaders had emerged that were not inextricably opposed to integration into the Philippines, as long as they were allowed to retain their sense of separate identity (Abinales, 2000; McKenna, 1998).

By the 1960s, however, tensions between Christians and Muslims in Mindanao had escalated and sporadic communal clashes emerged. This violence intensified in the early 1970s, particularly during electoral periods when rival politicians mobilized ethnic and religious militias to gather votes and intimidate their opponents. In 1972, with his second and constitutionally final term as president ending, Ferdinand Marcos declared martial law, justifying it largely on the basis of the ongoing violence in Mindanao. Martial law in turn provided the springboard for the Moro National Liberation Front (MNLF), which began the armed movement for a separate Moro state. The initial period of conflict was intense, but it quickly descended into military stalemate (Noble, 1981) and the separatist movement fragmented with the breakaway of the Moro Islamic Liberation Front (MILF) and later small groups such as Abu Sayyaf. A long process of negotiation between successive Philippine governments and the MNLF finally led to the creation of a new region with substantial autonomy, the Autonomous Region of Muslim Mindanao (ARMM), but the MILF and other groups rejected this solution, and conflict in the region has continued.

The final case that I consider is the Malaysian state of Sabah. Prior to achieving independence through merger with Malaya in 1963, Sabah – then known as British North Borneo – was administered as a separate colony, first under Chartered Company rule between 1886 and 1941, at which time it was occupied by the Japanese. Following the Japanese surrender, Sabah became a direct British protectorate. Sabah's inclusion in the formation of Malaysia was not initially supported by many key figures within the state, including the 'paramount leader' (*Huguan Siao*) of the largest indigenous grouping, the Kadazan-Dusun, Donald Stephens. While Stephens and others eventually accepted the logic – or at least the inevitability – of the formation of Malaysia, relations between Sabah and the federal government in Kuala Lumpur remained fractious. On at least three occasions, state leaders have raised, or stood accused of raising, the prospect of secession, but a popular movement for separation has never emerged, let alone a violent one (Brown 2004b, 2006). Sabah thus provides a useful comparator for the actively separatist cases explored here, by allowing us to identify commonalities and differences that may explain why regional discontent ultimately provided the grounds for violent mobilization in some cases but not others.

As already noted, a typical explanation of these separatist cases is located in the political geography of decolonization and the creation of ethnic peripheries to the independent states of Southeast Asia with weak historical and cultural linkages with the dominant group in the purported new nation state or even, in some cases such as Pattani, with strong links to a different nation state. It is these ethnic peripheries that have proved the breeding ground for all of the region's separatist movements.

Yet, to see separatist movements in Southeast Asia simply in culturalist terms as ethnonationalist resurgences seeking to 'correct' the arbitrary borders imposed by Western colonial wranglings would be insufficient. This is certainly a story that separatist organizations themselves are often keen to emphasize, framing their struggles in terms of 'ethnohistories' (Smith, 1986), which posit their respective insurgencies as the continuation of colonial-era resistance movements, with the ultimate aim of restoring legitimate pre-colonial polities. The timelessness of these 'natural', legitimate ethnic states are counterposed against the novelty and illegitimacy of modern territorial claims (for example, ASNLF, 1976; Misuari, 2000).

From a social scientific perspective, however, this appeal to ethnohistor-ical continuity is problematic for several reasons. Firstly, there is increasing evidence that such claims are based largely on erroneous historiography. On the one hand, the internal cohesion of separatist groups is historic-ally dubious. Thomas McKenna in particular has argued that the atavistic glorification of a precolonial Islamic polity in the southern Philippines is incorrect and that, in fact, the region was the site of incessant internal feuding between competing sultanates – primarily Sulu and Maguindanao – and their associated Datu elites (McKenna, 1998, 2002). On the other hand, external relations between the cultural predecessors of today's separatists and their denoted oppressors have not always exhibited the apparently timeless enmity that such ethnohistories propose. Horstmann (2004), for instance, observes that social relations in Pattani were historically largely harmonious, based on observance of cosmological commonalities between Muslim and Buddhist groupings rather than doctrinal differences.

Secondly, such ethnohistorical approaches cannot begin to explain why separatist movements emerge *when* they do and, indeed, why they *don't* emerge in other ethnically and historically distinct regions of modern nation states. Sympathetic analysts try to explain timing in terms of nationalist awakenings. Wearing his academic hat, Che Man (1990: 66), for instance, argued that the emergence of irredentism in southern Thailand was linked to the arousal of 'nationalist aspirations among the Muslims', driven by the attainment of independence by 'some subject peoples' in the postwar era. If this is the case, however, why did violent separatism not also emerge immediately in the southern Philippines – one of those states that did indeed achieve independence in the immediate postwar era? Why did the Acehnese enthusiastically throw their lot in with the Indonesia project during the anti-Dutch war, rather than seek to assert their own ethnonationalist past as the basis of an independent state, especially given the opportunity afforded by the lack of Dutch reoccupation?

While the political and cultural geography of postcolonial state formation in Southeast Asia undoubtedly provides the broad setting for the emer-gence of separatist movements, then, we are obliged to look deeper into the processes of social and economic transformation that preceded and accom-panied secessionism. We can begin by looking at how these new states initially sought to deal with 'problem' regions, which is largely a question of demography.

12.3   The demographic logic of separatism: State-sponsored migration and minoritization

Many of the post–Second World War states of Southeast Asia faced potential problems of ethnic peripheries, left over from the mismatch between colonial border-drawing and the patterns of precolonial settlement and state forma-tion. A typical response of these newly independent states was to encourage migration into the ethnic peripheries by more 'loyal' representatives of the putative nation state, often in the name of development. As we shall see in this and the next section, however, far from undermining the likelihood of secession, such policies typically exacerbated local grievances by adding to the sense of marginalization among peripheral communities.

This 'minoritization' policy was most extreme in the southern Philippines. Migration of Christianized Filipinos into Mindanao had been promoted since the American period, largely as a means of 'swamping' the rebel-lious Mindanao population, as well as providing the colonialists with a bedrock loyal population from which to staff their administration. By the time of Independence, Christians already outnumbered non-Christians in Mindanao as a whole, although they were not evenly spread – Muslims remain until today the majority in the southwestern parts of the island, and in the Sulu archipelago – the provinces that now constitute the ARMM.

After Independence, however, the new governments in Manila began encouraging even faster Christian migration to Mindanao (Figure 12.1). During 35 years of American control, between 1903 and 1939, just short of 70,000 migrants came to Mindanao; during just 12 years between 1948 and 1960, however, more than 1.2 million Christian Filipinos migrated to Mindanao, an annual increase of 6.7 per cent (Wernstedt and Simkins, 1965). State-sponsored resettlement schemes, with the ostensible aim of promoting rice production, brought thousands of poor Christians from Luzon and the Visayas islands to Mindanao, particularly around the Cotabato area (Abinales, 2000; Gutierrez and Borras, 2004). Although the growth in the non-Muslim population slowed considerably following the outbreak of viol-ence, it remained above the Muslim population growth rate between 1980 and 2000. The minoritization of the Muslims in Mindanao over the past century is stark. In 1903, Muslims constituted 76 per cent of the population; shortly after independence in 1948 they were already a minority with only 32 per cent of the Mindanao population; by 2000 this had decreased further to barely 20 per cent.

Similar population movement schemes were undertaken at various stages by the Indonesian and Thai governments. In Indonesia under the New Order, the largest state-sponsored resettlement scheme in history, the transmigra-tion (*transmigrasi*) programme relocated hundreds of thousands of families from Java and Bali across the archipelago; many more 'unofficial' migrants followed. The ostensible justification for the transmigration programme was

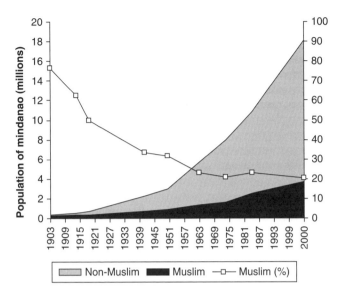

Figure 12.1 Population of Mindanao by religion, 1903–2000
Source: Author's calculations from 1990 and 2000 census samples and Che Man (1990).[2]

both developmental, based on the undoubted overpopulation in Java and Bali, and ideological, based on a nebulously defined need for 'national integration'. Tirtosudarmo (1995), however, suggests an alternative motive – to provide a bedrock of Javanese support for the territorially organized army, particularly in troublesome regions. Transmigration sites often took prime agricultural land and displaced local populations in constructing amenities and infrastructure to service the new developments (Leith, 1998). Moreover, transmigration sites were not evenly spread, but clustered in 'hot spots', one of which was Aceh. The choice of Aceh as such a hot spot was acknowledged by the government to be driven by security concerns (Kell, 1995). In the 1990 census, over 10 per cent of the population of Aceh was born outside the province, and a further 4 per cent of those born in Aceh were identifiably Javanese.[3]

Figure 12.2 shows the distribution of these migrants living in Aceh in 1990, broken down by the year of their arrival in Aceh and their place of birth. It is clear that migration into Aceh escalated considerably in the 1980s in two broad waves, firstly Java-born migrants who came between 1981 and 1984 – most likely through the transmigration programme – and latterly migrants from elsewhere in Sumatra, mostly the neighbouring province of North Sumatra. This surge of Javanese transmigration was, I will suggest below, particularly important for the dynamics of horizontal inequalities.

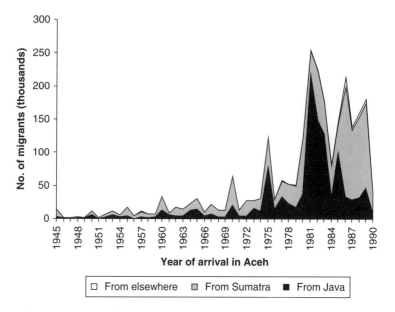

Figure 12.2   Indonesia – Migrants living in Aceh by year of arrival and place of birth, 1990
Source: Extrapolated estimates based on a random sample of the 1990 Indonesian Census.

In Thailand, relocation programmes saw resettlement of ethnic Thais into the Southern Region. Although this was on a much smaller scale than in either Indonesia or the Philippines, it nonetheless generated considerable resentment among the Muslim population (Che Man, 1990). However, higher reproductive rates among the Muslims have seen their position maintained within the three southernmost provinces (Table 12.1). Within the Southern Region as a whole, the Muslim population grew at an average 2.7 per cent per annum between 1960 and 2000, compared with 2.4 per cent overall.

Like the separatist regions under consideration here, the Malaysian state of Sabah has also experienced a significant influx of in-migration since joining the Malaysian Federation in 1963. Before joining Malaysia, the population of Sabah was divided into a number of indigenous ethnic groups, mostly Christian and animist, with some Muslim groups. Together with the indigenous groups of Sarawak and the peninsular Malays, these indigenous groups – jointly termed *bumiputera* or 'Sons of the Soil' – had certain constitutional privileges and, after 1969, were the beneficiaries of affirmative action programmes. In 1963, the Malay population of Sabah was minimal, while by 2000, around 10 per cent of the population was Malay, almost exclusively migrants from West Malaysia concentrated in the public sector in the state

Table 12.1 Thailand – Population of Southern Region by religion and province in percentage, 1960 and 2000

Southern Region	1960			2000		
	Buddhist	**Muslim**	**Other**	**Buddhist**	**Muslim**	**Other**
Chumphon	98.8	0.1	1.1	98.9	0.7	0.4
Krabi	61.3	38.1	0.6	65.2	34.7	0.1
Nakhon Si Thammarat	94.4	4.9	0.7	93.1	6.2	0.7
Narathiwat	20.7	78.2	1.1	17.9	82.0	0.1
Pattani	21.8	77.8	0.4	19.2	80.7	0.1
Phangnga	80.8	17.9	1.3	76.3	23.2	0.5
Phatthalung	91.5	8.0	0.5	88.3	11.1	0.6
Phuket	81.2	17.1	1.7	81.6	17.1	1.3
Ranong	87.2	11.9	0.9	88.5	10.9	0.6
Satun	16.8	82.9	0.3	31.9	67.8	0.3
Songkhla	77.9	18.6	3.5	76.6	23.2	0.2
Surat Thani	96.5	2.0	1.5	97.3	2.0	0.7
Trang	86.2	12.1	1.7	86.0	13.7	0.3
Yala	28.5	61.1	10.4	31.0	68.9	0.1
Total	72.9	25.3	1.8	71.6	28.0	0.4

Source: Thailand (1962) and data provided by the National Statistical Office of Thailand.

capital of Kota Kinabalu. This situation generated considerable resentment among many native Sabahans as it was seen to contravene the 'Borneonization' policy agreed during the Malaysian negotiations, which guaranteed that Sabah would be allowed to retain its distinct identity. A notable difference between Sabah and the other cases considered here has been the extent of *international* immigration. By 2000, almost a quarter of the population of Sabah were noncitizens, the vast majority from the Philippines or Indonesia. Over 80 per cent of these noncitizens were Muslim. Starting in the 1970s, officially sanctioned, or at least tolerated, migrants began arriving in Sabah from the Philippines and Indonesia (Table 12.2). Some were officially classified as refugees from the Moro conflict, but many more were economic migrants. Both academics and political activists alike have seen this influx as an attempt by successive pro-Muslim state administrations, backed by the national government in Kuala Lumpur, to change the nature of Sabah society (Sadiq, 2005).

We have thus seen that a typical state response to potentially troublesome ethnic peripheries was to encourage, to varying extents and with varying degrees of formality, migration into the region by peoples considered more 'loyal' to the central state. The next section examines how these demographic processes created or exacerbated socioeconomic horizontal inequalities and group grievances.

Table 12.2   Ethnic and religious distribution of Sabah, 2000 census

	Percentage of total population	Religious distribution (% within group)			
		Islam	Christian	Buddhist	Other
Malaysian Citizens	76.4	57.7	31.5	8.3	2.5
Bumiputera	61.6	64.4	33.1	0.6	1.9
Malay	11.7	100.0	–	–	–
Kadazandusun	18.4	21.0	74.8	0.6	3.6
Bajau	13.2	99.8	0.1	–	0.1
Murut	3.3	13.8	82.7	0.3	3.2
Other *bumiputera*	15.0	70.0	25.8	1.7	2.5
Non-*bumiputera*	14.9	30.0	24.7	39.9	5.6
Chinese	10.1	3.3	31.1	58.8	6.8
Other non-*bumiputera*	4.8	86.1	11.4	0.4	2.1
Non-Citizens	23.6	83.0	16.0	0.3	0.7
All Sabah	100.0	63.7	27.8	6.4	2.1

Note: 'Other' includes the census classifications of 'Hindu', 'Confucian/Taoism and other traditional Chinese religions', 'tribal/folk religions', 'others', 'no religion' and 'unknown'.
Source: Author's calculation based on Sabah (2002).

12.4   The economic logic of separatism: Horizontal inequalities

This section examines the dynamics of horizontal inequalities in the separatist regions considered here, again including Sabah as a comparator. When considering the role of horizontal inequalities in the emergence of violent separatism, there are two important dimensions worth considering. Firstly, the inequalities between the level of development in the separatist region vis-à-vis the rest of the country, which I term 'spatial inequalities' (cf. Kanbur and Venables, 2005; Murshed and Gates, 2005). The second dimension of horizontal inequalities I shall consider are those between the indigenous ethnic groups within separatist regions and migrants or 'representatives' of the national would-be 'nation state', which I shall term 'ethnic horizontal inequalities'. The assumption here is that the *experience* of horizontal inequality is rooted in locality and day-to-day interactions. The sense of relative deprivation experienced by a marginalized ethnic periphery vis-à-vis a distant and unvisited capital region, for instance, may be of much less political importance than inequalities relative to local residents who are seen as 'representative' of the dominant ethnic group, even if these latter inequalities are less severe.

The disparity between Aceh's oil-boom wealth and the continued impoverishment of large sections of its population is often cited as one of the root causes of the separatist struggle in the province (for example Kell, 1995; Ross,

2003). Indeed, GAM's declaration of Acehnese independence in 1976 was partially justified in such terms, claiming that the province's revenue production was 'used totally for the benefit of Java and the Javanese' (ASNLF, 1976). In the three decades following GAM's declaration, the human development situation in Aceh has shifted sharply adversely compared with other Indonesian provinces. In 1980, Aceh was a mid-income province, ranking tenth out of 26 provinces in terms of regional GDP, with very low poverty rates – only two provinces had a lower poverty rate than Aceh. As the exploitation of its natural resources progressed, Aceh's GDP increased relatively more quickly than most other provinces. In 1998, more than 40 per cent of Aceh's GDP was due to oil. But this increase in wealth generation was accompanied by a drastic increase in poverty. Poverty in Aceh more than doubled from 1980 to 2002; over the same period, poverty in Indonesia as a whole fell by nearly half. By 2000, Aceh's regional GDP had risen to fourth out of 30 provinces, but its poverty rank had also increased to fifth.

The development of the gas and oil industry in Aceh was centred on the northern coast port of Lhokseumawe, which quickly developed into a major economic enclave, designated the Lhokseumawe Industrial Zone (ZILS). Migrant labour was brought in to staff the zone, which came 'to assume the obtrusive character of a high-income, capital-intensive, urban, non-Muslim, non-Acehnese enclave in a basically low-income, labor-intensive, rural, Muslim, Acehnese province' (Donald Emmerson, quoted in Kell, 1995: 17). A glimpse into the dynamics of inequality in the urban economy at the time of the re-emergence of separatism can be gained by examining the data in the 1990 census. We can compare the relationship between the Javanese and the Acehnese in Aceh with the relationship between the Javanese and the Batak in the neighbouring province of North Sumatra. In both provinces, the Javanese form the second largest ethnic group. The Batak are the largest indigenous group in North Sumatra, with a position roughly equivalent to that of the Acehnese in Aceh. As a migrant community from Indonesia's politically dominant island of Java, the position of the Javanese community is often a matter of contention for indigenous groups. In both provinces Javanese had settled for many generations, but the state-sponsored 'transmigration' programme saw many more arrivals after the 1970s. Aceh in particular has been a site of recent migration; in 1990, 56 per cent of the Javanese in the province were born outside Aceh, as compared to only 14 per cent in North Sumatra. Henceforth, the term 'migrant Javanese' will be applied specifically to those Javanese born outside their current province of residence.

In 1990, more than half the Javanese employed in the urban areas of Aceh were employed in the top strata of jobs: government officials, professionals and technicians, compared with only a third of Acehnese (see Table 12.3). In contrast, the urban Javanese in North Sumatra were considerably underrepresented in both the top rank of jobs and the middle rank of clerical, sales and service workers, partly due to the relative educational advantage of

Table 12.3 Urban occupational distribution by ethnic group, Aceh and North Sumatra, 1990

Percentage of ethnic group in employment category (urban)	Aceh			North Sumatra		
	Acehnese	Javanese	Province	Batak	Javanese	Province
Government officials, professionals, technicians	34.3	**57.1**	39.0	**23.1**	8.2	18.9
Clerical and related, sales and serviceworkers	**32.9**	19.0	31.2	**34.4**	32.7	33.3
Other occupations	**32.9**	23.8	29.8	42.5	**59.0**	47.8

Source: Author's calculation from 1990 Indonesian Census sample.
Note: Cells in bold denote above province average.

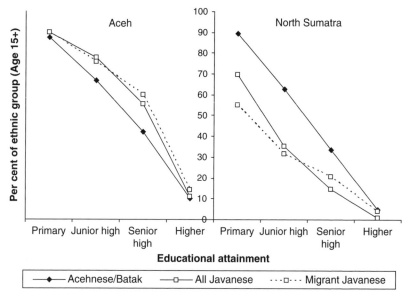

Figure 12.3 Educational attainment of largest two ethnic groups in urban areas, Aceh and North Sumatra, 1990
Source: Author's calculation from 1990 Indonesian Census sample.

the urban Javanese (Figure 12.3) and partly due to the relative disadvantage. Urban unemployment among the Acehnese, however, was twice as high as among the Javanese; among the more highly educated population, Acehnese unemployment was almost five times as high as Javanese (see Table 12.4).

These patterns suggest an iniquitous cycle of horizontal inequality in Aceh; the relative poverty of Aceh as a province – *spatial* horizontal

Table 12.4 Urban unemployment rates, Aceh 1990

Percentage of ethnic group aged 15+	Acehnese	Javanese	Province	Ratio A:J
All adults	**10.2**	4.7	8.2	2.19
Adults educated to Senior High or higher	**13.1**	2.7	9.1	4.85

Source: Author's calculations from 1990 Indonesian Census sample.
Note: Calculated as the ratio of unemployed job-seekers to the total working population.

inequalities – manifested itself in low education rates, which resulted in the in-migration of a substantial number of educated non-Acehnese to staff the higher ranks of the economy, particularly associated with the oil and gas industry. This in-migration in turn exacerbated local *ethnic* horizontal inequalities between Acehnese and Javanese, migrants and nonmigrants.

Thus far, we have considered only the urban population of the two provinces. A second insight into the dynamics of horizontal inequalities in Aceh and North Sumatra can be gained by comparing the educational attainment and landholding of the rural populations on the eve of the renewed rebellion. In educational terms, the ethnic profile in the two provinces was remarkably similar (see Figure 12.4). In both Aceh and North Sumatra, the indigenous group was considerably better educated in rural areas than the Javanese community. Almost half the rural Javanese population in both

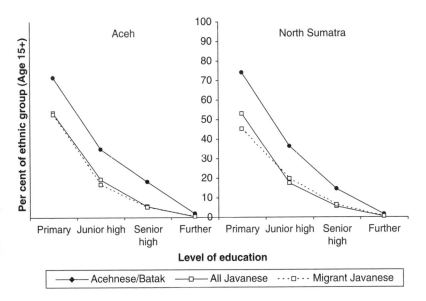

Figure 12.4 Indonesia, Aceh and North Sumatra provinces – Educational attainment of rural Acehnese, Batak and Javanese, 1990
Source: Author's calculations from 1990 Indonesian Census sample.

provinces in 1990 had not even completed primary schooling, compared with less than a third of Acehnese and Batak; at the other end of the scale, the proportion of Acehnese and Batak completing senior high school or further was more than three times the proportion of Javanese.

Where a noticeable difference between Aceh and North Sumatra emerges is in landholdings. In rural Aceh, the Javanese had much larger landhold-ings, with proportionately twice as many Javanese holding more than two hectares than Acehnese. These disparities are even higher if we compare the Acehnese population to the migrant Javanese, rather than those born in the province. In part these disparities are due the educational advantages of the Acehnese, who moved into nonagricultural activities to a greater extent than the Javanese. Seventy per cent of Acehnese work in the agricultural sector, compared to almost 90 per cent of rural Javanese in the province.

But considering only those within the agricultural sector, the Javanese maintained a distinct land advantage in Aceh (Figure 12.5). The proportion of Javanese holding more than one hectare was 15 per cent higher than the proportion of Acehnese; while at the two hectare level, this Javanese advantage increased to 45 per cent. This trend was even more marked among first-generation Javanese migrants, where the respective advantage over the Acehnese was 20 per cent and 68 per cent, suggesting that rural horizontal inequalities were increasing drastically. Indeed, among the Javanese who arrived in Aceh during the 1981–1984 migrant surge identified above, more

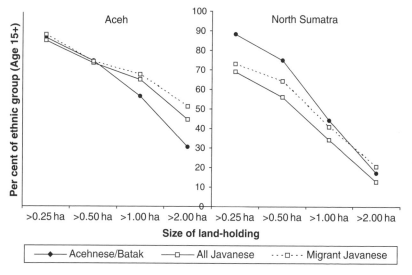

Figure 12.5   Landholding of rural Acehnese, Batak and Javanese in agricultural occu-pations, Aceh and North Sumatra, 1990

Source: Author's calculations from 1990 Indonesian Census sample.

than 70 per cent owned more than two hectares of land. Once again, the comparison with North Sumatra, where the Batak held a consistent land advantage over the Javanese, is marked.

The substantial landholdings of the Javanese population in Aceh are largely accounted for by the state-sponsored transmigration scheme. The horizontal inequalities between the ethnic Acehnese and the Javanese in the province help account not only for the separatist movement, but for the particularly anti-Javanese manifestation it took. As noted earlier, during the 1950s, the Darul Arqam rebellion in Aceh was more a struggle to *change the nature* of the Indonesian state than to secede from it. In contrast, the rebellions associated with the Free Aceh Movement, both briefly in the 1970s and since the early 1990s, have been characterized by often vitriolic anti-Javanese sentiment. GAM's *Declaration of Independence of Acheh-Sumatra*, specifically declares freedom from 'the foreign regime of Jakarta and the alien people of the island of Java', going on to describe how 'they have stolen our properties; they have robbed us from our livelihood; they have abused the education of our children; they have exiled our leaders; they have put our people in chains of tyranny, poverty, and neglect' (ASNLF, 1976). Although GAM denies it, it has been claimed that the 1990s saw 'the systematic attempt to cleanse Aceh of all Javanese presence' (Schulze, 2004: 39). At a deposition to the recent session of the UNHCR Working Group on Indigenous Populations, the Acehnese delegation placed specific emphasis on the transmigration programme as a source of grievance: 'With the drastic transmigration policy, the Javanese population in Acheh grew from negligible to over 10 per cent ... taking the most productive land areas and occupying the best jobs' (ASNLF, 2004).

Far from attempting to reduce economic horizontal inequalities in Aceh, then, the Indonesian government has in fact been the prime agent in creating such inequalities. The dynamics of this process have been reinforcing: lacking trust in the ethnic Acehnese, particularly young males who were assumed to be GAM sympathizers, the Indonesian government brought in outsiders, particularly Javanese, to manage and safeguard its economic interests in the province. Agricultural migration was also encouraged to provide a bedrock of support for the military presence in the province. This immigration, however, only reinforced Acehnese grievances against the central government and its Javanese 'agents', thus solidifying support for the rebellion.

In the case of Aceh, then, spatial horizontal inequalities revolving around the province's potential wealth as a natural-resource producer drove the emergence of a separatist movement in the late 1970s. This movement was relatively limited in scope and appeal, however, but reemerged a decade later, and during the intervening period significant *ethnic* inequalities had emerged between the ethnic Acehnese and the immigrant Javanese population.

In the case of the southern Philippines, historical data on both dimensions of horizontal inequality is sparse, but what is available presents an

Table 12.5　Philippines, ARMM – Socioeconomic indicators, 2000

	Incidence of poverty (%), 2000	Per capita income (PPP US$), 2000	Life expectancy at birth, 1997	Human Development Index	Rank (out of 77)
Maguindanao	36.2	1,306	53.2	0.431	73
Lanao del Sur	48.1	1,250	56.0	0.425	74
Basilan	63.0	1,077	59.8	0.420	75
Tawi-Tawi	75.3	1,218	50.4	0.378	76
Sulu	92.0	1,027	51.9	0.311	77

Source: HDN and UNDP (2002).

interesting picture. It is evident from the data that Mindanao in general, and the Autonomous Region of Muslim Mindanao in particular, is the most underdeveloped part of the Philippines. In the most recent National Human Development Report for the Philippines, the bottom five provinces in virtually every indicator of human development, and in the overall human development index, were the ARMM provinces (Table 12.5). The province of Sulu has ranked absolute bottom in every report since the first in 1994. In 2000, more than nine out of ten households in Sulu fell below the poverty line.

Regionally disaggregated GDP data are only available for the Philippines from 1975, three years after the insurrection broke out. Figure 12.6 tracks the relative GDP *per capita* of the three broad geographical zones[4] of the Philippines – Luzon, the large northern island that includes the capital, Manila; the Visayas archipelago in the middle area; and Mindanao and the Sulu archipelago in the south. Two points are worth noting here. Firstly, at this broad level, spatial inequalities in the Philippines have remained remarkably stable, with little change in relative standing over the past three decades. Secondly, and more importantly for our purposes, while the Mindanao/Sulu zone is relatively poor compared to Luzon, it is not significantly worse off than the Visayas. Indeed, during the most intense period of separatist activity in the 1970s, Mindanao was better off than the Visayas in GDP terms, and this relative advantage was broadly *increasing* until the mid-1980s.

Data limitations again make it difficult to get a picture of income disparities between the migrant Christians and the Muslims in Mindanao prior to the outbreak of conflict. However, a suggestive picture of the relative socioeconomic standing of the Christian and Muslim groups comes from educational data from the 1990 Philippines census. Figure 12.7 shows the proportion of the population who never attended school, broken down by age when the conflict began and by religion. It is clear that both religious groups made major advances in educational participation, at least at the very basic level. Yet, while nonenrolment in at least one year of education was virtually eradicated among the Christian population by 1970, it remained a

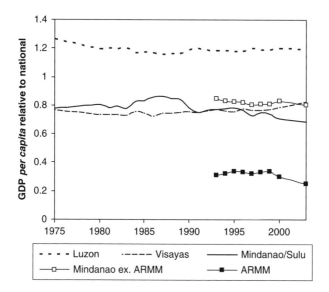

Figure 12.6 Philippines – Relative GDP *per capita* by broad geographical zone, 1975–2003

Source: Data provided by the National Statistics Office of the Philippines.

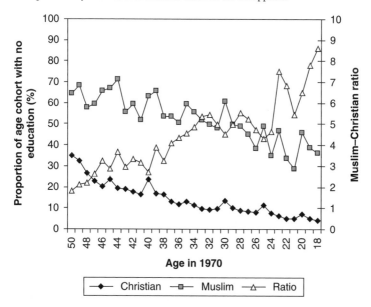

Figure 12.7 Mindanao, Philippines – Proportion of Christian and Muslim population with no schooling, by age in 1970 and religion

Source: Author's calculations, based on 1990 census sample.

significant problem for the Muslim community. If we consider the specific population sector that might be considered the 'usual suspects' for recruitment to rebel organizations – males between the ages of 15 and 30 (in 1972) – the situation is stark and clear: less than 4 per cent of Christians within this population had never attended school, but more than a third of their Muslim counterparts had no schooling.

Qualitative analyses of the Mindanao conflict also point to the importance of religious disparities in land ownership and landlessness, brought about by the introduction of land registration laws initiated by the American colonial state. Although legally entitled to register land in their names, registration created problems for the Muslim population on two fronts. Firstly, many of them were illiterate, unused to the processes of the modern bureaucratic state, or simply did not understand the registration process. But more important were the traditional cultural attitudes towards land among the Muslims. Within the traditional *adat* (customary law) systems of all the major Moro-Muslim ethnic groups, land was not an alienable commodity. The contemporary economy was predominantly a subsistence one, and land was generally communally held. While certain individuals could hold the right of usufruct over a given portion of land privately – usually at the discretion of the local *datu*, or local chief – no one had *ownership* of the land *per se*, not even the *datu* (Scott, 1982; Stewart, 1988). Land registration was thus anathema in this system, contravening both the inherently public nature of land in the Moro system and the role of the *datu* as the arbiter of land use claims. Survey research shows that such attitudes persist. While most Moros appear now to be familiar with the concept and practice of land ownership, less than one in five interviewees believed the secular courts to be the appropriate venue for resolving land disputes, preferring instead resolution through traditional *adat* or Islamic institutions and practices (Fianza, 1999).

During the 1950s and 1960s, then, substantial in-migration of Christians, combined with land laws alien to the Moro population, resulted in the emergence of significant horizontal inequalities in ownership of and access to land in Mindanao. At the same time, the paternalistic patron–client relationships that characterized the political make-up of the Philippines combined with monopolistic laws on commodity exports to allow a number of politically linked Christian families to gain vast plantation landholdings which tended to employ Christian labourers at the expense of Moros (Che Man, 1990; Gutierrez and Borras, 2004). Thus, not only were the Moro displaced from their 'traditional' lands, they were also denied access to the emerging money economy. By 1965, observers were already noting that Christian 'penetration' of Mindanao was causing 'unrest and strife', with the dispute settlement processes usually favouring the Christians as 'the better educated Christian has been able to present a stronger case to the courts... while Muslim litigants have been viewed as obstructionists and anachronists' (Wernstedt and Simkins, 1965: 101). A quantitative study of the geographical concentration of this preseparatist communal violence at the municipality level between 1970 and the declaration of martial law in 1972 found a measure of relative deprivation had the most significant correlation with the intensity of that conflict (Magdalena, 1977).

In the case of the Philippines, then, spatial inequalities between Mindanao and the rest of the Philippines appear not to have played a significant role in fostering Moro Muslim discontent. More inflammatory, rather, was the emergence of severe socioeconomic ethnic inequalities between the migrant Christian population and the Muslims *within* Mindanao. At least initially, violent mobilization took the form of communal conflict between the local religious populations. How this mobilization turned against the state itself will be discussed in the next section.

The final separatist case is southern Thailand. Analyses of the period of intense insurgency in southern Thailand in the 1950s and 1960s are at odds over the extent to which economic grievances can explain the separatist movement. Suhrke (1970: 533) argued that the Thai Muslims did not constitute 'an economic minority in the sense of having a particular economic structure or unique economic difficulties', arguing that while the south is undoubtedly a relative poor region, this is a regional, rather than ethnic, problem. Forbes (1982: 1066), however, claimed that 'Thai Malay dissatisfaction with their backward economic status is also a continuing problem for Bangkok', pointing out that not only are the Malay-dominated provinces relatively poor, what wealth there is accrues disproportionately to Chinese-origin businessmen and plantation owners. More recently, Srisompob and Panyasak (2006) have argued that while economic discontent may have played a role in earlier periods of insurgency, this can no longer be the case as the Malay-dominated provinces have improved their economic situation in the past 20 years.

In fact, the situation is not as rosy as Srisompob and Panyasak suggest. Over the past 25 years, since Thailand began producing provincial GDP statistics, two of the mainly Malay-Muslim provinces – Yala and Narathiwat – have experienced a significant decline in their relative socioeconomic standing (Figure 12.8), each falling by around 20 per cent of relative GDP *per capita*. Pattani has done better, but remains significantly below the national average. Looking at changes in absolute *per capita* incomes (Figure 12.9) further illustrates the relatively poor performance of the three Muslim majority provinces not only in relation to Thailand as a whole, but also notably compared with neighbouring Songkhla province, the Thai-dominated province that in effect provides the 'border' between the Malay-dominated provinces and the rest of the country.

It is important to note, however, that even Narathiwat is by no means the poorest province in the country. Thailand is a country of extreme regional disparities, with the northeast region in particular beset by problems of chronic poverty far worse than in the south. In Pattani, Yala and Narathiwat,

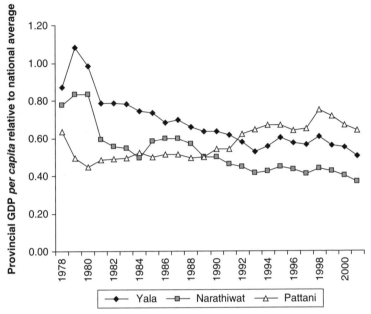

Figure 12.8 Thailand – Relative GDP *per capita* in three Malay-Muslim dominated provinces, 1978–2003
Source: Data provided by the National Statistical Office Thailand.

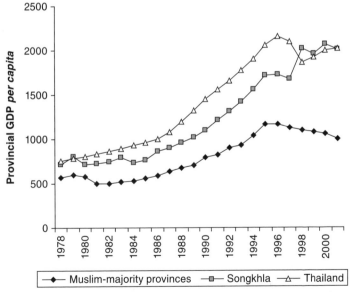

Figure 12.9 Thailand – GDP *per capita* in constant US$ (PPP 2000), selected provinces
Source: Data provided by the National Statistical Office Thailand.

poverty rates in 2000 were, respectively, 25.5 per cent, 28.1 per cent and 35.1 per cent, well above the national rate of 14.1 per cent but still nowhere close to some of the northeast provinces such as Yasothon and Nong Bua Lam Phu, both with poverty rates above 50 per cent.

Time series data on the evolution of ethnic inequalities within the Southern Region are not readily available. The 1987 Demographic Health Survey of Thailand gives a snapshot view of these inequalities, however. We can differentiate Central Thai speakers, Southern dialect speakers and Malay speakers. All the Malay speakers in the sample were Muslim, as were around 4 per cent of Central Thai-speakers. Southern dialect speakers were split 76 per cent Buddhist, 24 per cent Muslim.[5] Table 12.6 shows the average level of male and female education and a synthetic measure of household assets.[6]

It can clearly be seen that Muslims are disadvantaged overall vis-à-vis their Buddhist counterparts across all dimensions, both in the region as a whole and in the rural areas where Muslims are concentrated. In rural areas, the asset differential is not statistically significant, but all other differentials are. Taking language into account, Central Thai-speakers do better than Southern-dialect speaking Muslims, and far outstrip the Malay-speaking Muslims – with on average between four and five years extra education for both men and women and almost double the asset score. As mentioned above, despite state-sponsored schemes, Buddhist migration into the Southern Region has not significantly reduced the Muslim proportion of the population, but has nonetheless generated serious grievances. This data suggests that this is because Central Thai Buddhists, including assimilated Chinese, have taken up a dominant position in the socioeconomic scale. This picture is reinforced by the data on occupational distribution (Table 12.7). Just short of three-quarters of Muslim males are engaged in agricultural

Table 12.6 Educational and asset inequalities in Southern Thailand, by language and religion

Southern Region (Rural and Urban)	Female education (years)			Male education (years)			Household asset score		
	Buddhist	Muslim	Total	Buddhist	Muslim	Total	Buddhist	Muslim	Total
Central Thai	7.807	–	7.807	9.197	–	9.197	0.736	–	0.736
Southern dialect	5.253	3.627	4.863	6.140	4.079	5.642	0.443	0.400	0.433
Malay	–	2.920	2.920	–	3.524	3.524	–	0.405	0.405
Total	5.565	3.366	4.893	6.507	3.878	5.702	0.479	0.402	0.455
Southern Region (Rural)									
Central Thai	6.809	–	6.809	8.151	–	8.151	0.541	–	0.541
Southern dialect	4.948	3.546	4.587	5.788	4.091	5.349	0.331	0.317	0.328
Malay	–	2.785	2.785	–	3.401	3.401	–	0.316	0.316
Total	5.088	3.264	4.472	5.962	3.839	5.246	0.347	0.317	0.337

Source: DHS Survey Data (1987).

Table 12.7 Thailand – Male occupational distribution by religion and language, Southern Region (% of group)

	Buddhists			Muslims			All groups
	Central Thai-speaking	Southern dialect-speaking	Total	Southern dialect-speaking	Malay-speaking	Total	
Professional, technical and management	11.34	4.37	5.13	0.47	3.40	1.56	4.01
Clerical	4.82	1.38	1.75	0.00	1.03	0.38	1.32
Sales	27.09	7.03	9.23	5.23	6.13	5.56	8.08
Services	9.50	3.69	4.32	1.17	4.38	2.36	3.70
Agriculture	16.46	68.07	62.42	72.34	74.28	73.06	65.77
Self-Employed	12.13	59.11	53.97	57.83	46.75	53.73	53.90
Employee	4.33	8.96	8.45	14.51	27.53	19.33	11.87
Manual labour	30.79	15.48	17.15	20.79	10.78	17.09	17.13
Skilled	27.71	13.55	15.09	11.70	9.45	10.87	13.77
Unskilled	3.08	1.93	2.06	9.09	1.33	6.22	3.36
Total	100	100	100	100	100	100	100

Source: DHS Survey data (1987).

occupations, whether Southern dialect- or Malay-speaking. While Southern-dialect speaking Buddhists are also largely agricultural – albeit more self-employed rather than as employees – less than one in five Central Thai speakers are in the agricultural sector. While Central Thai-speakers account for less than 10 per cent of the population in the south, they account for more than 20 per cent of employees in professional, clerical and sales sectors.

Thus far, then, we have seen that the ethnic minorities in the separatist regions in Southeast Asia considered here were typically on the losing end of a double form of horizontal inequality, becoming socioeconomically disadvantaged vis-à-vis a largely migrant community in their 'own' regions, which were simultaneously experiencing relative economic decline. How does the nonseparatist comparator, Sabah, perform? When Sabah joined the Malaysian federation in 1963, its level of socioeconomic development was in some respects well below that of the urban areas of Malaya. When the first reliable poverty data became available in 1976, poverty rates in Sabah were in excess of 50 per cent, around 50 per cent higher than on the peninsula, but its wealth of natural resources meant that its overall GDP *per capita* was in fact around 20 per cent higher than the national average. In the ensuing three decades, poverty in Sabah undoubtedly reduced significantly, but at a much slower rate than in the peninsula, such that by 2002 poverty rates in Sabah were more than three times that of the peninsula (Table 12.8). A revised methodology for estimating poverty increased this disparity, showing the peninsular Malaysian poverty rate as 3.6 per cent in 2005 and the Sabah rate as 23.0 per cent. In terms of GDP *per capita*, Sabah also lost significantly in relative terms. While Sabah's GDP *per capita* was around 20 per cent higher

Table 12.8 Malaysia – Relative poverty rates in Sabah and Peninsular Malayasia, 1976–2005

	1976	1984	1987	1990	1995	1999	2002	2005 – Old methodology	2005 – New methodology
Sabah (%)	51.2	33.1	35.3	34.3	22.4	20.1	16.0	16.5	23.0
Peninsular Malaysia (%)	35.1	18.4	17.3	15.0	7.7	6.6	4.7	3.1	3.6
Ratio		1.46	1.80	2.04	2.29	2.90	3.04	3.42	5.32	6.39

Source: Author's calculation, from Malaysia (1981, 1986, 1991, 2001, 2006).

than the national rate in 1970, by 2003, GDP *per capita* was more than a third below the national average (Figure 12.10). While the economy of Malaysia over this period registered an impressive average GDP *per capita* growth of 4.0 per cent in real terms per annum, Sabah managed barely half this rate, averaging only 2.1 per cent. By 2000, Sabah ranked bottom of all the Malaysian states in all the indicators in the government's own socioeconomic development index (Malaysia, 2001).

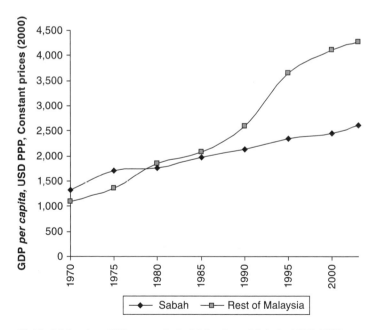

Figure 12.10 Malaysia – GDP *per capita* in Malaysia and Sabah, 1970–2003
Source: Author's calculations from Sabah (various years) and World Bank WDI dataset.

Table 12.9   Average relative *per capita* household expenditure by ethnic group, 1982, 1987 and 1989

Ethnic group	1982	1987	1989
Malay	1.44	1.44	1.41
Kadazan/Dusun	0.78	0.66	0.69
Bajau	0.70	0.83	0.80
Murut	0.41	0.57	0.67
Other *Bumiputera*	0.77	n.a.	n.a.
Chinese	1.67	2.00	1.95
Others	2.94	n.a.	n.a.

Sources: 1982 figures from Sabah (1991: 225); other years calculated from Shireen (1998: 111 and 123).

As in the other separatist cases, the demographic transformation of Sabah also generated significant ethnic inequalities, in particular an increasing demarcation between Muslim and non-Muslim *bumiputera*. As throughout Malaysia, the Chinese population of Sabah, accounting for around a quarter of the population in 1970, was markedly better off than the indigenous groups. By the 1980s, however, a further significant inequality had emerged with the influx of Malays from the rest of Malaysia, many of whom filled high-ranking positions within the state civil service. By 1982, the Malay population of Sabah, which by then accounted for significant proportion of the population, was significantly better off than the *bumiputera* groups native to Sabah. Through the 1980s, *average per capita* household expenditure among Malays was around double that of the Sabah *bumiputera*, although still lagging behind the Chinese (Table 12.9).

By the early 1980s, then, many Christian Kadazans in Sabah were doubly marginalized. Firstly, the state as a whole was being left behind in Malaysia's otherwise astounding economic growth. Secondly, within the state itself, Kadazan dominance was being threatened demographically by the influx of Muslim migrants and economically by the promotion of Malays into high-ranking positions in the state. By 1980, over 80 per cent of 'Echelon I' and 'Echelon II' civil servants in the state were identifiably Muslim (Lim, 2006).

In this section, then, we have seen that each of the separatist regions of Southeast Asia have been characterized by a 'double whammy' of spatial and ethnic horizontal inequalities. In all cases, including Sabah, this process drove a popular movement for autonomy. Whereas in Mindanao, Pattani and Aceh this movement turned into violent mobilization for secession, however, this was not the case in Sabah.

12.5 The political logic of separatism: The turn to violent mobilization

Thus some shared trends led to political mobilization in the separatist regions, including their status as 'ethnic peripheries' left over from colonial-era border demarcation, state-sponsored or abetted in-migration, and the concomitant emergence of significant horizontal inequalities, both regionally, with respect to the rest of the nation, and internally, with respect to ethnoreligious groups closer to the central state. Yet these trends also largely applied to our nonseparatist case, the Malaysian state of Sabah. In the final section of this chapter, I argue that this turn to violence can best be explained by the central state's response to demands for autonomy.

In the southern Philippines, even in the early decades of independence, migration and associated land tensions were the cause of increasing strife between Muslim Moros and Christian Filipinos in Mindanao, yet this did not yet take the form of a widespread rejection of the Philippine state by the Moro population. Conflicts remained localized and intercommunal, that is, community-versus-community rather than community-versus-state. Noble notes that while sporadic demands for Mindanao independence were made by Muslim leaders throughout this period, this was largely used as a bargaining mechanism for political patronage from Manila: 'Muslim leaders did not want to secede; they wanted rewards for not seceding' (1975: 456).

In the late 1960s and early 1970s, however, a series of events drove the *politicization* of Moro resentment towards the Christian state in Manila rather than the migrant population in Mindanao. The first of these was the 'Corregidor Incident' or 'Jabidah massacre' of 1968. Corregidor Island, in the Manila bay, was the site for the secret training of a group of Muslim volunteers recruited by the Philippine Armed Forces, apparently for a planned infiltration of Sabah, to which the Philippines retained a territorial claim. In March 1968, the trainees mutinied and were massacred by their Christian officers. Whether this mutiny was caused by their perception that the planned 'invasion' of Sabah was unjust or for the more prosaic reason that the recruits did not receive their promised pay cheques is unclear, but whatever the reason, the massacre of Muslim recruits by Christian officers raised Muslim resentment against Manila (Noble, 1976; 1981). Shortly afterwards, the Muslim governor of Cotabato province, Datu Udtog Matalam, announced the formation of the Mindanao Independence Movement (MIM), explicitly in response to the Corregidor Incident, although the MIM manifesto also asserted the theme of historical separateness elucidated above (Lingga, 2004).

Subsequently, in 1970, ongoing disputes over land between Christian and Muslim groups escalated into fighting, with the Philippine Constabulary intervening on the Christian side. These fights themselves stemmed largely from the competing cultural perceptions of land, and thus the inability of the Christians and Moros to agree even on a suitable legalistic *venue* to resolve their disputes, 'since their was no agreement on legal systems or judges' (Noble, 1975: 455). Fighting intensified as elections drew near and rival politicians mobilized ethnic and religious militias to gather votes and intimidate their opponents. In 1972, with his second and constitutionally final term as president ending, Ferdinand Marcos declared martial law. This provided the trigger for the Moro National Liberation Front (MNLF), which began the armed movement for a separate Moro state.

In southern Thailand, the turn to violence both in the 1940s and the ongoing episodes of violence can be linked to state policies which sought, to varying degrees, to force assimilation upon the Malay Muslims. Between 1938 and 1944, when Thailand was under the strongly nationalist regime of Pibul Songkhram, the Malays were subject to severe restrictions on their cultural expression, including discriminatory language regulations, the revocation of *shari'a* law and even the banning of the Malay *sarong* dress (Forbes, 1982). Following Pibul's fall in 1944, the new regime sought to placate the south with an 'Islamic Patronage' decree that reasserted their right to cultural distinctiveness. It was Pibul's return to power through a coup d'état in 1947 and his subsequent refusal to guarantee the continuation of the Islamic Patronage policy that provided the spark for the initial episode of conflict.

The military leader Sarit Thanarat, who took over from Pibul's in another coup d'état, continued a largely militaristic line towards the south, which was rewarded with continuing insurgency. After his death in office, however, a series of regimes sought a more conciliatory approach. Sarit's successor, Thanom Kittikachorn, embarked on a programme of basic infrastructural development in the south, providing electrification and sewerage facilities, and increased cultural recognition for Muslims, including state funding for the construction of a large mosque in Pattani. These policies 'worked well', depriving the separatist organization of significant support (Forbes, 1982). Subsequently, the regime of Prem Tinsulanond (1980–1988), himself a southerner, although ethnically Thai, 'brokered a kind of social contract in the area' (McCargo, 2006a: 3). The Southern Border Provinces Administrative Centre (SBPAC) was established as a venue for Muslim grievances; development projects were increased and local Muslims promoted in the civil service. This policy was largely reversed by the Thaksin administration, which came to power in the wake of the 1997 financial crisis. Thaksin viewed the south with suspicion, not because of its separatist tendencies *per se*, but because of its strong links to Prem who, although having resigned power in 1988, remained a central figure in Thai politics as part of a bloc associated with the monarch (McCargo, 2006b). In order to undermine Prem's continuing influence, Thaksin ordered a massive reorganization of security arrangements in the south. The SBPAC was disestablished, Thaksin's old police comrades were promoted into key security positions in the region and Muslim protest was met with considerable force, in turn further inflaming local sentiment. Most notorious here was the death of around 80 Muslims who suffocated in the back of military trucks after they were arrested at a protest demonstration. Amid escalating violence, Thaksin was deposed in a September 2006 coup d'état. The coup leader, General Soonthi Boonyaratglin, is a Muslim from the south, with strong links to Prem and the monarchy. Soonthi and his appointed prime minister, retired general Surayud Chulanont, have raised the prospect of negotiations with the insurgents.

In Aceh, the situation was rather more directly military. As already noted, the first insurgency in 1977 lacked widespread support – Kell (1995: 65) cites local sources suggesting the entire movement comprised less than 200 people. But the Indonesian military response was substantial and draconian. Following its experiences in East Timor and other trouble spots, the Indonesian military stamped down on Aceh, including the assassination of suspected GAM activists and forced mobilization of civilians. The oppressive and repressive Indonesian military reaction is largely credited for the drastic increase in support experienced by GAM following its re-emergence in 1989 (Aspinall, 2002; Robinson, 1998).

We have seen, then, that in the three separatist cases under consideration here, a combination of demographic transformation and the emergence of spatial and ethnic horizontal inequalities created conditions ripe for conflict. In the Philippines, violence did emerge, but in the form of sporadic intercommunal rather than antistate violence. In Aceh, a separatist movement was launched, but with little popular support, and was thus quickly suppressed. In each case, the mobilization of *mass* support for an explicitly separatist movement was linked to changes in government policy that were interpreted by the ethnic minorities in question as evidence of direct state discrimination. While horizontal inequalities generated occasionally violent communal tensions, violent antistate mobilization was directly linked to politicization of horizontal inequalities and their association with the state *qua* state, rather than the 'other' ethnic group.

To support this argument, I will end by considering a pivotal episode in the political development of the nonseparatist case, Sabah. We have seen that by the 1980s, many Christian Kadazans in Sabah were feeling increasingly marginalized within their 'own' state. As in southern Thailand, this sense of economic marginalization was given political form by government policies that were interpreted as undermining the cultural distinctiveness of the Kadazan. Firstly, in 1980, the Muslim-led state administration announced that the previous distinctions between different *bumiputera* groups in government strategy would be subsumed under the broader term of *pribumi*. Kadazan and non-Muslim anger at this move was twofold: firstly, it was feared that this would enable further discrimination in favour of Muslims, which would go unrecorded in the new data collection format; secondly, because the term *pribumi* was to include noncitizen residents of Indonesian and Philippine descent – most of whom were Muslim – it was feared that the move would allow for the further marginalization of the Kadazan at the hands of noncitizens. The second issue that galvanized Kadazan opposition was the government move in 1984 to appropriate the annual Kadazan *Kaamatan* harvest festival as a statewide celebration. The leading Kadazan politician within the government Joseph Pairin Kitingan, in particular was fiercely critical of this, perceiving it as a move to de-ethnicize and assimilate the major Kadazan cultural festival, stating that the move had 'hurt the Kadazan people very much' (quoted in Kalimuthu, 1986: 818). Pairin resigned from the state government and formed his own party, *Parti Bersatu Sabah* (PBS – Sabah United Party), as a vehicle for non-Muslim discontent.

The 1985 state election thus proved to be a critical juncture, with a three-way contest pitting the PBS against the incumbent federally backed pro-Muslim (although nominally multiethnic) BERJAYA party, and against the more stridently pro-Muslim United Sabah Nation Organization (USNO), which had controlled the state assembly prior to BERJAYA. Despite the active support of Kuala Lumpur, the election saw BERJAYA forced into third place, winning only 6 out of the 48 seats. The PBS emerged victorious with 26 seats, the remaining 16 being taken by USNO. Although the PBS had thus won the election, constitutional provisions allowed the incoming administration to appoint an extra six state legislators. With these extra seats, a combined BERJAYA-USNO coalition would have been able to form a majority administration. The governor appointed Pairin, leader of the PBS, despite pressure from BERJAYA and USNO leaders. The controversy provoked a period of serious social unrest, with massive and violent demonstrations by BERJAYA-USNO supporters and a series of bomb blasts in the state capital Kota Kinabalu.

The civil unrest was widely blamed on a faction within BERJAYA or USNO seeking to force the federal government into imposing a State of Emergency in the state, with the likely result that it would use these powers to allow a BERJAYA-USNO administration to be formed, as it had done in Sarawak and Kelantan previously (Chin, 1997). It was at this critical moment, however, that Acting Prime Minister Musa Hitam intervened, mobilizing the Federal Reserve Units and instituting a dawn-to-dusk curfew in Kota Kinabalu. Crucially, however, the federal government in Kuala Lumpur publicly endorsed the election of Pairin as the democratic choice of the state.

It would, of course, be futile to speculate over the alternative trajectory that Sabah might have taken had Musa not endorsed the victory of the Kadazan party in 1985. But this episode nonetheless broadly supports the analysis of the preceding sections. While the emergence of a double socioeconomic disadvantage among the Kadazans of Sabah created the conditions for ethnic discontent, it was the direct politicization of these differences by the government that generated a popular movement against the state, bringing Sabah to the brink of violence. Whereas in Thailand, the Philippines and

Aceh, the central state intervened in similar circumstances in a way that was seen as discriminating against the regional minority group, the Malaysian government chose instead to concede local power at a critical juncture.

To conclude, this chapter has illustrated that the combination of regional and ethnic horizontal inequalities and demographic marginalization on 'ethnic peripheries' of modern nation states creates the potential for violent separatism, but the turn to violence is largely dependent upon the state itself and, in particular, the way in which it responds to protest and nonviolent mobilization.

Notes

1. The GAM/ASNLF prefer the spelling Acheh to Aceh.
2. Philippines Census sample data used throughout this chapter provided by Minnesota Population Center, *Integrated Public Use Microdata Series – International Version 3.0*. Minneapolis: University of Minnesota, 2007; original data collected by the National Statistics Office of the Philippines.
3. The 1990 census did not collect data on ethnicity, but it did collect language data. This figure is arrived at by assuming all those who reported Javanese as their mother tongue or language of use at home were ethnically Javanese.
4. These 'zones' are not used in the Philippines' own statistical aggregation; I use the term 'zone' to distinguish from the 'Regions' that the Philippines does employ.
5. Less than 1 per cent of the sample reported a different language from these three, or a different religion from either Buddhism or Islam. These respondents have also been excluded.
6. The household asset measure is based on answers to questions relating to access to or household ownership of: electricity, a radio, a television, a refrigerator, a bicycle, a motorcycle and a car. Each asset was weighted according to the proportion of the population that did *not* possess the asset (for example, 70.7 per cent of households reported ownership of a radio, so ownership scored 1–0.707=0.293). The measure was then normalized by the maximum score to create a variable between 0 (no assets) and 1 (all assets).

Part IV
Conclusions and Policies

13

Major Findings and Conclusions on the Relationship Between Horizontal Inequalities and Conflict

Frances Stewart, Graham K. Brown and Arnim Langer

13.1 Introduction

In this book we set out to explore the relationship between HIs and conflict: whether indeed such a relationship pertains in recent conflicts; which type of inequality is most important; and in which conditions conflicts are more likely to emerge. We did so by case studies of countries in three regions of the world, West Africa, Southeast Asia and Latin America, and also through more global analysis, using political-economy, econometric, historical and anthropological approaches. Throughout, we have aimed to contrast countries (and areas within them) that have managed to avoid serious conflict with those countries or areas that have experienced severe violent conflict in recent decades. The aim of this chapter is to bring together the main conclusions that emerge from these case studies. The final chapter of the book reviews policy conclusions of the analysis.

The book has focused especially on the experience of eight countries, in three continents:

- In Latin America: Bolivia, Guatemala and Peru;
- In Southeast Asia: Malaysia and Indonesia;
- In West Africa: Côte d'Ivoire, Ghana and Nigeria.

Each country is multicultural and one country in each region has avoided serious national conflict, while the other(s) has/have experienced considerable violent conflict in the recent past. Bolivia, Malaysia and Ghana are the countries that have succeeded in remaining broadly peaceful, while Nigeria has not had national-level conflict for several decades. In contrast, Guatemala, Peru, Cote d'Ivoire and Indonesia all suffered serious internal violent conflict in recent decades. The intention of the investigation was to learn from these contrasting situations and policies.

Some large HIs can be observed in these countries, as shown in earlier chapters.

For example, in Peru indigenous people have seven years of schooling on average, half that of whites, while the proportion with secondary schooling is only one-fifth that of whites (Chapter 11). The rate of extreme poverty among the indigenous population in 2002 was more than four times the rate among the nonindigenous (Chapter 11). In Bolivia, too, the sharpest HIs are between the indigenous and nonindigenous populations. For instance, in 2001, the indigenous population had on average almost four years less schooling than the nonindigenous population, and the infant mortality rate among the indigenous population was about 50 per cent higher than among the nonindigenous population (Gray Molina, 2007). In Guatemala, a similar picture emerges. Even though literacy rates among the indigenous population have improved considerably since the end of the 1980s, there is still a significant gap between the indigenous and nonindigenous populations: in 1998, while about 58 per cent of the indigenous population was literate, among the nonindigenous population that figure was about 79 per cent (Caumartin, 2005). Twenty per cent of the indigenous population in Guatemala were in extreme poverty in 2000, while the rate among the nonindigenous population was just 5 per cent (Chapter 11). In Ghana, the Northern Region's child mortality rate is nearly two and a half times that of Ghana as a whole, and three times that of the Greater Accra Region. Access to health services in the Northern Region of Ghana is less than a quarter of that in the Greater Accra Region (Chapter 4). In Nigeria, maternal mortality rates in the northeast are nine times those in the southwest. In Côte d'Ivoire, the literacy rate among the Northern Mande is just 23 per cent, half the rate among the Akan (Langer *et al.*, 2007). In Malaysia, despite considerable improvement, Chinese incomes were, on average, over 1.6 times those of Malays in 2005, while the percentage of professionals of Chinese origin was almost twice the percentage of Malays, even though they account for a much smaller proportion of the population than the Malays (Volpi, 2007). However, it must be noted that this summary focuses on groups where there are large socioeconomic HIs. There are other groups in the same countries between whom differences in achievements and resources are quite low – for example, as between the Ewes and the Akans in Ghana, or the Akan and Krou in Côte d'Ivoire.

The next section discusses the major findings of the book, derived from the experience of these eight countries, and some comparative analysis of a broader range of countries.

13.2   General findings on the relationship between horizontal inequalities and conflict

Ten major findings emerge from the analysis in this book, with supporting evidence drawn from other studies.

1. The probability of conflict occurring rises where socioeconomic HIs are higher

This is supported by intercountry analysis by Østby (Chapter 7), who shows a significant rise in the probability of the onset of conflict across countries, for countries with severe social and economic HIs, for 1986–2003. In her models she defines groups alternatively by ethnicity, religion, and region and finds a significant relationship between HIs and the onset of violent conflict for each definition. Social HIs are measured by average years of education and economic HIs by average household assets. The effect of HIs is quite high: the probability of conflict increases threefold when comparing the expected conflict onset at mean values of all the explanatory variables to a situation where the extent of HI of assets among ethnic groups is at the 95th percentile. In the case of the interregional HIs, the probability of conflict increases two and a half times, as HIs rise from mean value to the 95th percentile value (see also Østby, 2003, which comes to similar conclusions).

Other statistical cross work supporting this relationship includes Gurr's successive studies of relative deprivation and conflict (1968, 1993; Gurr and Moore, 1997), and Barrows' investigation of sub-Saharan African countries of the 1960s. Gurr finds a positive relationship across countries between minority rebellion and protests and relative deprivation, defined in economic, political and cultural terms. Barrows (1976) finds that HIs showed a consistently positive correlation with political instability across 32 sub-Saharan African countries in the 1960s, with measures of inequality including share of political power and socioeconomic variables.

There are also intracountry studies showing a positive relationship between the level of HIs and the incidence (or intensity) of conflict. In Chapter 6, Mancini uses district-level data to examine the relationship between HIs and the incidence of conflict in districts in Indonesia. After controlling for a number of intervening factors including population size, ethnic diversity and economic development, he finds that horizontal inequality in child mortality rates and its change over time are positively (and significantly) associated with the occurrence of deadly ethnocommunal violence. Other measures of HI, including measures of HIs in education, unemployment, landless agricultural labourers and civil service employment were also related to the incidence of conflict, but the effects were less than that of child mortality, and were not significant when HI in child mortality was included. Results also suggest that violent conflict is more likely to occur in areas with relatively low levels of economic development and greater religious polarization. Standard measures of (vertical) income inequality as well as other purely demographic indicators of ethnic diversity are found to have no significant impact on the likelihood of communal violence.

Studies in other conflict-ridden countries have found that the intensity of conflict is related to HIs. In a study of the Moro rebellion in southern Philippines, Magdalena (1977) finds relative deprivation of Muslims measured in terms of differential returns to education, strongly related to the intensity of the conflict. In Nepal, Murshed and Gates (2005), using a 'gap' measure of human development, find strong econometric support for a relationship between regional deprivation and the intensity of the Maoist rebellion across districts. A subsequent study by Do and Iyer (2007) replicates the finding of a relationship between regional deprivation and the intensity of conflict – in this case measured by the regional poverty rate and the literacy rate – and also find that caste polarization has an additional impact on conflict intensity.

While higher HIs are correlated with a higher risk of conflict, not all violent mobilization in high-HI countries is primarily identity-driven, at least in terms of discourse. This was the situation in the Peruvian and Guatemalan examples explored in Chapter 11, where the rebellions were presented in ideological terms and prominent leaders of the movements came from outside the deprived indigenous groups, motivated by ideology not ethnicity. In these societies 'race/ethnicity' and 'class' are virtually coterminous, that is they are ethnically 'ranked systems' (Horowitz, 1985: 22). In such societies, mobilization by *class* may alternate or substitute for moblization by ethnicity.[1] However, there was a strong ethnic dimension to the conflicts – indicated by the willingness among indigenous people to be mobilized against the state and the victimization – indeed the almost genocidal targeting – of indigenous peoples by the nonindigenous-dominated governments. For example, Francisco Bianchi, a government adviser in the early 1980s, openly declared that 'the guerrillas have collaborated extensively with the Indians, because of this the Indians are subversives. And how do we combat such subversion? Obviously, by killing the Indians[2]' (cited in CEH, 1999: 182[3]). These factors point to the role of HI as an underlying element in these conflicts, which is confirmed in the Guatemalan case by the finding of the commission which investigated the historical origins of the Guatemalan conflict that its roots lay in the 'exclusionary, racist, authoritarian and centralist' characteristics of the Guatemalan state, economy and society (ibid.: 81).

We should emphasize that what we (and others) have found are increased probabilities of greater incidence of conflict as HIs increase. Not all countries with high HIs experience conflict. Indeed in our own country studies, both Ghana and Bolivia have high socioeconomic HIs, yet have avoided substantial conflict. It is therefore important to investigate when high HIs lead to conflict and when they do not. While a few of the studies cited above include political HIs, most do not. The nature of political HIs is one factor that determines whether high socioeconomic HIs lead to conflict.

2. *Conflict is more likely where political and socioeconomic HIs are high and run in the same direction, or are consistent. Where they run in different directions, conflict is less likely*

Where political and socioeconomic HIs are severe and consistent, both leadership and the mass of the population in the deprived group(s) have a motive for mobilization – the leadership because they are politically excluded (that is, they suffer from political HIs) and the population because they suffer from socioeconomic HIs, and these inequalities can be used by leaders to mobilize people. The Côte d'Ivoire story illustrates this. During Houphouët-Boigny's time, there was political inclusion, and the country was peaceful, despite some severe HIs on a north–south basis, as shown by Langer's analysis in Chapter 8. Nonetheless, discontent with the socioeconomic deprivation and the lack of inequality in cultural status, particularly the lack of recognition of the Muslim religion, was articulated in the Chartre du Nord of 1992, which explicitly pointed to the unfairness of the system. But after the Houphouët-Boigny regime came to an end, explicit political exclusion occurred, as Alassane Ouattara, a presidential candidate from the north, was barred from standing in both the 1995 and 2000 elections. No concessions were made and violent conflict broke out in 2002.

The Nigerian civil war (1967–1970), which resulted in the deaths of hundreds of thousands of people, also illustrates the importance of the coincidence of political and economic incentives and interests in provoking violent conflict. Initially, the Igbos and Yorubas, as the more educated groups, shared many of the high-level posts in the new Federation. The coup d'état of 29 July 1966, led by Lt Col Murtala Mohammed, a northerner, resulted in the exclusion of the Igbos from power and initiated an increasingly anti-Igbo climate. Due to the widespread anti-Igbo feelings and attacks that followed, many Igbos migrated to their home regions in the eastern part of Nigeria and '... became a powerful lobbying group for an independent Biafra, in which they now had a vested economic interest' (Nafziger, 1973: 529). Both economic and political exclusion was compounded by the fear that, without political power in the Nigerian Federation, there would be an increasingly disadvantageous distribution of oil revenues, by then the most important source of government revenue, while the revenues promised an independent Biafra relative riches.

Socioeconomic deprivation tends to affect the mass of the people. This generates mass grievances which make mobilization for opposition or even violence possible. However, for effective mobilization both elite and mass participation is required, especially since most serious conflicts are organized, not spontaneous, and thus require strong leadership. The motives of the elite of a group, or its potential leaders, are particularly important, because the elite controls resources (including sometimes military ones), and they can rouse support by accentuating common identities, and denigrating the 'other', while increasing perceptions of intergroup inequalities. In Brass' terms, they play the role of 'conflict entrepreneurs'. However, where the group's elite enjoys power, they are not likely to encourage or lead rebellion. This also holds true when they are politically included without being dominant, as they can still enjoy the 'perks' of office, including opportunities for personal enrichment and the dispensing of favours to supporters. Consequently, even in the presence of quite sharp socioeconomic HIs, people are unlikely to take to violent conflict if their own group leaders are politically included, and even less so if they are dominant politically.

This is exemplified by the experience of Malaysia, and Nigeria after the civil war. In both countries, the group that is economically impoverished is politically advantaged, in both cases accounting for a majority of the population. In Malaysia, the *bumiputera* account for roughly two-thirds of the population (depending on the precise categorization), while in Nigeria northern peoples are estimated to account for over 50 per cent of the population.[4] In each country, this numerical advantage has translated into dominance of political power (continuously in the case of Malaysia and for most of the time in the case of Nigeria). Having political power – and the 'pork-barrel' gains this confers – obviously greatly reduces the motive of a group's elite to lead a rebellion. It also permits action to be taken to correct other inequalities. In the case of Nigeria, such action has been mainly confined to the political sphere (including the bureaucracy and army through the Federal Character Principle), but in Malaysia systematic action has also been taken in the socioeconomic realm through the New Economic Policy.

At a local level, contrasting the experiences of two Nigerian cities – conflict-ridden Warri and more peaceful Calabar – in Chapter 9, Ukiwo also shows the importance of consistency in HIs, in socioeconomic and political dimensions, if they are to lead to conflict. In this case, in contrast to the earlier ones, he shows that if socioeconomic HIs are not high, then political exclusion will not be sufficient to provoke conflict. In Warri, there were both political and socioeconomic HIs; but in Calabar, although the leaders of certain groups did feel excluded and tried to mobilize support, their potential group followers believed themselves to be well treated and consequently were not ready to be mobilized in protest.

Østby (Chapter 7) provides econometric support for the importance of consistency between socioeconomic and political HIs. She shows that while political exclusion on its own as an independent variable does *not* affect the probability of conflict, it has a strong interactive affect with interregional asset inequality. That is to say, asset inequality has a stronger effect in increasing the probability of conflict in the presence of political HIs. She finds a similar effect with educational inequality, but not a statistically significant one.

3. Inclusive (or power-sharing) government tends to reduce the likelihood of conflict

This is really a development of the previous finding, since where power is shared, political HIs are lower, hence making peace likely even where there are severe socioeconomic HIs. When there is genuine power-sharing, no single group dominates political power, but all (major) groups have some real sense of participation in government. Econometric evidence has shown that formal power-sharing arrangements do reduce the potential for conflict as argued by Lijphart (1997; 2004); for example Binningsbø (2005) explores the impact of proportional representation and territorial autonomy within countries; and Reynal-Querol (2002a) finds a positive impact of PR on the reduction of conflict-propensity). In the federal context, Bakke and Wibbels (2006) find that 'co-partisanship' between central and subnational governments, which implies shared political power (at least regionally) and consequently lower political HIs, significantly reduces the chance of conflict. In our studies, both Bolivia and Ghana have included deprived groups in government. In the case of Ghana, there is an informal tradition in the Fourth Republic that whenever a southerner is president, the vice-president is northern. In Bolivia, informal arrangements have involved the political participation of indigenous representatives for much of recent history. In contrast, Guatemala, Peru and Indonesia, each conflict-ridden at certain times, practised exclusionary government prior to their conflict periods.

The implication of this finding, it is important to note, is that the political cooption of the leadership of disadvantaged minorities by the dominant group is often sufficient to prevent conflict without the necessity of undertaking policies to improve the socioeconomic position of these groups. This has arguably been the case with respect to the Indian population of Malaysia, which is represented in the governing coalition through the Malaysian Indian Congress, but which has received little in the way of targeted developmental aid, despite severe pockets of socioeconomic deprivation (Loh, 2003). Also in Nigeria, as noted above, while northern political power has helped avoid major north–south confrontations, the northern part of the country has remained seriously deprived in socioeconomic terms. It does not follow that this is a satisfactory situation, given that severe HIs are undesirable in themselves, in addition to their instrumental role in fomenting violent conflict. Nonetheless, political inclusion does appear to play an important role in preventing violence, and may constitute an important step towards more inclusive development as ethnic leaders who do not 'deliver' development to their constituency are likely to be challenged in the long run by new leadership contenders more willing to press their group's developmental claims.

4. Citizenship can be an important source of political and economic exclusion

Citizenship brings a variety of economic and political entitlements, as Gibney showed in Chapter 2. Not only political participation but also entitlements to a range of social and economic benefits frequently depend on citizenship. Exclusion from citizenship is a form of HI in itself and also constitutes an important source of inequalities in other dimensions. For example, noncitizenship may deny people the right to work, to join a union or to receive government assistance. Denial of citizenship is often a deliberate political act, taken for a variety of reasons, as elucidated by Gibney. Historically, indigenous groups in the Latin American countries were denied citizenship rights of both a political and economic nature. Moreover in some countries, there are, informally at least, local as well as national citizenship rights.

Sources of loss of citizenship rights vary. Migration (legal and illegal) is a common source, and in some cases the loss of citizenship is handed down across the generations. Less common are instances when states explicitly revoke citizenship rights, as happened to the Jews in Nazi Germany, and to the Asians in Uganda. A third way in which citizenship can be lost occurs when the state itself changes form. Gibney cites the case of the Roma population, who became stateless when the Czech Republic separated from Slovakia in the 1990s.

At a national level, denial of citizenship has been critical in inciting rebellion in the case of Côte d'Ivoire (Chapter 8). Similarly, in Nigeria, the settler/indigene distinction has been the source of many local-level conflicts (Bach, 2006; Human Rights Watch, 2006), while it has also been a major source of local conflicts in Ghana (see, for example, Jönsson, 2006; Tsikata and Seini, 2004).

Gibney suggests three principles upon which citizenship might be based: first, that everyone should be a citizen somewhere, and those without citizenship should be given it in the country where they are located; secondly, that *de facto* membership of a state should confer the right to citizenship, where *de facto* membership is defined by contributions and ties to the society; and thirdly that an extended period of residence should confer citizenship rights.

It is where any or all of these three principles are breached for significant numbers of people, particularly if they belong to a common ethnic or religious group, that denial of citizenship can provoke conflict. Moreover, given the close connection between citizenship and other economic and social benefits (such as the right to work, or access to state services or land), exclusion from citizenship can also be a profound cause of other socioeconomic HIs.

5. Inequality of cultural recognition among groups is an additional motivation for conflict and cultural 'events' can act as a trigger for conflict

Cultural status inequalities (explored by Langer and Brown in Chapter 3) can be extremely important. In the first place, culture (ethnicity or religion) itself is often the factor binding people together as a group. Hence the more important it becomes in the way people see themselves and others, the more likely it is that they mobilize along group lines. Cultural status inequalities can increase the salience of group identity. As argued in Chapter 3, there are three important elements involved in cultural recognition: differential treatment with respect to religion and religious observation, language recognition and use and ethnocultural practices. In some countries, conscious efforts are made to give equal recognition with regard to each element. This is notable in Ghana, for example. In others, there have been periods of explicit cultural discrimination (for instance, against the use of indigenous languages in Peru and Guatemala), or informal discrimination (such as towards non-Muslims in Malaysia or non-Christians in Côte d'Ivoire). Such inequalities make other inequalities (socioeconomic or political) more powerful as mobilizing mechanisms. Culturally discriminating events are also frequently a trigger for riots and even conflict, as exemplified by the Orange marches in Northern Ireland, which set off the 'Troubles' in the 1970s, as well as by language policy in Sri Lanka, and the desecration of religious buildings and sites in India and Palestine, which have acted as triggers for major conflicts.

6. *Perceptions of horizontal inequalities affect the likelihood of conflict*

Much of this book has been concerned with reporting on observable HIs. Yet people take action because of *perceived* injustices rather than on the basis of data of which they might not be aware. Normally, one would expect perceived and observed inequalities to be related, so these 'objective' HIs are clearly relevant to political action. Yet it is also important to investigate perceptions and their determinants, since leaders/media/educational institutions can influence perceptions of inequality, even when the underlying reality remains unchanged. Chapter 10 reported on such an investigation in Ghana and Nigeria. The results were particularly interesting in four respects. First, in both countries, the majority of those questioned perceived very little difference in educational access according to group despite the fact that records of school attendance show large differences (Chapter 10). This may be because perceptions of difference are based on opportunities at the local level and much of the recorded difference is between regions. Secondly, in both countries, respondents considered their religion to be much more important than ethnicity in the private sphere (for example, in relation to social interactions, including marriage) but ethnicity was much more important in the public sphere, in terms of their views on government jobs and contract allocation, pointing to the importance of maintaining ethnic balance in the political-administrative sphere. Thirdly, in general, Nigerians felt ethnicity to be more important to them than did Ghanaians, both in terms of their view of their own individual identities and also, they believed, as determinants of the allocation of government jobs and contracts. Finally, significantly greater numbers of respondents in Ghana stated that their national identity was important to them than in Nigeria. These last two findings may, in part, be a result of Nigeria's more turbulent political history, and may also be accounted for by differences in national leadership and the ways that political and educational systems have developed. The differences in perceptions of the importance of ethnicity may be one factor explaining why Nigeria has experienced more interethnic conflict than Ghana.

The importance of the role played by perceptions in provoking action means that leaders, institutions and policies that influence perceptions can affect the likelihood of political mobilization. In Côte d'Ivoire, post–Houphouët-Boigny there was an active campaign by political leaders to 'market' identities and differences via the media (Akindès, forthcoming). In Ghana, Nkrumah himself, the first postcolonial leader, put a huge emphasis on national unity, in contrast to leaders in Nigeria who had a much more regional perspective. Educational institutions are relevant here too. In Ghana, boarding schools dating back to colonial times have brought the future elite together from across the country and have contributed to a national project. These factors may partly account for the finding that Ghanaians valued their national identity more highly than Nigerians.

Perceptions can be influenced by a variety of actions (including symbolic ones). For example, both Nkrumah and Houphouët-Boigny initiated programmes of investment in the deprived Northern Regions with the intention of reducing inequalities. Although they were insufficient to close the gaps, these measures led people to believe that there was some attempt to produce a fairer distribution of resources. Moreover, the elites in the North benefited particularly from some of the programmes through, for example, the allocation of contracts and this reduced their incentive to mobilize their members for group conflict. The postconflict support for indigenous social and economic programmes in Guatemala, while also too small to make a major difference, has changed perceptions of inequality, with more people thinking the society is inclusive.

7. The presence of natural resources can be a significant cause of separatist conflict, as well as of local conflict, often working through the impact this has on HIs

There is a well-established econometric link between the presence of natural resources, such as gas and oil, and the incidence of conflict, but the precise causal mechanisms are disputed (Humphreys, 2005; Le Billon, 2001; Ross, 2004). In addition to encouraging increased competition for power among the elite (because of the greater 'spoils' from controlling the state), our research suggests that the conflict-inducing potential of natural resources is often mediated through their impact on HIs, and that this can translate into both separatist struggles and local-level conflict (Brown, Chapter 12; Tadjoeddin, 2007). The discovery of natural resources can generate sharp increases in regional inequality, and where these resources are located in ethnically or religiously distinct regions of the country, separatist conflict may emerge, particularly if the groups are relatively underdeveloped or feel they are not benefiting from the exploitation of the resources.

In Brown's analysis of separatist movements in Southeast Asia (Chapter 12), he finds that the discovery of natural resources in the Indonesian province of Aceh was a vital development in the transformation of Acehnese discontent. The objective of the rebellion changed from securing local rights to secession from Indonesia altogether. Similarly, Tadjoeddin (2007) argues that natural resources in Indonesia have generated an 'aspiration to inequality' in provinces where they are located. Likewise, Treisman (1997) argues that natural resources played an important role in stoking ethnic separatist claims in postcommunist Russia. The discovery of oil was also a major transformative factor in the Sudanese civil war.[5]

This is the source of a major dilemma, and the cause of much debate in places such as Indonesia and Nigeria. Do the people in resource-rich regions have some special rights over resources found in the region? If these are conceded, then HIs will arise as the resource-rich regions become much richer than others. Or, should the state redistribute the revenues (as, for example, with the INPRES programme in Indonesia under Suharto and the redistributive formula in Nigeria), which will moderate HIs, but may also lead to unrest. Revenue-sharing agreements are consequently a vital component of successful negotiation of peace agreements where natural resources are important.

Natural resources are also often associated with local-level conflicts, as in the Niger Delta region in Nigeria. Here too, the distribution of the resources among local groups, or between local groups and companies, is often unequal and can consequently feed local-level conflict. Local conflict in the Indonesian province of North Maluku was also instigated by ethnic disputes over control of a gold mine (Wilson, 2005).

8. *The nature of the state is of enormous importance in determining whether serious conflict erupts and persists*

Although highly repressive regimes can prevent conflict (for example, the New Order regime in Indonesia was effective in preventing communal conflict in much of the country), an aggressive state can also fuel and sustain a conflict. In Guatemala, and in Indonesia with respect to separatist conflicts, the harsh and aggressive state reaction to rebellion sustained conflict for many years, causing deaths on a massive scale and provoking further rebellion. In Guatemala, state reaction to rebellion has been described as 'a campaign of state terror' (Caumartin, 2005: 22) with massive killings, particularly focused on the indigenous population. In Indonesia, the viciousness of the Indonesian armed forces' response to the original, small-scale Acehnese rebellion boosted support for the movement when it re-emerged (Chapter 12; Kell, 1995).

The review of separatist conflict in Southeast Asia (Chapter 12) showed that a major difference between Sabah, which never developed into a separatist movement, and the others which did was the more accommodating stance of the Malaysian state.

Similarly, the state's handling of disputes in Ghana and of some local-level conflicts in Indonesia has dampened some conflicts and avoided others. In contrast, in Nigeria, it seems, state action is often late and one-sided, making the conflicts more severe than they need have been. This is exemplified by recent events in the Middle Belt. The government's passive and late reaction to the emergence of the violence between Muslims and Christians on 7 September 2001 in the Jos area is illustrative. It took the Nigerian military and police forces more than 12 hours to arrive at the scene of the violent conflict and many areas were left without security for the first 24 hours of the crisis (Higazi, 2007). Moreover, the intervention of the security forces was perceived to be biased against Muslims and they alleged that police forces had killed innocent people, including women and children (ibid.).

Local institutions are also important in determining the trajectory of violence. This has been shown by research in Indonesia, Ghana and Nigeria. For example, Asante (2007) has shown how in Ghana a conflict between adherents of the Ga traditional religion and some Christian Churches over drumming was prevented from escalating by the way it was handled by local institutions, particularly through the implementation of bylaws regulating noise-making in Accra by the Accra Metropolitan Authority. A similar pattern is found in many other incidents in Ghana (Tsikata and Seini, 2004). In the conflict in and around Jos in 2001, by contrast, local authorities did little to stop the conflict, and indeed may have contributed to it, leaving any solution to national forces (Higazi, 2007).

9. Some HIs are very persistent, even lasting centuries

We showed how persistent HIs can be in Chapter 4. Many HIs have colonial origins, caused by colonial powers privileging some groups or regions (or both), but they are sustained by a variety of ongoing elements. The colonial origin was indicated in all our studies. In Latin America, inequalities were caused by the privileged settlers taking the best resources for themselves and sustaining their privilege through discrimination and unequal access to every type of capital. Postcolonial policies have done little to correct these inequalities. Figueroa has shown that today not only do indigenous people in Peru have much less access to education than the *mestizo* population, who in turn have less than the whites, but also that for any particular level of education the *returns*, in terms of additional incomes earned as a result of such education, are significantly lower for the indigenous population than for the *mestizos*, which are again lower than the returns the whites secure.

This is due to a combination of poorer-quality education, less productive social networks and discrimination in employment (Chapter 4).

In West Africa, the inequalities were partly due to geographical and climatic differences, but these were made worse by colonial economic policies that favoured the south of each country in terms of economic and social infrastructure. Again postcolonial policies, including structural adjustment policies, have failed to correct the inequalities. In Malaysia, the colonial 'ethnic division of labour' (Brown, 1997) ensured that the Malays remained in subsistence agriculture, while migrant Chinese came to dominate the domestic economy. But in Malaysia, systematic policies have narrowed the differences.

The persistence of these inequalities is due to cumulative and reinforcing inequalities arising from unequal access to different types of capital – including financial, land, education and social capital. Asymmetries of social capital, in particular, arising because group members have stronger contacts within their group than across groups, have made it almost impossible for some groups to escape from these inequalities.

However, there are cases of 'catch-up', where group differences are reduced over time. Mostly these are policy-related, where a conscious and systematic effort has been made to correct the inequalities, as in Malaysia after 1970. In a few cases, groups have succeeded in catching up without government support – Chinese and Vietnamese immigrants in the US are an example of this. Their success seems to have been partly due to the selective immigration policy – which only allowed the more educated to enter the US – and partly to the culture of work, education and achievement which they brought with them, cultural capital of a type which is typically absent in long-deprived groups. The nature of the interlocking forces which typically perpetuate HIs over generations implies that very comprehensive policies are needed if these multiple handicaps are to be overcome.

10. International policies and statistics are too often blind to the issue of HIs, though national policies are often more progressive in this respect

Little attention is paid to HIs by the international policy community. The prime concerns of international donors are poverty reduction and the promotion of economic growth – neither agenda includes considerations of HIs. Vertical inequality is beginning to be recognized as a problem (Cornia, 2004; Kanbur and Lustig, 1999; UNDP, 2005; World Bank, 2006) because inequality has risen in the majority of countries in recent years and because high and growing inequality makes poverty reduction more difficult. Even so, vertical inequality has not received serious policy attention, and there is still less attention paid to horizontal inequality.

The growth supporting policies advocated internationally consist mainly of macropolicies designed to secure economic stability and openness, and mesopolicies intended to support economic infrastructure and enhance the role of the market in order to improve efficiency. Poverty reduction policies are mainly derived from the Poverty Reduction Strategy Papers (PRSPs). These focus particularly on social sector expenditures and on some special schemes for the poor such as microcredit. According to one review, 'the participation of minorities or indigenous peoples is either often overlooked or simply regarded as impractical due to their marginalisation' (Booth and Curran, 2005: 12). An analysis of the content of PRSPs shows universal inclusion of the 'normal' macro conditions, and policies to promote the social sectors. Gender equity is considered in a substantial majority of cases, but protection of ethnic minorities is mentioned in only a quarter of the cases. The cases where ethnic minorities were *not* mentioned include countries which are evidently heterogeneous, such as Azerbaijan, Benin, Burkina Faso, Chad, Guyana, Malawi, Mali, Mauritania, Mozambique, Niger, Rwanda, Tanzania and Uganda (Stewart and Wang, 2006).

More attention, however, is beginning to be devoted to HIs in analyses of conflict-prone situations (for example, DFID, 2007; World Bank, 2005), but it does not form a systematic part of reporting, and rarely enters policy discussions, apart from the regional dimension. Indeed, national policies which are explicit in addressing HIs, such as the Federal Character Principle in Nigeria and the Malaysian NEP, are frequently criticized by international donors.

International policies towards political systems also tend to ignore the question of HIs. Thus the widespread advocacy of multiparty democracy can lead to exclusionary politics in heterogeneous societies. In some postconflict societies, the issue is so obvious that power-sharing arrangements have been supported, as in Bosnia Herzegovina and Lebanon. But wider acknowledgement of the need to rethink the design of democratic systems is rare.

A dearth of international statistics on the issue reflects this lack of focus. For example, neither the World Bank nor the UNDP includes statistics on ethnic, religious or regional HIs in their well-known datasets, although some national-level Human Development Reports, such as those on Kosovo and Nepal, have provided ethnic or religiously disaggregated data. A notable exception is the Demographic and Health Surveys (to date covering 77 countries) funded by USAID with contributions from other donors. These contain ethnic and religious variables in quite a number of cases, permitting the investigation of relationships across countries (Østby, Chapter 7). But these surveys do not cover all countries, and are not carried out at regular intervals. Nor do they include political variables or other variables of obvious interest, such as household income.

As far as national policies are concerned, there is a much higher consciousness of the importance of HIs in many heterogeneous countries, and a vast array of policy approaches have been adopted, as will be indicated in the next chapter. Nonetheless, by no means all culturally diverse countries acknowledge the importance of HIs, or take policy action towards them, some because, like the international community policies they often adopt, they are blind to these issues, while others are deliberately exclusionary.

In the countries studied in this book, among the Latin American cases deliberately exclusionary policies were practiced in colonial times and carried over into independence. More recently, formally policies have been more inclusionary, but informally there is a great deal of inequality and little effort to correct this, especially in the cases of Peru and Guatemala. Bolivia has been more inclusionary politically, but has done little in terms of economic inequalities. After the conflict in Guatemala ended, some of the country's high inequalities, notably with regard to education and culture, have begun to be tackled. In West Africa, policies have varied over time. Since independence there have been weak attempts to correct inherited socioeconomic HIs, but these have been largely offset by macroeconomic policies which have pulled in the opposite direction. On the political front, Ghana has generally adopted informal inclusionary policies, and Côte d'Ivoire had a similar stance for several decades until exclusionary policies were adopted after Houphouët-Boigny. Nigeria, in contrast, has made a conscious attempt to correct political HIs via the Federal Character Principle (Mustapha, 2007), but has done little to correct socioeconomic HIs. In Southeast Asia, Malaysia has been most explicit, systematic and effective in correcting socioeconomic HIs via the NEP. A national coalition government involved all groups in society and thus, although Malays predominated, political HIs were partially kept in check. In Indonesia, there was a conscious but limited attempt to secure regional equity via the INPRES programmes, but political HIs were sharp under Suharto. Since democratization, extensive political and fiscal decentralization has effectively reduced these problems by making the district the main object of political power. An equalization formula is also in place to ensure that poorer districts receive a greater proportion of central funds.

In sum, national policies seem to be greatly in advance of international ones in the arena of HIs.

13.3 Conclusions

In summary, this book has elucidated the meaning of HIs, pointing to the multidimensionality of the concept. We have shown that severe HIs can be an important source of conflict, especially where they are consistent across dimensions. While socioeconomic HIs generate generally fertile ground for conflict to emerge and cultural status inequalities act to bind groups together, political HIs provide incentives for leaders to mobilize people for rebellion. In conditions of severe HIs, abrupt changes in political HIs, or cultural events in which important cultural or religious symbols are attacked, often constitute powerful triggers to conflict.

In the introductory chapter, we put forward four hypotheses about the relationship of HIs to violent conflict. Evidence in this book has supported the first three:

- that conflict is more likely where there are significant political or economic HIs, or both;
- that political mobilization is especially likely where HIs are consistent;
- and that cultural recognition or status inequalities are also provocative.

We were unable to explore the fourth hypothesis systematically – that political mobilization and possibly conflict is more likely to occur when HIs are widening – because of a dearth of accurate evidence on HIs over time, although evidence for districts in Indonesia (in Chapter 6) supported the hypothesis. Thus this hypothesis remains a presumption, supported at present by piecemeal evidence.

Other factors are, of course, also important in determining whether a conflict emerges. One is the nature of the state and its reactions, another is the role of local institutions in pacifying or dynamizing conflict once it has started, a third factor is the presence of natural resources, often working through the impact this has on HIs. For the most part, especially among the international community, little attention is paid to the issue of HIs, and the policies advocated can sometimes accentuate them. This is true both of economic policies, such as structural adjustment, and political polices, such as multiparty democracy. The next chapter discusses what policies would be appropriate once the importance of the issue has been acknowledged.

Notes

1. Ideological motivation was much more common in the Cold War. Following the demise of most communist regimes, ethnic mobilization has become more common.
2. *'La guerrilla se ha traido muchos colaboradores indios, por lo tanto los indios son subversivos. ¿Y como combater la suberversión? Evidentemente matanda a los indios'*
3. Caumartin (2005: 28).
4. Political resistance to censuses in Nigeria casts doubt on all population estimates.
5. *Sudan Update*, 'Raising the stakes: Oil and conflict in Sudan', December, 1999.

14
Policies towards Horizontal Inequalities

Frances Stewart, Graham K. Brown and Arnim Langer

14.1 Introduction

This book has argued that severe Horizontal Inequalities (HIs) predispose countries to violent conflict as well as reducing individuals' well-being. Relevant HIs include socioeconomic, political and cultural status dimensions, and they are particularly damaging when they are consistent across dimensions. In the light of these findings, this chapter reviews policies towards reducing HIs.

There are many considerations to be taken into account in designing development policies, particularly in a postconflict environment, in addition to those directed at HIs. Thus, political policies usually aim to introduce democracy and the rule of law and to protect human rights generally; economic policies aim to achieve macroeconomic stability, promote efficiency and growth and reduce poverty; and in postconflict societies, policies also aim to reintegrate combatants, to reconstruct basic infrastructure and to address other important causes of conflict, such as unemployment and opportunities for rent-seeking. Policies towards HIs do not displace these other policy objectives or the relevant instruments to achieve them, but they may sometimes involve some trade-offs in policy objectives and some modifications in instruments. Moreover, the exact nature of policies is clearly context-specific and what is appropriate in one country may not be appropriate in another.

This chapter reviews the range of policies which could contribute to alleviating the impact of HIs on conflict likelihood and its recurrence. The relationship between 'objective' HIs and conflict is complex and mediated by at least two intervening factors – the perceptions of HIs and the political salience of group identities. This relationship is depicted in a very stylized form in Figure 14.1.

Objective HIs affect both perceptions of inequality and the political salience of group identities. The latter two factors are in turn closely linked. Dealing with perceptions of inequality is particularly complex from a policy perspective because different groups may have different views on what a just

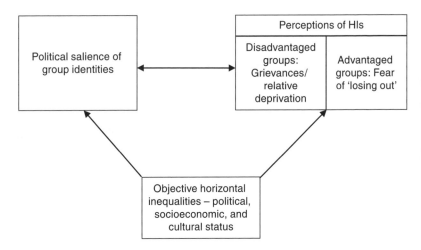

Figure 14.1 Schematic representation of conflict-inducing elements of horizontal inequalities

system would be, and on the origin of the observed inequalities. For relatively disadvantaged groups, particularly those experiencing persistent HIs, HI correction is likely to be seen as necessary to reverse historical injustices; for their relatively advantaged counterparts, however, HIs may be seen simply as a product of greater industry or a better work ethic on the part of the dominant group, and hence HI correction may be interpreted as unjust. Moreover, there may be a mismatch between 'objective' and perceived HIs. In this chapter we focus predominantly on policy options for reducing objective HIs. But securing accurate perceptions about inequalities is another important aspect of policy.

HIs are more likely to lead to conflict where cultural differences are believed to be marked. Moreover, the more entrenched the cultural differences, the more difficult it can be for members of deprived groups to overcome their disadvantage because of prejudice and discrimination. Hence, reducing the sharpness and salience of group distinctions might also be an objective of policy – if achieved, it should reduce the propensity to mobilize along group lines, and might contribute to the reduction of HIs. We describe policies aimed at reducing group salience as 'integrationist'.[1]

The chapter is organized as follows. Section 14.2 introduces a typology of policy approaches drawn from the schematic model above and briefly reviews some measurement issues. Sections 14.3, 14.4 and 14.5 consider the range of policy options available in the political, socioeconomic and cultural dimensions, respectively. Section 14.6 considers issues related to managing the proposed changes. Section 14.7 concludes.

14.2 Approaches to policy and measurement

Drawing on case studies and the work reviewed in this book, it is clear that different countries have taken different approaches to dealing with HIs. In this section, we introduce a typology of policy approaches. The policies are ultimately aimed at substantially reducing group inequality in economic well-being, political participation and cultural recognition. In practice, however, the policies have to be directed at processes affecting these outcomes, rather than the outcomes themselves.

Policies across each of the dimensions can take either a direct or indirect approach towards correcting group inequality. Direct approaches involve targeting groups, positively (for the deprived) and negatively (for the privileged). Indirect approaches aim to achieve the same HI-reducing impact indirectly via general policies, but because of their design in relation to the circumstances of the various cultural groups, they reduce HIs. Ethnic quotas for education or ethnic electoral rolls fall into the first category, while regional expenditure policies or the decentralization of power across the country fall into the second. The first type of policy unavoidably increases the salience of identity difference, while the second is broadly neutral in this respect, and may indeed contribute to greater integration over time. Given the objective of reducing salience, it is desirable for the first type of policy to be time-limited. A third type of policy is explicitly directed at reducing the salience of group boundaries by increasing integration (and less concerned with HI reduction). Examples are incentives for shared economic or political activities across groups.

Table 14.1 summarizes some examples of HI-reducing and integrationist policies across the three main dimensions: political, socioeconomic and cultural status. In subsequent sections, we discuss policy options in more detail. But first we briefly discuss the need for a careful country assessment, including measurement of HIs and identification of their major sources, before devising policy.

Knowledge about the nature of HIs and their major sources is an essential background for designing policies to reduce HIs. Evidence is needed on the multiple dimensions of HIs, the most relevant being dependent on country context. Is it, for instance, a matter of access to education, or poor economic opportunities, or both? Does access to land or employment show the sharpest inequalities, and which is most important to people? Data availability constraints are often severe and those areas that are fundamental to well-being should have priority for data collection. Apart from income, these include land and other assets; employment; educational access at various levels; and health outcomes such as infant and child mortality. Where the data permit, it is again desirable to compare performance in these nonincome dimensions across the distribution, rather than relying simply on comparisons of average performance.

Table 14.1　Examples of approaches to reducing horizontal inequalities

Dimension	Policy approach		
	Direct HI-reducing	Indirect HI-reducing	Integrationist
Political	Group quotas; seat reservations; consociational constitution; list proportional representation.	Design of voting system to require power-sharing across groups (for example, two-thirds voting requirements in assembly); design of boundaries, and seat numbers to ensure adequate representation of all groups; human rights legislation and enforcement.	Geographical voting spread requirements; ban on ethnic/religious political parties (national party stipulations).
Socioeconomic	Quotas for employment or education; special investment or credit programmes for particular groups.	Antidiscrimination legislation; progressive taxation; regional development programmes; sectoral support programmes (for example, Stabex).	Incentives for cross-group economic activities; requirement that schools are multicultural; promotion of multicultural civic institutions.
Cultural status	Minority language recognition and education; symbolic recognition (for example, public holidays, attendance at state functions).	Freedom of religious observance; no state religion.	Civic citizenship education; promotion of an overarching national identity.

However, before measurement, it is necessary to identify the relevant groups – that is those that seem to be most salient and most likely to be a source of mobilization. This can be drawn from a review of the history and politics of the society and from information about people's own perceptions of what group categorization is important and relevant. It is often helpful to adopt a variety of group classifications.

Apart from defining the relevant groups, a scoping exercise should address four further questions, relevant to policy design:

- Whether the salient groups are ranked hierarchically, that is, most members of one group are better off than the other group(s), or unranked, such that each group contains significant elements of rich and poor individuals (Horowitz, 1985).
- Whether groups are geographically concentrated or dispersed.
- Whether groups are specialized on particular economic activities (for example, one particular group mainly consists of traders, another of subsistence farmers, and another of cash-crop farmers).
- Whether the government is politically inclined to tackle inequalities or instead wishes to preserve them.

Measurement issues were discussed extensively in Chapter 5. From the perspective of policies in particular countries, 'adding-up' HIs over all groups for the country as a whole is not particularly relevant – this is more relevant to comparisons across countries. Much more important is to identify the magnitude and change in HIs in the main dimensions. This is most frequently represented by comparing the average *per capita* incomes of different group. However, this conceals distributional differences within groups. Yet from a policy perspective, how groups compare at different points in the distribution may be relevant since policies need to be directed towards the income quantile experiencing large inequalities. Hence it is important to ascertain how HIs vary across the income distribution, as discussed in Chapter 5, where we explored alternative measures that might be used to compare HIs at different points in the distribution.

Socioeconomic data broken down by the relevant ethnocultural categories are often scarce. Sometimes – as, for example, in Nigeria – ethnocultural variables are not included in surveys because of their political sensitivity (Okolo, 1999). For quick assessment, it may be necessary to use some other characteristic as a proxy for ethnocultural difference. Two such options are region and language. Regional data are often more readily available. Whether they are useful for HI assessment depends on the extent to which identity groups are geographically segregated. As a rule of thumb, region is a useful proxy if more than half the members of the relatively deprived group are concentrated in the targeted region(s) while less than half of the privileged group are in the targeted region(s). In many African countries, ethnic and religious groups are regionally concentrated so that regional inequality may be a suitable proxy, while in some cases, region itself defines group identities. An alternative proxy is language, on which information is sometimes available when ethnic variables are not – as in Indonesian surveys in the New Order period (Chapter 6).

Political HIs can be analysed through information on the group distribution of salient groups of positions in parliament, government and bureaucracy, and so forth. A key concept here is that of 'relative representation' (Langer, 2005), defined as each group's share of the positions available divided by its share of the population, which can be used as a measure of political HIs. This clearly requires knowledge of the background of the relevant officials or politicians. In some cases this may be publicly available (for example, in Nepal, see Brown and Stewart, 2006). Where it is not, however, 'name recognition' techniques may be employable in some contexts to attribute group background (see, for example, Langer, 2005).

The first need in any country is to conduct an inventory of available data. Potential data sources include the following:

- Census data, which often include ethnicity or language, and sometimes religion.
- Demographic and Health Surveys (DHS), many of which include ethnic identification along with information on access to social services and ownership of domestic assets.
- Regional data from the census, household surveys, and public expenditure accounts.
- Specific sectoral data (for example, from schools and hospitals) which often contain ethnic and regional information.

Urgent data gaps can be filled by 'light' surveys and the use of focus groups.

The next three sections discuss relevant policies on the basis of experience across the world. Design of policy in a particular context may be informed by such experience, but must ultimately rest on in-depth knowledge of the society in question.

14.3   Policies towards political horizontal inequalities

Political exclusion is likely to alienate group leaders, and hence give more incentives for group mobilization. Therefore, action is needed to ensure that each group participates in political decision-making processes and political power. This does not happen automatically in either democratic or nondemocratic systems. Both formal and informal mechanisms can play a role in ensuring such political participation (or indeed exclusion). Political power is located at many levels – the executive, the legislative, and the judiciary; at the centre and in local government; in the army and the police. Group participation needs to be identified at each of these levels, and appropriate policies devised. Although the appropriate constitutional solution must be country specific, depending on a country's history, geography, and demographic composition, it is possible to make some points that are generally relevant.

Major considerations in tackling political HIs include the definition of citizenship (discussed in Chapter 2), the design of the electoral system and rules of political competition, the composition of the executive and the way decisions are taken, the extent and nature of decentralization, and policies towards employment in the bureaucracy, the police and army.

14.3.1 The electoral system and political party regulations

There has been extensive discussion about the appropriateness of different forms of electoral arrangements for multicultural societies. Two dominant approaches are the consociationalist approach, associated primarily with Arend Lijphart (1977; 2004), and the integrationist approach, associated with Donald Horowitz (1985). These broadly correspond, respectively, to a direct approach to reducing political HIs and more indirect approaches intended to reduce both political HIs and the salience of group divisions.

Consociationalists typically promote the institutionalization (formally or informally) of a 'grand coalition' of groups as the basis of political office – in effect, ensuring all major groups are represented in government. In contrast, the integrationist approach is less concerned with achieving a 'balance of power' between major groups than with devising mechanisms to reduce the incentives for group mobilization, which might or might not be associated with reduced political HIs. But if integrationist approaches do not succeed in reducing group imbalances in power, the system may break down – as has occurred in a number of cases (for example in Lebanon and Sri Lanka).

Turning to more specific measures, one set of political HI-reducing policies consists of electoral mechanisms designed to ensure balanced group representation in parliament, government, and the executive. Lijphart (1986) has suggested that the simplest way of ensuring ethnic representativity is to create separate electoral rolls with seats allocated by group rather than by geographic boundary, as has been implemented in Cyprus and in New Zealand. An alternative mechanism is to create a single electoral roll but to reserve certain seats for certain groups. In India, around 15 per cent of parliament seats are reserved for Scheduled Castes, but registered electors from all groups in the constituency vote for them.

These mechanisms ensure a minimum balance of political representation at the expense, possibly, of entrenching identity politics as the basis of electoral mobilization. More indirect electoral mechanisms are also possible which may encourage group balance. For example, most forms of proportional representation (PR) are likely to achieve a greater degree of group balance than first-past-the-post systems, under which minorities 'tend to be severely underrepresented or excluded' (Lijphart, 1986: 113). In general, it appears that PR is an effective system to ensure that all groups are represented broadly in proportion to their population size, so long as the system has low thresholds for the minimum votes needed to justify election. Nonetheless, there may be a 'fair' electoral system, but minorities may still be excluded from government, while exclusion can occur in the determination of who is entitled to the vote.

In multiethnic societies, there is a strong tendency for political parties to become 'ethnic' as this seems to be an effective way of mobilizing votes (Horowitz, 1985). More broad-based coalitional parties can be encouraged by the electoral system – again through systems of 'list' PR, or a single transferable vote in multimember districts (adopted, for example, in Malta and Ireland). Without some such constraining influences, political parties can be highly divisive in multicultural societies, with elections sometimes leading to conflict (Snyder, 2000; Stewart and O'Sullivan, 1999). Restrictions on political parties themselves are another integrationist policy. Thus in both Ghana and Nigeria, political parties have to have representatives throughout the country, and given the geographic concentration of ethnic groups this promotes multiethnic parties.

14.3.2   Power-sharing in the executive

While the electoral mechanisms discussed may reduce group exclusion from parliamentary assemblies, groups may still be excluded from political power unless there are arrangements to ensure power-sharing in the executive.

The group background of the executive itself – the head of the executive, particularly, but also the cabinet – is of crucial importance for decision-making. In many countries, the group that dominates the executive distributes resources in a way that favours its own members. Moreover, group exclusion has powerful symbolic importance which can lead to group mobilization.

In many postconflict societies, formal mechanisms are introduced to 'share' the top governmental positions among cultural groups. For example, in Lebanon, the top three political offices are reserved for members of the three main ethnoreligious groups, and in Cyprus, Greek Cypriots vote for the president, Turkish Cypriots for the vice-president. Power-sharing can also take place over time. In Bosnia-Herzegovina, for instance, the chair of the three-member presidium rotates between the representatives of the Bosnian, Croat, and Serb communities.

The policies discussed above are mostly *formal* mechanisms, but in many countries *informal* practices or customs have emerged with similar outcomes. In Côte d'Ivoire, for instance, former president Houphouët-Boigny applied an informal policy of ethnic balancing such that all major ethnic groups were represented within the most important political institutions and positions, while in Ghana, a general expectation has evolved that the presidential and vice-presidential slates should include both a northerner and a southerner (Langer, 2005).

Informal mechanisms can be more extensive and flexible, and less open to the charge of entrenching identity politics, than formal ones, while even apparently good formal mechanisms for power-sharing can be subverted – for example by giving only minor posts to some groups. Moreover, formal and informal mechanisms can complement each other. However, informal mechanisms may be easier to subvert than formal, constitutionally enshrined ones, as illustrated in the case of Côte d'Ivoire, where the informal *compromis* of Houphouët-Boigny gave way under his successors.

14.3.3   The composition of the bureaucracy and the security services

Power-sharing is an important issue throughout the system, including, especially, at high levels in the bureaucracy, the army and the police. In some countries, HIs in the civil service reflect political dominance. For example, in Kenya, the Kikuyu, who form around 20 per cent of the population, accounted for over 30 per cent of the permanent secretaries in the civil service during the Kikuyu-dominated regime of President Jomo Kenyatta, but dropped to just 11 per cent in 1994 after a decade of rule by his successor, Daniel arap Moi. Meanwhile, the proportion from Moi's own ethnic group – the Kalenjin – increased from 5 per cent in 1978 to 35 per cent in 2001 (Kanyinga, 2006). Some countries rely mainly on informal conventions to secure balanced representations. More explicit policies are needed, however, where there are gross inequalities. An unusual example is Nigeria's federal character principle, which requires balance in appointments in a comprehensive way (Mustapha, 2007). In Ethiopia, too, the constitution requires ethnic proportionality at each level of government. Public appointment commissions for the bureaucracy can also be mandated to ensure a degree of ethnic balance in appointments and promotions as occurs in Ghana where the Council of State, which has the responsibility for making recommendations for high level promotions and appointments, is constituted by balanced representation from the regions.

14.3.4   Diffusion of power

Where power is concentrated in one body, it is easier for a single group to dominate and for others to be excluded than where power is more diffused. Diffusion can occur via division of powers at the national level through 'checks and balances', or via the decentralization of power. The US constitution provides a famous example of 'checks and balances' with power divided between executive, legislature and judiciary. Similar divisions of powers have quite frequently been adopted elsewhere, but they do not ensure comprehensive group participation if some groups are excluded from each of the branches of government, and/or one of the branches effectively dominates. Thus in the US case, the system has not been effective in ensuring full black participation in government. In many developing countries adopting a similar presidential system, the president effectively monopolizes power, as in the case of Suharto's Indonesia.

Where groups are geographically concentrated, a federal constitution can empower different groups, by allowing them control over many areas of decision-making, the degree of empowerment depending on the allocation of powers. Federal systems have been adopted in the multiethnic states of Belgium, Bosnia-Herzegovina, Ethiopia, India, Malaysia, Nigeria, and Switzerland, among others, with the extent of devolved powers varying considerably among them – for example, Malaysia and Nigeria are both argued to be highly centralized, despite their federal constitutions.

Decentralization can contribute to power-sharing in a similar way to federalism. But again much depends on which powers are given to the decentralized units and whether finance is also devolved. There are many cases of apparent decentralization with little real devolution (Crook and Manor, 1998). Even where there is real devolution, decentralization can replace one set of power-brokers with another. For example, decentralization in Uganda and Nigeria has empowered majority groups in the local government area, but disempowered minority groups (Green, 2006; Ukiwo, 2006). Econometric analysis, however, has shown that decentralization is associated with lower levels of communal and secessionist violence (Brancati, 2006).

In designing federal or decentralized institutions for the management of political HIs, a major consideration is how subnational boundaries should be drawn. Consociationalists argue for subnational boundaries to be drawn, as far as possible, 'around' ethnic groups; federalism is seen as a means of allowing national minorities a degree of autonomy over their own affairs. In contrast, proponents of integrationism argue that boundaries should be drawn 'through' ethnic groups, in order to moderate ethnic political claims (Horowitz, 1985). Critics of 'ethnofederalism' have pointed to the collapse of the post-Soviet federations – Yugoslavia, Czechoslovakia, and the USSR itself, as well as Nigeria before the Biafran civil war – as evidence of its weakness (Snyder, 2000).

14.3.5   Conclusions on policies towards political horizontal inequalities

Some general conclusions on appropriate policies towards political HIs can be drawn, but details must be country specific. Most important is the need to accept the objective of power-sharing across groups at many levels of government. While the easiest way to achieve this is with formal, direct mechanisms, there are many indirect mechanisms which contribute to realizing the objective. But with the latter, especially, it is important to monitor outcomes and be sure that they do indeed deliver a reduction in HIs. In sharply divided societies, formal direct mechanisms may be essential to persuade the various groups that power-sharing will indeed occur. This was the case historically in Belgium and Switzerland. Both are examples of quite explicit and formal power-sharing that has survived for centuries and produced peace, although, perhaps as a consequence, the various identities remain distinct in a way that is generally not the case in other European countries with more integrationist arrangements.

14.4 Policies towards socioeconomic horizontal inequalities: Affirmative action

The term 'affirmative action' has been defined as 'positive steps taken to increase the representation of women and minorities in areas of employment, education, and business from which they have been historically excluded' (Fullinwider, 2005). Essentially, this would cover any policy for improving HIs, whether direct or indirect and this is how we use it here. While direct policies target the disadvantaged group(s) it is also usually possible to devise HI-reducing policies that take a more indirect approach to supplement, or make unnecessary, the more direct policies.

There is a large range of policies that can constitute such affirmative action. This is because: (i) alternative approaches may be used to bring about an improvement in HIs – for instance, legal approaches, expenditure-led approaches, quantitative targets and quotas, and redistributionary approaches; (ii) there are many categories in which improvement may be sought – for example, within the social sector, access to health services at many levels, access to various types of education and training, housing, water, and so forth; and within the economy, access to employment at many levels, to many different types of asset and so on; and (iii) in the economic sphere, there are several levels of policy (macro, meso and micro).

We cannot be taxonomic in this review, but will, rather, touch on some important issues.

14.4.1 Indirect approaches

These include progressive tax policies and general antipoverty programmes which *ipso facto* benefit deprived groups relative to privileged ones. They also include regional and district tax and expenditure policies where groups are spatially concentrated. Other indirect measures use the legal system, for example, through the recognition and enforcement of economic and social human rights and through strong and well-enforced antidiscrimination legislation. For example, in Peru, a Human Rights Ombudsman (*Defensorio del Pueblo*) has been instituted to help enforce the rights of indigenous peoples.

Where regional disparities overlap with group identities, regional development policies can be a useful way of addressing HIs indirectly. Yet, in many countries the regional distribution of infrastructure actually accentuates existing imbalances rather than correcting them. For example, in both Peru and Mozambique the spatial distribution of public infrastructure has been very uneven, favouring more privileged regions (Escobal and Torero, 2005; Stewart, 2002).

However, even where regional inequalities are high, correcting such inequalities may not reduce all group inequalities. In Nepal, for instance, regional development policies would be likely to improve the conditions of the *Janajāti* ethnic groups, which are regionally concentrated, but would have less of an impact on the overall position of the *Dalit* (untouchable) castes, which are fairly evenly spread across the country (Gurung, 2005). In Ghana, over 30 per cent of traditionally northern groups migrated out of the region and are in fact located in the south.

Ethnic specialization in different sectors of the economy, often resulting from the colonial division of labour (see, for example, Brown 1997), also offers possibilities for reducing HIs by targeted programmes that benefit the economic sectors in which the relatively deprived groups are concentrated.

In general public expenditure can be a powerful tool for improving HIs. Three aspects of government expenditure need to be distinguished: the construction of publicly financed facilities, such as infrastructure; the running of public facilities (for example, the group composition of health-sector workers); and the beneficiaries of the facilities (Stewart *et al.*, forthcoming). Attempts to trace the (vertical) distributional impact of government expenditure have almost exclusively focussed on the third phase (Chu *et al.*, 2004; van der Walle *et al.*, 1995). Yet government investment accounts for a very large proportion of total investment in many developing countries, and the beneficiaries of contracts to carry out this expenditure are especially visible and their selection politically provocative. Government employment also typically constitutes a large proportion of total formal sector employment, and the distribution of these 'good' jobs is an important aspect of HI reduction in employment.

The tax system can also be designed to favour regions, districts, or sectors where deprived groups are concentrated. For example, the revenue-sharing formulae in Indonesia's decentralization programme was intended to improve the fiscal position of poorer districts. Similarly, specialized productive activities or sectoral concentration of groups makes it possible to use the tax system to differentiate among groups. In many contexts, particular groups are concentrated in trading, and taxes on wholesale and retail trade would alleviate HIs. Since the poorest people and groups are generally not in the formal sector direct taxes on the formal sector in general will help. In Niger, for example, most people in the informal sector are in a different ethnic group from those in the government and the formal sector generally (Barlow and Snyder, 1993).

14.4.2 Direct approaches

Partly because indirect policies take time and are not always effective, and often because of political pressure from particular groups, direct approaches have quite often been adopted both in the North (such as in the US, New Zealand, and Northern Ireland) and the South (such as in Fiji, India, Malaysia, South Africa, and Sri Lanka). These examples are instructive in pointing to the variety of policies possible. Some of the programmes have been introduced by disadvantaged majorities – for example in Fiji, Malaysia,

Namibia, South Africa, and Sri Lanka – and some by advantaged majorities for disadvantaged minorities – for example in Brazil, India, Northern Ireland, and the US. The latter show that affirmative action can be introduced even where the political situation appears unfavourable. While there is not space here to detail all policies, the following illustrative list shows the range of direct policies possible:

- Assets

    o Policies to improve the group ownership of land via redistribution of government owned-land, forcible eviction, purchases, and restrictions on ownership (Malaysia, Zimbabwe, Fiji, and Namibia).
    o Policies towards the terms of privatization (Fiji).
    o Policies towards financial assets such as bank regulations, subsidization, and restrictions (Malaysia and South Africa).
    o Credit allocation (Fiji and Malaysia).
    o Preferential training (Brazil and New Zealand).
    o Quotas for education (Malaysia, Sri Lanka, and the US).
    o Policies towards public sector infrastructure (South Africa).
    o Policies towards housing (Northern Ireland).

- Incomes and employment

    o Public sector procurement policies (Malaysia, Northern Ireland, South Africa, and the US) (see McCrudden, 2007).
    o Employment policies, including public sector quotas (Malaysia, Sri Lanka, and India), and a requirement for balanced employment in the private sector (South Africa).

- Education

    o Quotas for university entrants (Malaysia, Sri Lanka, and Nigeria).
    o Language policy used to strengthen the position of some groups and weaken that of others in school and university (Malaysia and Sri Lanka).

- Health

    o Policies to improve health access and services in relatively deprived areas (Northern Ghana and in relation to the black population in the US).

Most of these policies involve targets and/or quotas and public expenditure directed at bringing about a more balanced distribution.

14.4.3   The need for economy-wide restructuring as well as fiscal and expenditure policies

Experience shows that policies directed towards improving a group's human assets (notably education) are generally insufficient to improve economic HIs, particularly because poor groups are often handicapped by asymmetric social capital and inequality in economic assets and opportunities. Where improvements are made in human capital alone, through education, a group's economic progress is still held back by these asymmetries. Although something can be done to improve economic opportunities via special credit programmes and directed infrastructural investment, this is likely to be insufficient without a broad restructuring of the economic activity across groups in the economy. This was recognized in Malaysia's New Economic Policy which explicitly aimed to change the colonial division of labour. But more often economic policy is 'blind' to these issues. This applies, notably, to structural adjustment policies the design of which does not take into account the group distributional implications of the policies, and can result in a substantial worsening of the position of deprived groups. This appears to have occurred in Ghana, Mozambique, Uganda, Nigeria, and South Africa, for example, where structural adjustment policies favouring tradable products raised incomes among the more privileged elements (and groups). In Ghana, despite flows of public and NGO investments to the north, less than 1 per cent of private capital from outside Ghana has gone to the north in recent years, while it is claimed that in South Africa the economic model has perpetuated economic apartheid.[2] Privatization is another element in adjustment packages which frequently has strong group distributional implications, implications that are rarely taken into account in formulating policy. For example, in Mozambique the benefits of privatization were monopolized by one (already privileged) group.

The implications of particular macro-policy packages for HIs need to be explored and, where they widen HIs, policies either need to be modified or compensatory action taken.

Many countries have adopted a partial approach to correcting HIs, adopting some of the policies detailed above, with limited results (for example, Brazil). However, two countries provide instructive examples of how a comprehensive effort can improve socioeconomic HIs (both discussed in greater detail in Chapter 4):

- In Malaysia, the New Economic Policy was introduced in 1971, aiming to reduce inequalities between the Malays and the Chinese following anti-Chinese riots in 1969, with the aim of securing national unity. A two-pronged approach included the objective of eradicating poverty and 'to accelerate the process of restructuring Malaysian society to correct economic imbalance so as to reduce and eventually eliminate the identification of race with economic function' (Malaysia, 1971). Besides a variety of antipoverty policies, restructuring policies included expanding the *bumiputera* (an umbrella term for indigenous groups in Malaysia) share of capital ownership to 30 per cent; allocating 95 per cent of new lands to Malays; instituting educational quotas in public institutions in line with population shares; and credit policies favouring Malays with credit allocations and more favourable interest rates. The ratio of *bumiputera* average incomes to Chinese incomes moved from 0.42 to 0.57 between 1970 and 1999 (with the greatest improvement happening in the first ten years), the ratio of share ownership from 0.03 to 0.23, and the *bumiputera* share of registered professionals went from 8 per cent to 47 per cent over the same period (Malaysia, various years).

• In Northern Ireland, following centuries of strong discrimination and persistent HIs, a concerted effort was made to correct this from the late 1970s through housing policy, education policy, and fair employment legislation, backed up by the EU and the British government, who reserved their contracts for firms that did not discriminate. From the late 1970s to the late 1990s, the ratio of Catholics to Protestants in higher education moved from 0.39 to 0.81, inequality in the share of the population in the high-income category between Catholics and Protestants went from 0.55 to 0.77, and in the proportion of the population in houses with three or more rooms from 0.5 to 0.9. By 2004, inequalities in higher education and in access to basic health services had been eliminated (Cain Web Service[3]; Gallagher, 1995; McWhirter, 2004).

14.4.4 The role of international aid

International aid could also play an important role in reducing HIs. Where domestic governments are already committed to implementing HI-reducing policies, aid in the form of general budgetary support may be the most appropriate mechanism for helping countries tackle their HIs. Where governments are unwilling or unable to implement HI-reducing policies, however, project aid may be more appropriate through, for instance, basic service provision in relatively deprived regions. International aid can also contribute to reducing HIs in countries where HIs have clear sectoral aspects, through such programmes as the EU's Export Earnings Stabilization System (Stabex), a compensatory financial scheme to stabilize export earnings derived from primary agricultural commodities. This and similar schemes could be devised to support the crops of the poorer groups. For instance, in West Africa case Stabex-type policies could be applied to support the cultivation of cotton and peanuts, which is mainly concentrated in the deprived northern regions.

However, in practice international aid often reinforces existing inequalities. Data for aid distribution in Mozambique (which financed much of the country's infrastructure) shows a strong bias towards the relatively privileged south. In 1997, average *per capita* aid disbursements for 1995–1997 were

$18.5 in the north; $71.87 in the centre; and $103.98 in the south. Stabex as it is currently implemented may in fact be contributing towards increasing HIs – for instance in Ghana, the vast majority of the €141 million Stabex transfers received since 1975 have gone to the cocoa and timber producers located in the southern regions.[4] Structural adjustment policies, supported by the aid community, also often reinforce rather than offset existing HIs.

International NGOs and local NGOs seem to direct their activities more towards reducing HIs, by providing basic services to deprived areas. For instance, in Ghana a wide range of international NGOs focus their activities in the relatively deprived northern regions, for example by setting up schools, developing water supplies and providing other basic services.

Aid donors need to review their activities generally in the light of the need to reduce HIs. Probably the most important contribution international donors could make at this stage is to include the need to correct HIs in policy discussions, including in discussions of the Poverty Reduction Strategy Papers, thereby putting the issue on the policy agenda.[5]

Monitoring distributional outcomes is essential in order to assess the effectiveness of policies. Yet data are often lacking. Even information on the regional distribution of government expenditure is often not available, as is the case in Ghana, for example.

14.4.5   Integrationist policies

While direct policies tend to enhance the salience of identities and indirect policies are neutral in this respect, integrationist policies aim to reduce the salience of group boundaries. For example, in the realm of social policies, support for multicultural schools and social clubs and restrictions on exclusive schools/clubs may contribute; and in the economic sphere, policies that encourage intergroup economic engagement. Fiscal or other direct economic incentives for interethnic (intergroup) economic activities is one option. Such incentives, however, apply only to the formal economy and will not reach deprived groups concentrated in the informal sector. An example here is the rules governing the flotation of companies on the stock exchange in Malaysia, which stipulate a minimum apportionment of share capital to *bumiputera* stockholders for new flotations. The Malaysian system has been accused of creating a so-called 'Ali Baba' phenomenon in which a politically linked *bumiputera* investor (Ali, a common Malay name) provides the license and/or listing requirements for a Chinese entrepreneur (Baba, from a slang Malay term for the Chinese) but remains otherwise a silent partner (Heng and Sieh Lee, 2000; Jesudason, 1997). But recent research suggests that the approach has been successful in generating genuine interethnic partnerships in the SME sector (Chin, 2004).

14.4.6   Standards and efficiency

A common criticism of affirmative action policies is that they reduce standards (in the case of education) and efficiency (in the case of economic affirmative action). In theory, there are reasons for expecting the efficiency impacts to include both negative and positive elements. On the negative side, there is the interference in normal competitive processes which might prevent resources being allocated according to their most efficient use; but on the positive side is the reduction in economic exclusion and relative deprivation which itself contributes to inefficient resource allocation, thereby allowing the greater realization of potential. Even policies that create 'positive' discrimination in favour of deprived groups may be offsetting the deep bias against groups suffering long-term deprivation, which removing current obstacles alone is insufficient to reverse and may therefore have a positive impact on efficiency in the medium term.

There is no significant empirical evidence that such policies reduce efficiency, though careful evaluations are relatively rare. The most extensive studies of the efficiency impact have been with respect to US affirmative action towards blacks. Some studies show positive impact, while none show negative (Farley, 1984; Keister, 2000). In Malaysia, the high economic growth that accompanied the affirmative action policies also suggests that such policies are highly unlikely to have had any substantial negative efficiency impact, and may have had positive impact.

It is sometimes argued that, while affirmative action and other HI-reducing policies reduce intergroup inequality, they *increase* intragroup inequality. This is not inevitable but depends on whether the policies mostly extend the opportunities and services for lower-income classes (for example, unskilled employment; investment in poor regions; and primary education) within the deprived group(s), or mostly affect upper-income opportunities (professional employment; financial asset ownership; and higher education). Systematic evidence on this is lacking. In the case of Malaysia, intragroup inequality fell during the decade when the policies were most effective (Shireen, 1998). In contrast, in South Africa, it seems that intra-black inequality has risen since the policies were introduced (van der Berg and Louw, 2004). The business 'empowerment' policies in South Africa, for example, seem mainly to enrich a black elite.[6] In both cases, of course, many other influences were simultaneously affecting income distribution (such as the antipoverty policies in Malaysia and the liberalization policies in South Africa) so the changes cannot be attributed to the affirmative action policies alone.

The possibility of some adverse impact of HI-reducing policies on efficiency and intragroup equity suggests that one should aim to design policies which tend by themselves (or in conjunction with other policies) to enhance efficiency and to improve income distribution. From an efficiency perspective, this might mean a greater emphasis on process reform and subsidies rather than quotas; and from an equity perspective it would mean putting emphasis on employment and basic services as well as infrastructure development in poor regions. It should also be noted that even if the policies potentially reduce efficiency and worsen intragroup income distribution, these effects would need to be weighed against their likely impact in reducing violence, which would itself have a positive effect on growth and efficiency and poverty reduction.

14.4.7 Conclusions on policies towards socioeconomic horizontal inequalities

There is a large range of potential policies, both indirect and direct, for alleviating socioeconomic HIs, many of which have been adopted in parts of the world. Indirect policies are attractive in avoiding entrenchment of difference, but they tend to be slow and partial in their impact. Monitoring is important to ensure that such policies are effective. Economic policies that incorporate considerations of group equity are rare – and absent altogether in the case of macro and structural adjustment policies. Yet we find that only if there are economic as well as social policies to correct HIs is substantial improvement realized (see Chapter 4).

14.5 Policies towards cultural status horizontal inequalities

Cultural status inequalities were defined in Chapter 3, and a range of policies towards reducing such inequalities was identified there. Here we summarize some of that discussion. Cultural status inequalities arise from differences in recognition of the cultural and religious practices of groups within society, by the state and others. Such inequalities can lead to resentment and group mobilization, especially where there are also other political or socioeconomic inequalities.

An important difference in policies towards cultural status inequalities from those towards political or socioeconomic inequalities is that the latter generally involve some *redistributive* policies, while rectifying cultural status inequalities is often a matter of *recognition* rather than redistribution. Relevant policies relate to the three main areas of cultural status: religious practices, language policy, and ethnocultural practices. The main objective of policy in this area is to achieve 'cultural status equality'.

14.5.1 Religious practices

Appproriate policies to bring about cultural equality across religions depend on the nature of the inequalities – whether they derive, for example, from one religion being officially recognized as a state religion, or from more informal sources of inequality. In general, complete equality is not possible if the state recognizes only one 'official' religion. But even in such a context, countries can move towards greater equality of status of different religions. Policies to promote equality in religious recognition include ensuring equal opportunity to construct places of worship and burial grounds; recognition of religious festivals and, where appropriate, public holidays to commemorate them; inclusive laws regarding marriage and inheritance; and representation of all major religions at official state functions.

14.5.2 Language

The privileging of one or a few languages over others often signals the dominance of those for whom these languages are the mother tongue and as the Human Development Report 2004 notes, 'Recognizing a language... symbolizes respect for the people who speak it, their culture and their full inclusion in society' (UNDP, 2004: 9). Language policy raises complex questions. Designating one language as the national language is often seen as a means of promoting a cohesive and overarching national identity and possibly generating economic benefits, but it can also cause resentment among minority-language speakers. UNESCO recommends a 'three language formula' promoting the use of an international language, a *lingua franca*, and mother tongue.

Recognition of several languages has been successful in a number of multilingual societies. For example in Singapore, 'official' recognition is given to all four widely spoken languages – Malay, Mandarin Chinese, Tamil, and English – and government business is conducted in English but Malay is designated the 'national' language and used for ceremonial occasions (Spolsky, 2004). In Nigeria, the three main indigenous languages of Hausa, Yoruba, and Igbo are recognized as 'national languages', although this causes resentment among speakers of the many other minority languages. There are also informal aspects to language recognition policy. In Ghana, for example, English is the official language but successive governments have also actively promoted the study and teaching of (currently) 15 major Ghanaian languages (Bemile, 2000). In Belgium, convention now requires that the prime minister employs both French and Dutch in parliament and in dealing with the media, even to the extent of switching language midspeech.

The education sector is obviously hugely important in relation to language recognition. Promoting cultural status equality in multilingual countries requires education in more than one language, though the specifics will vary across countries (see, for example, Watson, 2007). While there are some costs of teaching more than one language at school, the benefits of multilingual education are educational as well as cultural. Evidence suggests that where pupils are educated in their mother tongue and taught a national *lingua franca* they generally perform much better.

14.5.3 Policies towards ethnocultural/religious practices

The state's recognition of, and support, for the cultural practices of different groups is another important dimension of cultural status inequalities. Once again, large variations can be observed. At one extreme are explicit prohibitive restrictions. Even where states are broadly tolerant of cultural diversity, however, official practices can privilege the dominant cultural group – through national holidays, naming conventions (of buildings, streets, and so on) and the promulgation of national 'heroes' and histories closely associated with the dominant cultural group. Cultural status equality requires that the state make an explicit effort to treat the practices of different groups equally.

Often this may require recognition of customary law practices. Plural legal systems increase the access of these minorities to the legal system, as well as their overall sense of being respected. Since the civil war, the Guatemalan government, for example, has made a conscious effort to provide recognition of indigenous communities' judicial norms (UNDP, 2004: 59). Similarly, in Nigeria, the introduction of Islamic *shari'a* in many of the country's northern states has contributed to a sense of public recognition and acknowledgement among Muslims.[7]

14.5.4   Conclusions on policies towards cultural status inequalities

Policies towards cultural status inequalities must take into account the country-specific histories, politics, and demographies of cultural interaction. Having said this, the preceding discussion has highlighted a number of policy conclusions which appear to be common across a large range of countries.

The first conclusion is that there are important symbolic steps that states can take across all three main issues discussed here – religion, language, and ethnocultural practices – that would increase the visibility and recognition of different cultural groups without significant economic costs, although there may be political repercussions. State recognition and support for religious festivities, informal language-use practices, and nonexclusive dress codes are examples.

In other policy areas, however, there are much more tangible trade-offs and dilemmas because of the cost implications. Language education and plural legal systems are examples. However, the trade-off may be exaggerated and compromise solutions can be possible, as in the Singapore language example.

In this section we have reviewed state policies, yet the private sector, notably the media, plays an equally important role in conferring a sense of belonging or inferiority to particular groups with respect to all three areas of policy discussed. The state can set the broad framework for the operation of the media (by, for example, outlawing 'race-hate' speech), and can subsidize media outlets presenting inclusive and/or alternative group visions. The (informal) cultural norms of a society – determining what is or is not acceptable – are of more importance in this realm however.

14.6   Managing change and policy obstacles

In this section we discuss some general problems of initiating, implementing, and managing policy change in horizontally unequal societies. This raises important issues, first because the policies may meet vigorous opposition from the privileged groups who would lose, at least relatively, which may prevent the policies being initiated; or, in extreme cases, if poorly handled, HI-corrective policies can themselves contribute to the escalation of conflict, as seems to have been the case in Sri Lanka and Fiji. In the Indonesian provinces of Maluku and Central Sulawesi, also, a major cause of conflict after the fall of Suharto was Christian resentment against pro-Muslim policies implemented in the last decade of his rule, which had seen their historical dominance severely undermined (G. K. Brown *et al.*, 2005). Secondly, as noted above, the policies can entrench ethnic difference. Hence it is important to introduce policies in a way that avoids these consequences to the extent possible.

14.6.1   Initiating horizontal inequality–management policies: Getting support for the policies

Much depends on the demographic composition of the population, and in particular whether the group which is deprived from a socioeconomic perspective forms a majority or a minority of the population. From a political perspective, corrective policies are clearly easiest to introduce when the socioeconomically deprived group forms a majority. This was the case in Malaysia, South Africa, and Sri Lanka, which made the initiation of HI-reducing policies politically feasible. Yet even this type of demography does not invariably lead to corrective action. For example, in Nigeria, northerners and Muslims form the deprived groups and are in a demographic majority, yet there is little corrective socioeconomic action. In such situations, it seems, the elite are satisfied with political power, and the associated economic benefits they acquire, and do not translate this into economic and social improvements for the broader group population. But such a situation may threaten the support and leadership position of the group elite if it persists. Of course, if there is no democracy, the minority privileged group may dominate the political system as well as the economic one – as in apartheid South Africa – and then changes are even less likely.

Where the disadvantaged group constitutes a minority and the national government represents a dominant group, initiating HI-corrective policies is much more problematic. Many Latin American countries, where indigenous people form a small proportion of the total population, provide examples. In such cases, there is a need to persuade decision-makers of the importance of avoiding severe HIs for social and political stability. As noted above, this situation does not invariably form a decisive obstacle; some governments have introduced programmes to correct HIs where the deprived group is a minority – for example, in Ghana in relation to the north and in Brazil and the US in relation to their black populations. Action is more likely when minority groups mobilize to improve their position; such mobilization was a factor leading to affirmative action in the US, for example.

Correcting political HIs so that all groups participate in decision-making is likely to make the initiation of policies to correct socioeconomic HIs more feasible politically. But this assumes a readiness to share power on the part of the majority group. Such a readiness may emerge from a general agreement on the importance of securing national unity and stability, which is an underlying reason for shared power in Ghana and Nigeria, for example, and in many 'post'-conflict societies such as Lebanon and Bosnia-Herzegovina. Power-sharing is more likely to emerge, however, if international norms move strongly in this direction.

14.6.2　Managing the implementation of horizontal inequality policies: Avoiding resistance

Where governments do implement HI-correction policies, there is a possibility that the policies generate resentment among losing groups and consequently arouse social tensions. The perceived loss (or reduction) in a position of dominance consequent on HI-corrective policies may itself then become a source of conflict.

Ensuring that advantaged groups do not lose in *absolute* terms even as their relative advantage is eroded may be important as a means to encourage such groups to accept HI-corrective policy processes. The experience of Malaysia is instructive here. In its early years, 'the NEP was widely accepted across ethnic lines, especially after the traumatic May 1969 events [ethnic riots]' (Jomo, 2004: 3). Moreover, the high economic growth of this period ensured that the Chinese gained in absolute terms, even as the *bumiputera* were improving at a faster rate. In contrast, the Sri Lankan policies came at a time of high unemployment among the educated population, making job losses among the educated Tamil youth particularly provocative (ILO, 1971). It seems that where the resources for HI correction mainly come from the benefits of strong economic growth, the policies are less likely to be politically contentious.

One important issue in getting widespread acceptance of HI-correcting policies relates to varying perceptions of the causes of HI and, hence, the 'fairness' of remedial policies. Dissemination of objective research on the nature and causes of HIs may make a contribution to correcting false perceptions and securing national support for policies to correct such inequalities. Broad transparency in policy implementation is also important in providing legitimacy for HI correction. In Malaysia, lack of transparency is behind current criticisms of the NEP, which is sometimes seen as no more than a rhetorical policy to justify clientalism which favours a select few (Gomez, 1994; Gomez and Jomo, 1997).

14.7   Conclusions

Sharp HIs can have many adverse consequences, the most serious being mobilization for violent conflict. It is therefore important to introduce policies to correct them. Action is needed to correct political inequalities and those in cultural status, as well as in socioeconomic HIs. The appropriate policies depend on the particular context and a first step in designing policies is a full analysis of that context and the dynamics of HIs.

There are many policies that have an impact on group distribution and that might be adopted to moderate HIs, as reviewed in this chapter. We differentiate two approaches: a direct approach and an indirect one. The first involves giving entitlements to people, whether political or economic, because of their group affiliation, while the second involves correcting HIs by more general policies that have the effect of improving HIs but without specifying group affiliation. In general, the indirect policies have the advantage that they are less likely to enhance the salience of ethnicity, and may indeed contribute to integration, while the direct policies tend to reduce integration may 'entrench' the salience of group difference.

HI-correcting policies have been introduced extensively across multiethnic countries, but mostly in a piecemeal way. Policies towards political HIs appear to be more common than policies towards socioeconomic ones, perhaps because political exclusion is a more obvious cause of mobilization and conflict than socioeconomic inequalities. Perhaps surprisingly, policies that tackle both political and socioeconomic inequalities are relatively rare. Where socioeconomic policies are put into effect in a piecemeal way they do not seem to have a big impact. But where policies are put into effect systematically, across social and economic dimensions, they can be effective in reducing HIs and in sustaining peace. Northern Ireland and Malaysia are examples briefly discussed in this chapter. There is no evidence that such policies have reduced efficiency or growth.

While governments in heterogeneous countries quite often introduce some such policies, they rarely form part of the international policy agenda. Despite their importance, policies to correct economic and political HIs do not, in general, seem to feature in a significant way in the recommendations made by donors for development or postconflict policy change, as discussed in the previous chapter.

Policies towards HIs *are*, however, related to three different strategies which are currently widely advocated internationally – poverty reduction, the elimination of social exclusion, and the Human Rights approach. HI reduction would generally contribute to the poverty reduction and Millennium Development Goals strategy, although poverty reduction strategies alone are not sufficient to bring about HI reduction in a systematic way. An HI approach would help reach some otherwise intractable areas of policy for poverty reduction – notably where discrimination is at the root of the prevalent poverty, as for example in some Latin American countries. Secondly, policies to eliminate social exclusion – which also require a multidimensional approach – are closely related to policies towards HIs, but there is more precision about HIs than social exclusion; however, although some important HIs occur without being so extreme as to merit the term 'social exclusion', effective policies towards social exclusion would contribute greatly to reducing HIs.[8] Thirdly, the Human Rights approach to development also has much to contribute to the reduction of HIs. In particular, on the political side, enforcing the International Covenant of Civil and Political Rights would assist in reducing political HIs; on the social, economic, and cultural side, promoting the realization of the International Covenant of Economic, Social and Cultural Rights would contribute greatly to reducing socioeconomic and cultural status HIs; while eliminating discrimination would contribute to reducing HIs of all kinds.

Finally, it must be emphasized, as noted at the beginning of this chapter, that policies to address HIs are, of course, not the only policies needed for development, generally or in a specifically postconflict environment.

The existence of other policy objectives means trade-offs between realizing objectives may occur. How severe these trade-offs are depends on whether meeting one objective really is at the expense of another. It is possible to exaggerate this. Thus, there is no evidence that improving HIs needs to reduce growth, since it involves extending education and resources to people whose potential has previously been underused. Moreover, if HIs are so severe that conflict threatens, avoiding this is necessary to promote growth and poverty reduction in the long run. But in the short run, at least, there can be trade-offs; in such a situation, an elected government must consider how much they value an inclusive political and economic system compared with their other objectives.

We have noted that in many contexts there is political resistance to policies to correct HIs. While these policies may encounter difficulties, the more that consideration of group inequality becomes part of the norms of policy-making in peace time as well as in postconflict situations, the more likely that action towards HIs will become part of routine policy-making.

Notes

1. Our concept of 'integrationist' policies corresponds closely to 'integrationism' within the literature on managing ethnically divided countries, which emphasizes policies that seek to encourage ethnic moderation and compromise and is most associated with the works of Horowitz (1985; 1989).
2. 'In general, neoliberal policies promoted by the World Bank and adopted by the ANC have helped black elites but done little for the black majority while largely preserving the status quo' (Schneider, 2003: 45).
3. http://cain.ulst.ac.uk

4. EU-Ghana Development Co-operation Annual Report 2004; downloaded from http://delgha.ec.europa.eu/en/publications/EC%20Ghana%20Annual%20Report%202004.pdf (last accessed 12 February 2007).
5. See Brown and Stewart (2006) for a more detailed discussion of how aid might be directed at reducing HIs.
6. *Financial Times*, 'Black South Africans grow impatient over pace of change', 5 January 2007.
7. The law only applies to Muslims, however, and the court of appeal remains civil.
8. See Stewart (2004) for a more detailed discussion of the relationship between the HI and Social Exclusion approaches.

References

Abinales, P.N. 2000. *Making Mindanao: Cotabato and Davao in the Formation of the Philippine Nation-State*. Quezon City: Ateneo de Manila University Press.

Abraham, C.E.R. 1997. *Divide and Rule: The Roots of Race Relations in Malaysia*. Petaling Jaya: Institute for Social Analysis.

Acemoglu, D., and Robinson, J.A. 2006. *Economic Origins of Dictatorship and Democracy: Economic and Political Origins*. Cambridge: Cambridge University Press.

Achen, C.H. 2002. Toward a new political methodology: Microfoundations and ART. *Annual Review of Political Science* 5: 423–450.

Adato, M., Carter, M., and May, J. 2006. Exploring poverty traps and social exclusion in South Africa using qualitative and quantitative data. *Journal of Development Studies* 42(2): 226–247.

Adejumobi, S. 2001. Citizenship, rights, and the problem of conflicts and civil wars in Africa. *Human Rights Quarterly* 23(1): 148–170.

Advisory Board on Human Security. 2004. *Denial of Citizenship: A Challenge to Human Security*. Report prepared for the Advisory Board on Human Security. New York: Advisory Board on Human Security.

Agyeman, D.K. 1998. Ethnic conflicts and politics in Ghana. In Nnoli, O., ed., *Ethnic Conflicts in Africa*. Dakar: CODESRIA Books.

Akindès, F. 2004. The roots of the military-political crises in Côte d'Ivoire. *Research Report No. 128*. Uppsala: Nordiska Afrikainstitutet.

Akindès, F. Forthcoming. *The marketing of Identities in Côte d'Ivoire*, CRISE Working Paper. Oxford: Centre for Research on Inequality, Human Security and Ethnicity, University of Oxford.

Alba, R., Lutz, A., and Vesselinov, E. 2001. How enduring were the inequalities among European immigrant groups in the United States? *Demography* 38(3): 349–356.

Albó, X. 2002. *Pueblos indios en la política*. La Paz: CIPCA.

Alderton, E.C. 1947. Reorganization of Efik-Qua-Efut Native Authority. National Archives, Ibadan (NAI), File No. 8/1/215.

Alesina, A., and Perotti, R. 1996. Income distribution, political instability, and investment. *European Economic Review* 40(6): 1203–1228.

Alesina, A., Devleeschauwer, A., Easterly, W., Kurlat, S., and Wacziarg, R. 2003. Fractionalization. *Journal of Economic Growth* 8(2): 155–194.

Alexander, J., McGregor, J., and Ranger, T. 2000. Ethnicity and the politics of conflict: The case of Matabeleland. In Nafziger, E.W., Stewart, F., and Väyrynen, R., eds, *War, Hunger and Displacement: The Origin of Humanitarian Emergencies, Vol. 2*. Oxford: Oxford University Press.

Anand, S. 1983. *Inequality and Poverty in Malaysia: Measurement and Decomposition*. New York: Oxford University Press.

Anand, S., and Sen, A. 1995. Gender inequality in human development: Theories and measurement. *Human Development Report Office Occasional Paper*. New York: UNDP.

Anderson, B. 1983. *Imagined Communities: Reflections on the Origin and Spread of Nationalism*. London: Verso.

326

André, C., and Platteau, J.-P. 1996. Land tenure under unendurable stress: Rwanda caught in the Malthusian trap. *Cahiers de la faculté des sciences économiques et sociales de Namur No. 164.* Namur: Centre de Recherche en Economie du Développement (CRED), Facultés Universitaires Notre-Dame de la Paix.

Ansión, J., Tubino, F., and Villacorta, A. 2004. Educación ciudadana intercultural para los pueblos indígenas de América Latina en contextos de pobreza. *Mimeo*, Pontificia Universidad Católica del Perú, Lima.

Antlöv, H. 2003. Village government and rural development in Indonesia. *Bulletin of Indoneian Economic Studies* 39(2): 193–214.

Arendt, H. 1986. *The Origins of Totalitarianism.* London: Andre Deutsch.

Asante, R. 2007. Cultural differences and political stability of Ghana. *CRISE Internal Paper.* Oxford: Centre for Research on Inequality, Human Security and Ethnicity, University of Oxford.

ASNLF (Acheh Sumatra National Liberation Front) 1976. Declaration of Independence of Acheh-Sumatra.

ASNLF (Acheh Sumatra National Liberation Front) 2004. Achehnese delegation paper. *22nd Session of the UNHCR Working Group on Indigenous Populations.* Geneva: UNHCR.

Aspinall, E. 2002. Modernity, history and ethnicity: Indonesian and Acehnese nationalism in conflict. *Review of Indonesian and Malaysian Affairs* 36(1): 3–34.

Assies, G., van der Haar, G., and Hoekema, A. 2000. *The Challenge of Diversity, Indigenous Peoples and Reform of the State in Latin America.* Amsterdam: Thela-Thesis.

Atkinson, A.B. 1970. On the measurement of inequality. *Journal of Economic Theory* 2(3): 244–263.

Auvinen, J., and Nafziger, E.W. 1999. The sources of humanitarian emergencies. *Journal of Conflict Resolution* 43(3): 267–290.

Azam, J.-P. 2004. Poverty and growth in the WAEMU after the 1994 devaluation. *Journal of African Economies* 13(4): 536–562.

Bach, D. 1997. Indigeneity, ethnicity and federalism. In Diamond, L., Kirk-Greene, A., and Oyediran, O., eds, *Transition Without End: Nigerian Politics and Civil Society under Babaniga.* Boulder: Lynne Reinner.

Bach, D. 2006. Inching towards a country without a state: Prebendalism, violence and state betrayal in Nigeria. In Clapham, C., Herbst, J., and Mill, G., eds, *Africa's Big States.* Johannesburg: Wits University Press.

Bakery, T. 1984. Elite transformation and political succession. In Zartman, W., and Delgado, C., eds, *The Political Economy of Ivory Coast.* New York: Preager Publishers.

Bakke, K., and Wibbels, E. 2006. Federalism and intrastate struggles: The role of diversity and disparity. Paper delivered at CRISE Workshop on *Federalism, Decentralisation and Conflict.* Oxford: Department of International Development, October 5–7.

Banégas, R., and Losch, B. 2002. La Côte d'Ivoire au bord la l'implosion. *Politique Africaine* 87: 139–161.

Banerjee, A.V., and Newman, A.F. 1993. Occupational choice and the process of development. *Journal of Political Economy* 101(2): 274–298.

Bangura, Y. 2001. *Ethnic Structure, Inequality and Public Sector Governance: A Comparative Study.* Geneva: UNSRID, http://unpan1.un.org/intradoc/groups/public/documents/UNTC/UNPAN018646.pdf.

Bangura, Y., ed. 2006. *Ethnic Inequalities and Public Sector Governance.* London: Palgrave.

Banks, M. 1996. *Ethnicity: Anthropological Constructions.* London: Routledge.

Bannon, A., Miguel, E., and Posner, D. 2004. Sources of ethnic identification in Africa. *AfroBarometer Working Paper No. 44.* Cape Town, SA: Institute for Democracy in South Africa.

Barlow, R., and Snyder, W. 1993. Taxation in Niger: Problems and proposals. *World Development* 21(7): 1179–1189.

Barrett, C., Marenya, P.P., Mcpeak, J., Minten, B., Murithi, F., Oluoch-Kosura, W., Place, F., Randrianarisoa, J.C., Rasambainarivo, J., and Wangila, J. 2006. Welfare dynamics in rural Kenya and Madagascar. *Journal of Development Studies* 42(2): 248–277.

Barrios, L. 2001. *Tras las Huellas del Poder Local: La Alcadía Indígena en Guatemala del Siglo XVI al Siglo XX*. Guatemala: Universidad Rafael Landivar.

Barrón Ayllón, M. 2007. Horizontal inequalities in Latin America: A statistical comparison of Bolivia, Guatemala and Peru. *CRISE Working Paper No. 32*. Oxford: Centre for Research on Inequality, Human Security and Ethnicity, University of Oxford.

Barron, P., Kaiser K., and Pradhan, M. 2004. Local conflict in Indonesia: Measuring incidence and identifying patterns. *World Bank Policy Research Working Paper No. 3384*. Washington, DC: World Bank.

Barrows, W.L. 1976. Ethnic diversity and political instability in black Africa. *Comparative Political Studies* 9(2): 139–170.

Barth, F. 1969. *Ethnic Groups and Ethnic Boundaries*. London: George Allen and Unwin.

Bastos, S., and Camus, M. 1993. *Quebrando el Silencio: Organizaciones del Pueblo Maya sus Demandas (1986–1992)*. Guatemala: FLACSO.

Bastos, S., and Camus, M. 2003. *Entre el Mecapal y el Cielo: Desarrollo del Movimiento Maya en Guatemala*. Guatemala: FLACSO.

Bauböck, R. 1997. Changing the boundaries of citizenship. In Bauböck, R., ed., *From Aliens to Citizens*. Aldershot: Avebury.

Beck, N., Katz, J.N., and Tucker, R. 1998. Taking time seriously: Time-series-cross-section analysis with a binary dependent variable. *American Journal of Political Science* 42(4): 1260–1288.

Behrman, J.R. 1990. The action of human resources and poverty on one another: What we have yet to learn. *LSMS Working Paper No. 74*. Washington, DC: World Bank.

Bemile, S.K. 2000. Promotion of Ghanaian languages and its impact on national unity: The Dagare language case. In Lentz, C., and Nugent, P., eds, *Ethnicity in Ghana: The Limits of Intervention*. Basingstoke: Macmillan.

Bertrand, J. 2004. *Nationalism and Ethnic Conflict in Indonesia*. Cambridge: Cambridge University Press.

Binningsbø, H.M. 2005. Consociational democracy and postconflict peace: Will power-sharing institutions increase the probability of lasting peace after civil war? Paper presented at the *13th National Conference in Political Science*, Hurdalsjøen, Norway, January 5–7.

Blau, P.M. 1977. *Inequality and Heterogeneity: A Primitive Theory of Social Structure*. New York: Free Press.

Blee, K.M., and Billings, D.B. 1996. Race differences in the origins and consequences of chronic poverty in rural Appalachia. *Social Science History* 20(3): 345–373.

Bogue, D.J. 1985. *The Population of the United States: Historical Trends and Future Projections*. New York: Free Press.

Booth, A. 2000. Poverty and inequality in the Soeharto era: An assessment. *Bulletin of Indonesian Economic Studies* 36(1): 73–104.

Booth, D., and Curran, Z. 2005. *Aid Instruments and Exclusion*. Report for the UK Department for International Development. London: Overseas Development Institute.

Borjas, G.J. 1992. Ethnic capital and intergenerational mobility. *The Quarterly Journal of Economics* 107(1): 123–150.

Borjas, G.J. 1995. Ethnicity, neighbourhood and human capital externalities. *American Economic Review* 85(3): 365–390.

Borooah, V., McKee, P., Heaton, M., and Collins, G. 1995. Catholic-Protestant income differences in Northern Ireland. *Review of Income and Wealth* 41(1): 41–56.

Bourguignon, F., and Chakravarty, S.R. 2003. The measurement of multidimensional poverty. *Journal of Economic Inequality* 1(1): 25–49.

Bourdieu, P. 1986. The forms of capital. In Richardson, J.G., ed., *Handbook of Theory and Research for the Sociology of Education*. New York: Greenwood Press.

Bourque, S.C., and Palmer, D.S. 1975. Transforming the rural sector: Government policy and peasant response. In Lowenthal, A.F., ed., *The Peruvian Experiment: Continuity and Change under Military Rule*. Princeton: Princeton University Press.

Brancati, D. 2006. Decentralization: Fueling the fire or dampening the flames of ethnic conflict and secessionism? *International Organization* 60(3): 651–685.

Brass, P.R. 1974. *Language, Religion and Politics in North India*. Cambridge: Cambridge University Press.

Brass, P.R. 1997. *Theft of an Idol: Text and Context in the Representation of Collective Violence*. Princeton: Princeton University Press.

Brass, P.R. 2003. *The Production of Hindu-Muslim Violence in Contemporary India*. Washington: University of Washington Press.

Breen, R. 2000. Class inequality and social mobility in Northern Ireland, 1973 to 1996. *American Sociological Review* 65(3): 392–406.

Brooks-Gunn, J., Duncan, G., Klebanov, P., and Sealand, N. 1993. Do neighbourhoods influence child and adolescent development? *American Journal of Sociology* 99(2): 353–395.

Brown, D. 1982. Who are the Tribalists? Social pluralism and political ideology in Ghana. *African Affairs* 81(322): 37–69.

Brown, D. 1988. From peripheral communities to ethnic nations: Separatism in Southeast Asia. *Pacific Affairs* 61(1): 51–77.

Brown, D. 1994. *The State and Ethnic Politics in South-east Asia*. London: Routledge.

Brown, G.K. 2004a. Civil society and social movements in an ethnically divided society: The case of Malaysia, 1981–2001. *PhD thesis*. School of Politics, University of Nottingham.

Brown, G.K. 2004b. Restraining autonomy: Sabah during the Mahathir years. In Welsh, B., ed., *Reflections: The Mahathir Years in Malaysia*. Washington, DC: Johns Hopkins University School of Advanced International Studies.

Brown, G.K. 2005a. Balancing the risks of corrective surgery: The political economy of horizontal inequalities and the end of the New Economic Policy in Malaysia. *CRISE Working Paper No. 20*. Oxford: Centre for Research on Inequality, Human Security and Ethnicity, University of Oxford.

Brown, G.K. 2005b. The formation and management of political identities: Indonesia and Malaysia compared. *CRISE Working Paper No. 10*. Oxford: Centre for Research on Inequality, Human Security and Ethnicity, University of Oxford.

Brown, G.K. 2005c. Horizontal inequality or polarisation? Inter-group economic disparity and its relationship with conflict. Paper presented at the IGCC Conference on *Disaggregating the Study of Civil War and Transnational Violence*. San Diego, CA: University of California Institute of Global Conflict and Cooperation, March 7–8.

Brown, G.K. 2006. Special autonomy as a conflict resolution mechanism: The Southeast Asian experience. Paper presented at the conference on *Federalism, Decentralization and Conflict*. Centre for Research on Inequality, Human Security and Ethnicity, University of Oxford, October 5–7.

Brown, G.K., and Stewart, F. 2006. The implications of horizontal inequalities for aid. *CRISE Working Paper No. 35*. Oxford: Centre for Research on Inequality, Human Security and Ethnicity, University of Oxford.

Brown, G.K., Tajima, Y., and Hadi, S. 2005 *Overcoming Violent Conflict: Peace and Development Analysis in Central Sulawesi, Vol. 3*. Jakarta: Conflict Prevention and Recovery Unit, United Nations Development Programme (CPRU-UNDP), Lembaga Ilmu Pengetahuan Indonesia (LIPI), Badan Pusat Perencangan Nasional (BAPPENAS).

Brown, I. 1997. *Economic Change in South-east Asia, c.1830–1980*. Kuala Lumpur: Oxford University Press.

Brown, M.K., Carnoy, M., Currie, E., Duster, T., Oppenheimer, D.B., Shultz, M.M., and Wellman, D. 2005. *The Myth of a Color Blind Society*. Berkeley: University of California Press.

Brown, T.N., Williams, D.R., Jackson, J.S., Neighbours, H., Sellers, S., Myriam, T., and Brown, K. 1999. Being black and feeling blue: Mental health consequences of racial discrimination. *Race and Society* 2(2): 117–131.

Brubaker, R., and Cooper, F. 2000. Beyond 'identity'. *Theory and Society* 29(1): 1–47.

Brukum, N.J.K. 1995. Ethnic conflicts in the Northern Region of Ghana: A study of the conflict in the Gonja District, 1980–1994. In Oquaye, M., ed., *Democracy and Conflict Resolution in Ghana*. Accra: Gold Type Press.

Buckland, P. 1979. *The Factory of Grievances: Devolved Government in Northern Ireland, 1921–1939*. Dublin: Gill & Macmillan.

Buhaug, H., and Gates, S. 2002. The geography of civil war. *Journal of Peace Research* 39(4): 417–433.

Bureau of the Census. 1996. *Detailed Tables for Educational Attainment in the United States: March 1995*. Washington, DC: Bureau of the Census.

Burr, M. 1998. 'Working Document II: Quantifying Genocide in Southern Sudan and the Nuba Mountains, 1983–1998', US Committee for Refugees, December 1998.

Buvollen, H.P. 2002. Cultural and legal barriers to justice in Guatemala. *UNDP Access to Justice Workshop*, Oslo, March 1. Downloaded from http://www.undp.org/governance/cd/documents/34.pdf (last accessed February 12, 2007).

Calla, R. 2003. *Indígenas, Política y Reformas en Bolivia: Hacia una Etnología del Estado en América Latina*. Guatemala: Ediciones ICAPI.

Canepa, G. 2007. The fluidity of ethnic identities in Peru. *CRISE Working Paper No. 46*. Oxford: Centre for Research on Inequality, Human Security and Ethnicity, University of Oxford.

Carens, J.H. 1995. Complex justice, cultural difference and political community. In Miller, D., and Walzer, M., eds, *Pluralism, Justice and Equality*. Oxford: Oxford University Press.

Carment, D. 2003. Secessionist ethnic conflict in South and Southeast Asia: A comparative perspective. In Ganguly, R., and Macduff, I., eds, *Ethnic Conflict and Secessionism in South and Southeast Asia*. New Delhi: Sage.

Case, W. 1996. *Elites and Regimes in Malaysia: Revisiting a Consociational Democracy*. Melbourne, Australia: Monash Asia Institute, Monash University.

Castles, S., and Miller M. 2003. *The Age of Migration*. 3rd ed. Basingstoke: Palgrave Macmillan.

Caumartin, C. 2005. Racism, violence and inequality: An overview of the Guatemalan case. *CRISE Working Paper No. 11*. Oxford: Centre for Research on Inequality, Human Security and Ethnicity, University of Oxford.

Caumartin, C. 2006a. CRISE Survey: Perceptions of identities, political and social cleavages in Guatemala. Paper presented at *Emerging Themes in Social Science Research in Guatemala*, Oxford, May 18.

Caumartin, C. 2006b. Indigenous people and politics? Issues in the measurement, and interpretation of political horizontal inequalities in Guatemala. Paper presented at *CRISE Latin America Workshop*, Santa Cruz, Bolivia, September 25.

Cayzac, H. 2001. *Guatemala, Proyecto Inconcluso: La Multiculturalidad, un Paso Hacia la Democracia.* Guatemala: FLACSO.

CEH (Comisión de Esclarecimiento Histórico). 1999. *Guatemala: Memoria del Silencio. Tomo I-V Oficina de Servicios para Proyectos de las Naciones Unidas (UNOPS)*, http://shr.aaas.org/guatemala/ceh/report/english/toc.html (last accessed June 7, 2007).

Chakrabarty, A. 2001. The concept and measurement of group inequality. *Centre for Development Studies Working Paper No. 315.* Thiruvananthapuram: Centre for Development Studies.

Chalk, P. 2001. Separatism and Southeast Asia: The Islamic factor in Southern Thailand, Mindanao, and Aceh. *Studies in Conflict and Terrorism* 24(4): 241–269.

Che Man, W.K. 1990. *Muslim Separatism: The Moros of Southern Philippines and the Malays of Southern Thailand.* Quezon City: Ateneo de Manila University Press.

Chin, J. 1997. Politics of federal intervention in Malaysia, with reference to Sarawak, Sabah and Kelantan. *Journal of Commonwealth and Comparative Politics* 35(2): 96–120.

Chin, Y.W. 2004. Ethnicity and the transformation of the Ali-Baba partnership in the Chinese business culture in Malaysia. In Cheah, B.K., ed., *The Challenge of Ethnicity: Building a Nation in Malaysia.* Singapore: Marshall Cavendish International.

Chirot, D. 2006. The debacle in Côte d'Ivoire. *Journal of Democracy* 17(2): 63–77.

Christie, C.J. 1996. *A Modern History of South East Asia: Decolonization, Nationalism and Separatism.* London: IB Tauris.

Chu, K.-Y., Davoodi, H.R., and Gupta, S. 2004. Income distribution and tax, and government social spending policies in developing countries. In Cornia, G.A., ed., *Inequality, Growth and Poverty in an Era of Liberalization and Globalization.* Oxford: Oxford University Press.

Chua, A. 2003. *World on Fire.* London: Heinemann.

Coghlan, B., Brennan, R.J., Ngoy, P., Dofara D., Otto, B., Clements, M., and Stewart, T. 2006. Mortality in the democratic Republic of Congo: A nationwide survey. *The Lancet* 367(9504): 44–51.

Cohen, A. 1969. *Custom and Politics in Urban Africa.* Berkeley: University of California Press.

Cohen, A. 1974. *Two-Dimensional Man: An Essay on the Anthropology of Power and Symbolism in Complex Society.* Berkeley: University of California Press.

Cojtí, D., and Fabian, E. 2005. *Resultados del Decenio Internacíonal de las 'Poblaciones' Indigenas del Mundo 1994–2004.* Guatemala: CEDIM (Centro de Documentación y Investigación Maya).

Collier, P. 2001. Implications of ethnic diversity. *Economic Policy* 16(32):127–166.

Collier, P., and Hoeffler, A. 1998. On economic causes of civil war. *Oxford Economic Papers* 50(4): 563–573.

Collier, P., and Hoeffler, A. 2004. Greed and grievance in civil war. *Oxford Economic Papers* 56(4): 563–595.

Committee of Concerned Itsekiri. 1998. *The Warri Crisis and the Solution.* Lagos: The Committee of Concerned Itsekiri.

Contamin, B., and Losch, B. 2000. Côte d'Ivoire: la voi étroite. *Politique Africaine* 77: 117–128.

Cooper, S., Durlauf S., and Johnson, P. 1993. On the evolution of economic status across generations. In *American Statistical Association, 1993 Proceedings of the Business and Economic Statistics Section.* Papers presented at the Annual Meeting of the American Statistical Association, San Francisco, California, August 8–12, 1993, under the sponsorship of the Business and Economic Statistics Section. Alexandria, VA: American Statistical Association.

Corcoran, M. 1995. Rags to riches: Poverty and mobility in the US. *Annual Review of Sociology* 21: 237–267.

Corcoran, M., Gordon, R., Laren, D., and Solon, G. 1989. Effects of family and community background on men's economic status. *NBER Working Paper No. 2896.* Cambridge, MA: National Bureau of Economic Research.

Cormack, R., Osborne R., and Thompson, W. 1980. Work? Young school leavers and the structure of opportunity in Belfast. *Belfast Fair Employment Agency, Research Paper No. 5.* Belfast: Fair Employment Agency.

Cornia, G.A., ed. 2004. *Inequality, Growth, and Poverty in an Era of Liberalization and Globalization.* Oxford: Oxford University Press.

Covello, V., and Ashby, J. 1980. Inequality in a divided society: An analysis of data from Northern Ireland. *Sociological Focus* 13(2): 87–98.

Crabtree, J., ed. 2006. *Construir Instituciones: Democracia, Desarrollo y Desigualdad en el Perú desde 1980.* Universidad Católica, Lima: Universidad del Pacífico y Instituto de Estudios Peruanos.

Crook, R. 1997. Winning coalitions and ethno-regional politics: The failure of the opposition in the 1990 and 1995 elections in Côte d'Ivoire. *African Affairs* 96: 215–242.

Crook, R., and Manor, J. 1998. *Democracy and Decentralisation in South Asia and West Africa: Participation, Accountability and Performance.* Cambridge: Cambridge University Press.

Cross Rivers State of Nigeria. 2000. *Views of the Cross River State Government on the Report of the Judicial Commission of Inquiry into the Crisis for the Selection of Obong of Calabar and Paramount Ruler of the Efiks.* Calabar: Government Printer.

CVR (Comisión de la Verdad del Perú). 2003. *Reporte Final, Vol. II Ch. 1. Lima: Comisión de la Verdad del Perú.* http://www.cverdad.org.pe (last accessed June 7, 2007).

Dahl, R. 2000. *On Democracy.* New Haven: Yale University Press.

Dalton, H. 1920. The measurement of the inequality of incomes. *Economic Journal* 30(119): 348–361.

Dary, C. 2003. *Identidades Étnicas y Tierras Comunales en Jalapa.* Guatemala: IDEI.

Das Gupta, J. 1970. *Language Conflict and National Development.* Berkeley: University of California Press.

Datcher, L. 1982. Effects of community and family background on achievement. *Review of Economics and Statistics* 64(1): 32–41.

Davenport, C. 2003. *Minorities at Risk: Dataset Users Manual.* College Park, MD: CIDCM, University of Maryland.

Davies, J.C. 1962. Towards a theory of revolution. *American Sociological Review* 27(1): 5–19.

Deaton, A. 1995. Data and econometric tools for development analysis. In Behrman, J., and Srinivasan, T.N., eds, *Handbook of Development Economics, Vol. 3.* Amsterdam: Elsevier Science.

Degregori, C.I. 1992. The origins and logic of Shining Path: Two views. In Palmer, D.S., ed., *The Shining Path of Peru.* London: Hurst and Company.

Deininger, K. 2003. Causes and consequences of civil strife: Micro-level evidence from Uganda. *Oxford Economic Papers* 55(4): 579–606.

Dembélé, O. 2003. Côte d'Ivoire: La fracture communitaire. *Politique Africaine* 89: 34–48.

Den Tuinder, B. 1978. *Ivory Coast: The Challenge of Success — A Report for the World Bank.* Baltimore: Johns Hopkins University Press.

Deutsch, J., and Silber, J. 2005. Measuring multidimensional poverty: An empirical comparison of various approaches. *Review of Income and Wealth* 51(1): 145–174.

Deutsch, K. 1961. Social mobilization and political development. *American Political Science Review* 55: 493–514.

Devine, J.A., Plinkett, M., and Wright, J.D. 1992. The chronicity of poverty: Evidence from PSID, 1968–1987. *Social Forces* 70(3): 787–812.

DFID (Department for International Development). 2007. *Preventing Violent Conflict.* London: HMSO.

Dickson, K.B. 1975. Development planning and national integration in Ghana. In Smock, D.R., and Bentsi-Enchill, K., eds, *The Search for National Integration in Africa.* New York: The Free Press.

Do, Q.T., and Iyer, L. 2007. Poverty, social divisions and conflict in Nepal. *World Bank Policy Research Working Paper No. 4228.* Washington, DC: World Bank.

Dordunoo, C.K., and Nyanteng, V.K. 1997. Overview of Ghanaian economic development. In Nyanteng, V.K., ed., *Policies and Options for Ghanaian Economic Development.* Accra: The Institute of Statistical, Social and Economic Research, University of Ghana.

Dorf, M. 2004. Can ethnic hatred be eliminated by eliminating ethnicity? Downloaded from http://writ.news.findlaw.com/dorf/20040414.html (last accessed June 7, 2007).

Douglas, W.A. 1988. A critique of recent trends in the analysis of ethnonationalism. *Ethnic and Racial Studies* 11(2): 192–206.

Dozon, J.-P. 2000. La Côte d'Ivoire entre démocratie, nationalisme et ethnonationalisme. *Politique Africaine* 78: 45–62.

Duclos, J.-Y., Esteban, J-M., and Ray, D. 2004. Polarisation: Concepts, measurement, estimation. *Econometrica* 72(6): 1737–1772.

Duncan, G.J., Gustafsson, B., Hauser, R., Schmauss, G., Messinger, H., Muffels, R., Nolan, B., and Ray, J.C. 1993. Poverty dynamics in eight countries. *Journal of Population Economics* 6(3): 215–234.

Dunkerley, J. 1988. *Power in the Isthmus.* London: Verso.

Durlauf, S.N. 2002. Groups, social influences and inequality: A memberships theory perspective on poverty traps. *SSRI Working Paper No. 2002–18.* Madison, WI: Social Systems Research Institute, University of Wisconsin-Madison.

Efik Eburutu Consultative Assembly. 2003. *Qua, Enough is Enough: Efik Reaction to Qua Memo.* Calabar: EECA.

Efut Combined Assembly. 2003. *The Position of Efut Nation on Moves by Government to Achieve Unity, Peace and Stability in Calabar, Cross River State of Nigeria.* Unpublished paper issued in Calabar.

Egreteau, R. 2006. Instability at the gate: India's troubled northeast and its external connections. *CSH Occasional Papers.* New Delhi: Centre de Science Humaines.

Ejobowah, J.B. 2001. The limits and possibilities of conflict-reduction strategies in Africa's polyethnic states. In Ike Idogu, E., ed., *The Issue of Political Ethnicity in Africa.* Aldershot: Ashgate.

Ellingsen, T. 2000. Colourful community or ethnic witches' brew? Multiethnicity and domestic conflict during and after the Cold War. *Journal of Conflict Resolution* 44(2): 228–249.

Ensari, N., and Miller, N. 2001. Decategorization and the reduction of bias in the crossed categorization paradigm. *European Journal of Social Psychology* 31: 193–216.

Escobal, J., and Torero, M. 2005. Adverse geography and differences in welfare in Peru. In Kanbur, R., and Venables, A.J., eds, *Spatial Inequality and Development.* Oxford: Oxford University Press.

Espiritu, L.Y. 1996. *Asian American Women and Men.* London: Sage.

Esteban, J.-M., and Ray, D. 1994. On the measurement of polarisation. *Econometrica* 62(4): 819–851.

Esteban, J.-M., and Ray, D. 1998. Conflict and distribution. *Journal of Economic Theory* 87(2): 379–415.

Ewusi, K. 1976. Disparities in levels of regional development in Ghana. *Social Indicators Research* 3(1): 75–100.

Faaland, J., Parkinson, J., and Saniman, R. 2003. *Growth and Ethnic Inequality – Malaysia's New Economic Policy*. Kuala Lumpur: Utusan.

Fair Employment Commission. 1998. *Monitoring Report No. 8: A Profile of the Northern Ireland Workforce – Summary of Monitoring Returns 1997*. Belfast: Fair Employment Commission.

Farley, R. 1984. *Blacks and Whites: Narrowing the Gap?* Cambridge, MA: Harvard University Press.

Fearon, J.D. 2003. Ethnic structure and cultural diversity around the world: A cross-national data set on ethnic groups. *Mimeo*. Stanford University.

Fearon, J.D., and Laitin, D.D. 1996. Explaining interethnic cooperation. *American Political Science Review* 90(4): 715–735.

Fearon, J.D., and Laitin, D.D. 2003. Ethnicity, insurgency, and civil war. *American Political Science Review* 97(1): 75–90.

Fianza, M. 1999. Conflicting land use and ownership patterns and the 'Moro Problem' in Southern Philippines. In Ferrer, M.C., ed., *Sama-Sama: Facets of Ethnic Relations in South East Asia*. Quezon City: Third World Studies Center, University of the Philippines.

Figueroa, A. 2003. *La Sociedad Sigma: Una Teoría del Desarollo Económico*. Lima: Catholic University of Peru Press.

Figueroa, A. 2006. Education, labour markets and inequality in Peru. Paper presented at the *CRISE Latin America Workshop*, Santa Cruz, Bolivia, September 18–20.

Figueroa, A., Altamariano, T., and Sulmont, D. 1996. *Social exclusion and inequality in Peru*. Geneva: International Labour Institute.

Figueroa, A., and Barrón, M. 2005. Inequality, ethnicity and social disorder in Peru. *CRISE Working Paper No. 8*. Oxford: Centre for Research on Inequality, Human Security and Ethnicity, University of Oxford.

Findlay, G.H. 1933. Intelligence Report on Efik Clan Organization, NAI/ File No. 27627, Vol. 2.

Flores Galindo, A., ed. 1976. Tupac Amaru y la sublevación de 1780. *Sociedad Colonial y Sublevaciones Populares: Tupac Amaru II-1780*. Lima: RETABLO.

Forbes, A.D.W. 1982. Thailand's Muslim minorities: Assimilation, secession, or coexistence? *Asian Survey* 22(11): 1056–1073.

Foster, J.E., Lopez-Calva, L.F., and Szekely, M. 2003. Measuring the distribution of human development: Methodology and an application to Mexico. *Estudios Sobre Desarrollo Humano*, PNUD Mexico, No. 2003–2004.

Foster, J.E., and Szekely, M. 2006. Is economic growth good for the poor? Tracking low income using general means. *Mimeo*. Vanderbilt University.

Fregene, P. 1997. Oil exploration and production activities: The socio-economic and environment problems in Warri Division- Itsekiri Homeland. Paper presented at the Friedrich Ebert Foundation Seminar on *Oil and the Environment*, Port Harcourt, Nigeria, May 14–15.

Frempong, K.D. 2001. Ghana's election 2000: The ethnic under current. In Ayee, J., ed., *Deepening Democracy in Ghana: Politics of the 2000 Elections*. Accra: Freedom Publications.

Friedman, J., and Levinsohn, J. 2001. The distributional impact of Indonesia's financial crisis on household welfare: A 'rapid response' methodology. *NBER Working Paper No.8564*. Cambridge, MA: National Bureau of Economic Research.

Frimpong-Ansah, J.H. 1991. *The Vampire State in Africa: The Political Economy of Decline in Ghana*. London: James Currey.

Frister, R. 2002. *Impossible Love: Ascher Levy's Longing for Germany*. London: Orion.

Fullinwider, R. 2005. Affirmative action. In Zalta, E.N., ed., *The Stanford Encyclopedia of Philosophy*, Spring 2005 edition. Available online at http://plato.stanford.edu/entries/affirmative-action/ (last accessed February 8, 2007).

Gaffney, P. 2000. Burundi: The long sombre shadow of ethnic instability. In Nafziger, E.W., Stewart, F., and Väyrynen, R., eds, *Hunger and Displacement: The Origins of Humanitarian Emergencies, Vol. 2*. Oxford: Oxford University Press.

Gallagher, A.M. 1995. *Majority Minority Review 1: Education in a Divided Society*, 2nd edition. Coleraine: University of Ulster.

Galor, O., and Zeira, J. 1993. Income distribution and macroeconomics. *Review of Economic Studies* 60(1): 35–82.

Gates, S., Hegre, H., Jones, M.P., and Strand, H. 2006. Institutional inconsistency and political instability: The duration of polities. *American Journal of Political Science* 50(4): 893–908.

Gbaramatu Clan Communities. 1997. *Memorandum Submitted to the Judicial Commission of Inquiry on the Warri Crisis*, Asaba, Delta State, May 26.

Ghana Statistical Service, 1998. *Core Welfare Indicators, Questionnaire (CWIQ) Survey, 1997, Main Report*. Accra: Ghana Statistical Service.

Gibney, M.J., and Hansen, R. 2003. Deportation and the liberal state. *UNHCR New Issues in Refugee Research Working Paper 77*. Geneva: UNHCR.

Glazer, N., and Moynihan, D. 1975. *Ethnicity, Theory and Experience*. Cambridge, MA: Harvard University Press.

Gleditsch, N.P., Wallensteen, P., Eriksson, M., Sollenberg, M., and Strand, H. 2002. Armed conflict 1946–2001: A new dataset. *Journal of Peace Research* 39(5): 615–637.

Glewwe, P. 1988. The distribution of welfare in Côte d'Ivoire in 1985. *Living Standards Measurement Study Working Paper No. 29*. Washington: World Bank.

Golder, M. 2005. Democratic electoral systems around the world, 1946–2000. *Electoral Studies* 24(1): 103–121.

Goldstein, H. 1995. *Multilevel Statistical Models*. New York: Halstead Press.

Goldstone, J.A. 2001. Demography, environment, and security. In Diehl, P.F., and Gleditsch, N.P., eds, *Environmental Conflict*. Boulder, CO: Westview.

Gomez, E.T. 1994. *Political Business: Corporate Involvement of Malaysian Political Parties*. Townsville: Centre for South-East Asian Studies, James Cook University of North Queensland.

Gomez, E.T., and Jomo, K.S. 1997. *Malaysia's Political Economy: Politics, Patronage and Profit*. Cambridge: Cambridge University Press.

Gonin, G. 1998. Ethnicity, politics and national awareness in Côte d'Ivoire. In Nnoli, O., ed., *Ethnic Conflicts in Africa*. Dakar: CODESRIA Books.

Government of Ghana, 2003. *Ghana Poverty Reduction Strategy (GPRS), 2003–2005, An Agenda for Growth and Prosperity*. Accra: Government of Ghana.

Grandin, G. 1997. To end with all these evils: Ethnic transformation and community mobilisation in Guatemala's Western Highlands, 1954–1980. *Latin American Perspectives*, 24(2): 7–34.

Gray Molina, G. 2007. Ethnic politics in Bolivia, 1900–2000: 'Harmony of inequalities'. *CRISE Working Paper No. 15*. Oxford: Centre for Research on Inequality, Human Security and Ethnicity, University of Oxford.

Green, E. 2006. Decentralization, district creation and conflict in Uganda. Paper presented at the *CRISE Conference on Federalism, Decentralization and Conflict*, Centre for Research on Inequality, Human Security and Ethnicity, University of Oxford, October 5–7.

Green, S. 2004. *The Politics of Exclusion: Institutions and Immigration Policy in Contemporary Germany*. Manchester: Manchester University Press.

Grindle, M., and Domingo, P., eds, 2003. *Proclaiming Revolution: Bolivia in Comparative Perspective*. Cambridge, MA: Harvard University Press.

Guichaoua, Y., Langer, A., Mancini, L., Stewart, F., and Ukiwo, U. 2006. The role of ethnicity in conflicts: Results of a perceptions questionnaire in Ghana and Nigeria. *CEMISS Final Report*. Oxford: Centre for Research on Inequality, Human Security and Ethnicity, University of Oxford.

Gurr, T.R. 1968. A causal model of civil strife: A comparative analysis using new indices. *The American Political Science Review* 62(4): 1104–1124.

Gurr, T.R. 1993. *Minorities at Risk: A Global View of Ethnopolitical Conflicts*. Washington, DC: United States Institute of Peace Press.

Gurr, T.R. 2000. *Peoples versus States: Minorities at Risk in the New Century*. Washington, DC: United States Institute of Peace Press.

Gurr, T.R., and Moore, W.H. 1997. Ethnopolitical rebellion: A cross-sectional analysis of the 1980s with risk assessments for the 1990s. *American Journal of Political Science* 41(4): 1079–1103.

Gurung, H. 2005. Nepal regional strategy for development. *ADB Nepal Resident Mission Working Paper No. 3*. Kathmandu: Asian Development Bank.

Gutierrez, E., and Borras, S. 2004. *The Moro Conflict: Landlessness and Misdirected State Policies*. Washington, DC: East-West Center.

Gyimah-Boadi, E. 2003. Ghana: The political economy of 'successful' ethno-regional conflict management. In Bastian, S. and Luckham, R., eds, *Can Democracy Be Designed? The Politics of Institutional Choice in Conflict-Torn Societies*. London: Zed.

Gyimah-Boadi, E., and Asante, R. 2006. Ethnic structure, inequality and public sector governance in Ghana. In Bangura, Y., ed., *Ethnic Inequalities and Public Sector Governance*. Basingstoke: Palgrave Macmillan.

Gyimah-Boadi, E., and Daddieh, C. 1999. Economic reform and political liberalization in Ghana and Côte d'Ivoire: A preliminary assessment of implications for nation building. In Mengisteab, K., and Daddieh, C., eds, *State Building and Democratization in Africa: Faith, Hope and Realities*. Westport, CT: Preager Publishers.

Hale, H. 2002. A political economy of secessionism in federal systems. Paper presented at the conference on *The Economics of Political Integration and Disintegration*. Université Catholique de Louvain, May 24–25.

Hansen, R. 2000. *Citizenship and Immigration in Post-War Britain*. Oxford: Oxford University Press.

HDP and UNDP (Human Development Network and United Nations Development Programme). 2002. *Philippine Human Development Report 2002*. Makati City: HDP and UNDP.

Hegre, H., Ellingsen, T., Gates, S., and Gleditsch, N.P. 2001. Toward a democratic civil peace? Democracy, political change, and civil war, 1816–1992. *American Political Science Review* 95(1): 17–33.

Hegre, H., and Sambanis, N. 2006. Sensitivity analysis of empirical results on civil war onset. *Journal of Conflict Resolution* 5(4):508–535.

Held, D. 1991. Democracy, the nation state and the global system. In Held, D., ed., *Political Theory Today*. Cambridge: Polity Press.

Heng, P.K., and Sieh Lee, M.L. 2000. The Chinese business community in peninsular Malaysia, 1957–1999. In Lee K.H., and Tan C.-B., eds, *The Chinese in Malaysia*. Shah Alam: Oxford University Press.

Hepburn, A.C. 1983. Employment and religion in Belfast, 1901–1951. In Cormack, R.J., and Osborne, R.D., eds, *Religion, Education and Employment*. Belfast: Appletree Press.

Herbst, J. 1993. *The Politics of Reform in Ghana, 1982–1991*. Berkeley: University of California Press.

Heryanto, A. 1998. Ethnic identities and erasure: Chinese Indonesians in public culture. In Kahn, J.S., ed., *Southeast Asian Identities: Culture and the Politics of Representation in Indonesia, Malaysia, Singapore and Thailand*. Singapore: Institute of Southeast Asian Studies.

Heshmati, A. 2004. Regional inequality in selected large countries. *Discussion Paper Series No. 1307*. Berlin: Institute for the Study of Labor.

Hewstone, M., Rubin, M., and Willis, H. 2002. Intergroup bias. *Annual Review of Psychology* 53: 575–604.

Higazi, A. 2007. Violence urbaine et politique à Jos (Nigeria), de la période colonial aux élections de 2007. *Politique africaine*, 106: 69–91.

Hoeffler, A., and Reynal-Querol, M. 2003. Measuring the costs of conflict. Oxford: Centre for the Study of African Economies.

Höfer, A. 1979. *The Caste Hierarchy and the State in Nepal: A Study of the Muluki Ain of 1854*. Innsbruck: Universitätsverlag Wagner.

Holsti, K.J. 2000. Political causes of humanitarian emergencies. In Nafziger, E.W., Stewart, F., and Väyrynen, R., eds, *War, Hunger, and Displacement: The Origins of Humanitarian Emergencies, Vol. 1*. Oxford: Oxford University Press.

Honig, B. 2001. *Democracy and the Foreigner*. Princeton: Princeton University Press.

Horowitz, D. 1981. Patterns of ethnic separatism. *Comparative Studies in Society and History* 23(2): 165–195.

Horowitz, D. 1985. *Ethnic Groups in Conflict*. Berkeley, CA: University of California Press.

Horowitz, D. 1989. Incentives and behaviour in the ethnic politics of Sri Lanka and Malaysia. *Third World Quarterly* 10(4): 18–35.

Horowitz, D. 1991. *A Democratic South Africa?* Berkeley, CA: University of California Press.

Horowitz, D. 1993. Democracy in divided societies. *Journal of Democracy* 4(4): 18–38.

Horowitz, D. 2001. *The Deadly Ethnic Riot*. Berkeley, CA: University of California Press.

Horowitz, D. 2002. Constitutional design: Proposals versus processes. In Reynolds, A., ed., *The Architecture of Democracy: Constitutional Design, Conflict Management, and Democracy*. Oxford: Oxford University Press.

Horstmann, A. 2004. Ethnohistorical perspectives on Buddhist-Muslim relations and coexistence in Southern Thailand: From shared cosmos to the emergence of hatred? *Sojourn* 19(1): 76–99.

Human Rights Watch. 2006. 'They do pot own this place': Government discrimination against 'non-indigenes' in Nigeria. *Human Rights Watch Index No. A1803*.

Humphreys, M. 2005. Natural resources, conflict and conflict resolution: Uncovering the mechanisms. *Journal of Conflict Resolution* 49(4): 508–537.

Huntington, S.P. 1993. The clash of civilisations? *Foreign Affairs* 72(3): 22–49.

Hylton, F. 2004. El federalismo insurgente: una aproximación a Juan Lero, los comunarios y la Guerra Federal. *Tinkazos: Revista Boliviana de Ciencias Sociales* 16: 99–118.

Ignatieff, M. 1995. The myth of citizenship. In Beiner, R., ed., *Theorizing Citizenship*. New York: State University of New York Press.

Ikime, O. 1967. The Western Ijo 1900–1950: A preliminary survey. *Journal of the Historical Society of Nigeria* 4(1): 65–88.

Ikime, O. 1969. *Niger Delta Rivalry: Itsekiri-Urhobo Relations and the European Presence 1884–1936*. London: Longman.

International Labor Organization (ILO) 1971. *Matching Employment Opportunities and Expectations. A Programme of Action for Ceylon*. Geneva: ILO.

Imai, K. and Weinstein, J. 2000. Measuring the impact of civil war. *CID Working Paper No. 51*. Cambridge, MA: Center for International Development (CID), University of Harvard.

Imobighe, T., Bassey, C.O., and Asuni, J.B., eds, 2002. *Conflict and Instability in the Niger Delta: The Warri Case*. Ibadan: Spectrum for Academic Peaceworks Associates.

INE (Instituto Nacional de Estadística) 2002. *Censo Nacional de Población y VI de Habitación del 2002*. Guatemala: INE.

INEI (Instituto Nacional de Estadística e Informática) 1995. *Migraciones Internas en el Perú*. Lima: Instituto Nacional de Estadística del Perú.

Irurozqui, M. 1994. *Armonía de las Desigualdades: Elites y Conflictos de Poder en Bolivia, 1880–1920*. Lima: Universidad de San Marcos.

Issacs, H.R. 1975. Basic group identity: The idols of the tribe. In Glazer, N., and Moynihan, D.P., eds, *Ethnicity: Theory and Experience*. Cambridge: Harvard University Press.

Itsekiri Ethnic Nationality. 2005. *A Memorandum Presented by the Itsekiri Ethnic Nationality to the National Political Reform Conference*. Abuja, Nigeria.

Jaggers, K., and Gurr, T.R. 1995. Tracking democracy's Third Wave with the Polity III Data. *Journal of Peace Research* 32(4): 469–482.

Jalan, J., and Ravallion, M. 2000. Is transient poverty different? Evidence for rural China. *Journal of Development Studies* 36(6): 82–100.

Jesudason, J.V. 1997. Chinese business and ethnic equilibrium in Malaysia. *Development and Change* 28(1): 119–141.

Jomo, K.S. 1990. Whither Malaysia's New Economic Policy? *Pacific Affairs* 63: 469–499.

Jomo, K.S. 2004. The New Economic Policy and interethnic relations in Malaysia. *Identities, Conflict and Cohesion Programme Paper No. 7*. Geneva: United Nations Research Institute for Social Development (UNRISD).

Jönsson, J. 2006. The overwhelming minority: Traditional leadership and ethnic conflict in Ghana's northern regions. *CRISE Working Paper No. 30*. Oxford: Centre for Research on Inequality, Human Security and Ethnicity, University of Oxford.

Joppke, C. 2005. *Selecting by Origin: Ethnic Migration and the Liberal State*. Cambridge: Harvard University Press.

Justino, P., Litchfiled, J., and Niimi, Y. 2004. Multidimensional inequality: An empirical application to Brazil. *PRUS Working paper No. 24*. Brighton: Poverty Research Unit at Sussex, University of Sussex.

Kabeer, N. 2002. Citizenship, affiliation and exclusion: Perspectives from the South. *IDS Bulletin* 33(2): 12–23.

Kalimuthu, R.K. 1986. The Sabah state elections of April 1985. *Asian Survey* 26(7): 815–837.

Kanbur, R., and Lustig, N. 1999. Why is inequality back on the agenda? In Pleskovic, B. and Stiglitz, J., eds, *Proceedings of the World Bank Annual Conference on Development Economics*. Washington, DC: World Bank.

Kanbur, R., and Venables A., eds, 2005. *Spatial Inequality and Development*. Oxford: Oxford University Press.

Kanbur, R., and Zhang, X. 1999. Which regional inequality? The evolution of rural-urban and inland-coastal inequality in China from 1983 to 1995. *Journal of Comparative Economics* 27(4): 686–701.

Kant, I. 1991. *Political Writings*. Cambridge: Cambridge University Press.

Kanyinga, K. 2006. Ethnicity, inequality and public sector governance in Kenya. In Bangura, Y., ed., *Ethnic Inequalities and Public Sector Governance*. Basingstoke: Palgrave Macmillan.

Keen, D. 1994. *The Benefits of Famine: A Political Economy of Famine Relief in Southwestern Sudan 1883–1989*. Princeton: Princeton University Press.

Keen, D. 1998. *The Economic Functions of Violence in Civil Wars*. Oxford: Oxford University Press.

Keister, L.A. 2000. *Wealth in America: Trends in Wealth Inequality*. Cambridge: Cambridge University Press.

Kell, T. 1995. *The Roots of Acehnese Rebellion, 1989–1992*. Ithaca, NY: Cornell University Modern Indonesia Project.

Khosla, D. 2000. Chinese in Malaysia: Balancing communal inequalities. In Gurr, T.R., ed., *Peoples versus States: Minorities at Risk in the New Century*. Washington, DC: United States Institute of Peace.

Kieffer, G.-A. 2000. Armée ivoirienne: le refus du déclassement. *Politique Africaine* 78: 26–44.

King, E.M., and Hill, M.A., eds, 1993. *Women's Education in Developing Countries: Barriers, Benefits, and Policies*. Baltimore: The Johns Hopkins University Press.

Knight, R. 2001. *Housing in South Africa*, http://richardknight.homestead.com/files/sisa-housing.htm (last accessed June 7, 2007).

Krishna, A., Lumonya, D., Markiewicz, M., Mugumya, F., Kafuko, A., and Wegoye, J. 2006. Escaping poverty and becoming poor in 36 villages of Central and Western Uganda. *Journal of Development Studies* 42(2): 322–345.

Kymlicka, W. 2004. Culturally responsive policies. *Background paper for Human Development Report 2004*. New York: United Nations Development Programme.

Ladouceur, P.A. 1979. *Chiefs and Politicians: The Politics of Regionalism in Northern Ghana*. London: Longman.

Laitin, D. 1986. *Hegemony and Culture: Politics and Religious Change among the Yoruba*. Chicago: University of Chicago Presss.

Langer, A. 2005. Horizontal inequalities and violent group mobilization in Côte d'Ivoire. *Oxford Development Studies* 33(1): 25–45.

Langer, A. 2007. The peaceful management of horizontal inequalities in Ghana. *CRISE Working Paper No. 25*. Oxford: Centre for Research on Inequality, Human Security and Ethnicity, University of Oxford.

Langer, A., Mustapha, A.R., and Stewart, F. 2007. Horizontal inequalities in Nigeria, Ghana and Côte d'Ivoire: Issues and policies. *CRISE Working Paper No. 45*. Oxford: Centre for Research on Inequality, Human Security and Ethnicity, University of Oxford.

Larson, B. 2002. Perú: guerra soberanía nacional y la cuestión 'indígena'. In Larson, B., ed., *Indígenas, Elites y Estado en la Formación de las Repúblicas Andinas 1850–1910*. Lima: IEP.

Le Billon, P. 2001. The political ecology of war: Natural resources and armed conflict. *Political Geography* 20(5): 561–584.

Le Pape, M. 2002. Chronologie politique de la Côte d'Ivoire, du coup d'état aux élections. In Le Pape, M., and Vidal, C., eds, *Côte d'Ivoire: L'Année Terrible, 1999–2000*. Paris: Karthala.

Lecomte-Tilouine, M. 2004. Ethnic demands within Maoism: Questions of Magar territorial autonomy, nationality, and class. In Hutt, M., ed., *Himalayan 'People's War': Nepal's Maoist Rebellion*. London: Hurst & Co.

Leith, J. 1998. Resettlement history, resources and resistance in North Halmahera. In Pannell, S., and von Benda-Beckmann, F., eds, *Old World Places, New World Problems: Exploring Issues of Resource Management in Eastern Indonesia*. Canberra: Australian National University, Centre for Resource and Environmental Studies.

Lemarchand, R. 1994. Managing transition anarchies: Rwanda, Burundi and South Africa in comparative context. *Journal of Modern African Studies* 32(4): 581–604.

Lentz, C., and Nugent, P. 2000. Ethnicity in Ghana: A comparative perspective. In Lentz, C., and Nugent, P., eds, *Ethnicity in Ghana: The Limits of Intervention*. Basingstoke: Macmillan.

Lewis, A. 1965. *Politics in West Africa*. Oxford: Oxford University Press.

Lichbach, M.I. 1989. An evaluation of 'does economic inequality breed political conflict?' studies. *World Politics* 41(4): 431–470.

Lijphart, A. 1977. *Democracy in Plural Societies*. New Haven: Yale University Press.

Lijphart, A. 1986. Proportionality by non-PR methods: Ethnic representation in Belgium, Cyprus, Lebanon, New Zealand, West Germany, and Zimbabwe. In Lijphart, A., and Grofman, B., eds, *Electoral Laws and Their Political Consequences*. New York: Agathon Press.

Lijphart, A. 1999. *Patterns of Democracy: Government Forms and Performance in Thirty-Six Countries*. New Haven: Yale University Press.

Lijphart, A. 2004. Constitutional design for divided societies. *Journal of Democracy* 15(2): 96–109.

Lim, R. 2006. Federalism, ethnicity and development in a Malaysian state: The case of Sabah, 1976–1985, *M.Soc.Sci. Thesis*, School of Politics, Universiti Sains Malaysia.

Lingga, A.S.M. 2004. Understanding Bangsamoro independence as a mode of self-determination. *Mindanao Journal* 27: 3–12.

Lloyd, P.C. 1974. Ethnicity and the structure of inequality in a Nigerian town in the Mid-1950s. In Cohen, A., ed., *Urban Ethnicity*. London: Tavistock.

Loh, K.W.F. 2003. The marginalization of the Indian community in Malaysia. In Siegel, J.T., and Kahin, A.R., eds, *Southeast Asia over Three Generations: Essays presented to Benedict R.O'G. Anderson*. Ithaca, NY: Cornell University Southeast Asia Programme.

Loury, G.C. 1981. Intergenerational transfers and the distribution of earnings. *Econometrica* 49(4): 843–867.

Loury, G.C. 2002. *The Anatomy of Racial Inequality*. Cambridge, MA: Harvard University Press.

Lundahl, M. 2000. Haiti: Towards the Abyss? Poverty, dependence and resource depletion. In Nafziger, E.W., Stewart, F., and Väyrynen, R., eds, *War, Hunger and Displacement: The Origins of Humanitarian Emergencies, Vol. 2*. Oxford: Oxford University Press.

Lundberg, S., and Startz, R. 1998. On the persistence of racial inequality. *Journal of Labor Economics* 16(2): 292–323.

Magdalena, F.V. 1977. Intergroup conflict in the Southern Philippines: An empirical analysis. *Journal of Peace Research* 14(4): 299–313.

Majumdar, M., and Subramanian, S. 2001. Capability failure and group disparities: Some evidence from India for the 1980s. *Journal of Development Studies* 37(5): 104–140.

Malaysia. 1971. *Second Malaysia Plan, 1971–1975*. Kuala Lumpur: Government Printer.

Malaysia. 1981. *Fourth Malaysia Plan, 1981–1985*. Kuala Lumpur: Government Printer.

Malaysia. 1986. *Fifth Malaysia Plan, 1986–1990*. Kuala Lumpur: Government Printer.

Malaysia. 1991. *Sixth Malaysia Plan, 1991–1995*. Kuala Lumpur: Government Printer.

Malaysia. 2001. *Eighth Malaysia Plan, 2001–2005*. Kuala Lumpur: National Printing Department.

Malaysia. 2006. *Ninth Malaysia Plan, 2006–2010*. Putrajaya: The Economic Planning Unit, Prime Minister's Department.

Mallon, F. 1987. Nationalist and anti-state coalitions in the War of the Pacific: Junin 1879–1902. In Stern, S., ed., *Resistance, Rebellion and Consciousness in the Andean Peasant World, 18th–20th Century*. Madison: University of Wisconsin Press.

Mancini, L. Forthcoming. An overview of HIs in six countries: Evidence from Demographic and Health Surveys. *CRISE Working Paper*. Oxford: Centre for Research on Inequality, Human Security and Ethnicity, University of Oxford.

Mandal, S. 2004. Transethnic solidarities, racialisation and social equity. In Gomez, E.T., ed., *The State of Malaysia: Ethnicity, Equity and Reform*. London: RoutledgeCurzon.

Manrique, N. 1981. *Campesinado y Nación: Las Guerrillas Indígenas en la Guerra con Chile*. Lima: Centro de Investigación y Capacitación, Editora Ital Perú.

Manrique, N. 1988. *Yawar Mayu: Socidades Terratenientes Serranas, 1879–1910*. Lima: Instituto Francés de Estudios Andinos, DESCO.

Manza, J., and Uggen, C. 2006. *Locked Out: Felon Disenfranchisement and American Democracy*. New York: Oxford University Press.

Margalit, A. 1996. *The Decent Society*. Cambridge, MA: Harvard University Press.

Marshall, M.G. 2006. Major episodes of political violence, 1946–2005 dataset. *Centre for Systemic Peace*. Downloaded from http://members.aol.com/cspmgm/warlist.htm (last accessed December 19, 2006).

Marshall, M.G., and Jaggers, K. 2003. *Polity IV Project: Political Regime Characteristics and Transitions, 1800–2001*. College Park, MD: CIDCM, University of Maryland.

Massey, D., and Denton, N. 1993. *American Apartheid: Segregation and the Making of the Underclass*. Cambridge, MA: Harvard University Press.

McCargo, D. 2006a. Rethinking Thailand's southern violence. *Critical Asian Studies* 38(1): 3–9.

McCargo, D. 2006b. Thaksin and the resurgence of violence in the Thai south: Network monarchy strikes back? *Critical Asian Studies* 38(1): 39–71.

McClintock, C. 1981. *Peasant Cooperatives and Political Change in Peru*. Princeton: Princeton University Press.

McCrudden, C. 2007. *Buying Social Justice*. Oxford: Oxford University Press.

McKenna, T.M. 1998. *Muslim Rulers and Rebels: Everyday Politics and Armed Separatism in the Southern Philippines*. Berkeley: University of California Press.

McKenna, T.M. 2002. Saints, scholars and the idealized past in Philippine Muslim separatism. *The Pacific Review* 15(4): 539–553.

McWhirter, L. 2004. *Equality and Inequalities in Health and Social Care in Northern Ireland: A Statistical Overview*. Belfast: Northern Ireland Department of Health, Social Services and Public Safety.

Melaugh, M. 1994. *Majority Minority Review 3: Housing and Religion in Northern Ireland*. Colreaine: Centre for the Study of Conflict, University of Ulster.

Melson, R., and Wolpe, H. 1971. Modernization and the politics of communalism: A theoretical perspective. In Melson, R., and Wolpe, H., eds, *Nigeria: Modernization and the Politics of Communalism*. East Lansing: Michigan State University Press.

Miller, R. 1983. Religion and occupational mobility. In Cormack, R.J., and Osborne, R., eds, *Religion, Education and Employment: Aspects of Equal Opportunity in Northern Ireland*. Belfast: Appletree.

Minority Rights Group International, ed. 1997. *World Directory of Minorities*. London: MRG.

Misión Indígena de Observación Electoral. 2004. *Informe Final, Elecciones Generales*. Guatemala: NALEB.

Misuari, N. 2000. A quarter of a century of illusory and fruitless pursuit of autonomy: The MNLF's urgent call for a realistic and pragmatic tactical and strategic approach. *Preparatory Meeting of the Senior Officials, 27th Islamic Conference of Foreign Ministers of the OIC*, Jeddah, Saudi Arabia.

Mogues, T., and Carter, M.R. 2005. Social capital and the reproduction of economic inequality in polarised societies. *Journal of Economic Inequality* 3: 193–219.

Molina, F. 2006. *Evo Morales y el Retorno de la Izquierda Nacionalista*. La Paz: Eureka.

Montalvo, J.G., and Reynal-Querol, M. 2005. Ethnic diversity and economic development. *Journal of Development Economics* 76(2): 293–323.

Montoya, R. 1998. *Multiculturalidad y Política: Derechos Indígenas, Ciudadanos y Humanos*. Lima: SUR Casa de Estudios del Socialismo.

Moore, W.H., Lindström, R., and O'Regan, V. 1995. Land reform, political violence and the economic inequality-political conflict nexus: A longitudinal analysis. *International Interactions* 21(4): 335–363.

Murray, D., and Darby, J. 1980. The vocational aspirations and expectations of school leavers in Londonderry and Strabane. *Fair Employment Agency Research Paper No. 6*. Belfast: Fair Employment Agency.

Murray Li, T. 2000. Articulating indigenous identity in Indonesia: Resource politics and the tribal slot. *Comparative Studies in Society and History* 42(1): 149–179.

Murshed, S.M., and Gates, S. 2005. Spatial-horizontal inequality and the Maoist insurgency in Nepal. *Review of Development Economics* 9(1):121–134.

Mustapha, A.R. 2005. Ethnic structure, inequality and governance of the public sector in Nigeria. *CRISE Working Paper No. 18*. Oxford: Centre for Research on Inequality, Human Security and Ethnicity, University of Oxford.

Mustapha, A.R. 2007. Institutionalizing ethnic representation. How effective is the Federal Character Commission in Nigeria? *CRISE Working Paper No. 43*. Oxford: Centre for Research on Inequality, Human Security and Ethnicity, University of Oxford.

Nafziger, E.W. 1973. The political economy of disintegration in Nigeria. *Journal of Modern African Studies* 11(4): 505–536.

Nafziger, E.W., and Auvinen, J. 2002. Economic development, inequality, war and state violence. *World Development* 30(2): 153–163.

Neumayer, E. 2003. Good policy can lower violent crime: Evidence from a cross-national panel of homicide rates, 1980–1997. *Journal of Peace Research* 40(6): 619–640.

Nicholas, C. 2000. *The Orang Asli and the Contest for Resources: Indigenous Politics, Development and Identity in Peninsular Malaysia*. Copenhagen: IWGIA.

Noble, L.G. 1975. Ethnicity and Philippine-Malaysian relations. *Asian Survey* 15(5): 453–472.

Noble, L.G. 1976. The Moro National Liberation Front in the Philippines. *Pacific Affairs* 49(3): 405–424.

Noble, L.G. 1981. Muslim separatism in the Philippines, 1972–1981: The making of a stalemate. *Asian Survey* 21(11): 1097–1114.

Nurmela, J. 2006. Does the use of communication media add to social capital? In Iisaaka, L., ed., *Social Capital in Finland – Statistical Review*. Helsinki: Social Statistics Finland.

O'Phelan Godoy, S. 1985. *Rebellions and Revolts in Eighteenth Century Peru and Upper Peru*. Vienna: Colonia.

Okolo, A. 1999. The Nigerian census: Problems and prospects. *The American Statistician* 53(4): 312–325.

Olson, M. 1965. *The Logic of Collective Action*. Cambridge, MA: Harvard University Press.

Omatete, O.O. 2003. Let my people live, http://www.waado.org/UrhoboHistory/West ernNigerDelta/Omatete/Appeal.htm (last accessed on June 7, 2007).

Østby, G. 2003. Horizontal inequalities and civil war: Do ethnic group inequalities influence the risk of domestic armed conflict? *Cand Polit. Thesis*, Department of Sociology and Political Science. Norwegian University of Science and Techonology (NTNU), Trondheim, Norway.

Østby, G. 2005. Dissaggregated inequalities and conflict in developing countries. Paper presented at the *Polarization and Conflict* (PAC) summer meeting, Konstanz, Germany, June 2–5.

Østby, G. 2008. Polarization, horizontal inequalities and civil conflict. *Journal of Peace Research* 45(2) (in press).

Østby, G., Nordås, R., and Rød, J.K. 2006. Regional inequalities and civil conflict in 21 sub-Saharan African countries, 1986–2004. Paper presented at the *47th Annual Convention of the International Studies Association*, San Diego, CA, March 22–25.

Otite, O. 1990. *Ethnic Pluralism and Ethnicity in Nigeria*. Ibadan: Shaneson C.I.

Paredes, M. 2007. Fluid identities: Exploring ethnicity in Peru. *CRISE Working Paper No. 40*. Oxford: Centre for Research on Inequality, Human Security and Ethnicity, University of Oxford.

Parekh, B. 2004. Redistribution or recognition? A misguided debate. In May, S., Modood, T., and Squires, J., eds, *Ethnicity, Nationalism, and Minority Rights*. Cambridge: Cambridge University Press.

Pastor, M., and Boyce, J. 2000. El Salvador: Economic disparities, external intervention, and civil conflict. In Nafziger, E.W, Stewart, F., and Väyrynen, R., eds, *War, Hunger and Displacement: The Origins of Humanitarian Emergencies, Vol. 2*. Oxford: Oxford University Press.

Pemberton, J. 1994. *On the Subject of 'Java'*. Ithaca: Cornell University Press.

Piel, J. 1995. *El departamento del Quiché Bajo la Dictadura Liberal (1880–1920)*. Guatemala: FLACSO.

PNUD, ILDIS, ASDI, and PLURAL. 2003. *Revoluciones del Siglo XX: Homenaje a los Ciencuenta Años de la Revolución Boliviana: Tenemos Pechos de Bronce pero no Sabemos Nada*. La Paz: Plural.

Podder, N. 1998. The implications of economic inequality for social welfare and social conflict. *International Journal of Social Economics* 25(6–8): 1244–1254.

Posner, D. 2004a. The political salience of cultural difference: Why Chewas and Tumbukas are allies in Zambia and adversaries in Malawi. *American Political Science Review* 98(4): 529–545.

Posner, D. 2004b. Measuring ethnic fractionalization in Africa. *American Journal of Political Science* 48(4): 849–863.

PPRU. 1993. *PPRU Monitor, Continuous Household Survey, Religion Report No. 1/93*. Belfast: Department of Finance and Personnel.

Premdas, R.R. 2006. Ethnic conflict, inequality and public sector governance in Trinidad and Tobago. In Bangura, Y., ed., *Ethnic Inequalities and Public Sector Governance*. Basingstoke: Palgrave Macmillan.

Pyong, G.M. 2006. Asian immigration. In Pyong, G.M., ed., *Asian Americans: Contemporary Trends and Issues*. London: Sage.

Qua Clans Constituted Assembly. 2003. *The Position of the Qua People of Calabar in the Current Move by Government to Achieve Unity, Peace and Stability in Calabar*. Calabar: OCCA.

Quah, D. 1996. Regional convergences clusters across Europe. *Centre for Economic Performance Discussion Paper No. 0274*. London: Centre for Economic Performance.

Rakindo, A. 1975. Indonesia: Chinese scapegoat politics in Suharto's 'New Order'. *Journal of Contemporary Asia* 5(3): 345–352.

Ramage, D.E. 1995. *Politics in Indonesia: Democracy, Islam and the Ideology of Tolerance*. London: Routledge.

Ranger, T. 1983. The invention of tradition in colonial Africa. In Hobsbawm, E., and Ranger, T., eds, *The Invention of Tradition*. Cambridge: Canto.

Ranis, G., Stewart, F., and Ramirez, A. 2000. Economic growth and human development. *World Development* 28(2): 197–220.

Reid, A. 1979. *The Blood of the People: Revolution and the End of Traditional Rule in Northern Sumatra*. Kuala Lumpur: Oxford University Press.

Reid, A. 2006. Colonial transformation: A bitter legacy. In Reid, A., ed., *Verandah of Violence: The Background to the Aceh Problem*. Singapore: Singapore University Press.

Republic of South Africa, 2005. *South Africa's Economic Transformation. A Strategy for Broad-based Economic Empowerment*, http://www.thedti.gov.za/bee/complete.pdf (last accessed June 7, 2007).

République de Côte d'Ivoire. 2001. *Recensement Général de la Population et de l'Habitation de 1998, Tome 1: Etat and Structures de la Population*. Abidjan: Institute National de la Statistique.

Reynal-Querol, M. 2001. Ethnicity, political systems and civil war. Barcelona: Institut d'Analisis Economic, Campus de la UAB, Bellatera-Barcelona.

Reynal-Querol, M. 2002a. Ethnicity, political systems, and civil wars. *Journal of Conflict Resolution* 46(1): 29–54.

Reynal-Querol, M. 2002b. Political systems, stability and civil wars. *Defence and Peace Economics* 13(6): 465–483.

Rimmer, D. 1992. *Staying Poor: Ghana's Political Economy, 1950–1990*. Oxford: Pergamon Press.

Robinson, G. 1998. *Rawan* is as *rawan* does: The origins of disorder in New Order Aceh. *Indonesia* 66: 126–157.

Roe, A., and Schneider, H. 1992. *Adjustment and Equity in Ghana*. Paris: Development Centre of the Organisation for Economic Cooperation and Development (OECD).

Rogowski, R., and MacRae, D. 2004. Inequality and institutions: What theory, history and (some) data tell us. Paper presented at the *APSA Conference*, Chicago, IL, September 2–5.

Ross, M. 2003. Resources and rebellion in Aceh, Indonesia. Bunche Hall: University of California, Los Angeles.

Ross, M. 2004. What do we know about natural resources and civil war? *Journal of Peace Research* 41(3): 337–356.

Rothchild, D. 1983. Collective demands for improved distributions. In Rothchild, D., and Olorunsola, V.A., eds, *State versus Ethnic Claims: African Policy Dilemmas*. Boulder, CO: Westview Press.

Ruane, J., and Todd, J. 1996. *The Dynamics of Conflict in Northern Ireland*. Cambridge: Cambridge University Press.

Rutstein, S., and Rojas, G. 2003. *Guide to DHS Statistics*. Calverton, MD: Demographic and Health Surveys, ORC Macro.

Sabah. 1991. *Buku Perangkaan Tahunan Sabah*. Kota Kinabalu: Department of Statistics, Sabah.

Sabah. 2002. *Yearbook of Statistics Sabah 2002*. Kota Kinabalu: Department of Statistics, Sabah.

Sabah. Various years. *Buku Perangkaan Tahunan Sabah.* Kota Kinabalu: Department of Statistics, Sabah.

Sadiq, K. 2005. When states prefer non-citizens over citizens: Conflict over illegal migration into Malaysia. *International Studies Quarterly* 49(1): 101–122.

Saenz de Tejada, R. 2005. *Elecciones, Participación Política y Pueblos Maya en Guatemala.* Guatemala: Instituto de Gerencia Política.

Sagay, J.O.E. (n.d.) *The Warri Kingdom.* Sapele: Progress Publishers.

Sakamoto, A., and Xie, Y. 2006. The Socioeconomic attainments of Asian Americans. In Pyong, G.M., ed., *Asian Americans: Contemporary Trends and Issues.* London: Sage.

Sambanis, N. 2001. Do ethnic and nonethnic wars have the same causes? *Journal of Conflict Resolution* 45(3): 259–282.

Satori, G. 1987. *The Theory of Democracy Revisited: The Contemporary Debate.* Chatham, NJ: Chatham House.

Schneider, G. 2003. Neoliberalism and economic justice in South Africa: Revisiting the debate on economic apartheid. *Review of Social Economy* 61(1): 23–50.

Schneiderman, S., and Turin, M. 2004. The path to *Jan Sarkar* in Dolakha district: Towards an ethnography of the Maoist movement. In Hutt, M., ed., *Himalayan 'People's War': Nepal's Maoist Rebellion.* London: Hurst & Co.

Schrire, R. 1996. The president and the executive. In Lane, J.-E., and Faure, M., eds, *South Africa: Designing New Political Institutions.* Newbury Park, CA: Sage.

Schulze, K.E. 2004. *The Free Aceh Movement (GAM): Anatomy of a Separatist Organization.* Washington, DC: East-West Center.

Scott, W.H. 1982. *Cracks in the Parchment and Other Essays in Philippine History.* Quezon City: New Day Publishers.

Sen, A. 1980. Equality of what? In *Tanner Lectures on Human Values.* Cambridge: Cambridge University Press.

Sen, A. 1992. *Inequality Reexamined.* Oxford: Clarendon Press.

Sen, A. 1997. *On Economic Inequality.* Oxford: Clarendon Press.

Shachar, A. 2007. Birthright citizenship as inherited property: A critical inquiry. In Benhabib, S., and Shapiro, I., eds, *Identities, Affiliations, and Allegiances.* Cambridge: Cambridge University Press.

Shapiro, I. 1999. Group aspirations and democratic politics. In Shapiro, I., and Hacker-Cordon, C., eds, *Democracy's Edges.* Cambridge: Cambridge University Press.

Shapiro, I. 2003. *The Moral Foundations of Politics.* New Haven: Yale University Press.

Shapiro, T.M., and Kenty-Drane, J.L. 2005. The racial wealth gap. In Conrad, C.A., Whitehead, J., Mason, P., and Stewart, J., eds, *African Americans in the U.S. Economy.* Lanham, MD: Rowman & Littlefield.

Shepherd, A., Gyimah-Boadi, E., Gariba, S., Plagerson, S., and Musa, W.A. 2005. Bridging the north south divide in Ghana. *Background Paper for the 2006 World Development Report.*

Sherer, G. 2000. Intergroup economic inequality in South Africa: The post-apartheid era. *American Economic Association Papers and Proceedings* 90(2): 317–321.

Shireen, M.H. 1998. *Income Inequality and Poverty in Malaysia.* Oxford: Rowman & Littlefield.

Shklar, J.N. 1991. *American Citizenship: The Quest for Inclusion.* Cambridge: Harvard University Press.

Sidel, J.T. 2006. *Riots, Pogroms, Jihad: Religious Violence in Indonesia.* Ithaca, NY: Cornell University Press.

Sieder, R. 2002. *Multiculturalism in Latin America: Indigenous Rights, Diversity and Democracy.* Basingstoke: Palgrave Macmillan.

Sigelman, L., and Simpson, M. 1977. A cross-national test of the linkage between economic inequality and political violence. *Journal of Conflict Resolution* 21(1): 105–128.

Smith, A.D. 1986. *The Ethnic Origin of Nations*. Oxford: Blackwell.

Smith, A.D. 1991. The nation: Invented, imagined, reconstructed? *Millenium: Journal of International Studies* 20: 353–368.

Smith, C.A., and Moors, M.M., eds, 1990. *Guatemalan Indians and the State, 1540 to 1988*. Austin, TX: University of Texas Press.

Smith, J.P., Thomas, D., Frankenberg, E., Beegle, K., and Teruel, G. 2002. Wages, employment and economic shocks: Evidence from Indonesia. *Journal of Population Economics* 15: 161–193.

Smith, R.M. 2002. Modern citizenship. In Isin E.F., and Turner, B.S., eds, *Handbook of Citizenship Studies*. New York: Sage.

Smith, R.M. 2003. *Stories of Peoplehood*. Cambridge: Cambridge University Press.

Smock, D.R., and Smock, A.C. 1975. *The Politics of Pluralism: A Comparative Study of Lebanon and Ghana*. Amsterdam: Elsevier.

Snyder, J.L. 2000. *From Voting to Violence: Democratization and Nationalist Conflict*. New York: Norton.

Songsore, J. 2003. *Regional Development in Ghana: The Theory and the Reality*. Accra: Woeli Publishing Services.

South-eastern State of Nigeria. 1972. *Conclusions of the Government on the Report and Recommendations of the Inquiry into the Obongship of Calabar Dispute*. Calabar: Government Printer.

Spolsky, B. 2004. *Language Policy*. Cambridge: Cambridge University Press.

Sriskandarajah, D. 2003. Inequality and conflict in Fiji: From purgatory to hell. *Asia Pacific Viewpoint* 44(3): 305–324.

Srisompob, J., and Panyasak, S. 2006. Unpacking Thailand's southern conflict: The poverty of structural explanations. *Critical Asian Studies* 38(1): 95–117.

StataCorp., 2003. *Stata Statistical Software: Release 8.2 (1) (User's Guide)*. College Station, TX: Stata Corporation.

Stefanoni, P., and Do Alto, H. 2006. *Evo Morales: De la Coca al Palacio, una Oportunidad para la Izquierda Indígena*. La Paz: Malatesta.

Stewart, J.C. 1988. The Cotabato conflict: Impression of an outsider. In Gowing, P., ed., *Understanding Islam and Muslims in the Philippines*. Quezon City: New Day Publishers.

Stewart, F. 2000a. The root causes of humanitarian emergencies. In Nafziger, W.E., Stewart, F., and Väyrynen, R., eds, *War, Hunger and Displacement: The Origins of Humanitarian Emergencies, Vol. 1*. Oxford: Oxford University Press.

Stewart, F. 2000b. Crisis prevention: Tackling horizontal inequalities. *Oxford Development Studies* 28(3): 245–262.

Stewart, F. 2002. Horizontal inequalities: A neglected dimension of development. *QEH Working Paper No. 81*. Oxford: Department of International Development, University of Oxford.

Stewart, F. 2004. The relationship between horizontal inequalities, vertical inequality and social exclusion. *CRISE Newsletter No. 1, Winter 2004*. Oxford: Centre for Research on Inequality, Human Security and Ethnicity, University of Oxford.

Stewart, F., Brown, G., and Cobham, A. Forthcoming. The distributional impacts of fiscal policies in post-conflict countries. *CRISE Working Paper*. Oxford: Centre for Research on Inequality, Human Security and Ethnicity.

Stewart, F., Fitzgerald, V., and Associates, 2001. *War and Underdevelopment: The Economic and Social Consequences of Conflict*. Oxford: Oxford University Press.

Stewart, F., and O'Sullivan, M. 1999. Democracy, conflict and development – Three cases. In Ranis, G., Hu, S.-C., and Chu, Y.-P., eds, *The Political Economy of Comparative Development into the 21st Century, Essays in Memory of John C.H. Fei*. Cheltenham: Edward Elgar.

Stewart, F., and Wang, M. 2006. Do PRSPs empower poor countries and disempower the World Bank, or is it the other way round? In Ranis, G., Vreeland, J.R., and Kosack, S., eds, *Globalization and the Nation State*. London: RoutledgeCurzon.

Strand, H., Wilhelmsen L., and Gleditsch, N.P. 2003. *Armed Conflict Dataset*. Oslo: International Peace Research Institute.

Strand, H., and Urdal, H. 2005. Differential growth, political instability and violent conflict. Paper presented at the *46th Annual International Studies Association Convention*, Honolulu, HI, March 1–5.

Suberu, R. 2001. *Federalism and Ethnic Conflict in Nigeria*. Washington, DC: United States Institute of Peace Press.

Subramanian, S. 2006. Social groups and economic poverty: A problem in measurement. In McGillivray, M., ed., *Human Well-Being: Concept and Measurement*. London: Palgrave Macmillan.

Suhrke, A. 1970. The Thai Muslims: Some aspects of minority integration. *Pacific Affairs* 43(4): 531–547.

Suhrke, A. 1975. Irredentism contained: The Thai-Muslim case. *Comparative Politics* 7(2): 187–203.

Suryahadi, A., Sumarto, S., and Protchett, L. 2003. Evolution of poverty during the crisis in Indonesia. *Asian Economic Journal* 17(3): 221–241.

Szereszewski, R. 1966. The Macroeconomic structure. In Birmingham, W.B., Neustadt, I., and Omaboe, E.N., eds, *A Study of Contemporary Ghana*. London: George Allen and Unwin.

Tabeau, E., and Bijak, J. 2005. War-related deaths in the 1992–1995 armed conflicts in Bosnia and Herzogovinia: A critique of previous estimates and recent results. *European Journal of Population* 21(2/3): 187–215.

Tadjoeddin, M.Z. 2003. Aspiration to inequality: Regional disparity and centre-regional conflicts in Indonesia. Paper presented at the *UNI/WIDER Project Conference on Spatial Inequality in Asia*, Tokyo, Japan, March 28–29.

Tadjoeddin, M.Z. 2007. A future resource curse in Indonesia: The political economy of natural resources, conflict and development. *CRISE Working Paper No. 48*. Oxford: Centre for Research on Inequality, Human Security and Ethnicity, University of Oxford.

Tadjoeddin, M.Z., Widjajanti, I.S., and Mishra, S. 2001. Regional disparity and vertical conflict in Indonesia. *Journal of the Asia Pacific Economy* 6(3): 283–304.

Tanaka, M. 2002. La dinámica de los actores regionales y el proceso de descentralización: ¿el despertar del letargo? *Working Paper No. 125*. Lima: IEP.

Taracena, A. 2002. *Etnicidad, Estado y Nación en Guatemala, 1808–1944, Vol. I*. Antigua Guatemala: CIRMA.

Taylor, J.G. 2003. *Indonesia: Peoples and Histories*. New Haven, CT: Yale University Press.

Thailand. 1962. *Population Census 1960*. Bangkok: Central Statistical Office.

Thernstrom, S., and Thernstrom, A. 1997. *America in Black and White: One Nation, Indivisible*. New York: Simon Schuster.

Tilly, C. 1998. *Durable Inequality*. Berkeley, CA: University of California Press.

Tirtosudarmo, R. 1995. The political demography of national integration and its policy implications for a sustainable development in Indonesia. *The Indonesian Quarterly* 23: 369–383.

Toft, M.D. 2003. *The Geography of Ethnic Violence*. Princeton, NJ: Princeton University Press.

Tomz, M., Wittenberg, J., and King, G. 2003. *CLARIFY: Software for Interpreting and Presenting Statistical Results*. Stanford University, University of Wisconsin, and Harvard University.

Treisman, D. 1997. Russia's 'ethnic revival': The separatist activism of regional leaders in a postcommunist order. *World Politics* 49(2): 212–249.

Tsikata, D., and Seini, W. 2004. Identities, inequalities and conflicts in Ghana. *CRISE Working Paper No. 5*. Oxford: Centre for Research on Inequality, Human Security and Ethnicity, University of Oxford.

Turton, D. 1997. War and ethnicity: global connections and local violence in North East Africa and Former Yugoslavia. *Oxford Development Studies* 25(1): 77–94.

Ukiwo, U. 2006. Horizontal inequalities and violent ethnic conflicts: A comparative analysis of ethnic relations in Calabar and Warri, Southern Nigeria. *D. Phil. thesis*. University of Oxford.

UNDP (United Nations Development Programme) 2000. *South Africa Human Development Report: Transformation for Human Development*. http://www.undp.org.za/sahdr2000/sahdr20002.html (last accessed July 7, 2007).

UNDP (United Nations Development Programme) 2003. *South Africa. Human Development Report – The Challenge of Sustainable Development*. http://www.undp.org.za/NHDRF.htm (last accessed July 7, 2007).

UNDP (United Nations Development Programme) 2004. *Human Development Report 2004*. New York: United Nations Development Programme.

UNDP (United Nations Development Programme) 2005. *Human Development Report 2005*. New York: Oxford University Press.

UNHCR (United Nations High Commissioner for Refugees) 2000. *State of the World's Refugees 2000*. Oxford: Oxford University Press.

UNHCR (United Nations High Commissioner for Refugees). 2006. *State of the World's Refugees 2006*. Oxford: Oxford University Press.

Urhobo Indigenes of Warri, 1997. *A Memorandum Presented to the Judicial Commission of Inquiry into the Ethnic Conflicts Between Ijaws and Itsekiris in Warri North, South and South West LGAs*.

van Binsbergen, W. 1976. Review of S.J. Natara "History of the Chewa". *African Social Research* 19: 73–5.

van Buren, L. 2005. Ghana: Economy. *Africa South of the Sahara 2006*. London: Routledge.

van Cott, D.L. 2000. *The Friendly Liquidation of the Past: The Politics of Diversity in Latin America*. Pittsburgh, PA: University of Pittsburgh Press.

van den Berghe, P. 2002. Multicultural democracy: Can it work? *Nations and Nationalism* 8(4): 433–449.

van der Berg, S., and Louw, M. 2004. Changing patterns of South African income distribution: Towards time series estimates of distribution and poverty. *South African Journal of Economics* 72(3): 546–572.

van der Walle, D., and Gunewardena, D. 2001. Sources of ethnic inequality in Viet Nam. *Journal of Development Economics* 65(1): 177–207.

van der Walle, D., Nead, K., and World Bank, 1995. *Public Spending and the Poor: Theory and Evidence*. Baltimore: Johns Hopkins University.

van Krieken, R. 1999. The barbarism of civilization: Cultural genocide and the 'stolen generations'. *British Journal of Sociology* 50(2): 297–315.

Vanhanen, T. 2000. A new dataset for measuring democracy, 1810–1998. *Journal of Peace Research* 37(2): 251–265.

Varshney, A. 2002. *Ethnic Conflict and Civic Life: Hindus and Muslims in India*. Oxford: Oxford University Press.

Varshney, A., Panggabean, R., and Tadjoeddin, M.Z. 2004. Patterns of collective violence in Indonesia 1990–2003. *UNSFIR Working Paper No. 04/03*. Jakarta: United Nations Support Facility for Indonesian Recovery (UNSFIR).

Volpi, M. 2007. *Horizontal Inequalities in Malaysia 1970–2007*. Presentation to *Centre for Research on Inequality, Human Security and Ethnicity seminar*, University of Oxford.

Walker, C. 1999. *Smoldering Ashes: Cusco and the Creation of the Republic of Peru, 1780–1840*. Durham: Duke University Press.

Warren, K.B. 1998. *Indigenous Movements and their Critics: Pan-Maya Activism in Guatemala*. Princeton: Princeton University Press.

Watson, K. 2007. Language, education and ethnicity: Whose rights will prevail in an age of globalisation? *International Journal of Educational Development* 27(3): 252–265.

Weller, M. 2005. The self-determination trap. *Ethnopolitics* 4(1): 3–28.

Wernstedt, F.L., and Simkins, P.D. 1965. Migration and the settlement of Mindanao. *The Journal of Asian Studies* 25(1): 83–103.

Whyte, J. 1983. How much discrimination was there under the unionist regime, 1921–68? In Gallagher, T., and O'Connell, J., eds, *Contemporary Irish Studies*. Manchester: Manchester University Press.

Williamson, J.G. 1965. Regional inequality and the process of national development: A description of the patterns. *Economic Development and Cultural Change* 13(4): 1–84.

Wilson, C. 2005. The ethnic origins of religious war in North Maluku. *Indonesia* 79: 69–91.

World Bank. 2004. *World Development Indicators 2004*. Washington, DC: Development Data Center, International Bank for Reconstruction and Development/The World Bank.

World Bank. 2005. *Toward a Conflict-sensitive Poverty Reduction Strategy*. Washington, DC: World Bank.

World Bank. 2006. *World Development Report 2006: Equity and Development*. Washington, DC: World Bank.

Yashar, D. 2005. *Contesting Citizenship in Latin America: The Rise of Indigenous Movements and the Postliberal Challenge*. Cambridge: Cambridge University Press.

Young, I.M. 2000. *Inclusion and Democracy*. Oxford: Oxford University Press.

Zartman, W., and Delgado, C., eds, 1984. *The Political Economy of Ivory Coast*. New York: Preager Publishers.

Zavaleta, D. 2006. CRISE perception survey: Results from Bolivia. Paper presented at CRISE Workshop, Santa Cruz de la Sierra, September 25.

Zavaleta Mercado, R. 1974. *El Poder Dual en América Latina: Estudio de los Casos de Bolivia y Chile con un Prefacio sobre los Acontecimientos Chilenos*. México: Siglo Veintiuno.

Zavaleta Mercado, R. 1990. *La Formación de la Conciencia Nacional*. La Paz: Los Amigos del Libro.

Zhang, X., and Kanbur, R. 2003. Spatial inequality in education and healthcare in China. *CEPR Discussion Paper No. 4136*. London: Centre for Economic Policy Research.

Author Index

Subject Index